# Historic Themes
## and
## Landmarks
### in
## Social Welfare
## Research

Harper Series in Social Work,
**Werner W. Boehm,**
*Series Editor*

# Historic Themes and Landmarks in Social Welfare Research

**Sidney E. Zimbalist**

*University of Illinois*

**Harper & Row, Publishers**
New York, Hagerstown, San Francisco, London

Sponsoring Editor: Dale Tharp
Project Editor: Renée E. Beach
Designer: T. R. Funderburk
Production Supervisor: Stefania J. Taflinska
Photo Research: Myra Schachne
Compositor: Maryland Linotype Composition Co., Inc.
Printer and Binder: The Maple Press Company
Art Studio: Vantage Art, Inc.
Cover: Wood engraving after Gustave Doré. (Granger)

HISTORIC THEMES AND LANDMARKS IN SOCIAL WELFARE RESEARCH

Library of Congress Cataloging in Publication Data

Zimbalist, Sidney Eli, 1922–
 Historic themes and landmarks in social welfare
research.
 (Harper series in social work)
 Includes indexes.
 1. Social service—Research—United States—
History. 2. Social surveys—United States—History.
I. Title.
HV85.Z55    361'.007'2073    76-43345
ISBN 0-06-047386-X

To Blanca

# Contents

# Part II
# Themes

# Foreword

For an editor, there are few books that provide more satisfaction than this one. When, a few years ago, Harper & Row established a textbook series in social welfare, we hoped to stimulate the production of books that would serve both the burgeoning undergraduate population and the graduate group of social work students. In so doing, we have been guided by the best judgments we could muster about the path we needed to follow both at a given point and in the foreseeable future. Thus we are trying to create textbooks that reflect both what is in the profession and what will be. Obviously, as time goes on we shall find that at times we hew too close to tradition and at other times we venture too far into the future.

This book felicitously and thoroughly combines past with present and forecasts the future. The author, a distinguished teacher and researcher in his own right, assesses and assays the development of research in social welfare. He brings to this assessment the perspective of the historian and a profound knowledge of the field of social welfare. These twin talents enable him to identify research cycles or themes that characterize the research efforts of leading contributors in the recent past. Moreover, the historical approach enables the author to place these research efforts in the context of both the social history of the United States and recent developments in the profession of social work.

The result is a book unique in its concept and invaluable in its usefulness to the student. Unique in concept because for the first time we see research examined not as a bundle of techniques but as a technical development that reflects ideology, values, and *zeitgeist*. Invaluable to the student because the student can now make the link between social welfare policy, research, and practice—a link all teachers devoutly wish for but seldom manage to achieve.

We have long hoped for a book that would be informed by historical perspective and would examine research in the context of social development; a book that manages to identify research gaps and shortcomings as well as achievements; a book that brings to the fore the special characteristics of research in social work and succeeds in forecasting the future in terms of the trends and aspirations of the profession.

Werner W. Boehm

# Acknowledgments

— • —

I am deeply indebted to a number of groups and individuals for assistance in the course of this work. The Lois and Samuel Silberman Fund, Inc., of New York City provided a generous grant for expenses entailed in the preparation of the text, and members of its Grants Committee made a number of very helpful suggestions. At an early point in planning, Dr. Rachel Marks, then editor of the *Social Service Review*, was highly encouraging and influential as a consultant.

The original dissertation on which this book is partly based was directed by Dr. William E. Gordon and the late Dr. William Burke of the George Warren Brown School of Social Work. Their vital assistance is greatly appreciated, as is the inspiration of the late Dean Frank J. Bruno, to whom the original thesis was dedicated.

The editor of the present volume, Dr. Werner W. Boehm, was most supportive throughout. His preceptive advice and guidance have been invaluable. Mr. Alvin A. Abbott of Harper & Row, Publishers, Inc., provided key inputs along the arduous way toward seeing the book into print.

My personal secretary for most of the text draft and its revisions was Mrs. Patricia Kratochwill, whose efficiency and ability to read and correct my handwriting never ceased to amaze me. Moreover, her freedom to let me know when something didn't make sense was extremely useful. My daughters, Linda and Judy, provided not only a critical and supportive audience but also tangible help with several essential tasks. And finally, my late wife, Blanca Wasserman Zimbalist, gave early encouraging and unstinting cooperation, without which this work would never have been carried forward.

I, of course, assume full responsibility for any shortcomings that remain.

Sidney E. Zimbalist

## SPECIAL COPYRIGHT PERMISSIONS

I would like to express my full appreciation and acknowledgments to the publishers of the following works for their permission to reprint the excerpts indicated below (presented in order of their appearance in the text:

Amos G. Warner, *American Charities*. 3d ed., revised by Mary Roberts Coolidge (New York: Thomas Y. Crowell Co. Inc., 1919) (1st ed., 1894), pp. 36–63.

Charles Booth et al., *Life and Labour of the People in London*. First Series: *Poverty*, vol. 1, pp. 1–26, vol. 2, pp. 20–26, final vol., pp. 16–19 and 210–216. (New York: AMS Press, 1970.) Reprinted from the edition of 1902–1904.

Paul Underwood Kellogg, ed., *The Pittsburgh District—Civic Frontage*, vol. 1 of The Pittsburgh Survey—Findings in Six Volumes (New York: Survey Associates, 1914), Preface and Appendix E, p. i and pp. 494–515. Copyright 1914 held by Russell Sage Foundation, New York.

Philip Klein et al. *A Social Study of Pittsburgh*. (New York: Columbia University Press, 1938), pp. xi–xvi and 877–884, by permission of the publisher and author.

A. Wayne McMillen, *Measurement in Social Work*. (Chicago: University of Chicago Press), 1914, Chicago, Ill.

Edwin Powers, "An Experiment in Prevention of Delinquency." *Annals of the American Academy of Political and Social Science*. vol. 261 (1939), pp. 77–88. Reprinted by permission of the American Academy of Political and Social Science.

Helen Witmer, "Value of the Study to Individual Boys" in Edwin Powers and Helen Witmer, *An Experiment in the Prevention of Delinquency: The Cambridge-Somerville Youth Study*. (New York: Columbia University Press, 1951), Chapter XXV, pp. 421–455. Reprinted by permission of the publisher and Dr. Witmer.

Leonard S. Kogan, J. Mc V. Hunt, and Phyllis Bartelme, *A Follow-up Study of the Results of Social Casework*. (New York: Family Service Association of America, 1953), pp. 91–103. Copyright 1953 by Family Service Association of America, New York.

Bradley Buell et al., *Community Planning for Human Services*. (New York: Columbia University Press, 1952), pp. 6–7, 9, 16, 84–85, 237, 260, by permission of the publisher.

Ludwig L. Geismar and Michael La Sorte, *Understanding the Multiproblem Family: A Conceptual Analysis and Exploration in Early Identification*. (New York: Association Press, 1964), pp. 15–21 and 52–93, by permission of publisher.

Irving Lukoff and Samuel Mencher, "A Critique of the Conceptual Foundation of the Community Research Associates", *Social Service Review*. 36, no. 4 (December 1962), pp. 432, 434, 438, 441–442, 443. Copyright 1962 © by the University of Chicago Press, Chicago, Illinois. Reprinted by permission of publisher.

Leonard Rutman, "The Demonstration Project as a Research and Change Strategy", *Journal of Sociology and Social Welfare*, 2, no. 2 (Winter, 1974) supplement: p. 264. Reprinted by permission of School of Social Work, University of Connecticut, Hartford, Connecticut.

Roland L. Warren, "A Multi-Problem Confrontation" and David Wallace and Jesse Smith, "The Study: Methodology and Findings," in Gordon E. Brown, ed., *The Multi-Problem Dilemma: A Social Research Demonstration with Multi-Problem Families*. (Metuchen, N.J.: The Scarecrow Press, Inc., 1968), pp. 91–94, 107–126, 143–151. Copyright © 1968 by the State Communities Aid Association. Reprint by permission of editor and publisher.

Roland L. Warren, "The Social Context of Evaluation", in William C. Sze and June C. Hopps, eds., *Evaluation and Accountability in Human Service Programs* (Cambridge, Mass.: Schenkman Publishing Co., 1974), pp. 20–21, by permission of publisher.

# Part
# I
# Background

# Chapter 1
# Introduction

## The Need for Historical Perspective

This volume is intended to fill a longstanding gap in the literature of social work, one that has been relatively neglected and has long needed attention. In brief, it consists largely of an original text—together with selected "landmark" readings—that aims at providing a perspective on the growth and development, the progress and pitfalls, and the major trends and landmarks of research in social welfare for the better part of a century. It represents an initial effort at providing a history of "scientific" social work from the standpoint of its shifting research concerns and conceptions over the decades. As such, it is hoped that it will contribute a significant facet to the history of the profession as well as the social history of the nation; it should also throw light on the development of an applied social science and the evolution of its scientific ideas.

It is the author's conviction that one of the most effective modes of insight into an emerging profession is through its developmental experience. In the case of an applied discipline such as social work, the growth of a distinct research tradition is likely to be particularly illuminating for a number of reasons.

In the first place, social work has long aspired to being a "science-based" helping art, and its successes and failures in approaching this goal should be instructive—not only to members of this profession but to other social professions and sciences as well. Futile quests and blind alleys might thus be better recognized, conceptual and methodological pitfalls avoided, and more promising strategies identified. In other words, the body of experience gained over several decades of social work research should have considerable significance for all who are concerned with the application of the research method to the solution of social problems and to the serving of human needs. The potentials and limitations of research effort in this field, spanning close to a century of trial and error, warrants attention as an informative example of the attempt to inject the scientific method and rational procedures into human affairs.

In the second place, social workers generally need to know more about the major works and turning points in the long struggle to make social welfare a more scientific and scholarly field, and about the key leaders and forces in this continuing enterprise. It is difficult to visualize a truly science-oriented profession in which the practitioners are not knowledgeable about some of the main research contributions—and their contributors—of the past as well as the present. Without such familiarity and appreciation, research is apt to be honored in rhetoric rather than in reality, in lip service rather than in tangible support and participation. Too often this has tended to be the case, and it is hoped that greater recognition of the long-term role of research in the field may make for a more constructive balance between the pragmatic art and the hopeful science of social work.

Finally, the author is persuaded that a powerful entree into the understanding of research methodology in this field may be gained by reviewing and analyzing its halting growth over the years in the immediate context of the contemporary issues and priorities with which the field has grappled. It is evident that the study of *current* research methods and reports is also vital to a full knowledge of the subject, but an informed and firsthand appreciation of the "classics" in this area can provide an essential time dimension and thereby throw light on the *why* of present-day social work research philosophies and techniques. In this way we may be better able to discern their underlying assumptions and temporal constraints and, it is hoped, better equip ourselves to transcend them.

Until now no such book has been available in social work, and the profession therefore has lacked a ready source of perspective on its evolving knowledge base and "scientific history." A broad view embracing past research gains and setbacks should have great value for a field still struggling for a firm sense of identity and direction.

Almost twenty years ago such a work was recommended in the volume on research in the 1959 *Curriculum Study* of the Council on Social Work Education, edited by Dr. Werner W. Boehm and written by the late Dr. Samuel Mencher. Dr. Mencher noted the gap as follows:

> There is definite need . . . for the development of historical materials in the field of social work research to supply the background for analysis of current studies and trends . . . to gain perspective both on the growth of social work knowledge and on factors influencing the nature of this growth.[1]

Today this important niche in the professional literature is still open, and the present volume is intended to make a start in filling it. It should be stressed, however, that this is not a historical work in the technical sense of historiography; that is, it does not undertake to discover new data or evidence from primary source materials. It does not seek to add to historical knowledge regarding the times, events, or personalities involved in social work research, much as such study is needed. Rather, the author has sought mainly to collate and interpret a synthesis of scientific ideas and effort from secondary materials in the field's published sources (see section on "Procedures" for fuller detail).

The importance of such an approach is well recognized in other social disciplines. Thus the prominent sociologist Paul F. Lazarsfeld has stated that

> detailed analysis of the way in which different disciplines formulate their problems—the exploratory models they set up—should also give impetus to productive interdisciplinary work. By showing that two or more branches of the social sciences are concerned with the same kind of problems however different the terminology they may use, such analysis may lead to important integrations of existing knowledge, and its significant prescription for future interdisciplinary efforts.[2]

And, in his book on the philosophy of the social sciences, Abraham Kaplan has expressed the point strongly as follows: "A study of the history of science, in a variety of disciplines and problematic situations, is likely to be far more rewarding for the actual conduct of inquiry than a preoccupation with an abstract logic of science."[3]

The philosophically minded reader will note a connection here between the intended exposition and related subject areas such as epistemology, logic, ethics, and the philosophy of science.

### Focus and Boundaries

The focus of this book is on research in social work and social welfare in the United States from the 1870s—with the emergence of the National Conference on Charities and Corrections—to the mid-1960s. To start with the temporal limits, this span of almost 100 years was selected as embracing practically the whole history of organized social work in this country, together with the related research experience. The cutoff in the middle 1960s was deliberately drawn so that the inclusion of "themes" and "landmarks" would not tread too closely on recent or current research. Some degree of distance and detachment is obviously desirable in order to maintain a minimal perspective in the viewing of trends in any field. However, selective reference is made to major research developments into the 1970s.

In terms of geography, we have restricted coverage mainly to social work research in the United States. This was done primarily in terms of convenience. The great European poverty studies of Frederick Le Play, B. Seebohm Rowntree, and Arthur Bowley had a powerful influence on the development of social work research in this country, but it was felt that the effort to do justice to these seminal works would take us too far afield. Certainly the wealth of material to be reviewed and sifted in the American experience comprises a more than adequate base for this kind of a volume. Accordingly, only passing reference will be made to the English and continental pioneers in this field where appropriate. However, one major exception to this limitation has been made in the case of the late-nineteenth-century "poverty studies" of Charles Booth in his monumental *Life and Labour of the People in London,* which pointed the way for American social welfare research for decades thereafter.*

Within this obviously ambitious scope, the following efforts have been made:

To identify and summarize the major historic research "themes" or "cycles" that have marked the scientific development of this field over the decades.

---

* See discussion in Chapter 3, pp. 74–75, and selected excerpts, pp. 97–113.

To place these salient research emphases within the context of the social and professional trends of the times.

To select, review, and excerpt certain key "landmark" studies within these major themes in order to convey some flavor of the style and views of contemporary researchers.

To provide an overview of the research perspectives, premises, and methodologies employed, in order to permit their assessment in the light of present-day scientific standards.

## Definitions

### "Historic Research Themes"

Clarification of several concepts in the foregoing section is needed in order to communicate the author's meaning. What is intended, for example, by the term *historic research theme* in social welfare? In the course of the investigation of the development of research in this field, it was found that there have been a number of distinct "waves" or "cycles" of emphasis in research interest and activity over the years. While they overlap each other considerably and in some instances have been either recurrent or continuous through many decades, nevertheless they tend to be more or less self-contained, coherent, and cumulative trends over a given period. In most cases they may be said to reflect current research "fashions" in the field—swings of the scientific pendulum, as it were—that arose out of current professional and social priorities, crystallized and proliferated to a peak of popularity, and then often subsided or stabilized (much in the manner of a social movement or "cause").

In identifying such themes the author chose to deal selectively only with those emphases in social work research that were sufficiently extensive and integrated to present a discernible identity and continuity in time. A research theme ideally had to have a "life history" of sorts, an incremental sequence of growth or change over a period of years. Thus it was not sufficient for inclusion that a type of study was prominent at a particular time or was frequently represented in the literature or research activity of the profession, unless there was also a distinguishable trend in approach, content, methods, or auspices. The writer did not presume to "catalog" everything that had been done in the field, nor to report isolated, unrelated pieces of research, even though in the aggregate the pieces might add up to a substantial total.

In addition to substance, there had to be coherence and continuity. On the basis of these criteria several large, and many small, blocks of research output in this field were excluded. The themes that were finally selected within these limits were the following (in roughly the chronological order in which they first emerged in the field):

research on the causes of poverty

measurement of the prevalence of poverty

the social survey movement

quantification and indexes in social work

evaluative research on social service effectiveness

study of the multiproblem family

Conspicuously absent from the preceding list are such broad study areas as administrative research in social welfare, research on social work theory, child welfare research, and the relatively recent "rediscovery" of poverty study in the 1960s. The first three of these areas, despite their frequency of occurrence and great significance to the field, did not yet appear to present'a sufficiently cumulative pattern to meet the criteria of continuity and coherence referred to earlier.* Finally, the exclusion of the veritable explosion of research on poverty and related community action programs in the heyday of the Great Society of the 1960s was due to a number of factors: its comparative recency, making sufficient objectivity and detachment for a balanced appraisal difficult; the overwhelming volume and diversity of material, making summarization and interpretation much too large a task for the present undertaking—a separate volume (or volumes) would be warranted; the relative accessibility of many of the reports and publications; and finally, the availability of many review articles and books on these subjects in the current literature.

## "RESEARCH LANDMARKS"

Within a particular theme, as defined in the preceding section, an attempt was further made to select one or two "landmark" re-

---

* Some "administrative research" activities are reported under "quantification in social work" (in the sense of service measurement and accounting) and "evaluative research" (in the sense of certain administrative experiments and demonstrations). (See pp. 271–278.) Moreover, the topic of theory testing in social work research—omitted from the list for the same reasons—are given special attention in a section of Chapter 9. The field of child welfare research is noted where appropriate in other chapters (e.g., Chapters 6 and 7), and its theoretical status is discussed in Chapter 9.

search works that in some sense appeared to epitomize the trend under consideration. These "classics" are given special attention in the text of the appropriate chapter and are also used as the source of extended excerpts in the "selected readings" section of the chapter. (See the section on "Organization of the Text.") The purpose of these excerpts—together with their discussion in the respective chapters—is to help convey to the reader the style, flavor, and ambiance of the study, to the extent feasible, from the vantage point of the original researcher and his era. Thus an opportunity is provided for firsthand contact and familiarity with the field's most influential research writings.

Several criteria have been kept in mind in making this selection. In the first place, the "landmark" studies have been limited to those that might be considered to be examples of *social work research* (as distinct from works primarily in sociology, psychology, or the other social sciences). Admittedly, this is a faint and fine line to draw at best, and the effort involves the obvious risks of a too parochial and narrow focus; it is, however, considered justified on the basis of the general objective here—namely, to provide a needed sense of continuity and professional identity to a disparate, evolving, and highly variegated field of applied study.*

By this limitation we are obviously excluding many "classics" from the more basic social sciences that may very well have had a greater impact on the field—directly or indirectly—than the "inside" studies included. The research of people like Emil Durkheim, Robert K. Merton, Robert F. Bales, Richard Cloward, Lloyd Ohlin, and the Chicago school in sociology; of I. Pavlov, B. F. Skinner, Gordon Allport, Carl Rogers, Abraham Maslow, and the Gestalt school in psychology; and of Kurt Lewin and Donald T. Campbell in social psychology come immediately to mind, to mention only a few related fields.

Within these limits, however, an attempt was made to identify several outstanding studies in social work research for excerpting and special discussion. While the specific selections were arrived at subjectively by the author,† several criteria were utilized in their determination:

---

* For interpretations of "social work research" as used in this text, see pp. 11–12 in this chapter; for its changing interpretations through the decades, see Chapter 2, pp. 25–26.

† A more "democratic" approach, of course, would have been to designate a panel of judges and have them make (or ratify) the final choice of the most significant research contributions in this field. While such a procedure would provide greater assurance of consensus and objectivity, it would also have obviously, been extremely cumbersome and time-consuming.

1. The work should have a wide and continuing influence, as demonstrated in citation, emulation, and impact either on social policy or practice, or on research methodology in this field.

2. The research should represent a large-scale, systematic *empirical* inquiry, that is, one based on documented evidence.

3. It should introduce new or revised content to the field in the form of theory, concepts, policy, practice methods, or research techniques.

4. The study should exemplify the best standards of research design and execution prevailing at the time.

5. It should have reached publication either in book or monograph form.

6. The published work should include a sufficiently detailed description of research procedure to allow for assessment of its adequacy in relation to the study's purpose and findings.

While not all of these criteria necessarily applied to each selection, they were taken into account in arriving at the final choices.*

### "SOCIAL WORK" and "SOCIAL WELFARE"

These global terms will not be specifically defined here; rather, the reader is referred to related articles in the 1971 *Encyclopedia of Social Work* for a full delineation of these notoriously nebulous concepts.[4] Suffice it to say at this point that for the present historical work it was considered appropriate to include in the domains covered by these phrases that content which was so recognized by the professional leadership and literature of the time—a circular definition in a sense, but perhaps as operational as any for our purpose. Obviously, the interpretation of these rubrics in the nineteenth century was different from that of the 1930s, which in turn is distinct from that of the 1970s, and on. It was thought best to accept the contemporary meaning of these terms rather than to attempt to impose a current viewpoint retroactively.

Moreover, in view of the constantly shifting content of these concepts and the relatively recent emergence of social work as a specialized entity within social welfare, it was thought best to treat these phrases more or less interchangeably and synonymously in this text. Certainly they were so considered in the early decades of social work research, and it was felt that it would be simpler and more consistent to avoid the attempt to distinguish between them in their varying nuances over the years.

---

* For the classics selected in this way, see excerpts listed in the table of contents.

"SOCIAL WORK RESEARCH" AND "SOCIAL WELFARE RESEARCH"

Similarly, with our interpretation of the terms *research* and *scientific method* we will consider the various ways in which these concepts were applied at different stages in the field's development—that is, the existing "state of the art" in social work research. Thus, for example, when the charity organization movement applied the phrase "scientific charity" to its approach to dealing with poverty, we will examine the contemporary sense and implications of this usage. In the next chapter some modern definitions of "research" are presented for use in assessing the diverse activities invoked in its name in this field.

It is important, however, to distinguish here as best we can between social work research and research in other social sciences such as sociological research, psychological research, and economic research. Such demarcations, slippery and ambiguous as they must be, are at the core of the selectivity that entered into the choice of "landmarks" discussed previously, as well as the historical analysis of research in this field. The difference must obviously be one of degree rather than of kind and more subjective than objective, but no less crucial for the task before us. The following criteria were employed in identifying social work research in the present text:

> 1. Research on a problem or question arising in the practice of—or in the planning of—any of the usually recognized social welfare services or social work programs of the period.
> 2. Research conducted by a professional social worker (or the contemporary equivalent thereof).
> 3. Research conducted under the auspices of a social work agency, including schools of social work.
> 4. Research financed by social work agencies or funding bodies.
> 5. Research published in social work journals or through other channels dealing primarily with social work.

Needless to say, the foregoing benchmarks could not be applied rigidly or mechanically but, rather, were used as rough guidelines. It was not necessary that all factors be present to include a given work—one or two might suffice to help confirm the judgment that a particular study lay within bounds.

Finally, it should also be noted that we did not attempt to draw a line between "social *work* research" and "social *welfare* research." This is because in the early decades of the field's development such a differentiation would have been untenable; and to undertake it even today would perhaps entrap us unnecessarily in semantic quicksands. In any case, we preferred to cast a wide

and flexible net and when in doubt to include rather than exclude. Accordingly, we have used these phrases flexibly and interchangeably, along with related phrases such as "welfare research,"
"social service research," "research in social welfare," and "research in social work."

## Sources and Procedures

This book is based in part on a complete rewriting, updating,
and reorganization of the author's 1955 doctoral dissertation,
"Major Trends in Social Work Research."[5] In addition, as discussed earlier, selected excerpts from the major landmarks in the
field have been incorporated at appropriate points within the
text. A couple of chapters of the original thesis were subsequently
revised and published as separate journal articles.[6] These versions
were drawn upon and modified in the present work as well.

The method employed for culling source materials in the
earlier dissertation was essentially a systematic review of the
periodical and serial literature of social work, supplemented by
reference to the major social work research reports and publications referred to in this literature. The major sources screened in
this manner were the following: *The Child, The Proceedings of
the National Conference of Social Work, Public Welfare, Smith
College Studies in Social Work, Social Casework* (formerly *The
Family*), *Social Security Bulletin, Social Service Review, Social
Work* (formerly *Compass*), *The Social Work Year Book* (now the
*Encyclopedia of Social Work*), *Survey Graphics and Survey Mid-
Monthly* (formerly *Charities and the Commons*), and *United
States Children's Bureau Publication Series*. While the emphasis
was initially on literature published between 1900 and 1950—the
period of increasing professionalism in social work and the emergence of social work research—close scrutiny has also been given
to earlier issues of the preceding sources and to prior research
landmarks. The geographic coverage, as previously noted, was
limited to this country, with the major exception of Charles
Booth's critically influential poverty studies in England.

For the updating of trends into the 1960s and 70s, a parallel
procedure was followed, but necessarily much more selectively
in view of the rapid acceleration of research productivity in social
work.

It should be stressed that this approach yields a view of research
largely as seen from *within* the field of social work—an "inner
perspective" of scientific trends, ideas, methods, and attitudes, as
it were. Such limitation obviously runs the risk of excluding much

that is significant in the way of external critique and broader perspective in the literature of the other social disciplines bearing upon social work research. However, in view of the huge volume of material involved, it was thought best to concentrate on internal sources. This decision was based on the assumption that, for the purposes of this text, valuable information and understanding of the nature of the field could be gained through an analysis of its own content.

Accordingly, the basis of this work was primarily material drawn from social work sources, defined as: periodical publications in the field of social work; material published under social work auspices; reports of studies conducted under social work auspices, including schools of social work; or the work of people identified as social workers. In any case, only published material was ordinarily considered, on the premise that the most important contributions in the field would be likely to reach print in some form.

As has been indicated, the primary base of material tapped was the periodical and serial literature of social work. The thinking here was that the research activities and issues that have had a significant impact on the field would probably be reported in the professional journals and other periodical literature and, therefore, that concentrating on this source would provide an initial core that could be supplemented by reference to selected works elsewhere.

### Organization of the Text

The nine chapters of this book fall into three categories as follows: (1) The first two chapters are of an introductory and background nature; (2) the next six chapters are each devoted to one of the major "historic themes" in social work research; (3) the concluding chapter presents a "retrospect and prospect" on the development of social work research based on the perspectives gained, including a section on theoretical research in social work.

In each of the six thematic chapters in the second group, selected excerpts from one or more related "classics" are included as recommended readings. These extended excerpts are placed at the end of the body of each chapter, immediately preceding the chapter summary. It is hoped that in this way the selected readings will be viewed as integral to the volume as a whole and that they will whet the reader's interest in fuller portions of the landmark texts cited.

## Recapitulation

In sum, then, this book is intended to add a new dimension to the study of social work research—the dimension of time. It is hoped that a historical perspective on the evolution of research in this field will place it in parallel and meaningful context with the study of the development of social welfare policy, services, and practice. Such an approach should also lend itself to the articulation of social work and social work research with American social history and with the history of the allied social sciences. Finally, it is intended that the present work will help underscore the fact that social work research is a vital, evolving discipline—with many edifying gains and losses along the way—and that both research and the profession have much to gain, particularly today, by taking the "long view."

### NOTES

[1] Samuel Mencher, *The Research Method in Social Work Education,* vol. IX of Werner W. Boehm, ed., *Social Work Curriculum Study* (New York: Council on Social Work Education, 1959), p. 38.

[2] Paul F. Lazarsfeld and Morris Rosenberg, eds., *The Language of Social Research: A Reader in the Methodology of Social Research* (New York: Free Press, 1955), p. 5.

[3] Abraham Kaplan, *The Conduct of Inquiry* (San Francisco: Chandler, 1964), p. 407.

[4] Robert Morris et al., eds., *Encyclopedia of Social Work: Sixteenth Issue* (New York: National Association of Social Workers, 1971).

[5] Sidney E. Zimbalist, "Major Trends in Social Work Research: An Analysis of the Nature and Development of Research in Social Work, as Seen in the Periodical Literature, 1900–1950," doctoral dissertation, Washington University, George Warren Brown School of Social Work, 1955, 420 pp.

[6] Sidney E. Zimbalist, "Index-Making in Social Work," *Social Service Review,* 31, no. 3 (September 1957): 245–257, and "Drawing the Poverty Line," *Social Work,* 9, no. 3 (July 1964): 19–26.

# Chapter 2
# The Emergence of
# Social Work Research

—————— • ——————

### Scientific Origins

Social work in this country has had a long and ambivalent relationship with research going back to the very beginnings of organized social welfare over 100 years ago. It may come as a surprise today to many social workers—and social scientists—to learn that the earliest predecessor of the organization now known as the National Conference on Social Welfare first met as a section of the American Social Science Association (the forerunner of the American Sociological Association. For five years, from 1874 to 1879, the social work group—referred to as the "Section on Social Economy"—met as a constituent part of the American Social Science Association.[1]

But the social sciences of that day differed in many respects from those of today. Then the American Social Science Association embraced essentially the same pragmatic goals of social reform and rehabilitation that social work has traditionally stood for.[2] The prevailing cultural climate was one of eager emancipation from the religious dogma and mysticism that had long obstructed the objective study of society and human problems, and unbounded faith in the application of rational intelligence—and its keenest instrument, the scientific method—to the solution of the mounting social ills of the time.[3] Thus for a brief period a century ago social work and social science stood together at the brink of what was optimistically hoped to be the dawn of a new era of scientific enlightenment and the logical solution of social problems.

Inevitably, differences of emphasis and temperament arose between social practitioners on the one hand and social theorists and researchers on the other. Practitioners found themselves immersed in the immediate practical problems of agency policies and procedures, practice standards and techniques, and the broad gamut of responsibilities involved in the meeting of human needs. Theoreticians and researchers became engrossed in the development and refinement of the scientific method, the objective analysis of social phenomena, and the building of models and concepts to explain social processes. Increasingly, they tended to disassociate from their earlier humanitarian emphases in the interest of greater scientific detachment. Essentially, it came down to a matter of personal and professional priorities; it is difficult indeed to be equally and concurrently concerned with the urgent problems of the individual (or community) on the one hand and, on the other, with the construction and testing of an objective conceptual framework to analyze these problems. As Robert M. Mac Iver, a leading sociologist and president of the American Sociological Association, later put it, "the reformist, moralistic sociology of the nineteenth century was undermined by new schools of thought seeking and claiming a neutral scientific objectivity."[4]

Thus, whether for good or ill, the union of social work and social science a century ago was a short-lived one. In 1878 the Wisconsin delegations to the Conference of Boards of Public Charities, as the organization was then called, refused to attend the sessions so long as it met as the "Section of Social Economy" of the ASSA. The delegation explained its refusal on the basis that the meetings of the Section were taking on the nature of a scientific association rather than a conference of professional practitioners consulting on common concerns.[5] From that point on, starting in 1879, the Conference of Boards of Public Charities met independently, and the resulting separation has persisted to the present time.

The immediate effect of independence was apparently salutary, since it quickly resulted in heightened Conference activity, with an expanded constituency and a more varied program. In the long run, however, the cleavage may well have hampered the scientific status and progress of the profession. The Conference soon lost its earlier identity as a body strongly committed to research and turned its attention primarily to problems of administration and practice.[6]

The significance of this very youthful flirtation and parting of ways for the future of social work research is great indeed. The underlying conflict waxes and wanes in succeeding years, but enters to some degree into every relationship between social work and research. The tension between objectivity and commitment, between tentativeness and confident action, between theory building and theory using, which is no doubt necessary and healthy in the practice of most professions, becomes heightened and sharpened when a largely unscientific art is placed against a research framework. By virtue of this early division of fields, social work was largely stripped of scientific skills and manpower and cut off from formal connection with the major sources of theoretical social thought of that era. On the other hand, independence enabled social work to adapt and borrow more flexibly, from a wider range of disciplines, than might otherwise have been the case. It also gave social work free rein to develop its own historical experience and identity.

Departure from the social science parent body did not, therefore, "solve" the research problems of the nascent profession. It may have helped pose them, perhaps in different form than would otherwise have been the case. The study of poverty and its causes, the need for a factual base for social reform, the demand for service measurement and evaluation, together with the many operational data requirements of a fast-growing field, put continuing pressure on the profession for systematic inquiry. As a result the early literature—before and after the turn of the century—was packed with pleas and exhortations for fact finding and research, perhaps to a greater extent than has been true since that time.

The research vacuum created by the field's "withdrawal" from the social science community was eventually filled in a variety of ways, some constructive, others questionable. In the latter category, as we shall see later, was the "scientific charity" movement of the last century, in which early casework efforts were ambitiously equated with the scientific method itself. The blurring of the two processes that resulted led to considerable confusion and the pursuit of misleading tangents. Another dubious response was the basic rejection of research and scientific inquiry as inapplicable or inappropriate to this human art. On the more positive side was the gradual evolution of research capability within the profession, which was now forced to look within itself for trustworthy answers to its growing need for verifiable knowledge.

## From Social Research to Social Work Research

It will be useful at this junction to review the early semantics of research usage in this field and their structural counterparts. The shifting language of research during the first few decades of social work in this country casts a revealing light on the current understanding and perception of "research" and "scientific method"* in the field.

One definitional trend of considerable significance was the slow and belated crystallization of the phrase "social work research" (or, alternatively, "research in social work"). In fact until some three or four decades ago little attention was paid to any formal distinction between social research in general and social work research in particular. It was assumed that the field of "charity work," "philanthropy," or "social economy"—as it was variously referred to—constituted a broad area of inquiry within the social sciences, but its boundaries and identity were largely unspecified. Thus the American Social Science Association upon its organization in 1865 declared its province to be "whatever concerns mankind in their social . . . relations [and] shades off easily and imperceptibly into metaphysics on one side, philanthropy on the other, and political economy on a third."[7]

One early attempt in the direction of establishing social work as a separate scientific discipline warrants mention, however. This was the essentially abortive effort of Dr. Amos Griswold Warner and others, toward the end of the last century, to launch a new science of charity. The cumbersome rubric chosen to designate the hoped-for field was "philanthropology."[8] Its major expression was the definitive text on social work of the time, *American Charities: A Study in Philanthropy and Economics,* completed by Dr. Warner in 1894. This was an extensive compendium of contemporary social work practice and problems, collating descriptive and statistical materials from various sources. It stood for several decades as the authoritative work in its field, though its "almost fatally statistical pattern" was not favorably received in some quarters.[9] (We shall later review and excerpt selected aspects of this important work—see pp. 38–41 and 50–67.)

---

* We use the terms *research* and *scientific method* interchangeably throughout the text.

Aside from this exception, however, research in social work was for the most part not differentiated from social research in general for several decades. Thus at the 1908 National Conference of Charities and Correction John Koren—chairman of its Committee on Statistics for several years—observed that "in common parlance this term [social research] covers almost every kind of exposition of social and social-economic conditions."[10]

Mary Richmond's classic, *Social Diagnosis* (1917), continued this usage of "social research" as incorporating and designating research in social work. She wrote of the "laborious and learned seeking for truth which deserves to be termed social research,"[11] and elsewhere went on to state:

> "Social research," with its precious freight of original discovery in all fields covered by social work, has also the secondary task of assembling facts in order to reinterpret them for use in social reform, in group work, and in case work.[12]

Even as late as 1929 the first volume of the *Social Work Year Book* gave its main article on research the title "Social Research."

Gradually, however, a distinction began to emerge in the literature. In 1933, for the first time, the *Social Work Year Book* carried an article on "Research in Social Work." Finally, in 1937 Helen R. Jeter laid down the gauntlet in the following manner: "The term 'research in social work' has been used in recent years as synonymous with the term 'social research.' This interchange of terms is no longer permissible."[13]

Over the years the differentiation between the two fields of research has been made on the basis of various criteria; prominent among these have been *auspices* and *function*. Definition in terms of auspice has the obvious advantage of permitting a ready identification, though it still begs the question of what is really different (if anything) about such research. The answer more likely lies in its function or purpose. The earliest attempt to define social work research on the basis of social work function was made by Helen Jeter in the same *Social Work Year Book* article: "Research in social work is inquiry into the techniques used by social workers in meeting certain human problems, whether these be individual or community-wide."[14] She went on to indicate that in addition to the study of social work practice (i.e., "techniques"), social work research also included the investigation of social needs and problems to which social work services are actually or potentially applicable. For example, she stated:

> Family welfare agencies sometimes study the incidence of tuberculosis in their districts. This is *not* research in social work *unless* it is directed toward a plan for meeting the problem of tuberculosis among the poor.[15] (emphasis added)

Notice here the repudiation of a definition based exclusively on the auspices within which it is conducted, and the emphasis on the study of social work programs and the need for such programs.

The functional interpretation of the special province of social work research has been quite influential over the years. In 1948 a highly significant workshop on "Research in Social Work" was held in Cleveland, sponsored by the American Association of Social Workers (now the National Association of Social Workers) and the School of Applied Social Science of Western Reserve University. Its influential published report drew a similar distinction:

> Social research is directed toward the advancement of any of the basic social sciences while research in social work deals with the problems faced by professional social workers and by the community in its concern with social work functions. In social work research the problem is always found in the course of doing social work or planning to do it. . . .[16]

This 1948 workshop may have constituted the unofficial launching of the "modern era" in social work research, bringing together as it did the leading social work researchers around the central research issues of the period. It helped crystallize the identity and definition of the newly emerging specialization of social work research, and sparked the organization of the first formal structure for carrying forward its common interests. This was the Social Work Research Group (SWRG), established in 1949 to provide a channel of communication for interested professionals. The Group soon began publishing its own bulletin, the *SWRG Newsletter,* under the editorship of Dr. Genevieve Carter, then research director of the Welfare Planning Council, Los Angeles Region.

In 1955, the membership of the SWRG was "blanketed into" the newly merged National Association of Social Workers (NASW) as its Social Work Research Section, one of its five "predecessor" organizations. By 1959, its membership numbered approximately 600, and local sections were functioning in 11 NASW chapters. Later, with the restructuring of the NASW in 1963, the Section became its Council on Social Work Research. The impact of these organizational developments on the growth and visibility of social work research over the years has been extensive and crucial to the strengthening of this special component of the field, and to its clarification.

In 1951 the Committee on Research Function and Practice of the recently organized SWRG issued its first report, combining both "auspice" and "function" elements in a definition of social work research. This, they stated, is "research of the type that is or should be carried on under social work auspices and which deals directly with the materials of social work—its concept, operation, personnel and clientele."[17] There apparently was a degree of controversy over this restriction of scope, since some members "would see social work research as including study of needs for services that are not in themselves social services."[18] Thus an issue was raised as to whether the field should be limited to services and needs that are generally recognized as social work in character at the time, or whether it should be interpreted more broadly to include the study of other societal problems and community deficits in such areas as housing, health, discrimination, and crime. The consensus of the group then apparently leaned toward the more specialized interpretation, as reflected in the first definition.

Coming down to more recent times, Mary E. Macdonald, writing in the first major textbook on the subject—*Social Work Research,* edited by Norman Polansky under the aegis of the Research Section of the NASW and published in 1960—further sharpened the functional criterion as follows:

> Neither subject matter nor method serves to define and delineate social work research. The idea of function is more useful. The function of social work research is to contribute to the development of a dependable body of knowledge to serve the goals and means of social work in all its ramifications.[19]

She went on to state: "Social work research begins with practical problems, and its objective is to produce knowledge that can be put to use in planning and carrying out social work programs."[20] The reader is referred to Professor Macdonald's full discussion of the special as well as general features of research in social work for an incisive and authoritative statement that has been drawn upon frequently in the subsequent literature.[21]

In this section, we have attempted to show that in the early decades of organized social work in this country little or no formal distinction was made between social research in general and social work research in particular. Only in the late 1930s and thereafter did a special identity begin to crystallize for research in this field. The distinctive characteristics of this new "specialization" were first sought in the auspices under which it was performed. A more useful and meaningful criterion, which gained wide acceptance in the field, was based on the function of the research, that is, the production of knowledge that can be utilized in planning and carrying out social work programs. Again we end up with a circular definition, but—it is hoped—a definition that helps focus the area of interest in pragmatic terms at least.

This trend involves more than the mere manipulation of words. The importance of this terminological shift from social research to social work research lay in its potential for the more intensive development and growing maturation of a specialized field of inquiry. It seems unlikely, for example, that the rapid expansion and strengthening of research in this field over the past thirty years or so would have taken place to the extent and in the form that it did if an identity and a corresponding structure for "social work research" had not crystallized.

The change in phrase was symbolic of the emergence of a distinct channel for the conduct, organization, and funding of research in social welfare. As we have seen, it provided a rallying point for a growing number of specialized researchers in this broad but roughly distinguishable study area. Such professional and scholarly interchange, under a common label, and later facilitated through organizational structures such as the SWRG in the late 1940s and 1950s (now the Council on Social Work Research of the NASW) should not be underestimated in its significance for a developing field.

It is interesting to note that this "declaration of independence" from social science came much later for research than for social work as a whole. As we have seen, the first national social welfare organization separated from the American Social Science Association in 1879; the gradual differentiation of social work research from social science research crystallized in the late 1930s, over half a century later. Understandably, the original fusion between social work and social science persisted much longer in the borderline and overlapping zone of research than in the core area of social work practice.

At the same time, it should be stressed that such research boundaries are ultimately arbitrary and man-made. In the literature of social work research there is strong and recurring recognition of the wide overlap with social science research and the impracticality—as well as undesirability—of seeking to impose a sharp demarcation on the essential continuum of research interest, and the underlying unity of social knowledge.

## Definitions of Research

Aside from the foregoing gradual differentiation of social work research from social research, a variety of other changes and controversies characterized the interpretation of these terms during this period. Space will not be taken to detail these issues here.[22] They dealt with such questions as the perennial dilemma of theoretical vs. applied emphasis in the definition of research in this field, the role of inductive vs. deductive methods, the question of the centrality of statistical and quantification procedures, the extent of the research process that needs to be encompassed for an undertaking to be considered "research," the feasibility of applying the scientific method to the study of a single "case," and so on. Some of these historic debates have been resolved with the passage of time; others are still with us.

Our approach here will be to adopt a rather broad and comprehensive view of research, preferring to include rather than exclude. A strict "either-or" interpretation of the meaning of research would run the risk, in a work like this, of ruling out much that has historically been viewed as research in the field, and could well defeat the purpose of providing a developmental, "inside" view of the subject.

For our purposes, therefore, we believe that the previously cited delineation of social work research presented by Professor Macdonald in *Social Work Research* provides a useful springboard. In Macdonald's terms, "research may be defined as systematic investigation intended to add to available knowledge in a form that is communicable and verifiable."[23] In elaborating on the terms in this definition she makes the important point that the "knowledge" being sought may involve various levels of generality ranging from the specifically factual to the universal. Thus research is seen as embracing both fact—finding to discover answers to applied questions on the one hand, and general theory building or testing on the other, a catholicity that appears to be particularly appropriate for research in an applied discipline such as social work as long as the essential criteria and standards of research method are adhered to.

These criteria, as stated in the preceding definition, include the requirement that the research be "communicable" and "verifiable." These terms are interpreted as follows:

> To be communicable means that the results are presented in a form that is comprehensible to others. Hence the terms are defined precisely and statements are substantiated with the evidence on which they are based. To be verifiable means that the

investigation is capable of being repeated by others. . . . Others who copy his method diligently should obtain the same results.[24]

One addendum to this interpretation appears to be in order. It is obviously not always feasible for a study to be "repeated by others," particularly when the data sources (as in an interview survey) are no longer accessible in a primary sense. An extension of the definition of "verifiability" might therefore be considered to include studies in which the factual evidence—and the procedures by which it was obtained—is set forth in sufficient detail to enable other competent observers to review them and arrive at an independent judgment as to whether or not the findings are justified. Note that the communication of the results of research to "others," and their review by "other competent observers," is the basis of the distinction between private and public knowledge, or between what is frequently referred to as "subjectivity" and "objectivity." In a sense, the crucial contrast is basically between two forms of subjectivity—the "intrasubjectivity" of the single individual in his private, internal judgment on the one hand and, on the other, "intersubjectivity," or the consensual agreement among indepedent, competent observers whose individual judgments or preceptions can then be compared. There are of course many semantic and philosophic land—mines in the foregoing language—for example, the nature and meaning of "systematic investigation," "factual evidence," "competent observers," "perception," and the like—but these matters might best be left to standard research textbooks and the philosophies of social science.

**NOTES**

[1] Frank J. Bruno, *Trends in Social Work* (New York: Columbia University Press, 1948), p. 42.

[2] Robert M. MacIver, "Sociology and Social Work," in *Social Work Year Book* (1933), pp. 497–500.

[3] Bruno, p. 25.

[4] MacIver, p. 498.

[5] Ibid., p. 6.

[6] Ibid., p. 7.

[7] Bruno, p. 4.

[8] Amon G. Warner, *American Charities: A Study in Philanthropy and Economics* (New York: Crowell, 1894), p. 401.

[9] Bruno, p. 101.

[10] John Koren, "Report of the Committee on Statistics," *Proceedings of the National Conference of Charities and Corrections,* 1908, p. 214.

[11] Mary E. Richmond, *Social Diagnosis* (New York: Russell Sage Foundation, 1917), p. 52.

[12] Cited in *Social Work Year Book,* 1935, p. 421.

[13] Helen R. Jeter, "Research in Social Work," in *Social Work Year Book,* 1937, p. 419.

[14] Ibid., p. 420.

[15] Ibid.

[16] *Research in Social Work* (Cleveland: American Association of Social Workers and School of Applied Social Sciences, Western Reserve University, January 1948), p. 6.

[17] Social Work Research Group, Committee on Research Function and Practice, "The Function and Practice of Research in Social Work," mimeographed, 1951.

[18] Ibid., p. 3.

[19] Mary E. Macdonald, "Social Work Research: A Perspective," in Norman A. Polansky, *Social Work Research* (Chicago: University of Chicago Press, 1960), p. 1.

[20] Ibid., p. 3.

[21] Ibid., pp. 1–5.

[22] For a treatment of these trends and issues, see the author's doctoral dissertation, "Major Trends in Social Work Research: An Analysis of the Nature and Development of Research in Social Work, as Seen in the Periodical Literature, 1900–1950" (Washington University, 1955), pp. 21–45.

[23] Macdonald, p. 2.

[24] Ibid.

# Part II
# II
# Themes

# Chapter 3
# The Search for
# the Causes of Poverty

## The Scientific Charity Movement

One of the first expressions of the scientific aspirations of the new field of social work took shape within the charity organization movement.[1] An important facet of this movement, one that surfaced quite early (first in England and then more sharply here), was its emphasis upon and identification with the "scientific method." In place of outdoor relief and indiscriminate alms giving, the charity organization movement offered intensive case investigations and individualization of the recipient; it proposed to conduct a thorough evaluation of the characteristics, worthiness, "cause" of need, and prospects for rehabilitation of each applicant for relief. As described by Frank J. Bruno, "it was hailed by many as an application of scientific method to that particular problem in human relations."[2]

The charity organization movement reached this country in 1877 with the establishment of the first society in Buffalo, New York. One of the early American leaders, Josephine Shaw Lowell, boldly staked out a claim to scientific territory, writing in 1884:

> I speak of "our science" because fortunately the task of dealing with the poor and degraded has become a sci-

ence, and has its well-defined principles, recognized and conformed to, more or less closely, by all who really give time and thought to the subject.[3]

Even earlier, in 1880, D. O. Kellog of the Philadelphia Charity Organization Society stated before a meeting of the American Social Science Association: "Charity is a science, the science of social therapeutics, and has its laws like all other sciences."[4]

"Scientific Charity" was the title of a paper presented to the National Conference of Charities and Corrections by Glendower Evans in 1889.[5] Evans summed up the essence of the then "modern" charity as follows:

> Thus scientific charity, far from bidding us cease to give alms, only bids us not to give them when they will be harmful; it bids us pause, when possible, to consider what their effect will be; and it bids us try, along with alms, to give some better gift, which may by and by put the poor beyond their need.[6]

Aside from the tenor of nineteenth-century "Lady Bountiful" paternalism in these statements, there is apparent a rather sweeping trust in science to guide the hand of the practitioner. Today, almost 100 years later, we may be somewhat sadder and, if not wiser, at least more realistic about the difficulties and complexities inherent in the application of the scientific method to human behavior. The problematic prospect was not entirely lost on the early enthusiasts, however, since Mrs. Evans went on to acknowledge that "it must be observed, however, that the application of this theory of scientific charity is far less simple than is the statement."[7]

One further quotation, from the National Conference of the following year (1890), expresses this early scientific optimism in rather extreme form:

> It was the admitted need of more authentic knowledge which called Charity Organization into existence, and bade it apply itself first and foremost to investigation. The promoters of the movement saw that the sorrows of millions of their fellow creatures . . . could not be healed until their miseries were measured, traced home, and the inexorable laws of social deterioration [or] restitution discovered.[8]

These few quotations from the early literature of the charity organization movement, which might readily be multiplied, may perhaps suffice to indicate the extent to which the "new look" in late-nineteenth-century philanthropy was preceived by its spokesmen to embody the scientific method. As expressed by Roy Lubove, the movement produced "a vast amount of rhetoric concerning the importance of a thorough understanding of the background of each case of dependency, combined with a series of preconceived moral judgments and presuppositions about the character of the poor and about human nature."[9]

An important problem here is the extent to which this early charity work may be identified with the scientific method or research process. The question of the relationship between social work practice and research is a crucial one in the history of this field, and in some ways the issue is still very much with us today.

Was the relationship one of "rhetoric," as suggested by Roy Lubove, or one of reality, as affirmed by the early leaders, or some mixture of both? The way in which the charity organization movement differed from earlier methods consisted partly of its special emphasis on the understanding of the individual client through a thorough investigation of his factual background. Presumably, the worker approached the client with general questions more or less clearly formulated, such as "What is the cause (or causes) of this family's dependency?" "How may it best be restored to self-sufficiency," and so on. He or she would then proceed to gather data from the family and collaterals, and the data would be interpreted to throw light on the problem and the prospects of rehabilitation through available means. The conclusions arrived at might then be "tested" and progressively revised through further observation and experience in working with the family until an optimal solution was arrived at. A similarity to the research process is undoubtedly discernible here. The question is, how meaningful is this similarity?

The answer of course depends on the criteria or standards of research one employs. The earlier general definition would appear to make charity organization practice *potentially* eligible for research or scientific status, but only under certain conditions that were rarely if ever met in actuality. According to this formulation, research might conceivably enter into the casework process if specific questions or hypotheses were formulated in explicit terms, and if these questions or hypotheses were then satisfied in such a way that the data and procedures involved could be subjected to scrutiny and concurrence by others. It is clear, however, that such conditions were not ordinarily fulfilled in practice. Questions or hypotheses were not often posed in formal, observable terms; the original observations of data sources were rarely documented in detail; and the full framework of study design and concept was not usually spelled out and accessible to review and agreement by others. The charity worker's conclusions were essentially based on private observations and judgment rather than on public knowledge openly and systematically arrived at.

It is of course an easy matter (and not very "sportsmanlike" at that) to deflate the scientific claims of nineteenth-century social work, particularly if one applies a modern research framework to the appraisal, as we have. The reason for doing so is not to point with scorn but to establish a baseline against which later social work practice may be compared in relation to such scientific ambitions. As Carol Germain has observed, "scientific charity" reflected the general intellectual climate of the times, with its optimistic faith in scientific progress and its "naive notions" of positivistic scientism.[10] Measured against the nineteenth-century yardsticks of "science," both in the view of the general public and in that of the social sciences of the day, social work was not knowingly overstating its case.*

It is understandable, therefore, that this terminology gained ascendancy in the field, and with little or no challenge to its scientific presumptions. It was attacked, however, on moral grounds. John Boyle O'Reilly, the popular Irish-American poet, wrote in 1886 of

> The organized charity scrimped and iced
> In the name of a cautious, statistical Christ[11]

And Jane Addams of Hull House deplored the resulting frustrations experienced by the poor: "When they see the delay and caution with which relief is given, these do not appear to them to be conscientious scruples, but the cold calculating action of the selfish man."[12]

From today's vantage point, then, it might be said that despite a surface analogy between "case investigation" and the research process, the relationship was more one of metaphor than one of identity. It represented hopes and aspirations rather than reality. As interpreted by Carol Germain, "scientific charity" expressed a *commitment* to the scientific method by the fledgling field, a commitment that has helped shape the evolution of social casework and is yet to be fulfilled.[13] Roy Lubove has usefully interpreted the scientific bent of early American social work as an affirmation of the goal of *rationality* in the nascent profession, a broader and perhaps more appropriate term that accommodates much of what then went on in the name of science, without im-

---

* See footnote, p. 35.

plying the rigor or technical standards of what is now considered to be the scientific method.[14]

Perhaps enough has been said to demonstrate the way in which the language and trappings of science took hold in the first decades of American social work. If the research verbiage appears in large part to be overblown today, it did not seem so to the early leaders of the profession, nor to their contemporaries.* And the impact of these scientific ambitions on the later development of the field, its professionalization, its university-based training programs, its various schisms and subcultures—and its persisting dilemmas—can hardly be exaggerated. It is sobering to consider that a century hence (in whatever form social work may then exist) our present use and perception of research may seem as simplistic and misplaced as that of "scientific charity" seems today—perhaps more so, in view of the accelerating pace of scientific and intellectual change. Within this perspective a measure of scientific and professional humility becomes us all.

By the end of the nineteenth-century, in any case, the vocabulary of "scientific charity" was no longer current in the literature, having fallen perhaps because of its own weight and overreach. Moreover, the beginnings of what was more specifically seen as "research" in the field during the late 1880s and 1890s may also have played a role in supplanting this broader usage. Research on the *causes* of poverty soon became a more specialized channel for the scientific aims of the youthful field.

### The Quest for Causation

The first major theme of empirical research to emerge in American social work was the search for the causation of poverty and related social ills, in the form of a series of statistical studies that ran their course largely before the turn of the century. Crystallization of interest in poverty and its causes in the late 1800s stemmed from several sources, including public concern over an apparent increase in the amount of "pauperism" and the

---

* It is intriguing in this connection to compare the "scientific charity" movement with the somewhat later "scientific management" movement. There are some possible parallels in terms of ambitiousness between the social work and industrial management approaches here. See Frederick W. Taylor, *The Principles of Scientific Management* (New York: Harper & Row, 1911); also, Samuel Haber, *Efficiency and Uplift: Scientific Management in the Progressive Era* (Chicago: University of Chicago Press, Midway Reprint, 1964).

growing burden of outdoor relief; the impetus of the "scientific charity" movement and its promise of the application of science to the solution of human problems; the "discovery of poverty" in nineteen-century literature, journalism, and art;[15] and the example of the great European poverty studies, particularly, of course, Charles Booth's *Life and Labour of the People of London*, of which the first report reached print in 1887.

It is interesting to speculate on the difference in focus between the American and English poverty inquiries during this period. Booth, for example, stressed the study of the nature and extent of poverty, with only a passing glance at causes. In the United States, by contrast, it was not until after the turn of the century that we began to see substantial research interest in the measurement and description of poverty per se. Perhaps the optimistic hope in this country for a simple "cure", once the source of the "disease" was scientifically determined, helped divert attention from the full extent and impact of the societal problem; moreover, the heavily moralistic and self-reighteous attitudes toward the dependent and "dangerous classes" in this country may have made systematic inquiry into the *size* of the problem appear less urgent than "diagnosis and treatment."

In any case, no American counterparts to the work of Charles Booth were undertaken until a decade or two later, and then in substantially different form (see Chapter IV). As described by Robert Bremner in his review of this period, "at the end of the nineteenth century Americans were still ignorant as to the actual extent of poverty in their midst. . . . Although only slight progress had been made in determining the amount of poverty in America, much attention had been given to its causes."[16]

Indeed, the National Conference of Charities and Corrections had as its initial raison d'etre the "search for the causes of human ills," according to Frank J. Bruno,[17] and at its first annual meeting in 1874 a report was given regarding a large-scale investigation being launched in New York State into the causes of pauperism.[18] It proposed the analysis of the records of some 15,000 inmates of poorhouses and almshouses on a case-by-case basis with the aid of case schedules—containing such questions as "Were [the parents] openly immoral, sensual, and debased?"[19] The study was referred to at later Conferences, but no final report was subsequently given to the forum.* Even with the help of an appropriation from the state legislature, the author of the 1874 paper, Dr. Elisha Harris, anticipated the task ahead soberly when

---

* Some of the results of this early effort are reported in the Warner "landmark" excerpt later in this chapter (see table and discussion, p. 61).

he stated: "It will be too great a task for any one mind to frame and inspire those inquiries, but what is worth doing at all in this field is worth doing well."[20] In any event, the strongly moralistic slant and the subjective case-by-case determination of causation (by the institutional physician or other responsible staff person in this instance) were typical of much of the early research on this problem.

Many theories of the causation of poverty had enjoyed a degree of public acceptance during the nineteenth century. In 1819 the New York Society for the Prevention of Pauperism listed immigration as the major cause and cautioned that New York was "liable to be devoured by swarms of people."[21] This concern over inundation by needy foreigners was a recurring theme in the welfare literature and public consciousness of the era. (In fact much social research—and social work research—up to World War I featured the analysis of social problems in terms of comparisons between native and immigrant segments of the population, as we shall have occasion to note. In more recent years such nationality breakdowns have tend to reemerge as racial and ethnic ones.) In the 1830s a leading welfare spokesman estimated that a significant portion of American poverty was due to the evils of drink.[22] Other prominent interpretations of the roots of poverty before 1900 included the several major economic theories— that is, those of Malthus, Marx, and Henry George—and the Darwinian and Spencerian theories of the survival of the fittest in biological and social evolution.

Along with the foregoing, of course, was the pervasive moralistic view that the poor were in some intrinsic manner the cause of their own plight, whether through sloth, shiftlessness, indolence, sinfulness, or other defects of spirit or character. Whether derived from traditional religious doctrine, the individualistic frontier ethic, the precepts of free enterprise, or other sources, the typical American attitude toward the poor tended to be more accusatory than sympathetic.[23] These values strongly colored the early history of social welfare in this country and clearly influenced the cast of causal inquiries for decades. As perceptively recounted by Frank Bruno

> It is significant that the first committees of the Conference [of Charities and Corrections], its papers, and its declared purposes spoke of the elimination of pauperism,* not of poverty. It was the weakness of the victims of destitution that called for study

---

* In nineteenth-century America the term *pauperism* was popularly used to refer to the state of extreme poverty that entailed dependency on public support or charity for maintenance.

. . . and not much attention was paid to those situations external to the dependent, which might throw some light upon the reasons for their dependence. There were hints from time to time that moral factors might not be solely responsible for the existence of need, especially in the dependency of children and widowhood. But they remained a minority, and not an influential minority, throughout the nineteenth century.[24]

Much of this early research in social welfare was incorporated in Amos Griswold Warner's classic *American Charities: A Study in Philanthropy and Economics,* published in 1894. This was perhaps the first definitive, comprehensive text on American social work. Dr. Warner, then professor of economics at Stanford University, had previously been an executive of the Baltimore Charity Organization Society. (His chapter on "Cause of poverty" is reproduced on pages 50–67.) Warner identified three main methods that had been employed in the study of poverty up to that time. These were (1) the deductive or philosophical method, as employed by Marx, George, and Malthus; (2) the inductive study which attempts to "ascertain in a large number of particular cases what causes have operated to bring about destitution;" and (3) the inductive study of "classes not yet pauperized" to identify impoverishing factors, as illustrated in Charles Booth's investigations.[25] He looked upon the third method as the most rigorous and pointed to Charles Booth's opus as the outstanding example of this form of inductive study.

However, the second category—referred to as the "case-counting" method—was the type most commonly carried out in this country, and the basis for Warner's compilation and summary in his book. He attempted to collate findings for nearly 28,000 cases of relief applicants investigated by a number of charity organization societies in 1887. The charity workers, utilizing this "case-counting" method, had classified the cases as follows:

| | |
|---|---|
| Worthy of continuous relief | 10.3 percent |
| Worthy of temporary relief | 26.6 percent |
| Need work rather than relief | 40.4 percent |
| Unworthy of relief | 22.7 percent[26] |

While the classification is based largely on the moralistic notion of the "worthiness" of the applicant, a causal implication is included with respect to the lack of available employment for the 40 percent in the "need work rather than relief" category. A "charity organization schedule" employing these categories had been in use by the participating societies during this period.*

Warner himself proposed a more sophisticated approach to the analysis of dependency, dividing the causes of poverty into "subjective" (i.e., within the individual) factors and "objective" (external or social) factors.[27] The first category included such traits as "shiftlessness," "abuse of stimulants," and "lack of judgement"; the second category included such characteristics as "evil association," "unwise [i.e., pauperizing] philanthropy," "inadequate education," "inadequate wages and irregular employment," and so on.[28]

Not content to compile the American experience alone, Warner went on to make a heroic attempt to incorporate European data as well, drawing upon Booth's findings in London and the reports of German investigations as well. While the comparability of these tabulations with each other—both within and between the studies—was obviously remote, and the author fully acknowledged the difficulties and hazards of aggregating such diverse groupings, he nonetheless proceeded with the effort in the apparent hope that its potential value would justify the risks.

In order to permit the fuller analysis of causes in this more comprehensive collation, several Charity Organization Societies followed a common framework of classification, adopting the one then in use by the Buffalo Society. The societies agreed that "only the chief cause" should be listed by the workers.[29]

The several specific categories were subsequently grouped under three headings: those indicating "misconduct," those indicating "misfortune," and those not classified or unknown. These groupings paralleled Warner's proposed distinction between subjective (or internal) and objective (or external) causation, and presumably reflected whether the "fault" was that of the person in need or that of the surrounding society.

The results were assembled into a combined table comparing the breakdown of poverty causes for applicants at 5 American societies, 2 of Booth's London district populations, and public relief recipients in 76 German cities. (Applied research is rarely as tidy as the textbooks say!) The percentage of cases whose

* The terms *worthy* and *unworthy* were dropped from these statistical forms by the year 1900 as a significant reflection of changing values and perceptions. In addition, the groupings "misconduct" and "misfortune" were at the same time changed to "causes within" and "causes outside" the family. Soon thereafter these categories were generally dropped. See Amos G. Warner and Mary Roberts Coolidge, *American Charities*, 3d ed., (New York: Crowell, 1919), footnotes, p. 44 and p. 134.

plight was judged to be due to "internal" causes, grouped under the heading of "misconduct," ranged from 12 to 31 percent among the American samples and from 3 to 42 among the European.[30] Warner took such findings as supporting the predominance of "objective" factors, external to the individual's control, in the etiology of dependency. In this regard he anticipated and helped lay the groundwork for the environmental emphasis and reform activism of social welfare in the early 1900s.

Warner went on to make the then customary obeisance to immigrant nationality comparisons in his poverty data, with an occasional stereotyping of one or another component of the American polyglot mix. In most respects, however, Dr. Warner was relatively farsighted and perceptive in his study and interpretation of poverty and its origins. In addition to serving as a kind of bridge between nineteenth-century moralism and twentieth-century reform, he was one of the first to stress the complexity and interaction of the "indefinitely numerous" factors producing poverty, and the futility of seeking any single cause or even any group of causes. He quoted Booth approvingly as stating that many of the poor are "the football of all the causes in the list."[31] He thus pointed the way for Mary Richmond and other later social work leaders to claim *multiple causation* as a professional core concept from the very start. Although his research and statistical methods are primitive by today's yardsticks, he helped carry forward the promise of a factual understanding of social problems and human needs.

One of the fixations in nineteenth-century interpretations of poverty was that it was in large part attributable to the "curse of drink," as noted earlier, and several investigations gave close attention to this problem. In his review of poverty factors Warner noted that intemperance varied between 8 percent and 20 percent as a main cause of poverty in American Charity Organization Societies—an appreciable minority, but a minority of cases nonetheless. In 1893, about the time Warner was completing his opus, a Committee of Fifty for the Investigation of the Liquor Problem was established. The Committee published a series of studies over the next ten years. The director of one of these inquiries—on the economic aspects of alcoholism—was John Koren, chairman of the National Conference Committee on Statistics.[32] He drew upon the data and records of charity organization societies, much as Warner had done previously. Special reports were prepared by workers in 33 societies for cases handled during a 3–12-month period. The findings indicated that some 25 percent of poverty cases were attributable primarily to alcoholism, a higher percentage than had been found in Warner's compilations.[33] In addition to other sources of inaccuracy and incomparability, the fact that the workers in this project were focusing their attention on the particular factor of alcoholism might very well have slanted their judgments. In addition, as Bremner observes, "the significance of this finding was undermined . . . by the growing conviction among professional social workers that it was unrealistic to attempt to pick out any single factor" in the explanation of poverty.[34]

## Critical Reaction

To challenge the research standing of these studies from a present-day vanatge point would be as impressive as shooting a squirrel with an elephant gun, and as unnecessary.[35] Their many weaknesses are self-evident, even to the layman. More significant for our purposes is the perception of these studies by their contemporaries. How were they used; to what extent were they accepted; what shortcomings were noted? As we have seen, Warner was cognizant of a number of limitations in his materials—the questionable comparability of judgment by different workers and agencies, the artificiality of seeking to identify the "chief" cause of dependency in a particular case, the preferability of broader social and population analyses (such as Booth's) to his own "case-counting" approach in seeking out the roots of poverty, and so on.

Other social work leaders raised questions about various aspects of these studies at an early point. In an 1877 paper a prominent National Conference officer—F. B. Sanborn—stated the case in favor of developing basic information on the *extent* of poverty before tackling the "delicate and difficult" work of uncovering *causes:*

> But the statistics of number and cost [of the poor] . . . are prior in practical consequences even to these tables . . . [on causes]. When armies are overrunning a country, it is of first importance to know where they are, how numerous are their forces, and what they are doing. At a later period . . . we may inquire how they came among us.[36]

These remarks were made in response to the major study then being conducted on the causes of pauperism in New York State institutions for the poor, which, as noted previously, had been reported by Elisha Harris to the first Conference in 1874. Sanborn saw the preoccupation with the causes of poverty as premature, urging more study of the "what" before inquiry into the "why." (Presumably, he would have preferred that we start with our own "Life and Labour of the People in New York.")

Aside from such concern with causal research in relation to its timing, another early Conference leader, Frederick H. Wines, attacked the method employed in the prevailing case-counting approach. He pointed out the "ex post facto fallacy" of retroactively identifying a factor present in an applicant as contributing to his dependency. For example, the fact that a needy person may also be a drunkard or "shiftless" or unemployed does not justify the conclusion that these are necessarily causes of his condition.[37] His drunkenness, shiftlessness, unemployment, and need may each have different roots, or they may all trace back to the same underlying sources, or the need may be the "cause" rather than "effect," and so on. In other words, Wines was in effect objecting to the tendency to interpret the possibly spurious association between factors in an individual case as indicating a casual relationship. Commenting on this early scientific critique, Dr. Bruno states:

> It is the only instance in these first thirty-five years of the Conference's activity that a rigid, scientific theorem of social research was mentioned. . . . Its careful observance, which would have led either to a more rational analysis of causes, or to abandoning the idea that a cause or any galaxy of causes could be found, might have saved the "scientific" efforts of an entire generation of fruitless searching for a definite clue to the perennial dilemma of why some men succeed and others, whose lot is not so very much different, fail.[38]

Closely related to this objection was the criticism of the *subjectivity* with which such interpretations were made. In practically all of these early studies one finds a single worker investigating an applicant or reviewing a record and on the basis of this personal evaluation arriving at a decision as to which cause or causes were responsible for his plight. This approach was amusingly punctured in the following account of then current data on the causes of crime:

> In New York City, where whiskey flows on every corner, 2 per cent of crime was the result of drink, but in that good state of Maine, where prohibition has been a wonderful success for at least a generation, 15 per cent is the result of drink. . . . It happens that in the Elmira Reformatory [in New York] there was a

gentleman at the head who felt that drink was not the cause of all the crime, but a result of it; and that result was 2 per cent. . . . The statistics are not of the slightest value.[39]

Obviously, when data are dependent on the judgment of different individuals they may reflect differences in judges as much as they do differences in the phenomena being judged. Until the reliability or extent of agreement between such judgments is determined and their validity considered, their compilation as statistics is dubious indeed.

Perhaps the sharpest attack on this type of research was later delivered by Lilian Brandt before the 1906 Conference. In it she not only drove home the point just made but also made some interesting observations on the early relationships between social workers and statistics. She stated:

> From the beginning the movement for intelligent charity has been characterized by a burning desire to get at causes of poverty and the early interest in statistics of dependent families . . . was due to the belief that they would show forth . . . all those human traits and social conditions which are responsible for dependence. We are still hoping for this, but we have changed our ideas as to the methods by which it can be done. . . .
>
> The old method of studying causes of poverty was an unfortunate one. The method consisted in tabulating the opinions of a large number of charity workers as to what was the cause of poverty in a large number of individual cases. It was unfortunate for two reasons: first, because it meant reliance on opinions, not on facts; and second, because the burden of deciding whether it was intemperance, lack of work, unwise philanthrophy, inefficiency or illness, in a given case, that brought the family to dependence, and the conviction arising that the decision could not be of much value, did much to make statistics in general hateful to charity workers.[40]

Whether or not we agree with her interpretation as to what makes statistics "hateful" to social workers, there was considerable contemporary support for her proposed alternative to the "case-counting" design for getting at the reasons for indigency, which she stated as follows:

> We are no less interested now in the causes of poverty, but we believe we shall learn more about them by a careful study of the conditions that are found in dependent families than by registering opinions as to which one of these conditions is responsible for the family's inability to support itself. . . .

> The primary object in collecting statistics of dependent families is, therefore, to get facts about the characteristics of the family.[41]

Thus Brandt recommended emphasis on a study of the objective factors found to be associated with poverty, rather than reliance on a subjective "diagnosis" of the worker in the attempt to identify causes. In a sense, too, she was replying to Wines' earlier criticism, in which he scored the ex post facto fallacy of retrospectively reading causes into case histories, by urging the abandonment of such causal interpretations and a focus on the more objective study of the associations between factors per se. Thus, Brandt was anticipating later emphasis in social science research that stress correlation analysis and other statistical measures of association rather than subjective cause-effect interpretations.

## Broader Inquiry into Causes

The twentieth century ushered in a social reform emphasis in social work that saw poverty and need as stemming primarily from societal shortcomings and inequities. The improvement of housing and working conditions, the achievement of a more humane and cooperative social and economic order, were objectives high on the social workers' list of priorities. It was a time in which the individual treatment approach was disparaged as a "retail" attack on a "wholesale" problem, and a status line was drawn between foresighted "prevention" and belated "treatment."[42]

This swing of the pendulum may have been in part a reaction against the stress placed on individual morality in the charity organization movement and in part a reflection of the general trend toward social and economic liberalism in England and America in the years before World War I. In any case, the moralistic classifications of the needy were largely discarded after 1900, as we have seen, and social work research was pressed into the service of environmental reform in the garb of the "social survey" (see Chapter 5). Studies of causation as such became less frequent in the face of the growing widespread conviction that society itself was the culprit.

At the same time, as noted earlier, there was already considerable early sophistication concerning the nature of causation itself in social work. Indeed Mary Richmond's *Social Diagnosis* reflected a quite mature expression of this appreciation of the multiple nature of social causation.[43] But now the search for causes was pursued with a difference, if not of kind, then of degree. Instead of attempting to reduce the complexities of human behavior and its determinants to labels, Richmond stressed the complex ramifications and interrelationships of the many causes entering into any particular situation. She wrote:

> The common inclination is to seek for one cause. Where cause must be sought in human motives, however, we must expect to find that it is not a single simple cause, but complex and multiple.[44]

She objected to any attempt to list simple causes in representing the forces that bring about need. "The one-word diagnosis," she maintained, "even when it names the general type of difficulty with correctness, is not social." She then continues: "Widowhood, desertion, illegitimacy—these are only isolated social facts having no diagnostic significance until their context in the particular instance is given." It was on the basis of authority such as this that the earlier practice of counting up specific "causes" read by workers into individual cases was largely abandoned.[45]

At the same time, it should be noted that Richmond's concept of causation was strongly influenced by the "medical model," in which the presenting problem or complaint was seen as traceable to underlying sources or forces, often related to the individual himself. This medical influence is described by Carol Germain as follows:

> It was during the Baltimore years that [Mary Richmond] wrote, for example, of pauperism as a "disease" and of the friendly visitor as a "social physician or general practitioner of charity" who is called upon to "heal" complex conditions. Although her writings contain references to what the teacher does with pupils, and to how the lawyer uses evidence, it was the medical or disease metaphor which was ultimately selected, developed, and refined by Mary Richmond and by later generations of case work theorists.[46]

Germain goes on to point out that "contrary to Mary Richmond's own involvement with environmental issues, yet inherent in the model, was a focus on individual processes which all but ignored the social context in which they are imbedded."[47]

After *Social Diagnosis* the gradual spread of Freudian theory and the "new psychology" further encouraged the approach to causation via an intensive psychodynamic study of the individual case. The impressive example of psychoanalytic literature gave impetus to numerous social work studies in which a handful of cases were closly scrutinized—usually in the course of treatment—for psychogenic patterns.

While this type of study has the same pitfalls of subjectivity and ex post facto error noted in the pre-1900 causual studies, as well as numerous other deficiencies, it also tends to differ from these in significant ways. As has been noted, the numbers involved were typically greatly reduced—a dozen as compared with thousands, say. While this limitation may make generalization more difficult, it also entailed a more intensive analysis of the individuals studied than was usually the case before. Moreover, the earlier moralistic theme was now largely discarded, and the later environmental emphasis muted, in favor of the new focus on psychodynamic factors and emotional interaction. In addition, the causal factors uncovered were likely to be expressed in complex, interrelated terms rather than simple, discrete categories.

Thus with each swing of the pendulum the factors fixed upon by preceding workers tended to be looked upon as superficial and "symptomatic" while the current ones were viewed as more basic. The later shifts of emphasis to environmental and institutional forces in the 1930s—and the rediscovery of poverty in the 1960s—continued this fluctuating pattern in professional and research orientation (see Chapter 5 and 7).

In recent decades there has been much less preoccupation in social work with the scientific search for the "causes" of poverty in the traditional sense in which we have been pursuing it here. During the Great Depression of the 1930s the self-evident economic basis of most unemployment and related dependency made such inquiry superfluous. Instead, the serious impact of economic crisis and unemployment on individual and family adjustment was stressed in a number of studies in this field.[48]

The "new look" at the persistence of poverty in the midst of an affluent society that surfaced in the early 1960s gave rise to a veritable Niagra of studies and statistical analyses of the characteristics, culture, and correlates of poverty. Indeed the poor became so popular an object of social inquiry that they began to resist the continuing invasion of their privacy, despite its being conducted in the name of knowledge. While concern with the causation and prevention of poverty was implicit in much of this investigation, the determination of causes was now rarely approached directly. More often the research focus was the social and individual characteristics associated with the incidence of poverty—such as race, education, geography, age, and family size—and with the measurement of the extent and distribution of poverty per se. (Further attention will be given to the latter area of study in the next chapter.) The avoidance of a frontal attack on the causes of indigency in later research on the subject probably reflects a more sophisticated "respect" for the imposing technical and conceptual complexities inherent in any such attempt.[49]

For the search for causes, in the discrete sense first undertaken in this field, was obviously overly optimistic—given the state of social science at the time—and insufficiently sensitive to the ambiguities and subtleties to be encountered in the study of social problems. The end of the nineteenth century was, however, a time of hope and faith in science, as we have noted, and social research boldly launched its experiment in human affairs. Though largely unsuccessful, the attempt nevertheless revealed the limitations of these efforts and thereby led to more promising approaches.

In 1918 a reviser of Warner's classic text—Dr. Mary Roberts Coolidge—trenchantly summarized what had taken place in social work since the turn of the century:

> Thus in one generation of social work the emphasis was transferred from the individual poor person and his deficiencies to society as a whole—to its faulty structure and its injustices. The word "causes" was from this time on superseded in the mouths of charity workers by the word "conditions" and the movement to ascertain what those adverse conditions are which produce dependency and delinquency and misery was pursued with cumulative vigor.[50]

This statement, though more than fifty years old, stands up impressively well—though we may not be quite so circumspect in avoiding any use of the term *cause* in accounting for economic need today. At that time, however, the reaction against the abuses of the concept was apparently so strong that some in effect adopted a "no-fault" policy toward the study of the poor. The earlier tendency to use the search for causes as a basis for pointing the finger of blame at the needy themselves led them to reject even the language of causation in the interest of shifting the locus of concern to societal "conditions."

## A Note on the Concept of Causation

Social workers are not the only ones to have had difficulty with the notion of causation. The concept has of course been the subject of controversy in philosophy and science for many centuries. Its clouded status goes back at least as far as Aristotle's attempt to deal with the slippery logic of cause and effect. Among more modern philosophers, John Stuart Mill undertook to elaborate the scientific implications in his "experimental canons." But many unresolved conceptual dilemmas remained, and David Hume was finally impelled to reject the entire notion and deny its empirical foundations. He undertook to replace the concept of "cause" with that of "association," the idea of one event merely being followed or paralleled by another.

Since then many physical scientists have followed Hume's lead by eliminating causation from their scientific glossary and stressing instead the concepts of chance and probability as the mainspring of action in the real world. For example, the late British mathematician and scientific interpreter J. Bronowski devoted several chapters to this fundamental shift in outlook in his book *The Common Sense of Science*. The following quotations may serve to suggest the general thrust of this argument:

> It was assumed in the classical science of the last century that such a phenomenon as radio-activity, or the inheritance of a blood group, or loss of nerve, or the rise in prices in a time of scarcity, is each the result of many influences; and that step by step these could be taken apart and the phenomenon traced to all its causes. In each case, what was happening could be treated as a laboratory experiment. It could be isolated from those events in the world which had no bearing on it, and lay as it were beyond the box of the laboratory. And within this box, the causes could be studied one by one, much as we study how the volume of a gas changes when the pressure is varied while we keep the temperature the same, and when the temperature is varied while we keep the pressure the same.
>
> But this picture of the phenomenon in isolation from the rest of the world and from the observer turns out to be false. There comes a time when it will not do any longer even as an approximation. Then it turns out that time and space, which Newton thought absolute, cannot be given physical meaning without the observer. The laboratory cannot exist in a void, and the experiment cannot be put in a box. And as we refine our measurements, the limitations of the observer look larger and larger.[51]

The alternative is the substitution of statistical "chance" for mechanical "cause":

This is the revolutionary thought in modern science. It replaced the concept of the *inevitable effect* by that of the *probable trend*. Its technique is to separate so far as possible the steady trend from local fluctuations. The less the trend has been overlaid by fluctuation in the past, the greater is the confidence with which we look along the trend into the future. We are not isolating a cause. We are tracing a pattern of nature in its whole setting. We are aware of the uncertainties which that large, flexible setting induces in our pattern. But the world cannot be isolated from itself: the uncertainty *is* the world. The future does not already exist; it can only be predicted. . . .[52]

Following these trends in physical science, many social scientists now focus their research on the determination of statistical associations (by means of measures of correlation, analysis of variance, factor analysis, path analysis, etc.)[53] Others have discarded causality in favor of newer systems concepts, which stress interacting configurations of forces in place of linear linkages and seem particularly compatible with social work phenomena.[54] Still others have built upon Mills' canons with various experimental and quasi-experimental designs while retaining the essence of cause and effect in the form of independent-dependent variables.[55]

A close reading of the schools of social research that presumably exclude causation suggests, however, that some version of the concept nonetheless tends to steal back in, whether in other guises or through later interpretation or implication. Causation seems to be one of those paradoxical philosophic concepts that we cannot do without and cannot do too well with either—at least in a rigorous empirical sense. Perhaps Kant was right in his transcendental view of causality, in maintaining that the human mind is structurally constituted so that "it cannot conceive of events save as effects of causes," as Abraham Kaplan interprets him.[56]

In any case, in an applied field such as social work, devoted as it must be to ameliorative change and prevention, it is hard to conceive of professional function without some notion of causation, whether single or multiple, linear or circular, interactive or transactive, proximate or ultimate, and so on. Inevitably we get caught up in semantics regarding what we really mean by *cause*, but in an action field we seem to be stuck with it or stuck without it.[57] For unless and until we are able to establish the sources of social pathology, it will be difficult to justify our efforts to reduce it, or to demonstrate their effectiveness.[58]

# Causes of Poverty

## AMOS G. WARNER

A new interest in the causes of dependence was created by the rise of humanitarianism, the development of political economy and of the evolutionary theory in the nineteenth century. Neither philosophers nor charity workers were satisfied to accept any longer the misused dictum, "The poor ye have always with you," as an excuse for merely palliative measures in dealing with them, nor with the current explanations of their misery. The students of the social sciences who have sought to ascertain the causes of poverty have employed three tolerably distinct methods. First, there are those deductive or philosophical thinkers who, from the well-known facts of social organization, have sought to deduce the causes tending to poverty, as a systematic writer on pathology seeks to set forth the inherent characteristics of the bodily organism which tend to make disease likely or inevitable. Secondly, there are those who make an inductive study of concrete masses of pauperism, usually separating the mass into its individual units, seeking to ascertain in a large number of particular cases what causes have operated to bring about destitution. This work resembles that of the practicing physician, endeavoring to ascertain the causes of sickness by a careful diagnosis of the cases under his care. Thirdly, there are those who study the classes not yet pauperized, to determine by induction what forces are tending to crowd individuals downward across the paper line, as the health officer of a city might undertake, by an examination of the drainage system or an analysis of the water or food supply, to ascertain the causes of disease in a given locality.

Examples of the philosophical or deductive method are found in the writings of men like Malthus, or Henry George, or Karl Marx, who, while they describe actual conditions at great length, still make the philosophical reasoning which is the heart of their work antecedent to their facts. The facts are given by way of illustration rather than of proof. Writers of this class are prone to think that they can find some single underlying cause of all the misery and destitution that exists. The three names just mentioned recall three explanations of poverty, each alleged to be universal, and the three mutually exclusive. Malthus was too wise a man to put forth his principle of population as an all-sufficient explanation of distress; but his followers have not been so wise. In the writings of certain economists it has been a fundamental thought that poverty exists mainly, if not entirely, because population tends to increase faster than food supply. All other causes are held to contribute to this, or to be derived from this. The pressure of population against the means of subsistence is held to guarantee that there shall always

From Amos G. Warner, *American Charities*, 3d ed., revised by Mary Roberts Coolidge (New York: Crowell, 1919) (1st ed., 1894), pp. 36–63. Reprinted with permission of publisher.

be a vast number of persons who can just manage to live miserably. A rise of wages will promote early marriages and rapid increase among laborers, until population is again checked by overcrowding and consequent misery and death. So wise a man as John Stuart Mill allowed his economic philosophy to be overshadowed by this idea.

Henry George ridiculed the Malthusian explanation of poverty, and offered an all-sufficient explanation of his own, which is, substantially, that poverty exists, on the one hand, because the landlord receives in rent so large a share of the annual product; on the other, because private property in land encourages the withholding of natural resources from use, the owners waiting to obtain an unearned increment. Since the owner of land receives wealth without labor to an increasing extent with the development of society, there must be an increasing number of those who labor but receive little or nothing.

Opposed to both these explanations of the existence of poverty is that of the socialists who follow Karl Marx's analysis of capitalistic production. Reduced to a sentence by Dr. Aveling, this explanation of poverty may be stated by saying that labor is "paid for, but not paid." The consumer pays enough for the product to remunerate the laborer, but the capitalist retains all except what will barely suffice to keep the laborer alive.

An explanation of poverty frequently offered by theologians is equally unsatisfactory. They inform us that all poverty comes primarily from vice and immorality—"Seek ye first the kingdom of God and his righteousness; and all these things shall be added unto you." They quote David as saying: "I have been young, and now am old; yet have I not seen the righteous forsaken, nor his seed begging bread." The temperance advocate, specializing upon the preacher's theory, assures us that the greater part of poverty comes from the abuse of intoxicants. The propagandist of purity tells us that it is undoubtedly the abuse of the sexual nature that leads to most of the social degradation and consequent poverty of our times. These different students of social science, if such they may be called, all say that what men need to make them prosperous is moral reformation or spiritual regeneration.

No one who has studied carefully modern industrial society can doubt that each one of these causes may produce a very considerable amount of destitution. But no one of them, nor all of them together, can be taken as an adequate explanation of poverty. For destitution is bound up with the facts of economic life and modern industrial life is infinitely complex. "The Malthusian," says Professor Seligman, "seizes upon redundant population, the communist upon private property, the socialist upon property in means of production, the single taxer upon property in land, the coöperator upon competition, the anarchist upon government, the anti-optionist upon speculation, the currency reformer upon metallic money, and so on. They all forget that widespread poverty has existed in the absence of each one of these alleged causes. Density of population, private property, competition, government, speculation, and money have each been absent at various stages of history without exempting society from the curse of poverty. Each stage has had a poverty of its own. The causes of poverty are as complex as the causes of civilization and the growth of wealth itself."[1]

To illustrate the complexity of the conditions of poverty more concretely: Suppose a second Robinson Crusoe on a desert island under exactly the same material conditions as the friend of our childhood; suppose he spent his time in distilling some kind of liquor, and subsequently getting drunk; suppose he allowed his mind to wander in dreamy and enervating revery upon debasing subjects; suppose that in consequence of these habits he neglected his work, did not plant his crops at the right time, and failed to catch fish when they were plentiful. Manifestly he would become poor and miserable, might become diseased from having insufficient food, and finally die in abject want. Poverty in such a supposititious case could not be traced to the fact that an employer had cheated the laborer of wages honestly earned, or to the fact that a landlord had robbed him by exacting rent, nor could it be traced to an excessive increase of population. Moreover, if Crusoe No. 2 had simply lacked judgment or skill, he might have become poor, although thoroughly pious and moral. If he had built a canoe that would not float, or a cave that crumbled in and injured him, or constructed a summer-house that he did not need, or had not the ingenuity to devise tools for his varied purposes, he might have failed to secure the necessaries of life, and have died in miserable destitution.

Now, if all these various causes are conceivably operative in the case of an isolated person, it is manifest that in actual industrial society as now organized, where the individual suffers not only from his own mistakes and defects, but also from the mistakes and defects of a large number of other people, the causes of destitution must be indefinitely numerous and complicated; and the man who says that he has found one all-embracing cause discredits himself as promptly as the physician who should announce that he found a single, universal and all-sufficient explanation of bodily disease.

The second method of seeking the causes of poverty, the inductive study of concrete masses of dependents, or case-counting, as it may be called, grew naturally out of contact with relief work. The systematized case records of relief societies and particularly the Charity Organization schedules of 1888, were expected to give more comprehensive results than they ultimately yielded; yet within a somewhat narrow scope these results are surprisingly definite. The limits of the method suggest themselves, if we reflect on the analogy of the physician standing by the sick-bed, and trying to learn the cause of the disease merely from an examination of the patient. He may learn the immediate or exciting causes of sickness, but back of these are the remoter causes which can only be learned by other methods of investigation. The competent physician will look for these in the hereditary constitution of the patient, or in bad conditions of public sanitation or personal hygiene, or in

[1] Seligman, "Principles of Economics," p. 591.

exposure to contagion, or in the revelations of bacteriology, or in unhealthy climate or occupation. But however thorough, he will scarcely be able to go farther afield than this to ascertain the ultimate economic and social conditions which may account for the patient's lack of physical resistance to disease.

This will become clear if we glance at the following analysis of the causes of poverty. It is not intended to be complete, but only to give in general outline a map of the field; and it was derived not from philosophical study but from practical experience as an agent of the Charity Organization Society of Baltimore and its adequacy tested by constant reference to concrete cases of destitution.

A statistical analysis of cases gives more light concerning the subjective causes of poverty than the objective causes, for in dealing with individuals their character is apt to be more studied than their environment. But even when environment is the primary cause of poverty, the immediate cause or coördinate result is often deterioration of character. As sickness is more obvious than bad sanitation, so is laziness than a malarial atmosphere, inefficiency than a defective educational system. One who attempts the analysis of cases is apt to be confused by the fact that under the operation of exactly similar general causes some

## ANALYSIS OF THE CAUSES OF POVERTY

**Subjective**

Characteristics
1. Undervitalization and indolence
2. Lubricity
3. Specific disease
4. Lack of judgment
5. Unhealthy appetite

Habits producing and produced by the above
1. Shiftlessness
2. Self-abuse and sexual excess
3. Abuse of stimulants and narcotics
4. Unhealthy diet
5. Disregard of family ties

**Objective**

1. Inadequate natural resources
2. Bad climatic conditions
3. Defective sanitation, etc.
4. Evil associations and surroundings
5. Defective legislation and defective judicial and punitive machinery
6. Misdirected or inadequate education
7. Bad industrial conditions
8. Unwise philanthropy

a. Variations in value of money
b. Changes in trade
c. Excessive or ill-managed taxation
d. Emergencies unprovided for
e. Undue power of class over class
f. Immobility of labor
g. Inadequate wages and irregular employment

families are destitute and some are not. One man is able to secure an adequate income under the most adverse circumstances—unhealthy climate, bad housing, unjust taxation, or lack of opportunities for education. Another man, under exactly the same conditions, will become destitute, and the observer must put down as the final and determining cause some defect in physique or character. Untrained charity workers who come immediately in contact with the poor are very prone to take short-sighted views of the causes of poverty. On the other hand, those who study the question from a philosophical standpoint are apt to lay too much stress on the influence of institutions or environment.

Each of these types of observers has, indeed, seized upon a portion of the truth; the questions of character are very far from insignificant, but so long as it is impossible to measure accurately all the forces within and without the individual which tend to push him above or below the line of economic independence, it will be necessary to study the combined operation of character, circumstance, and environment in accounting for his failure.

The results to be obtained from an investigation conducted on the case-counting principle will manifestly vary according to the particular class of destitute persons investigated. To count the cases of those who simply apply for relief will give different results from an investigation of the inmates of an almshouse. To study a group of distinctly pauper families having close inter-relations will give different results from an inquiry about all the poor in a given locality. A locality from which all the deaf and dumb, the blind, the feebleminded and the insane have previously been taken to institutions, will necessarily give different results from one in which these classes are still mingled with the general population. The first precaution, therefore, in drawing conclusions from charity cases as in every other kind of statistics, is to make sure that the classes compared are fairly comparable.

If the cases are those who have merely applied for relief, the first thing to be ascertained is how many of these applicants ought to have relief of any sort. A table of nearly twenty-eight thousand cases investigated by the Charity Organization Societies in 1887 gave these returns:

| | |
|---|---|
| Worthy of continuous relief | 10.3 percent |
| Worthy of temporary relief | 26.6 percent |
| Need work rather than relief | 40.4 percent |
| Unworthy of relief | 22.7 percent |

Charles D. Kellogg, commenting on this report, says that among all the societies in the country there is a "notable unanimity of opinion that only from thirty-one to thirty-seven percent, or perhaps one-third, of the cases actually treated were in need of the material assistance for which no offices of friendly counsel or restraint could compensate. The logical application of this generalization . . . is that two-thirds of the real or simulated destitution could be wiped out by a more perfect adjustment of the supply and demand for labor and a more enlightened and vigorous police administration."[2]

A more exact view of the same thing may be obtained if we consider 8,294 cases in three large cities—Baltimore, Boston and New York— when a fuller classification was used. In the summary for these cities in 1892 it was held that 35 percent of the cases should have work rather than relief: 9.1 percent should have no relief; 5.8 percent should be disciplined; 7.42 percent should have visitation and advice only. Altogether only about 42.64 percent needed direct relief of any sort.

The question most commonly in the minds of those who undertake to investigate the causes of poverty by a system of case counting is this: Is poverty a misfortune or a fault? No full answer to the question can probably be worked out by scientific methods, but the question is so frequently asked that it seems worth while to ascertain what light a case counting investigation of poverty can throw upon it. With this end in view, I have arranged a table [Table 1] giving a comparison of the results reached by German investigators, by Charles Booth, and by the American Charity Organization societies. These societies, as a result of their experience in the decade of 1877–1888 agreed upon a schedule of the causes of poverty and furthermore decided that only the chief cause should be given.

The specific causes given by the German, English and American tables are grouped under three heads: those indicating misconduct, those indicating misfortune, and those not classified, or unknown.[3]

In presenting such a table as this it is important to indicate clearly what it does not show. It deals, as already pointed out, only with the exciting causes of poverty, and yet this fact is often not kept in mind, even by careful writers. Mr. Booth, for instance, includes "pauper association and heredity" in this list of causes; and the American societies include "nature and location of abode." Both of these are by nature predisposing causes, rather than immediate or exciting causes and it is confusing to mix the two. Again, many of the persons whose cases are tabulated here have been as Mr. Booth says, "the football of all the causes in the list." Under such circumstances, to pick out one cause and call it the most important, is a purely arbitrary proceeding. Any one of the causes might have been inadequate to produce dependence had not others coöperated with it. A man is drunk and breaks his leg: is the cause accident or drink? When this question was submitted to a group of charity organization workers, it was very promptly answered by two

[2] These early figures are interesting because of the use of the word "worthy," which by 1900 was dropped from all relief statistics; and also for the appearance of "unemployment" as a chief cause. Matters of employment remain one of the two most significant of the conditions of destitution— *Reviser.*

[3] The American schedule was devised by the Charity Organization societies represented at the National Conference of Charities in 1888 and was based on one then in use by the Buffalo Society. *Reviser.*

Table 1[1] **Causes of Poverty—Misconduct vs. Misfortune**

| Locality | Baltimore | Boston | Buffalo |
|---|---|---|---|
| Report of | C.O.S. | A.C. | C.O.S. |
| Number of cases | 1385 | 2083 | 8235 |
| Year | 1890–2 | 1890–2 | 1878–92 |
| Causes | Percent | Percent | Percent |
| Drink | 8.0 | 20.5 | 7.8 |
| Immorality | — | — | — |
| Shiftlessness and inefficiency | 13.0 | 7.2 | 4.3 |
| Crime and dishonesty | 0.8 | 1.4 | — |
| Roving disposition | 1.4 | 0.8 | — |
| Total indicating misconduct | 23.2 | 29.9 | 12.1 |
| Imprisonment of breadwinner | 0.4 | 1.6 | 2.0 |
| Orphans and abandoned children | 0.9 | 0.7 | — |
| Neglect by relatives | 1.7 | 0.9 | — |
| No male support | 4.5 | 6.0 | 13.8 |
| Total—Lack of normal support | 7.5 | 9.2 | 15.8 |
| Lack of employment | 12.5 | 14.2 | 27.5 |
| Insufficient employment | 8.5 | 5.5 | 1.7 |
| Poorly paid employment | 5.0 | 0.9 | 6.0 |
| Unhealthy and dangerous employment | 0.3 | 0.4 | — |
| Total—Unemployment, etc. | 26.3 | 21.0 | 35.2 |
| Ignorance of English | 0.4 | 0.8 | — |
| Accident | 4.0 | 2.9 | 4.6 |
| Sickness or death in family | 20.2 | 24.0 | 24.6 |
| Physical defects | 6.0 | 2.4 | 5.3 |
| Insanity | 0.8 | 0.6 | 0.9 |
| Old age | 6.0 | 4.1 | — |
| Total—Personal incapacity | 37.4 | 34.8 | 35.4 |
| Total indicating misfortune | 71.2 | 65.0 | 86.4 |
| Unclassified or unknown | 5.6 | 5.1 | 1.5 |

[1] Slightly condensed from Table IV, p. 36, 1st ed. of Warner's "American Charities." *Reviser.*

of them—but their answers were different. A man has been shiftless all his life and is now old: is the cause of poverty shiftlessness or old age? A man is out of work because he is lazy and inefficient: one has to know him quite well before one can be sure that laziness is the cause. Perhaps there is hardly a case in the whole table where destitution has resulted from a single cause.

The writer was so thoroughly convinced of this that he urged, when the first of the case schedules were adopted in 1888, an arithmetical plan by which the tributary causes as well as the chief cause would be

| Cincinnati | New York | Stepney | St. Pancras | 76 German Cities | Total |
|---|---|---|---|---|---|
| A.C. | C.O.S. | Booth | Booth | Böhmert | |
| 4844 | 1412 | 634 | 736 | 95,845 | |
| 1890–92 | 1891 | 1892 | 1892 | 1886 | Average |
| Percent | Percent | Percent | Percent | Percent | Percent |
| 11.1 | 10.7 | 12.6 | 21.9 | 1.3 | 11.6 |
| — | — | 2.5 | 6.9 | — | — |
| 12.9 | 7.2 | 7.0 | 13.4 | — | 9.2 |
| 1.9 | 1.4 | — | — | — | — |
| 5.3 | 3.3 | — | — | 1.4 | — |
| 31.2 | 22.6 | 22.1 | 42.2 | 2.7 | 23.3 |
| 0.7 | 0.6 | — | — | 1.7 | — |
| 1.0 | 0.1 | — | — | 5.6 | — |
| 0.8 | 0.5 | — | — | 0.6 | — |
| 7.1 | 7.2 | 4.6 | 2.8 | 2.5 | — |
| 9.6 | 8.4 | 4.6 | 2.8 | 10.4 | 8.5 |
| 10.5 | 29.0 | 4.4 | 2.2 | 12.5 | — |
| 7.2 | 6.1 | — | — | — | — |
| 4.2 | 2.5 | — | — | — | — |
| 0.5 | — | — | — | — | — |
| 22.4 | 37.6 | 4.4 | 2.2 | 12.5 | 20.2 |
| 0.8 | 0.4 | — | — | — | — |
| 2.3 | 3.3 | 4.7 | 2.6 | 1.1 | — |
| 15.0 | 18.5 | 26.7 | 20.7 | 45.8 | 24.4 |
| 2.5 | 2.7 | — | — | 2.4 | — |
| 0.6 | 0.7 | 1.7 | 4.3 | 3.4 | — |
| 3.0 | 3.3 | 32.8 | 23.4 | 15.8 | — |
| 24.2 | 28.9 | 65.9 | 51.0 | 68.5 | 43.2 |
| 56.2 | 74.9 | 74.9 | 56.0 | 91.4 | 72.0 |
| 12.6 | 2.5 | 3.0 | 1.8 | 5.9 | — |

shown. The influences resulting in destitution being regarded as making ten units, the relative force of each cause would be indicated by a proportionate number of units. The system was rejected as too complicated; yet if the requisite amount of skill and care were used, it would give valuable results.[4]

[4] At the suggestion of Professor Warner the Reviser used this method in a study of "Almshouse Women"—see American Statistical Assoc., Sept., 1895; and the method was used later by Mayo-Smith, N. Y. C. O. S. Report, 1897; and by A. F. Simons and C. F. Weller, Am Jo. of Soc., March, 1898.

Charles Booth, without attempting to estimate the proportionate value of the different causes, tabulated them in his study of pauperism at Stepney and St. Pancras, with the results shown in Table 2.

The impossibility of giving an accurate statistical description of the facts is still clearer when we try to separate the causes indicating misconduct from those indicating misfortune. Back of disease may be either. The imprisonment of the bread-winner indicates misconduct on his part, but may only indicate misfortune on the part of his wife and children. The same is true in the case of abandoned children and neglect by relatives. This particular classification has been made in deference to popular inquiry, but in the writer's opinion its chief value consists in showing how little it is worth.

Table 2 **Principal Causes of Pauperism at Stepney**

| Principal or Obvious Causes | Males | Females | Total | Percent | Contributory Causes | | | |
|---|---|---|---|---|---|---|---|---|
| | | | | | Drink | Pauper Asso. and Heredity | Sickness | Old Age |
| 1. Drink | 53 | 27 | 80 | 12.6 | — | 23 | 11 | 11 |
| 2. Immorality | 6 | 10 | 16 | 2.5 | 3 | 3 | 3 | 1 |
| 3. Laziness | 10 | 2 | 12 | 1.9 | 6 | 5 | 1 | 3 |
| 4. Incapacity, temper, etc. | 17 | 7 | 24 | 3.8 | 4 | 5 | 2 | 6 |
| 5. Extravagance | 7 | 1 | 8 | 1.3 | 4 | 2 | — | 3 |
| 6. Lack of work or trade misfortune | 26 | 2 | 28 | 4.4 | 4 | — | 5 | 13 |
| 7. Accident | 25 | 5 | 30 | 4.7 | 4 | 2 | 1 | 14 |
| 8. Death of husband | — | 26 | 26 | 4.1 | 3 | 2 | 10 | 8 |
| 9. Desertion | — | 3 | 3 | 0.5 | 3 | — | 1 | 1 |
| 10. Mental derangement | 3 | 8 | 11 | 1.7 | 1 | 2 | — | 2 |
| 11. Sickness | 97 | 71 | 169 | 26.7 | 24 | 38 | 5 | 41 |
| 12. Old age | 113 | 95 | 208 | 32.8 | 22 | 18 | 44 | — |
| 13. Pauper asso. and heredity | 6 | 1 | 7 | 1.1 | 1 | — | 2 | 2 |
| 14. Other causes | 9 | 3 | 12 | 1.9 | 6 | 6 | 2 | 2 |
| Total number | 373 | 261 | 634 | 100 | 85 | 106 | 87 | 107 |
| Percent of total cases | — | — | — | — | 13.0 | 16.0 | 13.0 | 16.0 |
| Total for causes 1–5, "misconduct" | 93 | 47 | 140 | 22.1 | 17 | 38 | 17 | 24 |
| Total for causes 6–12, "misfortune" | 265 | 210 | 475 | 74.9 | 61 | 62 | 66 | 79 |

Source: Adapted from Booth's "Pauperism and the Endowment of Old Age," p. 10.

But after all possible allowance has been made for the personal equation of the investigator and for all the inevitable inconclusiveness of the figures, there is a residuum of information to be got from the tables made on the casecounting principle. They give, as well as such statistics can, the conclusions reached by those who are studying dependence at first hand. If the figures furnished by all the investigators were added together in one great total, and the figures reflect to some extent the actual conditions.

Returning to the discussion of Table 1 and considering for the present only the figures for American cities we notice that the percentages for all causes indicating misconduct vary only between 10 and 32 the most important of them being drink. The percentage for this cause averages 11.6, going as low as 7.8 in Buffalo and as high as 20.5 in Boston. Nearly, but not quite so important as drink, is shiftlessness and inefficiency. It goes as low as 4.3 in Buffalo and as high as 13 in Baltimore, and this, for the American societies, includes laziness. The other causes in this group appear to be insignificant.

The causes indicating misfortune are re-grouped under three heads: lack of normal support, matter of employment, and personal capacity. The most important of those in the first group is "no male support," which ranges from 4.5 to 13.8 percent. The high percentage under this cause in Buffalo and the corresponding small percentage of cases attributable to misconduct is perhaps due to the fact that a larger proportion of cases there were receiving public relief. It may be noted that the precentages under this heading (which includes desertion and death of husband) are tolerably constant, even in Germany and England.

Matters of employment account for some what more than one-third of the destitution dealt with by the American societies, varying from an average of 21 percent in Boston to 37.6 percent in New York. No one well acquainted with Charity Organization cases can doubt that a considerable portion of those whose poverty is said to result from lack of employment in ordinary times are to some extent incapable, or unreliable; but there will also be a varying proportion every year of workers, such as dock laborers, tailors, milliners and many others in the intermittent industries, out of work solely because of the seasonal nature of their occupation. In times of depression by far the larger part of the charity cases are the involuntarily unemployed whose slender resources cannot serve to carry them over in great emergencies.[5]

Under matters of personal capacity, accident and physical defect exert a minor but quite constant influence, the former somewhat greater than the latter even in the European figures. Old age was not at first included by the American societies among the causes of poverty and even in the schedules of 1888 the percentage is small. This may be attributed to the fact that they deal with people who are, for the most part, struggling against pauperism and who are still mixed with the

---

[5] The point of view with regard to unemployment as a cause of pauperism has materially changed since the first edition of 1894 was published. *Reviser.*

ordinary population. Manifestly, the results in such cases must differ from those of confirmed pauperism inside of institutions.

Sickness, though not the largest, is the most constant cause of poverty everywhere and at all times, so far as these figures show and according to all investigators. In both American and English experience the percentage sinks but once as low as 15 and never quite reaches 28, the average being 21. This is one of the most significant facts brought out by these statistics and one not anticipated by the writer when he began collating them. Yet it has been confirmed and reconfirmed in so many ways that the conclusion seems inevitable that the figures set forth the true conditions. Personal acquaintance with the destitute classes has further convinced him that most of the causes of poverty result from or result in, a weakened physical and mental constitution, often merging into actual disease.[6]

The general heading, incapacity, might furthermore serve to cover nearly all the causes. Six of them avowedly belong there and the five others tabulated under misconduct can be so classed if we are willing to include infirmities of character as well as of body. The conditions grouped under the head of lack of normal support may also be said to show that the dependents are personally incapable of self-support and through fault or misfortune on the part of their natural guardians, have been left to themselves. The four causes grouped under employment would seem to be of a different nature and to indicate that capable persons may suffer from enforced idleness to the extent of becoming paupers.

The English and German figures in Table 1 are not properly comparable with the American statistics, and yet there are enough points of similarity to make comparison useful. The essential differences can be for the most part accounted for by the type of pauperism studied. The great majority of the German and all of the English cases were inmates of institutions. The cases at Stepney are examples of chronic pauperism to a greater extent than any group in the American Charity Organization tables. At St. Pancras the pauperism is still more fixed and hopeless. The German figures are the only ones covering all the official relief work of a large number of cities.

The writer knows so little of the methods of German relieving officers that it is perhaps dangerous to venture an opinion; but we might explain the very high percentage attributable to sickness (45.8) and the very low percentage attributable to drink (1.3) on the assumption that they are strict in their methods of granting relief and disinclined to relieve those who because of drunkenness deserve punishment. This percentage is so unexpectedly low that Böhmert discusses it at some length. He points out that drink is a predisposing cause in many cases where the immediate cause is lack of work, accident, sickness, imprisonment, or abandonment of children. He makes a further analysis suggesting that about 7.54 percent of the cases may be held destitute through misconduct, though he puts little reliance upon the conclusion.

[6] "Armenwesen in 77 deutschen Städten," pp. 114–5.

His table of the causes of poverty in the cases of 13,252 children [Table 3] is interesting as showing that more than one fourth of these children are dependent through the fault of their parents or other guardians.

The American figures that can be most profitably compared with the German and English statistics are those collated by the New York State Board of Charities regarding the inmates of all state almshouses in 1874 and 1875 [See Table 4].

Table 3 **13,252 Dependent Children in German Cities**

| Cause of Poverty | Percent |
|---|---|
| Orphanage | 38.75 |
| Fault of guardian | 25.89 |
| Abandonment by guardian | |
| Abusement and neglect by | |
| Laziness of | |
| Drunkenness of | |
| Incapacity of guardian | 17.12 |
| Lack of work | |
| Large family | |
| Advanced age | |
| Defect, mental or physical | |
| Other causes | 18.24 |
| | 100.00 |

Source: Böhmert, pp. 115–116 and 127–128.

Table 4 **Existing Causes of Dependency, New York Almshouse Inmates, 1874–5**

| Causes of Dependency | Number of Inmates | Percent |
|---|---|---|
| Mental defect (insane, idiotic, epileptic) | 5,289 | 41.9 |
| Old age | 2,081 | 16.5 |
| Orphans and abandoned children | 1,956 | 15.5 |
| Sickness | 1,580 | 12.5 |
| Shiftlessness and inefficiency | 767 | 6.1 |
| Physical defect (crippled, deformed, blind, deafmute) | 589 | 4.7 |
| No male support | 278 | 2.2 |
| Imprisonment of breadwinner | 74 | 0.6 |

[1] Condensed from the original table in Report of the New York State Board of Charities, 1877.

Two facts are brought out prominently by this table: one is the tendency of statistics based on case-counting to degenerate into mere description of the personal characteristics or condition of the dependent; and the other is the tendency of drink as a cause of pauperism to disappear when we study chronic cases of long standing. In this table of "existing" causes it is not mentioned at all, its results only being registered.

The second question popularly asked regarding the causes of poverty would be: What are the indications as to the tendency of different nationalities or races to become poor? To find an answer to this question Table 5 was prepared, giving the facts concerning 7,225 cases.[7] Of the white and colored Americans, the Germans, the Irish and the English cases there are enough to make percentages tolerably trustworthy; while of the French, Polish, Spanish, Italian, Scandinavian and other nationalities the numbers are too few to be separately discussed.

**Table 5 Causes of Poverty; 7,225 American Cases, Classified By Causes of Poverty and Nationality (1890–1892)**

| | American, 2,698 Cases | German, 842 Cases | Colored, 545 Cases | Irish, 1,833 Cases | English, 632 Cases | Other Nationalities, Cases | Other Average 7,225 Cases |
|---|---|---|---|---|---|---|---|
| | % | % | % | % | % | % | % |
| Drink | 15.14 | 7.83 | 6.24 | 23.63 | 16.94 | 8.26 | 15.29 |
| Shiftlessness and efficiency | 9.19 | 7.48 | 5.69 | 5.79 | 7.13 | 7.57 | 7.52 |
| Other moral defects | 3.00 | 1.53 | 1.83 | 1.04 | 3.95 | 1.95 | 2.32 |
| No male support | 4.11 | 4.27 | 2.94 | 5.08 | 3.17 | 5.48 | 4.31 |
| Other lack of normal support | 1.91 | 0.57 | 2.02 | 1.97 | 3.16 | 2.14 | 2.02 |
| Lack of employment | 24.57 | 28.62 | 17.43 | 18.88 | 24.69 | 26.78 | 23.17 |
| Insufficient employment | 6.63 | 7.60 | 8.63 | 6.39 | 4.75 | 6.42 | 6.51 |
| Poorly paid, etc. | 2.18 | 2.84 | 1.10 | .87 | 1.43 | 5.48 | 1.90 |
| Accident | 2.66 | 3.56 | 1.47 | 3.11 | 2.69 | 3.48 | 2.86 |
| Sickness or death in family | 20.31 | 22.92 | 39.64 | 19.81 | 22.94 | 21.24 | 22.27 |
| Physical defect | 3.40 | 4.73 | 5.50 | 3.49 | 1.74 | 4.62 | 3.69 |
| Insanity | 0.92 | 0.71 | — | .91 | 1.26 | 1.12 | 0.85 |
| Old age | 2.81 | 2.73 | 4.58 | 6.97 | 3.63 | 2.37 | 4.00 |
| Unclassified or unknown | 3.17 | 5.20 | 2.93 | 2.06 | 2.52 | 3.09 | 3.28 |

As to "drink" we find a general average of 15.29 percent. The white Americans are slightly below and the English slightly above this average. The Irish have a larger percentage, 23.63, under this head than any other nationality, the Germans are far below it at 7.83, and the colored Americans are still farther below at 6.24.[8]

[7] By the courtesy of the General Secretaries of the Charity Organization Societies of Baltimore, New Haven and New York, and of the Associated Charities of Boston, original schedules of more than eight thousand cases were furnished which are recombined so as to afford information not obtainable in the published reports of 1890–1892.

[8] Koren, in "Economic Aspects of the Liquor Problem" (p. 176), concludes that few negroes are habitual drunkards; that intemperance is only accountable for a small part of the negro's poverty; and that only in exceptional cases are drinking habits a barrier to steady employment—*Reviser.*

In shiftlessness and inefficiency the white Americans lead all other well represented nationalities, having a percentage of 9.19 as against an average of 7.52. The Irish here fall much below the average with 5.79 percent. Totalizing the percentages of causes indicating misconduct we get a general average of 25.13, the Irish leading with 30.46 and the English and Americans coming next with 28.02 and 27.33, respectively. The Germans are far below the average with 16.84 percent and the colored Americans lowest of all with 13.76. These relative positions are not changed if we include the cases in which imprisonment of breadwinner, orphanage or abandonment and neglect by relatives, may be taken to indicate misconduct on the part of natural guardians. In no nationality, therefore, does the number of cases of destitution under the head of misconduct reach one-third of the total.

Matters of employment vary less than the personal causes, as between the different nationalities, and the same is true of accident and physical defect. Under the very important head of sickness we find one decided variation. The average of this cause is 22.27 percent and all except the colored Americans conform quite closely to this. The cases of colored people show a percentage of 39.64, nearly double the average and quite double that of the Irish.

Those who know the colored people only casually or by hearsay may be surprised to find the misconduct causes running so low among them, while sickness is of greater relative importance than in any other nationality. But to one who has worked in Baltimore and Washington it seems a natural result and indeed a confirmation of the reliability of these statistics. The colored people are weak physically, become sick easily, and often die without visible resistance to disease. At the same time they have a dread of being assisted, especially when they think an institution will be recommended; and this, together with a certain apathy, will often induce them to endure great privations rather than ask for help. Besides this, there are many associations among them for mutual help, and the criminal and semi-criminal men have a brutal way of making their women support them. That the percentage for lack of work, 17.42, is lowest and that for insufficient employment is the highest under these two heads, perhaps reflects their hand to mouth way of working at odd jobs rather than taking steady work.[9]

Because one must hesitate to put much weight on a general average of this kind, the constituent elements of the table have been collated separately for each city to find out how far the differences between nationalities are constant for different places and according to different observers. In the matter of drink the nationalities kept the same relative positions; and in every city sickness was of greater relative importance among colored people than among others. That a larger number of Americans were destitute because of shiftlessness and inefficiency than of any other nationality was confirmed by the experience of New

[9] It may also reflect the fact that they are not as eligible for the better-paid and steadier work as white workmen.—*Reviser.*

York and New Haven but not wholly by Baltimore and Boston. On the whole, however, there are no variations that need destroy our confidence in the general averages established in Table 5. The similarities are so constant that if a new table were given the writer, in which the numbers and percents were pre-arranged and the headings of the lines and columns left blank, he should expect to be able to write in the names of the leading causes and of the leading nationalities without serious error.[10]

A classification of more than four thousand cases in Boston and New York establishes the fact, already suggested by Table 1, that large families are a relatively unimportant cause of destitution [see Table 6].

Fifty-two percent of these cases had one to three children and only 18 percent had more than five children. The "families" of one person each are either widows or widowers. The largest single family was found among colored people but the largest proportion of relatively large families—those numbering from five to nine persons—was found among the Italians, Poles and Russians. The families of paupers or semi-dependents usually average smaller than those of the population as a whole, partly because the number among classes degenerate enough to be dependent is not as large as is ordinarily supposed; to some extent because of high infant mortality; and because the families of these classes tend to disintegrate rapidly, children drifting away from parents and aged parents in turn being shaken off by adult children. The family therefore which applies for relief is often only the fragment of a family.

A re-classification of applicants for relief in column one, Table 7, by marital condition, shows that about one-half are married people living together, and nearly one-third are widows and deserted wives.

Seven percent deserted wives may seem large to those unacquainted with the modern urban population but it is lower than many charity workers expected to find it. The differences between the work of the different societies is the principal thing reflected by the variations in the applications of single men.

A matter which is not brought out by the tables thus far given, but which is shown by the collateral investigations of the different agencies, is the large number of children either dragged into pauperism by the destitution of their parents or entirely abandoned by them. In the figures of almshouse pauperism this appears; but the condition there shown has now gone by as children have been drafted off to other institutions. But in the American experience of cases on the poverty line the large number of children is very striking. Out of 4,310 persons dealt with by the New York Charity Organization Society in 1891, over 40 percent were under fourteen; in Boston, out of 3,927 individuals dealt with, over 42 percent were under fourteen; in Buffalo, out of

[10] The original table on pp. 49–50 of the First Edition adds nothing to this statement of Professor Warner and is therefore omitted—*Reviser.*

Table 6  4,176 Boston and New York Cases, Classified According to Number in the Family and Nationality, 1890–1892

| Number in Family | American, 1,363 Cases % | Colored, 192 Cases % | English, 496 Cases % | French, 77 Cases % | German, 373 Cases % | Italian, 109 Cases % | Irish, 1,287 Cases % | Polish and Russian, 128 Cases % | Scandinavian, 22 Cases % | Other Countries, 129 Cases % | Total, 4,176 Cases % |
|---|---|---|---|---|---|---|---|---|---|---|---|
| 1 | 14.81 | 16.14 | 17.53 | 10.38 | 12.06 | 7.33 | 15.77 | 4.68 | 18.18 | 12.40 | 14.60 |
| 2 | 20.90 | 27.08 | 19.15 | 22.07 | 17.42 | 11.00 | 19.19 | 8.59 | 13.63 | 14.72 | 19.30 |
| 3 | 17.62 | 22.91 | 17.53 | 23.36 | 17.69 | 13.76 | 18.10 | 19.53 | 27.26 | 21.70 | 18.24 |
| 4 | 17.82 | 13.43 | 18.75 | 18.18 | 15.28 | 18.34 | 15.46 | 12.50 | 22.75 | 17.82 | 16.67 |
| 5 | 11.59 | 7.81 | 12.90 | 13.00 | 17.42 | 19.26 | 12.82 | 17.96 | 13.63 | 13.95 | 12.98 |
| 6 | 7.90 | 7.81 | 6.06 | 2.59 | 8.31 | 10.09 | 8.00 | 9.37 | — | 10.07 | 7.78 |
| 7 | 5.64 | 3.12 | 3.83 | 7.89 | 5.36 | 15.59 | 5.67 | 10.93 | 4.54 | 6.20 | 5.77 |
| 8 | 2.34 | 0.52 | 2.45 | 1.29 | 2.41 | 2.75 | 3.03 | 10.15 | — | 2.32 | 2.73 |
| 9 | 0.80 | 0.52 | 0.60 | 1.29 | 1.87 | 1.83 | 1.93 | 3.12 | — | 0.77 | 1.14 |
| 10 | 0.46 | — | 0.60 | — | 0.80 | — | 0.46 | 2.34 | — | — | 0.47 |
| 11 | 0.08 | — | — | — | 0.80 | — | 0.07 | 0.78 | — | — | 0.14 |
| 12 | — | — | 0.60 | — | 0.53 | — | — | — | — | — | 0.11 |
| 13 | — | 0.52 | — | — | — | — | — | — | — | — | 0.02 |
| Unknown | 0.10 | 0.03 | — | 0.06 | 0.05 | 0.05 | 0.04 | 0.05 | 0.04 | 0.05 | 0.05 |

Table 7 **Cases by Marital Condition and Cities**

| | New York,[1] Boston, Baltimore, New Haven, 1890–1892, 8,028 Cases | New York, 1896–1900, 8,638 Cases | Boston, 1899–1905, 5,529 Cases |
|---|---|---|---|
| | % | % | % |
| Married | 47.7 | 64.71 | 53.5 |
| Widows | 23.7 | 23.21 | 24.5 |
| Deserted wives | 6.9 | 5.89 | 9.3 |
| Single women | 5.6 | 2.39 | 6.5 |
| Deserted husbands and widowers | 4.8 | 2.30 | 2.7 |
| Single men | 10.6 | 1.02 | 2.7 |
| Orphans | 0.3 | 0.31 | 0.2 |
| Divorced | 0.4 | 0.13 | 0.6 |
| Miscellaneous | — | 0.04 | — |
| Total | 100.0 | 100.00 | 100.0 |

Source: Charity Organization Society reports.
[1] Arranged from Table XII, Warner, 1st ed.; columns 2 and 3 added by the reviser.

2,515 persons, 48 percent were under fourteen; only in Baltimore did the percentage of children fall as low as 15.8.

On the whole it may be concluded that while the leading cause of confirmed pauperism as investigated by Charles Booth in England, is the weakness of old age, the leading cause of incipient pauperism, as investigated by the American Charity Organization Societies, is the weakness of childhood. Taking this in connection with the large percentage of pauperism which is constantly and everywhere attributed to sickness and physical defect, we have a striking confirmation of the conclusion reached by Dugdale in his study of the Jukes. He says:

"Pauperism is an indication of weakness of some kind, either youth, disease, old age, injury, or for women, childbirth.

"Hereditary pauperism rests chiefly upon disease in some form, tends to terminate in extinction, and may be called the sociological aspect of physical degeneration."

If we assume, roughly, that the forces which tend to break down the physical man and to bring about various forms of degeneration, are those which are pushing him toward death, we may present them graphically by a modification of a diagram used by Dr. J. S. Billings[11] [see Figure 1].

[11] In the Cartright Lectures on "Vital and Medical Statistics" printed in *Med. Rec.*, December, 1889.

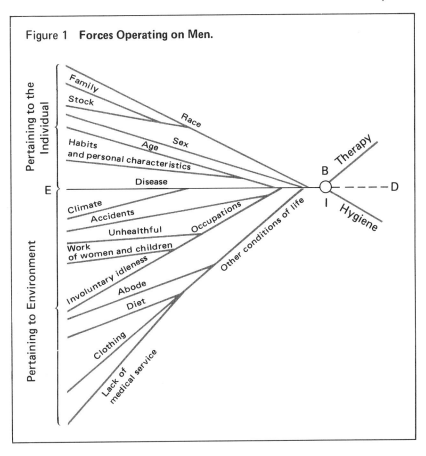

Figure 1  **Forces Operating on Men.**

Let the point B represent birth and the point D represent death. The individual I passes to the right along the line ED at a rate proportionate to the progressive exhaustion of his vital energies. The forces which retard his movement are grouped under two heads, those pertaining to the individual and those pertaining to the environment. The most constant force in producing incapacity from which pauperism results we have found to be disease, which is placed accordingly in the middle position among the forces tending toward death. In the next chapter we will consider some of the predisposing causes of disease and of other forms of degeneration which pertain to the individual; and in the succeeding chapter some of those which pertain to environment. It is an inquiry fraught with great difficulties. As Dr. Billings said in closing these lectures: In viewing the records of human life, disease and death, the variations which are at first most perceptible are often those which are most superficial, and which give little or no indication of the magnitude and direction of the great masses beneath.

## Chapter Summary

We have attempted here to trace some of the major features in early social welfare research on poverty causation. Such research constitutes the first identifiable "cycle" of social inquiry to crystallize within the embryonic field. Its emergence was related to the early identification of "scientific charity" with the rational analysis and alleviation of human dependency in American society.

The initial studies of causes in social work undertook a "case-counting" approach to the subject whereby individual cases of poverty were analyzed subjectively by charity workers and these causal judgments were then tabulated for large numbers of cases. In this pre-1900 period a heavily moralistic slant characterized the perception of poverty causes. The severe limitations of these subjective, ex post facto statistics were noted in the social work literature of the era. Amos Griswold Warner, the foremost codifier of nineteenth-century social welfare knowledge, recognized such liabilities in the data he compiled and questioned the very notion of discrete "causes" of so complex a social phenomenon as poverty.

Around the turn of the century the stance of social work began to move away from individual moral rehabilitation and toward social and institutional reform. Mary Richmond gave eloquent expression to the key social work doctrines of multiple causation and the complex interaction of social factors as opposed to the simple determination of poverty and other human needs. In the face of such developments, the quest for the major "causes" of poverty in individual cases soon gave way to study of the societal conditions associated with its occurence. The goal of social reconstruction overshadowed that of individual rehabilitation.

Though the very vocabulary of "causes" subsequently became a *lingua non grata* in the field for a time—through disillusionment and misuse—nevertheless this early phase of research in social work had its constructive side. With all of its scientific inadequacies and naiveté, it amassed a cumulative base of data and interpretation that helped the field overcome its initial tendency to see poverty as residing largely within the moral defects of the individual. In this way it assisted the emerging profession—and with it perhaps the nation itself—in shifting its attention to the social and economic concomitants of want.

The chapter closed with a complete excerpt from a key section of the revised edition Warner's "classic" *American Charities*, dealing with "Causes of Poverty" and reflecting contemporary research writing and thinking on the subject.

**NOTES**

1 For a recent review of the history of the "scientific charity" movement, see Roy Lubove, *The Professional Altruist* (New York: Atheneum, 1971), paperback, pp. 1–54. One aspect of this movement in Lubove's analysis involved the managerial efficiency, coordination, and organization dimension of "scientific charity"; another—the dimension we are primarily concerned with in this chapter—entailed the application of what was then understood to be the scientific method to the understanding and cure of individual and social problems (Lubove, pp. 6–7).

2 Frank J. Bruno, *Trends in Social Work* (New York: Columbia University Press, 1948), p. 98.

3 Cited in Virginia P. Robinson, *A Changing Psychology in Social Casework* (Chapel Hill: University of North Carolina Press, 1934), p. xii.

4 Cited in Carol Germain, "Casework and Science: A Historical Encounter," in Robert W. Roberts and Robert H. Nee, eds., *Theories of Social Casework* (Chicago: University of Chicago Press, 1970), pp. 8–9, footnote.

5 Glendower Evans, "Scientific Charity," *Proceedings of the National Conference of Charities and Corrections,* 1889, pp. 24–35.

6 Ibid., p. 32.

7 Ibid.

8 Charles D. Kellog, "Statistics: Their Value in Charity Organization Work," *Proceedings of the National Conference of Charities and Corrections,* 1890, p. 33.

9 Lubove, p. 7.

10 Germain, pp. 8–12.

11 Cited in Robert H. Bremner, *From the Depths: The Discovery of Poverty in the United States* (New York: New York University Press, 1956, p. 53.

12 Lubove, p. 10.

13 Germain, p. 7.

14 Lubove, p. 121.

15 Bremner, pp. 87–120.

16 Ibid., pp. 83–84.

17 Bruno, p. 220.

18 Elisha Harris. "The Statistics of Crime and Pauperism," *Proceedings of the First Conference of Charities and Corrections,* 1874, pp. 34–43.

19 Ibid., p. 34.

20 Ibid., p. 36.

21 Cited in Bremner, p. 8.

22 Ibid., p. 80. This was the early pioneer in American social welfare, Rev. Joseph Tuckerman.

23 That these attitudes still persist in large degree today is well documented from many standpoints. See, for example, Joe R. Feagin, "Poverty: We Still Believe God Helps Those Who Help Themselves," *Psychology Today,* November 1972, pp. 101–110.

24 Bruno, p. 27.

25 Amos G. Warner, *American Charities: A Study in Philanthropy and Economics* (New York: Crowell, 1894), p. 22.

26 Ibid., p. 30.

27 Ibid., p. 28.

28 Ibid.

29 Ibid., pp. 31–32.

[30] Ibid., p. 36.

[31] Ibid., p. 32. Warner went on to acknowledge that "under such circumstances, to pick out one cause and call it the most important, is a most arbitrary proceeding." Nevertheless he reluctantly makes use of such classifications in his analysis "in deference to popular inquiry" (Ibid., p. 38).

[32] Bremner, p. 56.

[33] Ibid., p. 81.

[34] Ibid.

[35] For a modern, technical critique of the "one-shot case study method," see Donald T. Campbell and Julian C. Stanley, *Experimental and Quasi-Experimental Designs for Research* (Chicago: Rand McNally, 1963), pp. 6–7 and Table 1, p. 8.

[36] F. B. Sanborn, "Statistics of Pauperism in the United States," *Proceedings of the Conference of Charities,* 1877, p. 23.

[37] Cited in Bruno, p. 76.

[38] Ibid.

[39] Samuel G. Smith, "Discussion on Legislation Concerning Charities," *Proceedings of the National Conference of Charities and Corrections,* 1901, p. 355.

[40] Lilian Brandt, "Statistics of Dependent Families," *Proceedings of the National Conference of Charities and Corrections,* 1906, p. 436.

[41] Ibid.

[42] Bruno, p. 111.

[43] Mary E. Richmond, *Social Diagnosis* (New York: Russell Sage Foundation, 1917), p. 93.

[44] Ibid., p. 100.

[45] Ibid., p. 259. For fuller discussions of these conceptual issues in social work, see Sidney E. Zimbalist, "Organismic Social Work Versus Partialistic Research," *Social Casework,* January 1952, pp. 1–8; also, Germain, op. cit.

[46] Germain, p. 13.

[47] Ibid., p. 15.

[48] See, for example, Ruth S. Cavan and Katherine H. Ranck, *The Family and the Depression* (Chicago: University of Chicago Press, 1938); also *Unattached Women on Relief in Chicago, 1937* (U.S. Women's Bureau, 1937).

[49] E.g., Hubert M. Blalock, *Causal Conferences in Non-experimental Research* (Chapel Hill: University of North Carolina Press, 1961).

[50] Amos G. Warner and Mary Roberts Coolidge, *American Charities* (New York: Crowell, 1919), pp. 135–136.

[51] J. Bronowski, *The Common Sense of Science* (New York: Random House, Vintage Books, 1954), p. 89.

[52] Ibid., pp. 87–88.

[53] Blalock, op. cit.

[54] Gordon Hearn, ed., *The General Systems Approach: Contributions Toward a Holistic Conception of Social Work* (New York: Council on Social Work Education, 1969).

[55] Donald T. Campbell and Julian C. Stanley, *Experimental and Quasi-experimental Designs for Research* (Chicago: Rand McNally, 1963).

[56] Abraham Kaplan, *The Conduct of Inquiry* (San Francisco: Chandler, 1964), p. 124.

[57] Another aspect of this issue is the perennial philosophic problem of determinism vs. free will in human affairs. See, for example, Kaplan, pp. 121–124. Ramifications of this conflict were reflected in social work in the earlier

diagnostic vs. functional controversy, and in the current existential vs. ego psychology viewpoints. See Scott Briar and Henry Miller, *Problems and Issues in Social Casework* (New York: Columbia University Press, 1971), p. 29; also, Roberts and Nee, chaps. 2 and 3.

[58] For further discussion of the conceptual and technical problems here, see Robert M. McIver, *Social Causation* (Boston: Ginn, 1942) and Hubert M. Blalock, *Causal Models in the Social Sciences* (Chicago: Aldine, 1971).

# Chapter 4
# The Measurement
# of Poverty

## The British Background

In a text dealing with major historic emphases in social work research it should not be surprising that the first two such themes to be elaborated—out of a half-dozen in all—pertain to the study of poverty. For social welfare emerged in large part out of the attempt to grapple rationally and systematically with this human blight, and it was natural and appropriate for the research arm of the field to lend support by attempting to "measure" poverty. One such effort was detailed in the last chapter, describing the search for the causes of poverty, and a separate but related thrust will be dealt with here, namely, the quantitative study of its level and extent.

Logically speaking, it might be argued that the measurement of a phenomenon should precede an attempt to attack its sources, and as we have seen this point was indeed made as early as 1877. It can be observed, however, that though history is chronological, it is not necessarily logical. In any case, American social welfare research turned first to causation and only later to taking stock of poverty as such. In England the alternative priority was followed, and indeed there was little British concern with the probe for "causes," in the American style at least. Perhaps if we had followed the other course some blind alleys might have been avoided.

But the United States did not have a Charles Booth at the time to "lift the curtain" of poverty with a massive and masterful inquiry. We did profit immensely, however, from his example and his findings. The first reports of his monumental undertaking began to appear in the *Journal of the Royal Statistical Society* in 1887, and the continuing publications had a marked impact on welfare leaders in this country. We have already noted that Amos Warner incorporated some of Booth's data on causes in his 1894 treatise, even though this was an incidental tangent to Booth's major focus. More important, Booth's model was widely quoted and admired as the ideal prototype for welfare investigation. His influence on the subsequent course of poverty research and the later social survey movement in this country was a profound one. Booth's example was so impressive that it towered above other efforts either in France or in this country in shaping the pattern of welfare research for years to come.[1] Despite its many inadequacies and inefficiencies by today's research criteria, *Life and Labour of the People in London* clearly stands unchallenged as the outstanding achievement of social work research in the nineteenth century.

Charles Booth was a most unusual businessman, a conservative and wealthy London shipowner whose intellectual interest in social problems and poverty was whetted in part by attendance at meetings at Toynbee Hall and Oxford House and in part by acquaintance with the settlement house workers he met there. A report in 1885 by the Marxist Social Democratic Federation in London had claimed that one-fourth of the working class lived in dire poverty, and Booth—refusing to accept this "incendiary" conclusion—determined to ascertain the facts of working-class life through objective, scientific investigation.[2]

It is clear that Booth had no idea what an extended voyage he was undertaking when he embarked upon these uncharted waters in 1886, a voyage to be completed seventeen years—and seventeen volumes—later. Though he still had not found all of the answers to the questions with which he started, he had thrown a strong new light on the nature and spread of urban poverty and pointed the way for modern community studies in social work and in the social sciences generally. He financed the project himself and wrote many of the reports, while gathering around him a talented group of assistants (including the writer Beatrice Potter, who later married Fabian socialist Sidney Webb).

In addition to focusing on poverty, Booth's seventeen volumes also covered industrial, religious, and other institutional forces bearing upon the lives of the London working class. He concluded finally that the estimate of one-fourth of the population living below the "poverty line," which had challenged him to tackle this huge project in the first place, was if anything too low—his own figure, so laboriously compiled, was closer to one-third (30.7 percent). In addition, Booth had amassed a vast store of facts and impressions about life in London at the close of the nineteenth century that opened the eyes of his contemporaries to some of the realities about them. His efforts helped pave the way for sweeping social reforms and the subsequent breakup of the Elizabethan Poor Law in England. Of this outcome, Beatrice Potter Webb later wrote:

> If I had to sum up, in a sentence, the net effect of Charles Booth's work, I should say that it was to give an entirely fresh impetus to the general adoption, by the British people . . . of the policy of securing to every individual . . . a prescribed national minimum of the requisites for efficient parenthood and citizenship. This policy may, or may not, be Socialism, but it is assuredly a decisive denial of the economic individualism of the 'eighties.[3]

Charles Booth, the conservative businessman, would probably have bristled at this terminology, though he did espouse what he referred to as a "limited socialism" in some of his recommendations (e.g., for old-age pensions as a means of combatting poverty among the elderly).[4]

Thus Booth's epic volumes apparently fell on highly fertile soil, more so than the work of his followers in this country. Perhaps the earlier emergence in England of the Industrial Revolution, with a resultant greater sense of public responsibility for its social consequences, brought about a greater concern for the mass implications of widespread poverty. Then, too, England had a longer-standing tradition of social and legislative reform, based on fact-finding investigations and royal commission inquiries, than was the case here.

Another important contribution to poverty research in England was made by B. Seebohm Rowntree's surveys of the provincial town of York, beginning with *Poverty: A Study of Town Life,* published in 1901.[5] Using rather different methods (see pp. 79–81), he nonetheless came up with a similar proportion living below the poverty line—27.8 percent as compared with Booth's 30.7 percent in London. Thus poverty was demonstrated to be a widespread component of the British population, similarly prevalent in both small town and metropolis.

## The Nature of Social Need

But what is meant by *poverty?* Can it be usefully defined and measured? As we shall see, it was recognized from the first that we are dealing here with a concept that is essentially judgmental and culturally determined. As such it is typical of a number of central social work concepts that are similarly grounded in value premises and community standards, such as "need," "adjustment," and "pathology." Generically, poverty measurement may be viewed as a form of "need research,"[6] that is, the study of a social need—in this case the need for a minimally adequate standard of subsistence.

The identification of what constitutes "social need" in the first place may be said to depend essentially on the prevailing cultural norms and expectations of the surrounding society. Whether or not a given social condition—illiteracy, for example—is viewed as reflecting a "need" calling for societal attention depends in the last analysis on the perception of that condition by the community, its importance to the functioning of the community, and the relative priority given to it.

All of which appears to leave the social work researcher in something of a dilemma. For if need research is value based, then where does research fit into this process? The logical problem here stems of course from the nature of an applied, helping profession such as social work. For in addition to the study of "what is" (i.e., facts, relationships, theories, laws, etc.), which has been the traditional domain of science, social work is equally concerned with "what should be"—the determination of goals, values, and ends. And this is a process of a quite different order.[7] Research, for example, can establish the standards of living and the distribution of income in a particular population. But the question of what the standard of living *should be* for a given segment of the population, say, the most impoverished class, is a value judgment. Stated otherwise, it is an act of community conscience—a matter of public preference rather than a matter of "fact."[8]

However, to say that goals and values are not fully ascertained by research is not to say that research cannot contribute to their clarification and delineation. Thus research may identify the values and attitudes held by the public; it may provide verifiable data on specified social conditions; it may throw light on the probable consequences of different social choices; it may analyze alternative means of approaching given objectives. The objectives or goals themselves derive ultimately from the community's values, which of course vary from culture to culture, and from age to age within a given culture. And this flexible nature of social need—more transient than permanent, more relative than absolute, more subjective than objective—can be seen with particular clarity in the study of the archetypal need of human beings for social survival in the form of a minimally adequate standard of living. As a research target it is a peculiarly frustrating one, receding as one approaches it. For man is a social creature, and the consensus as to what is necessary to his social nature shifts with the standards of society. Shakespeare put it well when he had King Lear admonish that if we

> Allow not nature more than nature needs,
> Man's life is cheap as beasts'.[9]

## Poverty and Its Gradations

It should be emphasized that in discussing poverty in Western society we are indeed referring to a "social need" as contrasted with a "physical" one. This, it will be maintained, is the case despite that fact that we do tend to speak of "material want," "tangible need," "physical destitution," and the like. Actually, in this part of the world starvation is rare (though malnutrition and disease related to malnutrition are not), and fatal exposure "to the elements" seldom occurs (though it does occur). In the area of nutrition certain physiological minimal requirements have been established for subsistence, but even here cultural standards enter in some degree into the selection of foods and into the manner of their preparation. For example, protein may be derived from either meat or vegetables, so that a choice must be made in the type (and hence the cost) of protein. Thus the 20 to 25 cents per person per day allocated for food in some United Nations refugee relief operations for mere physical survival would hardly be conceivable as a minimal American diet.* Similarly, while adequate shelter and clothing are essential to withstand winters in the upper latitudes, the form in which the minimum may be provided can vary quite widely in kind and cost.

* A recent report from the World Bank states: "Almost 650 million people in the developing world are considered to live in *absolute poverty, existing on annual per capita incomes of not more than $50*" (emphasis added). Cited in *Chicago Daily News,* August 26, 1975, p. 8.

It can therefore be maintained that in the Western countries poverty is perceived more as a social phenomenon than as a physical one. So the choice of what goods and services go into a "minimally adequate" standard of living, and how much, is more a matter of cultural standards than one of scientific evidence. It is also a political matter, not only because controversial attitudes and values are involved within a given body politic but also because public action and responsibility may be inferred from the poverty thus identified; income redistribution is implied.

In defining poverty Booth invented the useful notion of the "poverty line," the level of income dividing the "poor" from the "nonpoor." He also went on to identify eight standards of life in late-nineteenth-century London, four below the poverty line and four above, as follows:

| | | |
|---|---|---|
| | A. | The lowest class of occasional labourers, |
| "Very poor" | | loafers and semi-criminals |
| | B. | Casual earnings |
| | C. | Intermittent earnings |
| "Poor" | | |
| | D. | Small regular earnings |
| *Poverty line* | | |
| | E. | Regular standard earnings |
| | F. | Higher class labour |
| "Comfortable" | | |
| | G. | Lower middle class |
| | H. | Upper middle class[10] |

Booth recognized the subjectivity and relativity involved in establishing the poverty line in his definition as follows:

> The divisions indicated here . . . are necessarily arbitrary. By the word "poor" I mean to describe those who have a sufficiently regular though bare income, such as 18s to 21s per week for a moderate family, and by "very poor" those who from any cause fall much below this standard. The "poor" are those whose means may be sufficient, but are barely sufficient, for *decent, independent life;* the "very poor" those whose means are insufficient for this *according to the usual standard of life in this country*. My "poor" may be described as living under a struggle to obtain the necessaries of life and make both ends meet; while the "very poor" live in a state of chronic want. It may be their own fault that this is so; that is another question; my first business is simply with the numbers who, from whatever cause, do live under conditions of poverty or destitution.[11] (Emphasis added)

Booth thus provided for the breakdown of the global term *poverty* into several degrees or intensities of need, a pattern followed in one form or other by a number of his successors. B. S. Rowntree, for example, introduced a distinction between "primary" and "secondary" poverty, which was different from Booth's breadown of poverty into the "poor" and the "very poor." Rowntree defined "primary" and "secondary," respectively, as follows:

a. Families whose total earnings were insufficient to obtain the minimum necessaries for the maintenance of merely physical efficiency [i.e., 21s 8d per week for a family of five]. Poverty falling under this head was described as "primary" poverty.
b. Families whose total earnings *would have been sufficient* for the maintenance of merely physical efficiency *were it not that some portion of it was absorbed by other expenditure either useful or wasteful.* Poverty falling under this head was described as "secondary" poverty.[12] (Emphasis added)

Rowntree's cutoff criterion of 21s 8d per week for a family of five in 1899 was more specific than Booth's earlier figure of 18–21s; it also was somewhat more systematically derived in terms of constituent costs. For example, the food item was based on current understanding of minimal nutritional requirements. However, for reasons discussed earlier, such figures entail a large degree of judgment based on prevailing social standards.

Despite the differences in the internal classifications of poverty in the two studies, Rowntree was convinced that their total estimates were parallel. In his words, he had "no hesitation in regarding my estimate of the total poverty in York as comparable with Booth's estimate of the total poverty in London, and in this Mr. Booth agrees."[13] As a result York's 28 percent below the poverty line was considered roughly commensurate with London's 31 percent.

In 1913 the prominent mathematical economist Sir Arthur L. Bowley applied (with minor adjustments) Rowntree's criteria of "primary" poverty to the population of five middle-sized industrial towns.[14] In carrying out these investigations he is reputed to have been the first to have utilized population sampling in community research.[15] Since he limited his analysis to "primary" poverty, his totals are not directly comparable with the figures cited earlier. (His towns averaged slightly higher than Rowntree's 10 percent in "primary" poverty.) Some ten years later he repeated his surveys, publishing the results under the title *Has Poverty Diminished*. He concluded that it had, inasmuch as the "primary" poverty he was examining in 1924 was "little more than half that in 1913."[16] However, the trends in "hard-core" poverty may very well differ from poverty trends in general.

An instructive illustration of the latter point may be seen in Rowntree's 1936 replication of his York poverty study.[17] This time Rowntree followed Bowley's example in focusing on the "primary" poverty level, on the basis that it provided a more consistent and tangible measure than the more subjective "secondary" poverty category. In 1899, "secondary poverty" had been ascertained by the following procedure:

> The investigator, in the course of his house to house visitation, noted down the households where there were evidences of poverty, i.e., obvious want and squalor. Direct information was often obtained from neighbors, or from a member of the household concerned, to the effect that the father or more was a heavy drinker; in other cases the pinched faces of the ragged children often told their own tale of poverty and privation.[18]

In 1936, Rowntree abandoned the effort to measure this "secondary" level. As he explained,

> In this survey I have made no attempt to measure the amount of "secondary" poverty by direct observation, partly because the methods of doing this adopted in 1899 appear to me now as being too rough to give reliable results, and also because *even had I done so the results would not have rendered possible a comparison with 1899, for ideas of what constitutes "obvious want and squalor" have changed profoundly since then.* There is no doubt that in 1899 investigators would not have regarded as "obvious want and squalor" conditions *which would have been so regarded in 1936,* and on the other hand a large proportion of the families living below the 1936 poverty line *would not in 1899 have been regarded as "showing signs of poverty."*[19] (Emphasis added)

A more explicit recognition of the relativistic nature of the general poverty concept could hardly be given. Adhering, then, to the presumably firmer concept of "primary" poverty, Rowntree found—as Bowley had previously—that there had been a substantial reduction, by more than one-half, from 1899 to 1936 in this type of adject need. In actual proportions, the figure for those living in "primary" poverty in 1899 was 9.9 percent of the total population of York, and in 1936 it was 3.9 percent.[20] The same yardstick of income was used in both years, with only an adjustment to reflect the change in the value of money over $3\frac{1}{2}$ decades.[21]

In his 1936 replication, however, Rowntree derived a new measure of the "minimum" income required "to enable families . . . to secure the necessaries of a healthy life" at that time, based on the best available current estimates regarding minimal nutrition, housing, clothing, recreation, and other basic family needs. The budget he arrived at was 43s 6d per week (after rent) for a family of five.[22] (This figure is to be contrasted with 30s 7d per week, which was the equivalent—at 1936 prices—of the corresponding primary poverty yardstick in 1899.)[23] In applying his new "minimum" standard to the population of York in 1936 Rowntree found that 31.1 percent of the *working class* was living below this level. (In 1899 the portion of the working-class population of York in *either* "primary" or "secondary" poverty was 33.4 percent.)*

Rowntree rightly cautions the reader that these two figures have "no relation to each other,"[24] since they are based on quite different standards of need, and he therefore limits himself to the comparison of the "primary" poverty figures as the most uniform between the two periods, as noted previously. The important point for our purposes, nevertheless, is that his *conception* of what constitutes a suitable "minimum" did indeed rise appreciably over the years. The 43s 6d per week in 1936 was almost 50 percent higher than the 1899 poverty line in constant monetary terms; moreover, the portion of the wage-earning population below this shifting line was not greatly different in the two periods.

Finally, in the 1930s a *New Survey of Life and Labour of the People in London,* following and refining Booth's model prototype, was conducted under the direction of Sir Hubert Llewelyn Smith. Changes in life style and social conditions over the four decades spanned by these two studies made meaningful comparisons tenuous and difficult, though a number of parallels and contrasts were drawn in the nine-volume report.[25]

In this "new survey" no attempt was made to revise Booth's poverty yardstick in more modern terms. Rather, it was applied as an absolute measure (as Rowntree had applied it in parts of his second survey), and it was found, not surprisingly, that in this sense poverty had indeed declined in London—from 30.7 percent in the late nineteenth century to some 9.5 percent in 1929.[26]

In highlighting† this impressive corpus of English poverty

---

* It should be noted, however, that the portion of the *total* population of York below this line dropped from 27.8 percent living "in poverty" in 1899 to 17.7 percent living below the 1936 "minimum budget."

† Through the 1930s only; much more has since been done.

research we can distinguish two contrasting standards of measurement. One is an *absolute* (or "static") yardstick, in which the identical subsistence level, defined in constant monetary terms, is applied to different communities or periods; this fixed type of measure shows a striking improvement or reduction in the incidence of poverty over the decades. The second yardstick is a *relative* (or "flexible") one, reflecting the shifting norms and expectations of an advancing economy and way of life; this mobile standard tends to show a fairly consistent portion of the population "below par." These approaches to poverty measurement should be clearly distinguished. (At the same time, it should be kept in mind that the distinction here is *not* between "objective" *vs.* "subjective" standards, since, as has been pointed out, all modern poverty standards contain subjective elements.) A recent economics text puts it this way:

> Although the presently established "poverty line" [in the United States] exceeds the *average* income level in almost every other country in the world, it appears quite clear that we shall not be satisfied with that level . . . and will no doubt raise our sights. When most people think of poverty it is not the absolute level of income that they have in mind, but rather the relative level of income. And this turns out to be a much more stubborn problem to resolve.[27]

Taken as a whole, there was no group of poverty studies in the United States at all comparable with this remarkable series of investigations in England until we reach the decade of the 1960s. Only with the launching of the "Great Society" did the study of poverty in this country begin to approach the British efforts.

## Early Poverty Studies in the United States

Family budgetary studies in the United States go back at least as far as 1875, when a series of official household expenditure inquiries were conducted for the U.S. Bureau of Labor by Carroll D. Wright. Over 25,000 families were interviewed to obtain data on expenditure patterns and distributions.[28] However, it was not until the present century that intensive studies specifically aimed at establishing *minimum* budgetary standards were launched in this country.

### More's "Wage-Earner's Budgets"

One of the earliest such studies in social work was Louis B. More's *Wage Earner's Budgets,* conducted from 1903 to 1905 and published in 1907.[29] This was originally to be a study of living standards of families in the immediate vicinity of a New York settlement, Greenwich House. However, the problem of minimum budgetary needs and standards was taken up as part of the total study. The study provides an early illustration in this country of the method of supervised longitudinal account keeping by families as a means of obtaining detailed information on expenditures over time. (In this regard More's approach represents an American adaptation of a method introduced by the French social research pioneer, Frederic Le Play, in his *Les Ouvriers Européens,* published in 1855.)

Capitalizing on their intimate acquaintance and frequent contacts with the families in the neighborhood, More and her coinvestigators from Greenwich House persuaded some 50 families (about 200 were tried) to keep household budgets for periods varying from one week to one year.[30] A number of the resulting detailed accounts of income and expenditures were presented in full in her report, but the bulk of the analysis was in terms of averages for breakdown by nationality or by income level. The small number of cases in most of these categories, and the highly selective nature of the sample to begin with, render her conclusions from such comparisons dubious, however accurate the individual records may be.

Of particular interest here is the method of estimating the minimum income required for a "fair living wage." From a study of her budget data and her knowledge of the families, More arrived at the judgment that "a well-nourished family of five needed at least $6 a week for food."[31] This largely subjective figure was then used as a base in estimating the total income required, by establishing the "normal" percentage that food comprises of the total family budget. From her sample, More computed the average percentage of budget expended for food at 43.4 percent. This figure happened to coincide closely with one arrived at in a then current Bureau of Labor survey, and she therefore felt justified in applying it to her "minimum" *food* estimate in order to calculate the annual income required to provide such subsistence. Her "conservative conclusion" was that the yearly wage on this basis should be at least $728 per year, and she then arbitrarily revised it upward to $800–900 to allow for "a larger proportion of surplus than was found in these families, which is necessary to provide adequately for the future."[32] While this procedure was more systematic than Booth's method of drawing the line, the essentially arbitrary basis of the steps involved— the largely judgmental food item and the assumption that the "average" portion that food expenditures comprise of all budgets studied is appropriate at the marginal income level—made it hardly more "objective."

### CHAPIN'S "STANDARDS OF LIVING AMONG WORKINGMEN'S FAMILIES"

The best known of American social work studies of the type under discussion is probably the one conducted by Robert Coit Chapin in 1907–1908 at the request of the New York State Conference of Charities and with the backing of the Russell Sage Foundation.[33] In 1906 the New York State Conference considered at length the problem of living standards and decided to implement a longstanding interest in the scientific determination of how much relief was required to provide adequate sustenance for an average family. Accordingly, a committee was appointed (of which Dr. Chapin was made secretary) "to report what constitutes a normal standard of living, and the cost of such a standard for a definite social unit at this time, in the cities and towns of this state."[34] "Normal standard of living," according to the context, referred to the lowest level of living compatible with proper health and decency for a moderate-sized workingman's family.

After considerable trial and error in method of data collection, the use of volunteer interviewers was abandoned and a total of 551 schedules were executed by paid investigators. The sampling procedure was not a very systematic one. On this point Dr. Chapin states:

> The families were selected on the basis of their willingness and ability to give the information that was sought. Dependent families were excluded, and the visitors tried to find families of normal composition and of modern size, that is, both parents living and from two to four children under sixteen years of age. As to the amount of income, attention was concentrated on families having an income of from $500 to $1000 a year. [Note: The final income range used was $600–1100.][35]

Despite its unsystematic nature, the sampling may have provided an improvement over that followed in More's study inasmuch as a more homogeneous study group was selected for investigation. The restriction of family size and income may in a sense have strengthened the significance of the findings for that type of family, since the resulting averages no longer straddled such a wide range of values. At the same time, one has no way of knowing how much self-selection of the sample may have biased the findings.

A complicated, fifteen-page schedule was developed to bring out the information sought. The approach was retrospective, rather than longitudinal, in that expenditure data were based on the memory of the respondents rather than on account books kept continuously over time. For some items, such as food, Chapin asked for the weekly amount spent and multiplied it by fifty-two to obtain the annual estimate; for other items, such as fuel, he requested a yearly estimate directly. Schedules in which the estimate of annual expenditures thus arrived at exceeded by more than 5 percent the estimated annual income were ordinarily discarded as too inaccurate for use.[36] Schedules eliminated in this way, and through the application of the aforementioned criteria of size and income, reduced the number of schedules that could be used to 318, or about half the number originally completed.

The retrospective method of obtaining expenditure data is obviously subject to many inaccuracies and omissions, though its simplicity and economy as compared with the longitudinal method make it highly attractive. Moreover, the longitudinal approach by means of supervised record keeping is of course itself vulnerable to some bias by virtue of the inevitable self-selection of people willing to submit to such a regimen, and also the possibly distorting effect of the record-keeping and supervisory process.

Chapin's data were averaged by income level and by nationality. His comparisons within such classifications had limited generalizability in light of the sampling limitations noted earlier. For our purposes, his method of determining the minimum budget necessary for the maintenance of a "normal" standard is of special interest. The principle followed was basically that of determining, by the best means available, what the minimum expenditure in *each* major category of the budget should be in order "to keep soul and body together."[37] He then undertook to determine the income level below which the average expenditures for the various portions of the budget tended to fall short of the previously set levels, and above which the average expenditures tended to be over these amounts. Following this general method, Chapin arrived at the conclusion "that an income under $800 is not enough to permit the maintenance of a normal standard."[38] The correspondence to the minimum budget of $800–900 arrived at independently by More is striking.

This method of establishing the minimum food expenditure is unique and noteworthy. Chapin submitted the food schedules to an authority on physiological chemistry who reviewed them in terms of their nutritional adequacy. It was found that most families in which less than 22 cents per day was spent for food per member were not receiving sufficient nourishment "to maintain physical efficiency."[39] Accordingly, this monetary standard was applied to all the cases and used as a basis for classifying families as to whether or not they were adequately fed. As noted earlier, diet is one budgetary area in which a *partially* scientific determination of budgetary adequacy can be made. Minimum standards in the other budgetary categories were set more or less arbitrarily, partly with reference to the typical level of expenditure in the sample and partly with reference to what was thought to be necessary for proper maintenance.[40]

In comparing the More and Chapin studies several points at which Chapin profited by the experience of the Greenwich group may be noted. His sample was made more homogeneous; its total size was increased; his constituent budgetary standards were made more explicit; and his final minimum figure was arrived at through a more systematic application of his component standards. On the other hand, his retrospective method of data collection must be considered less reliable than More's longitudinal method of supervised budget keeping. In neither case, however, was the sample large enough, or sufficiently representative, to warrant the comparisons between nationality and income levels that both authors indulged in.

Many of these limitations were noted by social work critics of the time. An important point was stressed by Kate Claghorn in a paper before the 1908 National Conference:

> The skill of the housewife, which no way has been found as yet to measunre statistically, is as important an element in the problem as any of those that can be so measured. And this is not true merely in the preparation of food, but in the direction of all expenditure.[41]

Here indeed is a variable that would be hard to control but might very well vitiate the application of standards to individual families. By and large, the assumption in most budgetary studies appears to be that all families should be able to achieve an average, or even ideal, level of efficiency and skill in the utilization of their income. That this does not hold for many families, particularly those in economic hardships, hardly needs to be pointed out.

The recognition of such weaknesses in family budget studies led Claghorn to offer some good advice:

Realizing the difficulties of the undertaking, the cautious investigator of budgets will disclaim any attempt at elaborate generalization, and will even, with studied modesty, claim to make
none, offering his product as merely a bit of social history to be
used by anyone else who may find it useful.[42]

It is important to observe that these early poverty studies in the
United States focused more on the determination of *where* to
draw the poverty line than on the numbers and portions of the
general population above and below it. In this respect they
differed sharply in emphasis from the English prototypes of Booth
and Rowntree, which were aimed primarily at this latter question.

More's study of 200 families was drawn from the immediate
neighborhood of Greenwich House in Greenwich Village and
could not therefore be seen as representative of the general population. Her project in fact was undertaken as a description of
living standards "among different races and occupations" in the
area, and only secondarily got into the question of a poverty
line. Chapin's investigation was directed expressly at ascertaining
what an adequate standard of relief should be, at the request of
the New York State Conference of Charities. Here again we see
less propensity on the part of the early American studies to tackle
the mass implications of the spread of poverty than was the case
in England.

The impression should not be given, however, that *no* early
attempts were made to estimate the overall incidence of poverty
in this country; however, these were more journalistic than empirical research undertakings. For example, in 1892 Jacob Riis
hazarded the judgment that 20 to 30 percent of New York's population lived in want, and in 1904 Robert Hunter, a settlement
worker, published an admittedly crude national "guesstimate"
of 10 million Americans living in poverty.[43]

The American poverty yardsticks were incorporated into "standard budgets" by social agencies in this country and widely used
in the determination of the amount of relief that should be given
to indigent applicants. Referring to this budgeting tool and
criterion of need, Sophonisba Breckinridge later stated that it
was "one of the most radical devices invented by social workers,"[44]
and in the sense of providing a standard measure of economic deprivation there was certainly a "radical" potential in hand here.

These minimum budget "cutoffs" were frequently compared
with prevailing wages in the common working-class occupations
and industries in an attempt to point up the gross shortcomings

of existing wage policies. Thus, though we did not have any "great poverty study" in the British mold, the poverty line concept could still be used for public educational purposes.[45] For example, the Catholic economist John A. Ryan assumed in his book *A Living Wage* (1906) that a family of moderate size required approximately $600 per year to maintain an American standard of living. He went on to estimate that at least 60 percent of the adult male wage earners received less than this amount.[46] At about the same time, as we have just seen, the More and Chapin studies arrived at a somewhat higher subsistence level ($800–900 per year), which made the prevailing wage scales even more inadequate by comparison. And Warner's reviser, Mary Roberts Coolidge, cited a 1916 report by the U. S. Public Health Service in which four-fifths of American wage earners were classified as receiving less than $800 per year, which was then considered a "low" estimate for the poverty line.[47] That not more was made of these findings as approximations of the extent of poverty in early-twentieth-century America may have been due to the highly controversial and political nature of such huge estimates.

But increasingly now the center of gravity for such studies moved toward official governmental auspices, and into such fields as home economics and labor statistics. The reasons for this transfer of responsibility are interesting to speculate about. Probably the mass character and large investments of time and money required to make such studies worthwhile pointed inevitably toward public rather than private support. Too, the growing concern of social workers with individual psychological factors after the war may have contributed to our withdrawal from this broader type of social research. Another possible factor may have been the degree of technical specialization required in this difficult research area. Whatever the reason, after World War I there was little in social work in the way of budgetary studies that approached even the modest scope and significance of the earlier ones.

An official study by the Bureau of Labor Statistics in 1919 undertook some further refinement of the poverty line. A distinction was attempted among the following:

a. *The pauper or poverty level*—This represents roughly a standard of living just above where families receive aid from charity, or where they run into serious debt.

b. *The minimum of subsistence level*—This is based essentially on mere animal existence and allows little or nothing for the needs of men as social creatures*

c. *The minimum of health and comfort level*—This represents a slightly higher level than that of subsistence, providing not only for the material needs . . . but also certain comforts, such as clothing sufficient for . . . self-respect and decency, some insurance, . . . and expenditures for self-development.[50]

Because of wide differences in terminology, procedure, and context, detailed comparisons between the various poverty lines drawn in England and in this country are problematic at best. In recent years, as we shall see, more "official" poverty measures have been widely used in this country, and higher-level family budgets have also been developed for other purposes.

The earlier interest in comparing the expenditure patterns of different nationality groups appears to have disappeared in family budget research after World War I. According to one writer, the dropping of this variable from later studies, and the consequent averaging of all groups within American society falling in the same income level, was due to the finding that the various ethnic groups did not reveal any fundamental differences in living standards within a given income bracket. Hence, in later studies "income and locality were accepted as the principal factors affecting levels of living, and this means that the general consumption pattern was assumed to be the same for all workers in a community regardless of national origin or type of work."[51] On the basis of such evidence of homogeneity the resulting mass averages were considered appropriate for application to specific groups in the population.

While research of this type has largely passed out of the hands of social work in recent decades, it may be of interest to give brief notice to some of the later developments in this field of inquiry. During a twelve-month period in 1935–1936 the most extensive study of living conditions and household expenditures conducted in the United States to date was executed under the joint auspices of the U. S. Bureau of Labor Statistics, the Bureau of Home Economics of the U. S. Department of Agriculture, the National Resources Committee, and the Central Statistical Board. Known as the Consumer Purchases Study, it provided "for the first time in American statistical history an extensive and comparable body of data on the spending habits of major groups

* Compare with Rowntree's "primary poverty," p. 79.

of American consumers."[52] Earlier studies had generally been confined to limited segments of the population in particular localities, and especially concentrated on the urban laborer. Now all parts of the population were represented, and both rural and urban areas. This study was used as the basis of the first official Consumer Price Index until it was supplanted by more recent data. Its findings were variously drawn upon and utilized in subsequent formulations of standards and family budget studies. One development was the attempt to establish a budgetary standard on the basis of the relationships existing between the adequacy of diets and income level, by selecting the income level at which a given percentage—necessarily arbitrary—of diets were considered adequate. (Note the parallel to one portion of Chapin's work.) This approach obviously assumes a close correlation between dietary expenditure patterns and other areas of expenditure, an assumption that may not be fully warranted.[53]

An important innovation in the setting of a "minimum" budget was made in the 1948 study by the U. S. Bureau of Labor Statistics entitled *Worker's Budgets in the United States* and limited in scope to workers' families with two young children.[54] In this study the method of determining the "point of maximum elasticity" was introduced as a means of identifying the standard quantity required in all categories of expenditure save food and housing. The "point of maximum elasticity" of a good or service is a term used in economics to denote the "inflection point" on the income-quantity curve, that is, the point at which the increment in consumption of a commodity, for each unit of increment in income, has reached a maximum and thereafter declines with increasing income. In the case of clothing, for example, a curve would be drawn representing the relationship between income and the consumption of clothing in the population under study. It would be found, as might be expected, that the amount spent for clothes by families in the lower brackets was less than that spent by families in the higher income brackets, and that for each unit of increase of income there was a greater proportionate increase in clothing expenditures. That is, families with a $1000 income might consume $100 worth of clothing; families with a $2000 income might consume $300 worth; those with $3000 income might consume $700 worth; and so on, dealing in each case with average figures. Eventually, however, a point is reached at which the amount of increased expenditure for clothing for each $1000 of additional income will no longer be greater than the previous increase. That is, the increments in clothing consumption will begin to diminish, though the absolute total spent for clothes may continue to rise with higher income. This turning point is the "point of maximum elasticity" for this class of commodity in this particular population at this particular time. The corresponding quantity of these goods or services may then be taken as the aggregate judgment of the community, since it reveals in empirical fashion the priority that the population as a whole assigns to a particular category of expenditure, as reflected in its actual market behavior. Beyond this "maximum elasticity" point the community begins to give the commodity a lower priority in its expenditures; hence, the "minimum" standard for the commodity according to the current priorities set by the community for goods and services may be determined. It is interesting to note in this regard that the housing standards arrived at by the method just described coincided quite closely with the housing standards independently arrived at by the American Committee on Hygiene of Housing.

This econometric technique, therefore, provides a means for determining the existing economic values of a given population. Whether or not this particular set of values is accepted for social welfare planning purposes is a further value decision on the part of those responsible for such planning. Thus it is possible in this way to determine fairly objectively what a community considers to be a "minimum" standard of living for itself; but should this minimum standard be used for relief purposes, for minimum wage legislation, for the planning of new services? May the community as a whole be "too high" or "too low" in certain areas of expenditure? Is there a responsibility for professioanl leadership in modifying the existing market values of the community? For example, a population may place a very low priority in its spending patterns on protecting itself through insurance against the important hazards of modern life. Should the standard budget therefore also minimize the place of insurance, or should special provision be made for it? If such questions are answered affirmatively, then the setting of standards is again thrown open to the consensus of "competent observers." A similar problem arises in areas of expenditure where there may be "too high" a priority set by the population, from the standpoint of budgeting "experts." Should the community's standard for liquor consumption be included in the "minimum budget," for example? It thus seems clear that while the objective determination of existing community priorities, as provided by "the point of maximum elasticity," can contribute much to the establishment of budgetary standards, the role of outside value judgments is not thereby eliminated.

In the late 1940s the U. S. Bureau of Labor Statistics issued the. first of its "City Worker's Family Budgets" in response to requests for information as to what it takes for an urban wage earner's family to live at a "modest but adequate" level.[55] It should be emphasized that this budget was *not* intended as a poverty line, being aimed considerably above such a minimum standard. At the same time, it is below the average or typical family income level—actually some 15 to 20 percent below the mean income for such families.[56] Though not a poverty yardstick, this measure will be briefly described here, since it throws light on the range and interrelationships of related living standards. The City Worker's Family Budget was officially interpreted as follows:

> The "modest but adequate" level of living described by this budget standard is neither a "minimum maintenance" nor a "luxury" level. The budget does not show how an "average" family spends its money; neither does it show how a family should spend its money. Rather, it is an estimate of the total cost of a representative list of goods and services considered by 4-person city families of the budget type (employed husband, wife in home, with 8-year-old daughter and 13-year-old son) to maintain a level of adequate living according to standards prevailing in large cities of the United States in recent years.[57]

One of the important features of the City Worker's Family Budget was its incorporation of the previously discussed "point of maximum elasticity" concept into some of the expenditure calculations.[58]

This kind of a "modest but adequate" (or "moderate") budget level has been widely utilized over the years by social agencies for counseling, budget management, and fee-charging purposes. In a number of major cities the central councils of social agencies (later community welfare councils, health and welfare councils, community service councils, etc.) had long maintained similar "standard budgets" for use by local agencies in their service programs. The Chicago Standard Budget (going back as far as 1913) and the New York Family Budget Standard were well-known and influential guides of this type that antedated the Bureau of Labor Statistics' entry into the field. With the availability in the 1940s of an official governmental budget measure in the form of the City Worker's Family Budget, less responsibility for the maintenance of such a tool was felt by the voluntary sector; most councils have by now abandoned this service, which had usually been carried by their research departments. However, the Family Budget Standard prepared periodically by the Community Council of Greater New York has continued, in a rather elaborate and detailed fashion, as an important refinement and adaptation of the "moderate" city worker's budget level.

In 1967 the U. S. Bureau of Labor Statistics issued a major extension of its City Worker's Family Budget. In response to many requests for "higher" and "lower" budget levels in addition to the original "moderate" concept, it published such a breakdown for 39 metropolitan areas and 4 nonmetropolitan areas.[59] However, the "lower" level here is still far above the notion of a poverty line as discussed earlier; and the "higher" level is far from representing a luxury standard of living in current American terms. The average budget figure in 1967 for the "moderate" urban family of four in Chicago, for example, was $9076 (before taxes); for the "higher" standard it was $13,050; for the "lower" standard it was $5915.[60] (In the 1960s the official Office of Economic Opportunity "poverty" yardstick for a family of four was well under $4000 per year.) Thus this expansion of the City Worker's Family Budget really reflected various *gradations* of a "moderate" standard of living rather than a range extending from poverty to affluence. It constitutes, in any case, a highly useful contribution to this and other related fields in many areas of policy guidance and individual budget management. (In 1975, the "moderate" budget for an urban family of four was $15,318; the "higher" level, $22,294; the "lower" level, $9588.[61]

## The New Poverty Line

The reawakening of the nation in the 1960s to the existence of poverty in the midst of a prosperous society was an impressive social phenomenon and—to social workers with a long memory—a not unfamiliar one. The "scientific charity" movement was, as we have seen, in part a response to the recognition of the problem of pauperism in the late nineteenth century, with the hope of finding the key to the eradication of the ancient curse of penury. The "social survey movement," to be taken up in the next chapter, was in a sense a shift of the same motivation to another level of attack. In the national crisis of the 1930s it was self-evident that the mass poverty of the Great Depression was a societal breakdown demanding a societal solution.

The recent rediscovery of poverty was stimulated more by the writing of economists and journalists than by social workers. John

Galbraith's *The Affluent Society* (1958)[62] called popular attention to the persistence of individual "case" poverty and insular "pockets" of poverty, and Michael Harrington's *The Other America* (1962)[63] spotlighted "how the other *one-fifth* lives" (if one may rephrase the title of Jacob Riis' late-nineteenth-century classic). The national conscience was finally aroused after the quiescence of the late 1940s and 1950s, and with the interest of President Kennedy and the impetus of President Johnson the country embarked upon its too-brief "War on Poverty." This campaign unfortunately soon fell behind other national priorities, both military and domestic, and by the 1970s the plight of the poor had once more become a generally accepted part of the American scene.

In this new round with poverty, however, the social sciences were better equipped than previously with concepts and measurements. When the Office of Economic Opportunity got under way in the mid-sixties the nation had more knowledge of the subject than in prior encounters. Not only was there a widely accepted poverty line available, but it was soon applied and adapted to the demographic analysis of "who" and "where" the poor were—age, race, sex, family size, region, occupation, and so on. Mollie Orshansky, a research analyst with the Social Security Administration, published an illuminating series of articles in the early sixties, utilizing census data and budget yardsticks to develop an extensive base of statistical materials on the incidence of the problem.[64] Her method of calculating the poverty line was simple and direct. From recent expenditure survey data it was known that approximately one-third of the household budget of most American families was spent on food. Orshansky drew upon the U. S. Department of Agriculture's "economy" food plan, which is four-fifths of its regular "low-cost" plan and approximates the most inexpensive means of providing the essential nutrition in an American type of diet. It is intended for "emergency or temporary use" only.[65] This "economy" food plan was then merely multiplied by three, on the *assumption* that since the typical American family of three or more spends about one-third of its budget on food, then a borderline poor family should similarly be able to get by with three times its food budget. Note how this harks back to one aspect of the procedure followed by Louise More in 1906—except that at that time food represented close to one-half of the household budget of the working class. One common index of a rising standard of living is a decrease in the portion of family expenditures devoted to food.

This technique has the great advantages of clarity, understandability, and flexibility; since "economy" food budget estimates were available for different family sizes, ages, regions of the country, and so on, the conversion to a poverty line was ongoing, immediate, and direct. One deficiency of the 1960 census was that it did not break down families into sufficiently specific types by income so that the categories could readily be translated into population segments above and below the poverty line. However, this handicap was largely overcome through special tabulations, estimates, and sample surveys. In the 1970 census the poverty line was "built into" the census design from the outset, so that today a tremendous amount of detail on the distribution and characteristics of the poor, determined by the same method, is readily accessible.*

In 1959 (the income year utilized in the 1960 census) the poverty line so measured was $3165 per year for a nonfarm family of four. At the time it was estimated that some 39.5 million Americans, or about 22 percent of the population, were living in poverty.[66] In 1969 (the income year on which the 1970 census was based) the corresponding cutoff was $3745, and the resulting portion of the population living in poverty was 13.7 percent.[67] A later official sample survey conducted by the Bureau of the Census in 1971 yielded an estimate of 12.5 percent of the population below the poverty line, and the criterion used had risen to $4140 per year.[68] These increases were based on cost-of-living adjustments since the original calculations for 1959.† Significantly, in the 1970s the Bureau of the Census began to refer to the poverty line as the "low-income line," apparently preferring a less "loaded" phrasing.[69]

It is intriguing to consider the relative consistency across time and geography in the portion of a society deemed to be poor, even though this may have changed recently in this country. Up until the last few years studies of general poverty—regardless of where or when—often resulted in something like one-third of the populace being defined as living in want. As we have seen, Booth estimated 31 percent of late-nineteenth-century London to be

---

* Income," in this official poverty measure, is technically interpreted as pretax, posttransfer, cash income for the family unit over the calendar year, excluding capital losses and gains. See Robert D. Plotnick and Felicity Skidmore, *Progress Against Poverty: A Review of the 1964–1974 Decade* (New York: Academic, 1975), p. 32. This reference is a valuable and illuminating technical study of recent American trends in relative and absolute poverty.

† The latest official "poverty line," adjusted for changes in the Consumer Price Index since 1971, was $5500 per annum for an urban family of four as of April 1, 1976. *Chicago Sun-Times*, April 25, 1976, p. 120.

below the poverty line; Rowntree arrived at 28 percent "poor" in York at the turn of the century.

In this country there were no adequate studies of the general extent of poverty until much later. In 1937, in his second inaugural address Franklin Delano Roosevelt identified "one-third of a nation ill-housed, ill-clad, ill-nourished." In the early 1960s Orshansky reviewed various estimates of poverty in the United States, ranging from one-fifth to one-third.[70] However, the official 1960 census figure, as we have seen, was 22 percent, and the 1971 census estimate was down to 12.5 percent.

This apparent decline may be attributed to a real change in the incidence of disadvantage in our society. It is possible, on the other hand, that the static yardstick used for a poverty line since 1959—except for cost-of-living increases—no longer represents an appropriate measure in recent years, if indeed it did then. For example, it appears that the multiplier of three is not as valid today. Since rising standards of living are associated with decreasing percentages of income spent on food, it is probable that a *higher* multiplier than three would provide a better criterion today. Moreover, the use of an "economy" food plan—which was arbitrarily defined as four-fifths the low-cost food plan—may be challenged as an increasingly shaky base to which to apply the multiplier in the first place. It can be argued, therefore, that the 1971 annual income level of $4140 for an urban family of four yielded an understated poverty line at the time, and that with more reasonable assumptions regarding current life styles and consumption patterns something higher would be justified. If so, then the portion of Americans living in poverty might rise sharply from the present approximately one-eighth to an appreciably higher fraction (perhaps even to one-third!). Though the affluent sixties witnessed a reduction in the incidence of "absolute" poverty, they may also have raised the standards for participation in the social and economic life of the community. Stated otherwise, an increasingly technological society can well lift the minimal "takeoff point" for independent functioning even as it lowers the prevalence of dire need and destitution.

All of which brings us back to our starting point, that is, the essentially judgmental and value-based nature of any poverty defintion or measurement. Recognizing this relativistic core of the concept, some authorities[71] have recently suggested setting the poverty line at one-half the *median* family income. This approach would allow it to "float," so to speak, following the course of the economy while denoting in a flexible fashion the comparatively disadvantaged segment of the population.

# East London

## CHARLES BOOTH

The inquiry of which I am now able to publish the results, was set on foot in 1886, the subject being the condition and occupations of the inhabitants of London, and my grateful thanks are due to those friends who helped me at the outset in laying down the principles on which the inquiry has been conducted. It was decided to employ a double method, dividing the people by districts and again by trades, so as to show at once the manner of their life and of their work. Most of 1886 was occupied with preliminary work, in 1887 sufficed to complete the district inquiry in East London, and 1888 was spent on the trades and special subjects.

The special subjects connected with East London have started into great prominence during the time I have been at work. On the question of the "Unemployed" we have seen a house-to-house inquiry instituted by Government, which took as one of its selected districts St. George's-in-the-East. On the influx of poor Jews, under the name of "Foreign Immigration," we have had a Committee of the House of Commons; and there has been the Committee of the House of Lords on the "Sweating System," which is still prolonging its labours. In addition, the whole question of Poor Relief has been laid open by another Committee of the House of Commons, and we have seen a succession of Mansion House inquiries on the same subject. To meet this evident demand for information I offer the pages which follow. The facts as given have been gathered and stated with no bias nor distorting aim, and with no foregone conclusions.

For the district inquiry, resulting in the division of the people into 8 classes, I have relied upon information obtained from the School Board visitors, of whom there are 66 in the East London district, and my tables are based on three assumptions:

1. That the numbers of married men with school children in each section by employment imply a similar proportion in the same sections of married men without school children, and of other male adults. For the choice of employment is made before the epoch of school children, and the period of employment continued long after; the fathers of the school children of the day are but a section of a block which contains, all the while, old men and young, married and single, those with children and those without, in every trade. Hence, having scheduled the heads of families with school children, I feel justified in dividing the other male adults in similar proportions.

From Charles Booth et al., *Life and Labour of the People in London,* 1st Series: *Poverty,* vol. I (New York: AMS Press, 1970). Reprinted from the edition of 1902–1904. Excerpts reprinted with permission of publisher.

2. That likewise the number of children of scool age in each section implies the existence of brothers and sisters, older and younger, to be found living under the same home conditions. Hence I have added children and young persons of 13–20 to each section in proportion to the number of school children scheduled.

3. That the condition as to poverty of those with children at school in each section will safely represent the condition of the whole section; the younger men in some employments, and the older men in others, earn less money than those of middle age who are the fathers of the children at school, but both are at less expense. On the whole, therefore, the condition of the bulk will be better than that of the part we are able to test.

I have, however, assumed that as in the condition of the tested part—which amounts to fully one half of the population—so is the condition of the whole population; and I may here say that I have throughout my inquiry leaned to the safe side, preferring to paint things too dark rather than too bright, not because I myself take a gloomy view but to avoid the chance of understating the evils with which society has to deal.*

The School Board visitors perform amongst them a house-to-house visitation; every house in every street is in their books, and details are given of every family with children of school age. They begin their scheduling two or three years before the children attain school age, and a record remains in their books of children who have left school. The occupation of the head of the family is noted down. Most of the visitors have been working in the same district for several years, and thus have an extensive knowledge of the people. It is their business to re-schedule for the Board once a year, but intermediate revisions are made in addition, and it is their duty to make themselves acquainted, so far as possible, with new comers into their districts. They are in daily contact with the people, and have a very considerable knowledge of the parents of the school children, especially of the poorest amongst them, and of the conditions under which they live. No one can go, as I have done, over the description of the inhabitants of street after street in this huge district (East London), taken house by house and family by family—full as it is of picturesque details noted down from the lips of the visitor to whose mind they have been recalled by the open pages of his own schedules—and doubt the genuine character of the information and its truth. Of the wealth of my material I have no doubt. I am indeed embarrassed by its mass, and by my resolution to make use of no fact to which I cannot give a quantitative value. The materials for sensational stories lie plentifully in every book of our notes; but, even if I had the

* I undoubtedly expected that this investigation would expose exaggerations, and it did so; but the actual poverty disclosed was so great, both in mass and in degree, and so absolutely certain, that I have gradually become equally anxious not to overstate—C. B., 1902.

skill to use my material in this way—that gift of the imagination which is called "realistic"—I should not wish to use it here. There is struggling poverty, there is destitution, there is hunger, drunkenness, brutality, and crime; no one doubts that it is so. My object has been to attempt to show the numerical relation which poverty, misery, and depravity bear to regular earnings and comparative comfort, and to describe the general conditions under which each class lives.

For the trade inquiries and special subjects, I have been fortunate in obtaining the aid of others, and their work will speak eloquently for itself.

If the facts thus stated are of use in helping social reformers to find remedies for the evils which exist, or do anything to prevent the adoption of false remedies, my purpose is answered. It was not my intention to bring forward any suggestions of my own, and if I have ventured here and there, and especially in the concluding chapters, to go beyond my programme, it has been with much hesitation.

With regard to the disadvantages under which the poor labour, and the evils of poverty, there is a great sense of helplessness: the wage earners are helpless to regulate their work and cannot obtain a fair equivalent for the labour they are willing to give; the manufacturer or dealer can only work within the limits of competition; the rich are helpless to relieve want without stimulating its sources. To relieve this helplessness a better stating of the problems involved is the first step. "We are a long way towards understanding anything under our consideration, when we have properly laid it open, even without comment."* In this direction must be sought the utility of my attempt to analyze the population of London.

In order that the true, and not more than the true, significance and value may be given to the facts and figures produced, it may be useful to explain exactly the method that has been adopted in collecting them.

The 46 books of our notes contains no less than 3400 streets or places in East London, and every house and every family with school children is noted, with such information as the visitors could give about them. Here are specimens of each class of street:

### St. Hubert Street† (Class A)‡

|  |  |  | Class |
|---|---|---|---|
| 1. Casual Labourer | 1 room | 2 school children | B |
|  | (Now gone hopping). |  |  |
| Charwoman | 1 room, widow | 1 child at school and 1 baby | B |
|  | (The widow's sister also lives with her.) |  |  |
|  | 1 room | 1 family, no children at school |  |
| 2. Bootmaker | 1 " wife helps, | 2 school children | C |
| Casual Labourer | 1 " | 1 child at school and 2 babies | A |
|  | (Very low family. Also have one child at Industrial School.) |  |  |
| (?) | 1 room, widow | 1 child at school | B |
| Hawker | 1 room | 3 school children | A |
|  | (Queer character.) |  |  |
|  | 1 room | 1 family, no children at school |  |
|  | (One room—empty.) |  |  |

* "Autobiography of Mark Rutherford."

| | | | |
|---|---|---|---|
| 3. Hawker (female) | 1 room | 3 school children | B |
| | Husband in prison—mother lives with them—doubtful characters.) | | |
| Hawker | 1 room | 1 child at school | A |
| | (Two elder sons loaf about.) | | |
| Fish-stall Hawker | 1 room, wife helps, | 2 school children and 1 baby | B |
| | 1 '' | 1 family, no children at school | |
| 4. Casual Labourer | 1 '' | wife and children away | |
| Casual Carman | 1 '' | 4 school children and 1 baby | B |
| | 1 '' | a female of doubtful character | |
| Hawker of Flower Stands | 1 '' | no children at school | |
| 5. Sweep | 1 '' wife dead | 4 school children | B |
| (?) | 1 '' | 1 child at school | B |
| Hawker (female) | 1 '' | 1 '' '' | B |
| 6. Casual Labourer | 1 '' | 3 school children, 2 babies and | |
| | | 1 girl over age | B |
| | (Nos. 4, 5, and 6 are mixed up in some extraordinary fashion. All | | |
| | the inmates have to use one small yard with one water tap and w.c.) | | |
| 7. Cork-cutter | 1 room | 3 school children and 1 baby | B |
| | 1 '' | 1 family, no children at school | |
| 8 and 9. | Sawmills | | |
| 10 and 11. General Shop | 2 rooms, widow | 1 child at school and 2 help mother | E |
| | (Makes a fair living.) | | |
| A Disused Shop | 1 room | 1 family, no children at school | |
| Bootmaker (journeyman) | 1 '' wife chars | 3 school children, 1 over age | B |
| | (Dreadfully poor, deaf, decrepit, and rheumatic.) | | |
| Hawker | 1 room | 4 school children and 1 baby | B |
| | (Makes and sells flower stands.) | | |
| Hawker | 1 room | 1 child at school and 1 baby | B |
| Carver | 1 '' | 2 school children and 1 baby | B |
| | (Wretchedly poor.) | | |
| 12. Greengrocer's | 1 '' and shop | 2 school children and 1 baby | C |
| | (Wife's mother also lives with them.) | | |
| Bootmaker | 1 room | 3 school children | B |
| Casual Labourer | 1 '' | 3 '' '' and 1 at work | B |
| 13. Old Woman | 1 '' | 1 child at school | B |
| | (This is a nurse child, and what she receives for it is her only means of living.) | | |
| Casual Labourer | 1 room | 1 child at school | B |
| Casual Labourer | 1 '' | 2 school children | B |
| Tenement in yard at back of house, occupied by | | | |
| Match Box Maker | 2 rooms | 3 school children & 2 help father | B |
| | (All work at this—a wretchedly poor lot.) | | |

† The rear names of the streets are, for obvious reasons, suppressed.

‡ Note: The map that appears with this list is not included here.

The listing of inhabitants of St. Hubert Street continues for a couple more pages in this fashion and then concludes with the following description of the street.

*General Character*—An awful place; the worst street in the district. The inhabitants are mostly of the lowest class, and seem to lack all idea of cleanliness or decency. Few of the families occupy more than one room. The children are rarely brought up to any kind of work, but loaf about, and no doubt form the nucleus for future generations of thieves and other bad characters. The property is all very old, and it has been patched up and altered until it is difficult to distinguish one house from another. Small back yards have been utilized for building additional tenements. The property throughout is in a very bad condition, unsanitary and overcrowded; and it is stated (as a suggestive reason why so little has been done in the way of remedy) that until very recently the rent collector of the property was a brother of the Sanitary Inspector! A number of the rooms are occupied by prostitutes of the most pronounced order.

A dozen additional pages (Volume I) that immediately follow in the original text are omitted here; they consist of similar street-by-street listings of households in East London, with individual and general descriptions. Booth then continues as follows.

From notes such as these the information given in our schedules was tabulated, and from them also was coloured the map which now forms a part of that published in connection with these volumes. The people—that is those of them who had school children—were classified by their employment and by their apparent status as to means; the streets were classified according to their inhabitants. Such is the nature of our information, and such the use made of it. It was possible to subject the map to the test of criticism, and it was mainly for this purpose that it was prepared. It was exhibited at Toynbee Hall and Oxford House, and was seen and very carefully studied by many who are intimately acquainted, not with the whole, but each with some part, of the district portrayed. Especially, we obtained most valuable aid in this way from the Relieving Officers and from the agents of the Charity Organization Society. The map stood the test very well. There were errors, but on reference they were, in almost every case, found to be due to mistake in the transfer of verbal into graphic descriptions, or consequent on our having made a whole street the unit of colour, whereas different parts of the same street were of very different character. The map was revised, and now equally represents the facts as disclosed by this inquiry, and as agreed to by the best local authorities.

Our books of notes are mines of information. They have been referred to again and again at each stage of our work. So valuable have they proved in unforeseen ways, that I only regret they were not more slowly and deliberately prepared; more stuffed with facts than even they are. As it was, we continually improved as we went on, and may be said to have learnt our trade by the time the work was done. At first, nothing seemed so essential as speed. The task was so tremendous; the prospect of its completion so remote; and every detail cost time. In the Tower House Hamlets division, which was completed first, we gave on the average 19¾ hours work to each School Board visitor; in the Hackney division this was increased to 23½ hours. St. George's-in-the-East when first done in 1886 cost 60 hours' work with the visitors; when revised it occupied 83 hours. At the outset we shut our eyes, fearing lest any prejudice of our own should colour the information we received. It was not till the books were finished that I or my secretaries ourselves visited the streets amongst which we had been living in imagination. But later we gained confidence, and made it a rule to see each street ourselves at the time we received the visitors account of it. With the insides of the houses and their inmates there was no attempt to meddle. To have done so would have been an unwarrantable impertinence; and, besides, a contravention of our understanding with the School Board, who object, very rightly, to any abuse of the delicate machinery with which they work. Nor, for the same reason, did we ask the visitors to obtain information specially for us. We dealt solely with that which comes to them in a natural way in the discharge of their duties.

The amount of information obtained varied with the different visitors; some had not been long at the work, and amongst those who had been, there was much difference in the extent of their knowledge; some might be less trustworthy than others: but taking them as a body I cannot speak too highly of their ability and good sense. I also wish to express my warm thanks for the ready manner in which all—the Divisional Committees themselves, the District Superintendents, and the Visitors; lent themselves to my purpose. For without this nothing could have been done. The merit of the information so obtained, looked at statistically, lies mainly in the breadth of view obtained. It is in effect the whole population that comes under review. Other agencies usually seek out some particular class or deal with some particular condition of people. The knowledge so obtained may be more exact, but it is circumscribed and very apt to produce a distortion of judgment. For this reason, the information to be had from the School Board visitors, with all its inequalities and imperfections, is excellent as a framework for a picture of the Life and Labour of the People.

The population brought directly under schedule—viz., heads of families and school children coming under the ken of the School Board visitors, with the proportion of wives and of older or younger children all partly or wholly dependent on these heads of families and sharing their life—amounts to from one-half to two-thirds of the whole population. The rest have been scheduled by other means or in proportion, according to the three assumptions already noted.

The special difficulty of making an accurate picture of so shifting a scene as the low-class streets in East London present is very evident, and may easily be exaggerated. As in photographing a crowd, the details of the picture change continually, but the general effect is much the same, whatever moment is chosen. I have attempted to produce an instantaneous picture, fixing the facts on my negative as they appear at a given moment, and the imagination of my readers must add the movement, the constant changes, the whirl and turmoil of life. In many districts the people are always on the move; they shift from one part of it to another like "fish in a river." The School Board visitors follow them as best they may, and the transfers from one visitor's book to another's are very numerous.* On the whole, however, the people usually do not go far, and often cling from generation to generation to one vicinity, almost as if the set of streets which lie there were an isolated country village.

* A return prepared by one of the School Board visitors, who has a fairly representative district in Bethnal Green, shows that of 1204 families (with 2720 children) on his books, 530 (with 1450 children) removed in a single year.

The inquiry as to Central London was undertaken by a committee of six, and that for Battersea by Mr. Graham Balfour; the method adopted in each case being the same as had been employed in East London.

The remainder of this first volume consists of further detailing of conditions in East London, Central London, Outlying London (North of the Thames), and South London, along with separate chapters devoted to such topics as "Poverty," "Class Relations," "Common Lodging Houses," and "Homeless Men," and an overall summary and conclusion. The following excerpt is taken from Volume II, Chapter II, in which some of Booth's definitions, procedures, and findings regarding the measurement of poverty are presented.

## STATISTICS OF POVERTY

Before giving the figures by which I have sought to measure the poverty existing in London, it may be well to refer once more to their validity. The methods employed in the collection and tabulation of the information have been already indicated. These methods were adopted as suited to the peculiarities of the subject and the materials with which we had to deal; but are doubtless open to criticism from many points of view. Not only is exactness in this case out of the question, but even the most general results obtained are open to dispute. At every turn the subject bristles with doubtful points. For each one of these, as it has arisen (if it has been observed) the best available solution has been sought, or what has seemed the most reasonable course has been taken.

But it is manifest that in an inquiry such as this, a very slight bias may lead to serious error, and the bias might be quite unconscious. I can only say we have done our best to keep clear of this danger.

It is to be remarked further that apart from bias two distinct mental attitudes continually recur in considering poverty; and either of these, if not safeguarded in some way, might prove very misleading. On the one hand we may argue that the poor are often really better off than they appear to be, on the ground that when extravagances which keep them in poverty are constant and immediate in their action, the state of things resulting cannot reasonably be called poverty at all. For instance, a man who spends ten or fifteen shillings in drink one week, cannot be called poor because he lacks the money for some necessity a few days later. In support of this is certainly true that in many cases the homes appear no whit less poor whatever the earnings at the time may be. It often occurs too that the ordinary earnings are increased by accidental receipts capable, if judiciously applied, of meeting the occasional extra demands which keep men's pockets empty. On the other hand we may as logically, or perhaps more logically, disregard the follies past or present which bring poverty in their train. For how distinguish between degrees of folly more or less recent or remote? In this temper we prefer to view and consider these unfortunates only as they actually exist; constantly put to shifts to keep a home together; always struggling and always poor. And turning in this direction the mind dwells upon the terrible stress of times of sickness or lack of work for which no provision, or no adequate provision, has been made. According as the one or other of these two points of view is taken, thousands of families may be placed on one or the other side of the doubtful line of demarcation between class and class among the poor.

Of these two ways of looking at the same facts, the second is that which we have in theory adopted, and although in practice this theory will have been more or less modified, it is still probable that a good many families have been reported as poor, who, though they are poor, are so without any economic necessity. On the other hand it is likely enough that many a painful struggling life hidden under a decent ex-terior has passed in our books as "comfortably poor," to borrow a phrase used by one of the most sympathetic of the School Board visitors. Thus in the end, when I consider the figures, and the tale they tell, though I sway this way or that according to the mood of the moment, I am fully satisfied that the general conclusions are not very far from the truth, and I believe that my readers may fairly accept them in this light. In so far as there is any general error it will I think be found on the safe side—that is, in overstating rather than understating the volume of poverty which exists, or existed when the inquiry was made; and it is satisfactory to know that since the inquiry was made, times have been good, and poverty less pressing, than was the case previously.

The inhabitants of every street, and court, and block of buildings in the whole of London, have been estimated in proportion to the numbers of the children, and arranged in classes according to the known position and condition of the parents of these children. The streets have been grouped together according to the School Board subdivisions or "blocks," and for each of these blocks full particulars are given in the tables of the Appendix. The numbers included in each block vary from less than 2000 to more than 30,000, and to make a more satisfactory unit of comparison I have arranged them in contiguous groups, 2, 3, or 4 together, so as to make areas having each about 30,000 inhabitants, these areas adding up into the large divisions of the School Board ad-ministration. The population is then classified by Registration districts, which are like wise grouped into School Board divisions, each method finally leading up to the total for all London.

The classes into which the population of each of these blocks and districts is divided are the same as we were used in describing East London, only somewhat simplified. They may be stated thus.

A. The lowest class—occasional labours, loafers and semi-criminals.
B. The very poor—causal labours, hand-to-mouth existence, chronic want.

C and D. The poor—including alike those whose earnings are small, because of irregularity of employment, and those whose work, though regular, is ill-paid.

E and F. The regularly employed and fairly paid working class of all grades.

G and H. Lower and upper middle class and all above this level.

The Classes C and D, whose poverty is similar in degree but different in kind, can only be properly separated by information as to employment which was obtained for East London, but which, as already explained, the present inquiry does not yield. It is the same with E and F, which cover the various grades of working-class comfort. G and H are given together for convenience.

Outside of, and to be counted in addition to, these classes, are the inmates of institutions whose numbers are specifically reported in every census, and finally there are a few who, elude official enumeration and are not counted at all.

The proportions of the different classes shown for all London are as follows:

| | | | | |
|---|---|---|---|---|
| A (lowest) | 37,610 | or | .9 percent | In poverty, |
| B (very poor) | 316,834 | " | 7.5 percent | 30.7 per- |
| C and D (poor) | 938,293 | " | 22.3 percent | cent |
| E and F (working class, comfortable) | 2,166,503 | " | 51.5 percent | In comfort, |
| G and H (middle class and above) | 749,930 | " | 17.8 percent | 69.3 per- cent |
| | 4,209,170 | | 100 percent | |
| Inmates of Institutions | 99,830 | | | |
| | 4,309,000 | | | |

Graphically, the proportions may be shown thus:

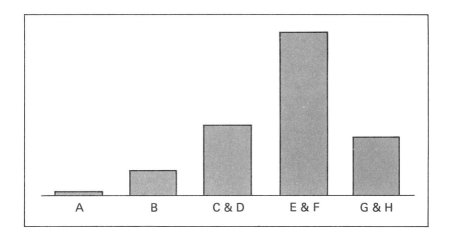

| A | B | C & D | E & F | G & H |

The description of these classes given already as to East London, may be taken as applying with equal force to the whole population. Much might be added to make the description more complete, but nothing need be taken away. The numbers of the lowest class (A), it is admitted, are given at a very rough estimate; they are hardly to be counted by families and so partly escape the meshes of our School Board net. They are to be found in the common lodging-houses and in the lowest streets, and a very full description of their lives and habits is given in the special chapters which treat of these subjects. Class B is fairly counted, and of what it consists, many examples are given in the description of specimen streets, but neither it nor any of the working classes, C, D, E, or F, can be dealt with properly apart from their trades or employments, as the conditions under which these people live, depend mainly upon the conditions under which they work or fail to find work. An account of the life of each of the several classes that are grouped under the letters G and H would be very interesting, but is beyond the scope of this book. I am, however, able to make a division in the figures which answers pretty closely, though not quite exactly, to that between upper and lower middle class. This division is provided by the line of rental value, beyond which the School Board do not go in making their schedules. Out of the 750,000 people included in Classes G and H, as nearly as possible 250,000 live in scheduled and 500,000 in unscheduled houses. These figures may be counted as representing roughly the lower and upper middle classes respectively. The wealthy classes are included with the upper middle class.*

Assuming that these figures are accepted as approximately correct, the view that is taken of them will depend partly upon what may have been pre-supposed. I imagine that bad as is the state of things they disclose it is better than was commonly imagined previous to the publication of the figures obtained for East London. On the other hand they are probably worse, especially in regard to the numbers of Classes C and D, than may have been anticipated by those who have studied and accepted the East End figures.

That is to say, the poverty of the rest of London as compared to East London is perhaps greater than most people have supposed. For myself it was so. In 1888 I made an estimate based on the facts as to East London, and the comparative density of population in other parts, on the theory that density would probably coincide with the degree of poverty. The result was to show a probable 25 percent of poor for all London, or nearly 6 percent less than we now get. South London and the district about Holborn are mainly responsible for the difference.

The following excerpt is taken from Booth's final volume and

---

* The unscheduled population has been estimated in proportion to the number of houses in some cases, and assumed by way of remainder in other cases, and in every instance the assumed number of servants has been added to Classes E, F, to which by position they may be taken to belong.

illustrates some of his influential and innovative—for his time—techniques of statistical analysis. These pages are from Chapter I.

## BIRTH-RATE AND DEATH-RATE

The effect of poverty and crowding upon births and deaths is a subject of the greatest importance, and upon it some light may now be thrown. As to births, I have taken the annual average of the five years 1891–5 for the fifty districts already named, and the rate has been calculated on the mean of the population returns 1891 and 1896. For the death-rate, the actual number of deaths have been obtained for 1894 and 1895, and the mean of these two years taken on the same basis of population. Special investigation (kindly permitted by the Registrar-General) was needed to adjust the deaths in hospitals, infirmaries and other institutions to the districts from which the patients had come. Only with regard to those who had been for a long time inmates of asylums or workhouses, does any error creep in, and to meet this an estimated allowance has been made.

That poverty and crowding go together on the whole we have already seen, and it was to be expected that they should. We can now point to other related conditions less easily foreseen, and show that both birth-rate and death-rate are high in proportion to the degree of poverty and crowding. The following table indicates this.

In the table (and the accompanying map) the fifty districts into which London has been divided are arranged in the combined order of these four tests of social condition, and it will be seen how slightly these individual tests vary from their mean.

The vagaries as between poverty and crowding have been already mentioned. They are in the main caused by diffierence in rates of rental, and (closely connected therewith) by the necessity in certain employ-ments for the workers to live near their work. But habit and the ac-cepted standard of life in different districts, or amongst different classes or races, and perhaps other causes, have also their effect.

As regards birth-rate and death-rate, though as a rule they follow the same order as that indicated by the combined test, there are exceptions which may easily be noted by merely glancing down the columns.

In St. George's in the East and the Shadwell the death-rate is at its highest, although this district stands only fourth in crowding, sixth in poverty, and eighth in its birth-rate. For this discrepancy there is no very obvious explanation. It is, however, probable that the high death-rate has been connected with the intermittent and exposed character of much river-side labour, and that as this tends to improve in status and decline in volume, and to be accompanied by an influx of foreign Jews, the relative figures will in all likelihood approximate to those of Whitechapel, a district which besides being far less poor than it is crowded, has a very high birth-rate undoubtedly due to the Jewish popu-lation, and proportionately an extremely low death-rate.

## Table of Districts Arranged In Order of Social Condition

| District | Order of Poverty 52%—5% | Order of Crowding 57%—7% | Order of Birth-rate 43⅓%—15½% | Order of Death-rate 25½%—11% | Combined Order |
|---|---|---|---|---|---|
| Waterloo and St. Saviour's | 1—52.0 | 3—54.1 | 3—39.4 | 2—24.7 | 1 |
| Old Street and South Shoreditch | 3—47.7 | 1—57.1 | 2—39.9 | 4—24.0 | 2 |
| S. George's in East and Shadwell | 6—44.8 | 4—53.7 | 8—36.6 | 1—25.4 | 3 |
| Bethnal Green | 4—47.0 | 2—55.0 | 4—38.9 | 12—21.2 | 4 |
| Whitechapel, Spitalfields, &c. | 22—33.1 | 6—53.1 | 1—43.3 | 7—22.4 | 5 |
| Bermondsey | 2—50.2 | 14—44.6 | 7—37.3 | 8—22.3 | 6 |
| Hoxton and Haggerston | 9—40.9 | 8—51.3 | 6—37.6 | 9—22.1 | 7 |
| Lamzeth | 13—36.6 | 10—48.3 | 5—38.3 | 6—23.1 | 8 |
| Gray's Inn and Clerkenwell | 5—45.0 | 5—53.5 | 21—31.6 | 13—21.1 | 9 |
| St. John's, Westminster | 7—44.7 | 7—52.2 | 27—30.0 | 15—21.1 | 10 |
| Poplar and Limehouse | 11—37.6 | 22—33.5 | 13—35.1 | 5—23.4 | 11 |
| Christ Church, Marylebone | 26—31.1 | 9—51.2 | 34—26.7 | 3—24.5 | 12 |
| Newington and Walworth | 18—35.0 | 20—35.4 | 11—35.7 | 10—21.9 | 13 |
| Somers Town and East Side Regent's Park | 21—33.1 | 12—47.7 | 22—31.3 | 18—20.2 | 14 |
| Rotherhithe | 10—40.2 | 25—31.9 | 12—35.4 | 20—20.0 | 15 |
| North Camberwell | 8—44.5 | 28—30.3 | 15—34.8 | 23—19.4 | 16 |
| Bow and Bromley | 16—36.1 | 29—30.0 | 9—36.1 | 17—20.5 | 17 |
| Mile End Old Town | 27—31.0 | 18—36.3 | 16—34.3 | 14—21.1 | 18 |
| Islington | 12—37.3 | 16—40.2 | 23—31.2 | 26—18.0 | 19 |
| St. Giles's and Strand | 29—30.5 | 13—45.9 | 38—25.0 | 11—21.4 | 20 |
| Battersea (East) | 17—35.9 | 27—31.5 | 14—34.9 | 31—17.6 | 21 |
| St. John's Wood | 24—32.2 | 17—38.7 | 37—25.2 | 16—20.7 | 22 |
| Fulham | 37—25.4 | 30—26.6 | 10—35.9 | 21—19.9 | 23 |
| Deptford | 19—34.6 | 37—20.4 | 18—32.5 | 24—19.1 | 24 |
| Soho and St. James's | 15—36.2 | 15—40.6 | 42—22.9 | 37—17.0 | 25 |
| Kentish Town | 33—27.1 | 19—35.5 | 28—29.9 | 30—17.8 | 26 |
| Kennington | 30—29.6 | 31—25.7 | 17—34.0 | 34—17.1 | 27 |
| Kensington Town | 23—32.8 | 24—32.9 | 36—25.4 | 28—17.9 | 28 |
| Peckingham and Nunhead | 20—33.4 | 40—18.6 | 20—31.7 | 25—18.8 | 29 |
| Tottenham Court Road | 39—21.3 | 11—48.0 | 44—22.1 | 27—18.0 | 30 |
| Greenwich | 14—36.4 | 41—18.4 | 26—30.4 | 29—17.9 | 31 |
| Chelsea | 41—19.3 | 21—33.6 | 33—27.8 | 22—19.7 | 32 |
| Paddington and Kensal Town | 34—26.7 | 26—31.6 | 30—29.2 | 36—17.0 | 33 |
| City of London | 25—31.5 | 23—33.1 | 49—17.5 | 19—20.0 | 34 |
| Battersea (West) | 23—30.8 | 39—18.7 | 24—31.0 | 35—17.0 | 35 |
| Upper Holloway | 31—28.8 | 33—25.1 | 29—29.3 | 41—16.0 | 36 |
| Hammersmith | 35—26.0 | 35—23.0 | 31—29.1 | 33—17.5 | 37 |
| Woolwich and Plumstead | 32—27.9 | 38—20.2 | 19—31.9 | 39—16.4 | 38 |
| Hackney (excluding Stamford Hill) | 38—24.3 | 36—21.4 | 25—30.5 | 32—17.5 | 39 |
| St. Margaret's, Westminster, and Belgrave | 47—15.5 | 32—25.2 | 45—21.0 | 38—16.7 | 40 |
| South Camberwell and East Dulwich | 46—15.7 | 48—11.3 | 32—27.8 | 40—16.1 | 41 |
| Wandsworth and Putney | 36—26.0 | 47—12.0 | 46—20.9 | 42—15.5 | 42 |
| Clapham | 40—19.4 | 43—13.9 | 41—24.3 | 44—15.0 | 43 |
| Brixton | 45—15.7 | 45—13.2 | 35—25.6 | 43—15.3 | 44 |
| Stoke Newington and Stamford Hill | 42—18.5 | 44—13.4 | 39—24.8 | 46—13.5 | 45 |
| Mayfair and parts of Marylebone and Paddington | 49—14.0 | 34—23.6 | 48—18.5 | 47—13.4 | 46 |
| Lewisham, Sydenham & Eltham | 44—15.8 | 50— 7.0 | 40—24.7 | 45—13.5 | 47 |
| Hampstead | 48—14.3 | 42—16.1 | 47—20.6 | 49—12.0 | 48 |
| Streatham, Norwood & Dulwich | 43—16.6 | 49— 7.2 | 43—22.8 | 48—12.5 | 49 |
| Bromton | 50— 4.9 | 46—12.3 | 50—13.5 | 50—10.9 | 50 |

Bethnal Green stands about fourth in everything except death-rate, which is as unaccountably low as that of St. George's in the East is high. Bermondsey, less crowded than it is poor, is otherwise quite normal.

Similar brief references to the status of other districts follow for another page or so and are omitted here with the exception of the following summary map.

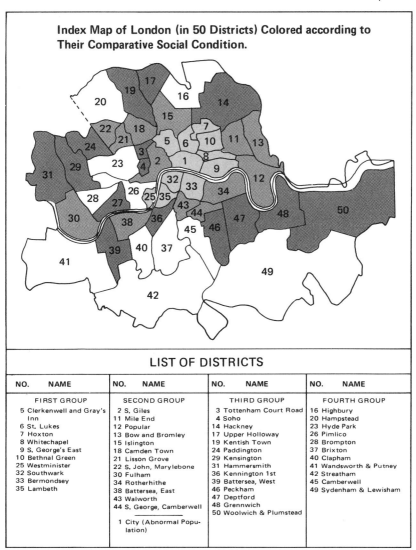

**Index Map of London (in 50 Districts) Colored according to Their Comparative Social Condition.**

## LIST OF DISTRICTS

| NO. NAME | NO. NAME | NO. NAME | NO. NAME |
|---|---|---|---|
| FIRST GROUP | SECOND GROUP | THIRD GROUP | FOURTH GROUP |
| 5 Clerkenwell and Gray's Inn | 2 S. Giles | 3 Tottenham Court Road | 16 Highbury |
| 6 St. Lukes | 11 Mile End | 4 Soho | 20 Hampstead |
| 7 Hoxton | 12 Popular | 14 Hackney | 23 Hyde Park |
| 8 Whitechapel | 13 Bow and Bromley | 17 Upper Holloway | 26 Pimlico |
| 9 S. George's East | 15 Islington | 19 Kentish Town | 28 Brompton |
| 10 Bethnal Green | 18 Camden Town | 24 Paddington | 37 Brixton |
| 25 Westminister | 21 Lisson Grove | 29 Kensington | 40 Clapham |
| 32 Southwark | 22 S. John, Marylebone | 31 Hammersmith | 41 Wandsworth & Putney |
| 33 Bermondsey | 30 Fulham | 36 Kennington 1st | 42 Streatham |
| 35 Lambeth | 34 Rotherhithe | 39 Battersea, West | 45 Camberwell |
|  | 38 Battersea, East | 46 Peckham | 49 Sydenham & Lewisham |
|  | 43 Walworth | 47 Deptford |  |
|  | 44 S. George, Camberwell | 48 Grennwich |  |
|  |  | 50 Woolwich & Plumstead |  |
|  | 1 City (Abnormal Population) |  |  |

This last excerpt from Booth is also from his final volume and comprises its concluding passage. These pages express a personal and philosophical perspective after many years of pioneer research effort.

## THE ROAD AND ITS DIFFICULTIES

Improvement must be sought, first of all, in the deepening of the sentimental of Individual Responsibility. This sentiment rests no doubt upon right feeling, but is subject to stimulation by the opinion of others, and may finally be enforced by law. Of these three, public opinion seems to me to be the most lax. The expectation of evil, the attributing of bad motives, and the ready acceptance of a low standard constitute the first difficulty we have to meet. Cynicism is accounted so clever that men pretend to be worse than they are rather than be thought fools. Clear views of right and wrong in matters of daily action, however firmly they may be rooted in the hearts of men, seldom find utterance; and when this polite rule is broken some surprise is always felt. It is no question of charitable construction of the acts of our neighbours, on the ground that, not knowing all, we hesitate to judge; an attitude for which, though it may be weak, something might be said; but it is that we deliberately refuse to know, in order that we may not need to judge. And this is not the worst, for without knowing or judging, or seeming to care at all, many, if not most men, in order to be safely sensible, indiscriminately assume rascality everywhere. This moral laxity applies to all classes, with some divergence as to the subjects on which the point of honour stands out and cannot be ignored; and by none is it exhibited more widely than by the great masses of respectable working men.

It would seem inevitable that the sense of duty must be weakened by the loss of the habit of judging and of the experience of being judged, as well as by laxity, but nevertheless I venture to assert that it is maintained at a far higher level than is generally thought or claimed. Thus legal enactment, if carefully aimed and measured, becomes doubly and trebly valuable, serving first to check the evil-doer, and secondly to awaken the individual conscience, while it also, by impressing an undeniable seal of condemnation, crystallizes the looseness of public opinion as to any particular offense. Legislation can never go far beyond the sanction of existing public opinion, but many may yet lead the way, and in many cases has done so.

The owner of a house, if he be given, and if he accept, his proper place, will be but the medium by which punishment will fall on the evil-doer and order be enforced; and by the performance of this service he will acquire a new and noble title to his property. By this means, and by this means alone, can houses of ill-fame be suppressed or controlled, and the difficulties of enforcing the Factory and Workshop Acts in minor establishments be overcome. It is not the ultimate owner and immediate landlord alone whose sense of responsibility may be strengthened, and upon whom new duties and new liabilities may justly be thrown: against others, too, besides the holders of licenses, penalties for breach of social regulation or moral order may wisely be enforced. In proportion to the degree of effective liability maintained in this respect do we see a rising standard of public judgment and expectation; and it would be the same throughout if responsibility could be enforced. The attempts made by special legal enactment to stamp their true character on unscrupulous money lending, on secret commissions, and on fraud in company promotion, though very difficult of execution, have undoubtedly had a considerable effect on public opinion. In addition, the giving or receiving of bribes in connection with the work of public officials deserves some special stigma of disgrace, and a public rec- ognition of this would probably be welcomed by all well-meaning officials.

It is in such ways that the sense of individual responsibility may be strengthened and used.

Private corporations and associations for the advancement or pro- tection of acquired interests are more frankly selfish than individuals. They provide a conservative element of the utmost value in the social structure, and may be expected to act up to the letter of the law. But even more than individuals, they need to be humanized by the influence of public opinion, or their giant strength may be abused. They constitute our second difficulty.

We then pass to political, philanthropic, and religious associations, which in their efforts to enlighten and advance mankind are the most zealous of all agencies. To them even more than to the direct working of public spirit in administration do we look for the methods of im- provement; but their zeal itself brings its difficulty. Each is too apt to cry 'I am the way,' and to be unable to admit any other possible salva- tion. It is not jealousy, for jealousy, like imitation, is a manifest form of approval, but positive hostility, due, it may be, to the feeling that our proposal traverses another; but far more to actual condemnation of the efforts made by others, however well-intentioned they may be. And from this feeling of antagonism it is that each effort is apt to draw its strength. To find a fulcrum which shall neither be nor involve hate is the third and greatest difficulty of all.

As to administration, this is at present in a highly experimental stage, particularly in London, and needs encouragement fully as much as criticism. It has to form its own experience, and to stand or fall, or change its ways, according to the results. Vast powers have been most deliberately conceded to local authorities, and these powers are in- creased every year. To suppose that they will not be used is to assume the ridiculous position of a father who, after giving a young man a latchkey and money to spend, expects him to be at home every evening by ten o'clock. It is not one experiment, but hundreds or thousands that are being made, by local bodies, large and small, all over the country, with varying aims and under varying auspices. The Local Government Board may cluck from its coop, but the young birds will run far, and, if they are ducklings, will take to the water. London differs only because of its size. It is the 'ugly duckling' of this story.

In 1888 the Conservative Government, by establishing the London County Council, took a great step in the development of the sense of local responsibility, relying for its success on the good sense of the people; and on this same foundation our hopes for the future rest. It is probable that the sphere of collective municipal action will gradually be defined, though it may be too soon yet to lay down rules. As trenching on the sphere of industry, one theory would confine it to necessary monopolies, another would extend it to all monopolies, while a third would create monopolies on purpose. Probably only experience can decide as to what shapes collective action, whether monopolistic or not, may wisely take. Democratic local government is at present in the making, but it is one of the points (for of these there are still several) in which I believe our country to be in advance of all others, and if we can keep the lead in this particular, we shall not fail to hold our great place in the economy of the world.

Finally, facts are still needed. But the spirit of patient inquiry is abroad; my attempt is only one of its children. Every year that passes produces valuable work in this direction, both official and voluntary. The various 'Settlements' are all centres of research, and the work often carries a small endowment. Moreover, the London County Council has in nothing shown a higher sense of its position or a more truly progressive spirit, than in the careful collection and liberal publication of statistical and social information.

These considerations have reconciled me to the incompleteness of my own work. At the best speed possible to me, it would have taken three more years, and I suppose three more volumes, to have dealt adequately with the new subjects touched upon in the preceding pages; an extension which the limits of my readers' patience (to say nothing of my own) absolutely forbade.

At this pont, therefore, my work ends. I have not attempted to make any direct inquiry into the habits of the people in their various classes, nor made any detailed study of administration as conducted by the various local authorities. But these subjects have naturally been continually before me, and a good deal of information has been gathered concerning them. Placed between saying nothing and saying what I could, I have chosen the latter alternative, and can only beg the indulgence of the reader for the presumption with which I have put forward my views on subjects so debatable and difficult.

Further than this it will be remarked that some subjects of extreme importance in connection with the life of London are hardly mentioned at all. The great Friendly Societies have been barely alluded to, and the system of popular life insurance has been neglected. Of Co-operative distribution, whether on its wholesale or retail side, little has been said, whilst the great question of Co-operative Production has been but incidentally spoken of. More noteworthy still is the omission of any reference to the influence on London life of Art and Literature, and especially to that branch of Literature which is termed *par excellence* "The Press." With regard to all these subjects I can only plead that in the absence of the body of special information needed, I could have offered but a few general and perhaps obvious remarks. There will doubtless be other subjects or points of view, the neglect of which may strike the reader, though perhaps none of quite equal importance, or so likely to be involved in future developments, as those I have mentioned. But besides any of which we may now be conscious, there will be others which coming years will unfold, when if this book should be consulted as a record of the past it will surely be with amazement at the failure to remark, or give their true significance to, the tendencies that will then appear to have been so evident; the stirrings of mighty movements, or the shooting of new life. How, it will inevitably be asked, is it possible that any one could have been so blind?

The last word I would add is this: the object of the sixteen volumes has been to describe London as it appeared in the last decade of the nineteenth century. Beyond this I have sought, however, imperfectly, to show what is being done to ameliorate its conditions and have suggested some directions in which advance might be made; but this last was no part of the original design, which was, solely, to observe and chronicle the actual, leaving remedies to others. To this attitude I would now revert. For the treatment of disease, it is first necessary to establish the facts as to its character, extent and symptoms. Perhaps the qualities of mind which enable a man to make this inquiry are the least of all likely to give him that elevation of soul sympathetic insight, and sublime confidence which must go to the making of a great regenerating teacher. I have made no attempt to teach; at the most I have ventured on an appeal to those whose part it is. Some individual views and convictions have been intentionally allowed to show themselves here and there in comments made, but no body of doctrine is submitted.

The dry bones that lie scattered over the long valley that we have traversed together lie before my reader. May some great soul, master of a subtler and nobler alchemy than mine, disentangle the confused issues, reconcile the apparent contradictions in aim, melt and commingle the various influences for good into one divine uniformity of effort, and make these dry bones live, so that the streets of our Jerusalem may sing with joy.

## Chapter Summary

Charles Booth's pioneering series of poverty studies in London had a major impact on American social welfare research in the late nineteenth and early twentieth centuries. His subjectively determined poverty line (with gradations), his intensive community focus, his thorough and painstaking empiricism, his Gargantuan labor of seventeen years and as many volumes, his effective use of social statistics, his manifest integrity and felicitous style left a deep imprint and a well-nigh unattainable standard for his immediate followers in England and in this country. The heyday of this type of study in American social work was between the turn of the century and World War I. Louise More's early budgetary study made use of a longitudinal method of supervised account keeping on the part of selected families. Robert Chapin, in his well-known study, *Standard of Living Among Workingmen's Families,* adopted the retrospective approach of relying largely on the family's memory of past expenditures. Chapin introduced the systematic formulation of "minimum" estimates for each category of expenditure and the use of a dietician's judgment in the analysis of the adequacy of food expenditures. Both More and Chapin arrived at a figure between $700 and $800 per year as the minimum standard for a living wage for a normal family in the early 1900s. These early efforts were severely limited in terms of size and representativeness of sample.

A few studies of this type were completed in social work after the war, with the trend in favor of the longitudinal approach to obtaining expenditure data. In recent decades the major inquiries along these lines have been conducted under governmental auspices and have become increasingly large-scale and specialized undertakings that now are conducted largely outside the field of social work. Of special interest is a relatively recent technique for objectively determining the current priorities in expenditures according to the judgment expressed by the community through its actual spending patterns. This is the so-called "point of maximum elasticity" method, reflecting the empirically determined value judgments of the community. Subjective adjustments may be required before it is finally applied, however.

The popular "moderate" budget standard of the U. S. Bureau of Labor Statistics, the City Worker's Family Budget, makes use of this technique at some points. It has recently added an "upper" and "lower" budget level—all well above the poverty line. This type of budget guide, and adaptations of it in the larger cities, have long been used by social agencies in a variety of ways.

The rediscovery of poverty in the 1960s found improved budget research tools available for the setting of a modern poverty line for United States families. The official measure is, quite simply, three times the cost of the U. S. Department of Agriculture's "economy" food plan for the given type of family. From 1959 to 1975 the poverty cutoff determined in this manner rose (on a cost-of-living basis) from $3165 to $5038, while the portion of the population living in poverty dropped from 22 to 12 percent. It appears probable that this official yardstick, based on studies stemming from the 1950s, is too static and outdated to provide a meaningful measure of poverty today.

In this and the preceding chapter we have seen that one of the central taproots of American social work lay in the study of poverty—first its causes and then its measurement. These research pursuits have now been largely given up to other disciplines, notably economics. Nevertheless it seems clear that social work must retain a basic concern for understanding and combatting poverty and its adverse human consequences if the profession is to remain true to its historic identity.

Extensive excerpts were quoted at the end of the chapter from Booth's epic study, *Life and Labour of the People in London,* which greatly influenced the course of social work research in this country.

## NOTES

[1] Robert H. Bremner, *From the Depths; The Discovery of Poverty in the United States* (New York: New York University Press, 1956, p. 71).

[2] Albert Fried and Richard M. Elman, eds., *Charles Booth's London* (New York: Pantheon Books, 1967), p. xvii.

[3] Quoted in Pauline V. Young, *Scientific Social Surveys and Research* (New York: Prentice-Hall, Inc., 1949), p. 56, 2d ed.

[4] Fried and Elman, p. xxxiii.

[5] Benjamin Seebohm Rowntree, *Poverty: A Study of Town Life* (London: MacMillan, 1902).

[6] See *The Use of Research Techniques in Determining the Need for Health and Welfare Services* (New York: Community Chest and Councils of America, Inc., 1950).

[7] Edward E. Schwartz, "Social Work Research," *Social Work Year Book* 1951, p. 502.

[8] See, for example, Abraham Kaplan, *The Conduct of Inquiry* (San Francisco: Chandler Publ. Co., 1964), pp. 370–405.

[9] William Shakespeare, *King Lear,* Act II, sc. 4.

[10] Charles Booth, *Life and Labour of the People in London,* 1st ser. vol. I (New York: AMS Press, 1970), reprinted from the edition of 1902–1904, p. 33.

[11] Ibid.

[12] Rowntree, pp. 117–118.

[13] Ibid., p. 355.

[14] Sir Arthur L. Bowley and A. R. Burnett-Hurst, *Livelihood and Poverty* (London: G. Bell and Sons, 1915).

[15] Young, p. 19.

[16] Sir Arthur L. Bowley and Margaret H. Hogg, *Has Poverty Diminished* (London: P. S. King and Son, 1925), p. 16.

[17] B. Seebohm Rowntree, *Poverty and Progress: A Second Social Survey of York* (London: Longman's, Green, 1941).

[18] Rowntree, *Poverty: A Study of Town Life,* pp. 148–149.

[19] Rowntree, *Poverty and Progress,* p. 461.

[20] Ibid., p. 108.

[21] Ibid., pp. 101–104.

[22] Ibid., p. 29.

[23] Ibid., p. 456.

[24] Ibid., p. 461.

[25] Sir Hubert Llewelyn Smith, *New Survey of Life and Labour of the People in London* (London: London School of Economics, 1930–1935). Nine vols.

[26] Ibid., VI *(Social Survey),* 3–4.

[27] Douglas C. North and Roger L. Miller, *The Economics of Public Issues* (New York: Harper & Row, 1971), p. 151.

[28] Dorothy W. Douglas, "Family Budgets," *Encyclopedia of the Social Sciences,* 1934, vol. 5–6, pp. 73–77.

[29] Louise B. More, *Wage-Earner's Budgets* (New York: Holt, Rinehart and Winston, 1907).

[30] Ibid., p. 4.

[31] Ibid., p. 269.

[32] Ibid., p. 270.

[33] Robert Coit Chapin, *The Standard of Living Among Workingmen's Families in New York City* (New York: Russell Sage Foundation, 1909).

[34] Cited in Lee K. Frankel, "The Relation Between Standards of Living and Standards of Compensation," *Charities and the Commons,* 17 (November 1906): 1049.

[35] Chapin, p. 26.

[36] Ibid., p. 33.

[37] Ibid., p. 246.

[38] Ibid., p. 247.

[39] Ibid., p. 126.

[40] Ibid., pp. 245–247.

[41] Kate Holladay Claghorn, "The Use and Misuse of Statistics in Social Work," *Proceedings of the National Conference of Charities and Corrections,* 1908, p. 242.

[42] Ibid., p. 239.

[43] Cited in Bremner, pp. 83–151.

[44] Sophonisba P. Breckinridge, "The Scope and Place of Research in the Program of the Family Agency," *Proceedings of the National Conference of Social Work,* 1931, p. 225.

[45] Cited in Bremner, p. 153.

[46] John A. Ryan, *A Living Wage* (New York: Arno Press, 1906). Reprinted 1971.

[47] Mary Roberts Coolidge, in Amos G. Warner and Mary Roberts Coolidge, *American Charities* (New York: Crowell, 1919), 3d ed., p. 157.

[50] Royal Meeker, "Tentative Quantity-Cost Budget Necessary to Maintain a Family of Five in Washington, D.C.," *Monthly Labor Review,* 9 (December 1919): 23.

[51] Dorothy S. Brady, "The Use of Statistical Procedures in Derivation of Family Budgets," *Social Service Review,* 23 (June 1949): 142.

[52] Mary Sydney Branch, "Consumer Expenditures in the Low Income Group," *Social Service Review,* 12 (June 1949): 258.

[53] Brady, p. 145.

[54] Ibid., p. 150.

[55] Ibid., p. 152.

[56] Helen H. Lamale and Margaret S. Strotz, "The Interim City Worker's Family Budget," *Monthly Labor Review,* 83, no. 8 (August 1960): 808.

[57] Ibid., p. 786.

[58] Ibid., p. 802.

[59] U.S., Department of Labor, Bureau of Labor Statistics, *Three Standards of Living for an Urban Family of Four Persons: Spring, 1967,* Bulletin 1570-5 (Washington, D.C.: GPO, 1968).

[60] Ibid., p. 5.

[61] U.S., Department of Labor, Bureau of Labor Statistics, Chicago Regional Office, June 15, 1976. (Personal communication)

[62] John Kenneth Galbraith, *The Affluent Society* (Boston: Houghton Mifflin, 1969).

[63] Michael Harrington, *The Other America: Poverty in the United States* (Baltimore: Penguin Books, 1962).

[64] See, for example, Mollie Orshansky, "Children of the Poor," *Social Security Bulletin*, 26, no. 7 (July 1965); also, her "How Poverty is Measured", *Monthly Labor Review*, vol. 5, no. 2, pp. 37–41.

[65] U.S., Department of Commerce, Bureau of the Census, *General and Economic Characteristics: U.S. Summary* (1970 Census PC1-C1), p. App.–3.

[66] U.S., Department of Commerce, Bureau of the Census, *We, the Americans: Our Incomes* (no. 5 in a series of reports from the 1970 Census), p. 15.

[67] Bureau of the Census, *General and Economic Characteristics*, p. 1–358.

[68] Bureau of the Census, *We, the Americans*, p. 15.

[69] Ibid.

[70] Orshansky, "Children of the Poor," *Social Security Bulletin*, 26, no. 7 (July, 1965): 11.

[71] Including an economist writing in a U.S. Chamber of Commerce publication! See Victor R. Fuchs, "Toward a Theory of Poverty," in *The Concept of Poverty* (Washington, D.C.: Chamber of Commerce of the United States, 1965), p. 75; also see S. M. Miller, Martin Rein, Pamela Roly, and Bertram Gross, "Poverty, Inequality, and Conflict," *The Annals of the American Academy of Political and Social Science*, 373 (September 1967): 20–21.

# Chapter 5
# The Rise and Decline of the Social Survey Movement

—————— • ——————

## Introduction

After the turn of the century the study of poverty in this country evolved into the famous and dynamic social survey movement. The story of this development has been told a number of times, and there is no need to spell out the full narrative here.[1] The present purpose, rather, is to appraise this major phase of social work in terms of its general research implications and its place in the development of research in the field

It may be difficult in this day and age to visualize the electrifying impact that the social survey idea apparently made on the young profession in the first years of this century. Somehow the soil and the climate of the times were ripe for a dramatic device like this to flourish and to well-nigh capture the field for some time. As an index of its dominating influence we may cite the fact in 1909 the major professional journal in social work of the day, *Charities and The Commons,* changed its name to *Survey.* This was shortly after the magazine helped launch the first modern social survey, conducted in Pittsburgh in 1907. Looking back on this dazzling era some years later one practitioner commented:

In the days when the survey appeared as a brilliant new star above our horizon, we eagerly sought to bring its light upon our case work problems and to produce statistics ourselves that might be included among its nebulae. What a famous town Pittsburgh was in those days![2]

It was as if some recent research development, such as systems analysis, were to grow in scope and popularity to the point at which the leading social work journal would be renamed for it and a major portion of professional attention devoted to it. What accounted for this striking growth? What factors brought about its later modification and decline? What were some of its technical strengths and weaknesses? These are some of the questions to be explored in the following pages.

## Historical Setting

As has been noted, the turn of the century marked a swing in social work emphasis away from the moralistic focus of the early charity organization movement and toward environmental and social thought, which was by then becoming more fully cognizant of the issues created by the accelerating industrialization and urbanization of American society. The Industrial Revolution reached full stride in this country in the second half of the nineteenth century, several decades later than in England. The new liberalism and "social democracy" of Theordore Roosevelt, Robert La Follette, and other progressive leaders of the early 1900s reflected this growing concern for political and economic reform. It was within this context that the famous crusading journalists and writers of the 1890s and 1900s—Jacob Riis, Lincoln Steffens, Upton Sinclair, and others—created a deep impression on the public mind with their graphic accounts of squalor and exploitation in the cities and slums of the nation.[3] Thus people were becoming aroused to the need for social change and action, and more receptive to proposals pointing the way toward needed reforms. To these factors may be added the growing status being accorded the scientific method by the public, as previously noted, stemming from its technological successes in the physical and medical sciences. These various influences helped pave the way for a dramatic attack on the social problems of the day—an attack that professed to be scientific, comprehensive, and effective in bringing about needed social change. Shelby M. Harrison, one of the leaders of the survey movement, identified the following as major factors accounting for the phenomenal success it enjoyed:

(1) growth of community problems, (2) scientific advances in solutions, (3) emphasis on social values, and (4) recognition of the interrelationship of problems.[4]

Within social work itself, additional contributory influences were in operation around this time. The "scientific" charity organization movement, which was now over two decades old, had not provided the solution to the problem of poverty that had been hoped for. Growing industrialization had created increasing needs and problems with which the movement apparently was not equipped to cope. The case-by-case approach of its workers was widely condemned as the use of "retail" methods at a time when a "wholesale" attack on the underlying social and economic evils was necessary.[5] Social workers were looking for more dramatic vehicles in a frontal assault on the growing social malaise of the time.

The settlement movement in social work also added impetus to these trends. Arising in the 1880s and 1890s first in London and then in New York, Chicago, Boston, and elsewere in the United States, dedicated groups of educated men and women took up "settlement" in centers in workingmen's neighborhoods and slums and undertook to know and serve their new neighbors. Such experiments provided first hand knowledge of the depressing circumstances and forces with which the underprivileged had to deal, and led to the conviction that social, economic, and housing reforms were necessary to effect improvement in their lot. Settlement workers played an active role in bringing about many reforms in their immediate environs as well as on the larger scene. Coming into immediate touch with social needs and problems, they saw the opportunity for objective studies of social conditions as a contribution to knowledge and to the planning of reforms. Indeed, as we have seen, part of the stimulus for Booth's *Life and Labour of the People in London* was said to have come from his contacts with Tonybee Hall.

In this country, the residents of Chicago's Hull House published a scholarly study of the people and living conditions in the neighborhood of the settlement in 1895. This was the well-known *Hull House Maps and Papers: A Presentation of Nationalities and Wages in a Congested District of Chicago,* which set forth in maps, charts, tables, and interpretive text various ethnic, racial, and socioeconomic characteristics and factors in its primary area and served as a prototype of neighborhood studies in social work for many years.[6] Other settlement houses published studies along these lines during the same period.[7] Unfortunately, however, the social settlement movement did not fulfill its early promise of research creativity. According to Bruno, this failure was due primarily to the burden of time, expense, and specialization that such undertakings required.[8]

Another factor making for the initial success of the social survey movement may be the seeming ease with which such "fact finding" can be accomplished. Note has already been taken of the many theoretical and methodological difficulties encountered in the pursuit of individual causation and the technical measurement of poverty. By comparison, the study of external social conditions must have appeared enticingly simple and straightforward. Census statistics, housing data, working conditions, wages, family composition, health and welfare facilities and services are relatively tangible and accessible characteristics. Therefore a large-scale assault on the external facts of life may have appealed to the field as a more effective and available outlet for its crusading energies. The limitations of this form of activity were only to emerge later.

Finally, mention should be made of the powerful model provided by Booth's earlier trail-blazing study of life and labor in London. According to Philip Klein, the Pittsburgh Survey (and its sequels) "certainly was stimulated by the impact of Booth's work on social welfare perspectives."[9] While there were differences in method and focus between the two approaches, there were important parallels as well: the concentration on a local community; the comprehensiveness of scope, embracing many aspects of urban life; the concern with the needs and problems of people, particularly those at the lowest income levels; the flexible use of descriptive study methods, both quantitative and qualitative; the combined interest in research and reform; and so on. Poverty per se was no longer stage center, however.

For reasons like these the first decade of the twentieth century witnessed a burst of fact-finding activity in social work, the like of which may not have been seen before or since. Stated one observer before the 1908 National Conference: "Every settlement worker, every college boy and girl, filled with enthusiasm for 'research' and 'statistics,' is roaming up and down the land, with open note-book and freshly sharpened pencil, to glean . . . precious speach of statistical fact."[10] Another complained: "The investigations of the ever-growing army of social workers sent up a constant sound like the hum of bees."[11] Apparently by 1908 these activities had become so extensive that John Koren, chairman of the Conference Commitee on Statistics, had to caution the field that "social research is dangerously near becoming a fad in several quarters."[12] It is interesting to note such comments almost seventy years ago in a field that today frequently castigates itself for its inadequate attention to research.

### The First Pittsburgh Survey

In 1905 the two leading social work periodicals of the time— *Charities* (the publication of the Charity Organization Society (COS) of New York City) and *The Commons* (the settlement house periodical put out by the Chicago settlement of the same name)—merged as *Charities and The Commons* under the editorship of Edwin Devine. The following year another journal, *Jewish Charity,* the official organ of the United Hebrew Charities of New York, was also absorbed into the new merger. Dr. Devine was a midwestern educator who had been attracted to the emerging field of social work and during this period was serving as executive secretary of the New York COS.[13] In order to give direction and impetus to the newly unified journal, as well as other publication projects, he organized a Charities Publications Committee, including such prominent reformers of the time as Jane Addams and Jacob Riis.[14]

Special numbers of the new journal were soon devoted to selected problems such as "The Negro in the Cities of the North" (1905–1906) and "Neglected Neighborhoods: In the Alleys, Shacks and Tenements of the National Capitol" (1906). These exposés aroused considerable interest in liberal and welfare circles around the country, and subsequently some of the leading citizens and social workers in the Pittsburgh area requested that the Charities Publications Committee consider a study of social conditions in that industrial center.

Among his many other leadership activities, Devine organized the first formal educational program in social welfare in the form of the Summer School of Philanthropy, sponsored by the New York COS and later affiliated with Columbia University. Paul Kellogg was a student in one of these classes, and the young midwestern journalist sufficiently impressed his mentor to be invited in 1902 to join the staff of *Charities* as assistant editor, an affiliation that was to last a half-century. When the appeal came from Pittsburgh in 1907, Paul Kellogg—by then managing editor of *Charities and The Commons*—was assigned the responsibility for meeting the challenge.[15]

The job was financed largely by the newly organized Russell Sage Foundation, which came into existence in 1907 and undertook support of the survey as one of its projects. This financial boost came just in the nick of time, since the meager funds with which the undertaking was launched—$1,000 from the Publication Committee and $350 from Pittsburgh contributors—would hardly have been sufficient for such a task! Russell Sage eventually contributed a total of $27,000 to the survey, plus $20,000 for its publication.[16]

From the very outset the underlying motivation was an interest in "spreading information through journalism."[17] The initial sponsoring committee was in the field of publication, and the survey was looked upon as a promising interpretive and educational device. One of the objectives in the overall planning was the eventual utilization of the material collected as the basis for a series of articles in *Charities and The Commons*. As stated in the initial prospectus, the purpose was to determine

> The facts of underlying needs through investigation by experts in sanitary and civic work; to supply unbiased reports in each field as a basis for local action; and to publish a special Pittsburgh number for distribution locally and for use nationally in movements for civic advance in other American cities.[18]

Thus, as Paul Kellogg described it in retrospect, the survey was "in its origin a journalistic project."[19] It will be well to keep this background in mind as the movement is reviewed.

After some preliminary exploration the first formal step in the project was taken. This consisted of sending "what might be called a flying wedge of investigators" into Pittsburgh. The investigators studied various aspects of the local situation for periods ranging from six to eight weeks.[20] In this way a number of brief reports were prepared covering the immigrant groups, the Negros, housing, the health and police departments, aldermen's courts, playgrounds, children's institutions, schools, factory inspection, child labor, industrial education, and general labor conditions.[21]

The second major phase was a closer examination of several problem areas that had been uncovered in the initial reconnaissance. These investigations, completed by a staff of special consultants over a period of one year, were published in several volumes as follows:

> 1. An inquiry into hours, wages, and labor organization in the steel industry, by John A. Fitch.[22]
> 2. A study of living conditions and household budgets, by Margaret F. Byington.[23]

3. A study of industrial accidents in terms of causes, consequences, and legislative provisions, by Crystal Eastman. [24]

4. A general review of the women-employing trades, by E. B. Butler.[25]

5. A study of the economic cost of typhoid fever in six representative areas of the city, by Frank E. Wing.[26]

6. A review of the child-helping institutions and agencies of Pittsburgh, by Florence L. Lattimore.[27]

Highlights of these studies were published in a series of articles appearing in *Charities and The Commons* starting in 1909.

It may be noted, to begin with, that the scope of coverage of the survey extended far beyond what is conventionally included within the primary focus of social work today. Moreover, the range of study approaches adopted, in accordance with the different subjects of study, was quite varied. In effect the Pittsburgh Survey was a series of independent studies of selected community problems, conducted concurrently and tied together in planning and execution through staff interchange. A final characteristic to be mentioned is the major emphasis that was placed on the study of general social and industrial problems, and the relatively limited place given to the study of social services per se.

In order to convey to the reader some feeling of the kind of work that went into the making of the Pittsburgh Survey, brief summaries of portions of the study will be given in the following paragraphs. In view of the fact that the findings were published in 35 different articles and 6 volumes, it will be understood that only the barest sampling of their contents can be presented here (see excerpts, pp. 143–163).

Perhaps the major theme that runs through the entire survey is the grim omnipresence of the steel mills, whose impact on the life and economy of this industrial center is seen on almost every page of the report. In many sections of the study problems directly connected with the industry are in the foreground of attention, as, for example, in the volume by Crystal Eastman on *Work Accidents and the Law,* published in 1910. The tone of the book is set by the frontispiece, which presents the "Death Calendar in Industry for Allegheny County," consisting of twelve months during 1906–1907 on which red crosses corresponding to fatal industrial accidents were entered on the appropriate dates. A total of 526 deaths were graphically portrayed in this manner. In the course of the study these individual accidents were followed up where feasible in order to determine their economic and social consequences to the families afflicted and to the community. In addition, 509 nonfatal accidents occurring in industry from April through June of 1907 were traced in the same manner. The names were obtained from the coroner's reports and hospital records. It was found that 63 percent of the accidental deaths were of individuals who were the "sole or chief support of a family."[28] And of these, 53 percent received no more than $100 in settlements from the companies involved! Only 22.5 percent of these accidents were thought to be due to the negligence of the worker, in whole or in part.[29] The families bereaved by industrial accidents were investigated where available, and in 132 families thus studied it was reported that 470 children were left fatherless and that 22 of these had been forced to leave school to go to work by the time of the follow-up.[30] A number of case histories were presented to illustrate the more intangible costs to the families and community in terms of suffering, loneliness, and maladjustment. In such ways as these a powerful indictment was built up of the industries and of the community that permitted this waste and tragedy to take place. The significance of the findings was spelled out in moving language:

> If we were to regard the year's industrial fatalities in Allegheny County as one overwhelming disaster in which the dead numbered 526, its most appalling feature would be that it fell exclusively upon workers, bread-winners. Among those killed were no aged, helpless persons, no idle merry-makers, no unresponsible children. The people who perished were of those upon whom the world leans.[31]

This combination of startling findings and eloquent rhetoric was apparently not without results. According to Mary Van Kleeck, writing in the *Social Work Year Book* for 1929, the "development of workmen's compensation may be traced to interest which was stimulated by the Pittsburgh Survey."[32]

Considerably closer to present-day social work was the study by Florence Larabee Lattimore, published under the title "Pittsburgh as Foster Mother." This had to do with the standards of service of children's institutions in Pittsburgh and the needs of their resident populations. It was determined that approximately 6000 children spent all or part of the year in institutions in Pittsburgh, the average number at any one time being around 3000.[33] A special intensive study of 663 children in five selected institutions was made in order to get a picture of their background and family characteristics and make some evaluation of factors entering into their becoming institutionalized. On the basis of this special study it was estimated that 10 percent of the cases were related to the incidence of industrial accidents or industrial diseases in their families.[34] When all "preventable" diseases and accidents were included, the portion went up to about one-fourth.[35] In another analysis 55 families out of the 275 from which the children had come were identified as being sufficiently self-maintaining and "moral" so that the children "should not have been separated" from the parents.[36] Furthermore, in a number of other situations where need was a factor, "the reasonableness of home allowances . . . was not considered," whereas if they had, "many of the children need never have been pronounced 'homeless.' "[37]

A number of additional criticisms were leveled at the institutions for lax standards of care. The following menu, described as typical in several institutions, was presented to document the point:

Breakfast:    Coffee, bread, and a little butter.
Dinner:       Stew, bread, water.
Supper:       Tea, bread, with spoonful of molasses on it.[38]

Lattimore's recommendations were numerous. She urged that greater attention be given to keeping the child in the home, including more careful investigations at intake, greater emphasis on conservation and rehabilitation of families, and "home allowances"—later achieved as "mothers' pensions" and Aid to Dependent Children. She further stressed the need for more foster homes, better standards and coordination of institutional care, more alert public opinion, and widespread social action and reform.[39]

## The Rapid Spread of the Survey Idea

The Pittsburgh Survey started a chain reaction that swept the field like wildfire. The boldness of the conception, the enthusiasm of its leaders, the eloquence of its literature captured the imagination of the field and of the public, and the social survey was hailed as a major development in the evolution of social work. It was (modestly) compared with the charity organization society movement and the settlement movement as a major stage in the development of the profession.[40]

Soon Buffalo, Syracuse, and other cities were jumping on the survey bandwagon, and by 1911 it could be stated that "east as far as Boston . . . and here and there through the country to Seattle, the cities, keenly alive to the value of self-knowledge, have taken some form of community inventory."[41] As early as 1912 enough cities desiring surveys had requested consultation from the newly christened *Survey* magazine and the Russell Sage Foundation to warrant the latter's setting up a permanent Department of Surveys and Exhibits. Shelby M. Harrison, a former member of the Pittsburgh Survey staff, was made its first director.[42] Within the first year of its existence the Department received requests from over 100 cities in 34 different states for surveys or for advice in organizing local surveys.[43] In 1913 the movement had reached such proportions that a cartoon was printed in a daily city newspaper, the *Scranton-Republican,* caricaturing the social surveyor as a figure suspended aloft by a balloon attached to his trousers, perusing a city below him through an enormous telescope.[44]

Significantly enough, the social survey movement began, and has continued, as a primary *social work* phenomenon. Its initial auspices were social work; its major support and promotion was social work; and much of its leadership was drawn from the field. Charles A. Ellwood pointed out this fact before the 1918 Conference when he stated: "It is to the credit of our scientifically trained social workers that they have done vastly more to develop and to perfect the social survey than have our academic social scientists. Much, however, remains to be done."[45] According to Pauline Young, the first surveys in which sociologists "took an active and leading part" were surveys of race relations, beginning as late as 1919 and thereafter.[46]

### Characteristics of the "Classic" Social Survey

Perhaps sufficient material on the Pittsburgh prototype of the social survey movement has been presented to warrant our pausing to take stock of this phase of the development of social work research. On the basis of our summary thus far, how may the "classic" social survey be characterized? What are its major strengths and weaknesses? How does it stand up in terms of scientific criteria?

RESEARCH ASPECTS

As has been seen, the social survey movement was first and foremost a means of publicizing the needs of a community in as compelling a manner as possible so as to galvanize the populace into taking remedial action. Facts were gathered and analyzed as a means to this end. Thus it aspired to be a social reform vehicle as well as a research tool. To this combination in itself there can be little objection in an applied field like social work. Ultimately, however, a line must be drawn between fact finding for the sake of answering questions and fact finding for the sake of impressing, shocking, alarming, or arousing.

As we interpret it, research begins with the explicit formulation of questions or hypotheses. The impression that one gains from these first surveys is that the ruling consideration in the search for facts was often the effect that they were likely to have on an audience rather than the light that they might throw on questions or hypotheses clearly formulated and impartially pursued. It was stated that "in the Pittsburgh Survey it was deemed expedient to sacrifice comprehensiveness to concentrated power of attack upon certain . . . enormities of the Pittsburgh situation."[47] Research must, of course, be selective; one cannot study "everything." But if the selectivity is based primarily on demonstrating how bad a situation is rather than on a balanced effort to obtain all relevant data bearing upon a problem or question, its results are inevitably suspect.

This is an issue that goes right to the heart of research in an applied helping profession, particularly in its specific fact-finding phases. Social work research is unavoidably linked with the advancement of social work programs and objectives; its data are intended to contribute to these ends. In this sense it may be argued that social work research cannot be "pure" research (if indeed this is possible in the inevitably value-laden social sciences). And yet in its research undertakings it might do well to lean over backwards in order to avoid selecting data primarily to "make a case," data that reflect mainly one side of a question, data that are deliberately intended to jolt the reader. In other words, social work research should be primarily question-centered in order to maintain its research identity and integrity. Only in this way can its conclusions be considered verifiable or reproducible, since the selection of data relevant to a clearly defined question or hypothesis is a process subject to greater discipline and control, and hence verification by others, than the selection of data primarily for the attainment of partisan ends or dramatic effect.

If, on the other hand, the primary criterion of selection is to bring about change, rather than obtain answers, then the process is closer to education or crusading or propagandizing than it is to research. These are, to be sure, fine distinctions, based on degree rather than kind, since the questions or hypotheses studied in social work research have practical goals in view, if not immediately then in the long run. But the differentiation is nonetheless significant in the continuing effort to develop a disciplined field of research inquiry within social work, and one that must be zealously guarded by researcher and practitioner alike if the research is to be something distinct from practice as such.

Since the avowed purpose of the survey movement was the bringing about of change, the selection and dissemination of facts had this overriding objective in view, and all else tended to be subordinated to this end. Witness the following statement by Francis H. McLean, quoted approvingly by Shelby M. Harrison: "A survey by itself is not of the slightest importance. There is nothing magical in it. A survey's value indeed is not to be estimated in the light of the breadth of depth of its researches . . . it is nothing unless it leads to action."[48] Where such an extreme attitude prevails, quality research—and quality journalism as well—must find it difficult to flourish. For the quality and excellence of a research product, even in an applied field, cannot be judged entirely by its external results; research and social action are essentially separate—albeit related—processes with quite different criteria of results and quality. While they can and should contribute to each other, the one cannot be made the test of the other without seriously jeopardizing their respective functions. When research is under pressure for quick, tangible results, it is difficult to avoid compromising some of the thoroughness, impartiality, and precision that are required to maintain the verifiability of findings and conclusions.

## WELFARE "STANDARDS" IN THE SURVEY

Along with publicity and action, the social survey purported to lay the factual foundation required for intelligent planning. "Facts were seen to be a primary requirement, first, as a means of interesting citizens in conditions calling for attention; and second, as a basis for concerted action."[49] But before facts can lead to plans for action there must exist a frame of reference within which these facts can be interpreted. Facts never really "speak for themselves," though positivistic doctrine may hold otherwise; there must always be a theoretical or contextual key to read their significance. In the case of the survey, there is an assumption that the facts will reveal certain "gaps" and "needs" in the services or resources of the community, thus pointing the way for remedial or preventive action. But any interpretation of need for services implies the existence of a "standard" or "norm" against which to measure that need. Although such a standard is necessarily subjective and value based where social needs are concerned, it would appear important to formulate it as specifically and empirically as possible if it is to be utilized in research. Otherwise the means by which conclusions are arrived at remain more private than public and are hardly subject to adequate verification by others. The "minimum budget," for example, was seen in the preceding chapter to be a basically subjectively determined standard that is then spelled out in concrete terms for use in practice or research. Standards in social work are rarely articulated this clearly, however, and are often buried implicitly in the conclusions and interpretations of a study.

From its outset the social survey movement was strong on selected fact gathering and recommendations but woefully weak in explicating its standards. Nevertheless the most important section of many survey reports was a more or less detailed listing of recommendations for change, presumably arising out of the data collected. The relationship, however, between the various tables and charts and tabulations, which often comprise the core of such reports, and the final recommendations, is seldom clear. The leap from the data to the conclusions often skips a number of important intermediary steps. While it is perhaps not entirely fair to take the survey movement to task for a shortcoming that characterizes much of social work, this type of investigation has been particularly vulnerable in this regard. This issue was recognized in the early surveys but was generally glossed over with glib references to "experience" and the "art of diagnosis." Thus at the outset Paul Kellogg described the survey as a form of "diagnosis" by which "the survey takes from the physician his art of applying to the problems at hand standards and experiences worked out elsewhere."[50] The obligation of the scientific diagnostician to formulate his "standards" and "experiences" in explicit terms for others either to accept or reject was, however, not fulfilled in most survey undertakings. There was talk about "focusing many cities on one" as a means whereby "we could rapidly apply standards which had been worked out by slow processes of reform elsewhere—measure Pittsburgh against the composite community made of the nation's best."[51] But this "best" composite was apparently achieved privately within the minds of the survey makers, for it was never shared with the public except as it was applied in the conclusions and recommendations of the survey authors.

The lack of welfare standards in survey work was retrospectively scored by Kate Claghorn in a *Survey* article in 1934. She wrote:

> In the development of the survey the question of standards was always cropping up, and the surveyors seemed to feel increasingly a need for supporting their evaluations and recommendations by some sort of proof. . . .

> Why should not a reliably established standard always have
> been used? Because in many fields of interest such standards had
> not been worked out. . . . The surveyor . . . had to fall back on
> his own convictions or those of other people, his or their "com-
> mon sense," or on the community standard.[52]

She then went on to make a significant point relative to the research status of many survey conclusions:

> We may look upon the standards on which recommendations
> were based as hypotheses to be tested by experiment, and the
> carrying into effect not a final conclusion, but the experiment
> needed to verify the hypothesis.[53]

This salutary conservatism was unfortunately rarely observed
in practice; the impression was given in most early surveys that
the conclusions and recommendations were "scientifically" determined and established through the elaborate survey process
despite their avowedly "journalistic" nature.

### OTHER SURVEY CHARACTERISTICS

A further characteristic of the early social surveys was the broad-
ness of their scope, as already noted. The first surveys were intended to be truly "general" ones, embracing many if not most
of the significant aspects of a community's social, economic, and
political life. Obviously such a goal was often not attainable
within the practical limitations of time and resources available,
and therefore the survey was forced to focus on certain selected
major features or problems in the local situation for particular
attention. However, the aim of achieving a community overview
of needs, problems, services, and social forces was never lost
sight of, even at the cost of occasional superficiality of investigation. As expressed by Kellogg, the survey is "a sizing-up process
that reckons at once with many factors in the life of a great civic
area, not going deeply into all subjects, but offering a structural
exhibit of the community as a going concern."[54]

It may also be noted that the early social survey was essentially
limited to a particular community at a particular time, and that
the findings and conclusions were highly specific in this sense.
Whereas something was learned in the making of each survey that
might be generally useful and applicable elsewhere, the primary
emphasis was on "diagnosing" a given community as it was "today" in a major, one-shot operation. The findings and conclusions
might have no direct bearing on any other community, or indeed
on the same community five years hence. In this sense the survey
may be looked upon as the documentation of a piece of social

history, which is put to educational use in the attempt to change that history.

Finally, the people actually doing the planning, administering, and interpreting of the typical survey were usually from outside the community. Specialists and "experts," either as representatives of state and local associations or as individuals, were called in to render judgment on the ills and deficiencies of the local community. Obviously, this recourse to outside experts has certain advantages and disadvantages in community studies. The stranger may be able to take a fresh look at local conditions, less encumbered by personal ties and biases than many "insiders." At the same time, his lack of intimate familiarity with local factors, attitudes, and relationships may easily lead him astray. In any case, the early survey movement definitely cast its lot with the "outsiders," possibly influenced by the "scientific management" movement then current, with its reliance on the outside "efficiency expert."

### DEFINITIONS OF THE CLASSIC SOCIAL SURVEY

How, then, shall we define the classic American social survey? The literature contains a multitude of survey definitions, some stressing certain of the characteristics discussed earlier, some stressing others.[55] Perhaps the best of these is the early definition given by Kellogg in setting down the distinctive features of the Pittsburgh Survey:

1. To bring a group of experts together to co-operate with local leaders in gauging the needs of one city in several lines.
2. To study these needs in relation to each other, to the whole area of the city, and to the civic responsibilities of democracy.
3. To consider at the same time both civic and industrial conditions, and to consider them for the most part in their bearings upon the wage-earning population.
4. To reduce conditions to terms of household experience and human life.
5. To devise graphic means for making these findings challenging, clear, and unmistakable.
6. To establish natural relations with local agencies, to project the work into the future.[56]

Recasting this definition in the light of later perspective, and taking into account the points brought out in the foregong discussion, the following descriptive statement might be offered. The early social survey was a process for effecting social improvement by means of a large-scale, one-time investigation of a community's social welfare needs. Its method consisted of bringing in a team of outside "experts" who, in close conjunction with local groups, gathered together a mass of information selected largely to demonstrate the most serious needs and problems of the community in a number of fields. This material was utilized as a basis for drawing conclusions and recommendations for social action, without much in the way of articulation of the specific standards of need applied. Major emphasis was placed throughout on publicizing the survey and its findings and conclusions as widely and effectively as possible so as to arouse the community to action and implementation of its recommendations.

## Reaction and Reevaluation

The enthusiastic and uncritical acceptance of the survey idea by the field persisted for some time. Increasingly, however, mutterings of dissatisfaction began to appear in the literature. A phase of questioning and doubting emerged, and probably reinforced some of the modifications that were already beginning to take place in the form and method of the survey. In part this reaction may be traced to the "overselling" of the potentialities of this device by its advocates. When it was discovered that surveys were not the panacea for all of the ills of a community that they were sometimes made out to be, that they had definite limitations and pitfalls, that they were expensive and time-consuming, the profession began to take critical stock of its high-flying offspring.

One of the first formal admonitions came from outside the field. It was presented by sociologist J. L. Gillin before the American Statistical Association in 1914. That he did not mince words is illustrated by the following extract:

> In the absence of established standards of survey work, the commercial social surveyor who depends upon his work for a living is a menace to the development of this form of social stock-taking. Now is the time to provide deliverance of the social survey from the hands of the man who does social surveying on a commercial basis. . . .
>
> The professional surveyor is likely to be open to criticism on a number of points. Too often he starts in on the social survey the victim of a preconceived hypothesis or of an established prejudice. He assumes that certain things are wrong. Unconsciously that conviction colors his findings. Having found certain things wrong in other communities, naturally he is looking for

the same things in the community now under observation. Again, the commercialized surveyor is prone to look only for bad conditions rather than to make a correct appraisal both of the good and the evil in the community's life. He is likely to feel that he must find the evil that employers have suspected, else he cannot justify his employment. In this respect he reminds one of the quack doctor who can secure business only by making out a bad case for the prospective patient. Such a surveyor may excite interest and secure employment for a time but his methods are sure to bring reproach upon the whole survey movement.

Again, the social surveyor desires publicity for his work. He has learned that muck-raking secures publicity. Therefore he emphasizes the evils in a community without stating them in their proper relations to the social assets of a community. Following the publication of a one-sided survey of this kind, there is bound to be a reaction on the part of those who know that the community is better than it has been painted.[57]

The hazards that Gillin points to are certainly realistic ones to be faced by every survey maker. To the extent that such abuses crept into the survey record, they certainly warranted its fall from public favor. In a paper before the National Conference of Social Work a little over a decade later (1927), George H. von Tungeln made some of the same criticisms of the social survey, concluding that it was best characterized as "constructive propaganda."[58]

The question of the efficacy of the social survey was raised by Arch Mandel before the 1924 Conference. He pointed to the fact that in Detroit, where no large-scale surveys had been launched, apparently greater social reform progress had been made than in Cleveland, where a number of very elaborate surveys had been conducted. He therefore expressed skepticism about the vaunted prowess of the survey, and went on to conclude that "the difficulty with the general survey is that it presents too much at one time for the public to assimilate properly." He recommended "continuous self-surveys by the local organization," calling in specialists only "if necessary"[59] instead of expending so much effort and expense on such a large-scale, one-shot affair. The idea of continuous rather than sporadic community stock taking is an important one, echoed many times in the later literature.[60]

A further criticism of the social survey was made by J. Howard T. Falk before the same Conference. Falk was concerned about the tendency in some surveys to impose the standards of an outside group on a local community or agency without sufficient local readiness for such a change. "The objective survey," he stated, "made on the initiative of an influence which wants reform, and directed as if it were against a delinquent who has not felt the desire for reform, is wrong in principle, and likely to be unsuccessful in fact." Such an approach to effecting change should be made use of only "as a last resource, when all other means have failed."[61] However, when the groups and agencies involved have given spontaneous indication of their desire to change and improve, then and only then can a survey be very useful.[62]

A caseworker's attitude toward the survey movement was expressed at about the same time by Corinne A. Sherman, writing in *The Family* in 1925: "Since [the Pittsburgh Survey] . . . we have become a little disillusioned. Some of us may feel, for instance, that different sets of figures are too often contradictory, . . . that after all tables and charts are not really descriptive of the human beings with whom we have to deal."[63]

By 1930 Francis H. McLean was quoted as stating "I am convinced that more money has been wasted upon surveys, and some mighty good surveys at that, than upon any other form of social effort."[64] He went on to make the point that a series of limited studies of special areas of service or need might be of greater value than the large-scale type of general survey. There was also the ever-present danger that "study" might forestall obviously needed action.

Such were some of the reactions in the literature to the challenge and pretensions of the original survey idea. But a number of significant changes were already taking place in the survey movement, some of them in line with the criticisms and suggestions just noted.

## The Decline of the "Classic" Social Survey

Quite early in the survey movement the classic Pittsburgh prototype of a large-scale, city-wide undertaking delving into many types of problems at once began to subdivide into a number of less ambitious varieties. As early as 1913 Shelby Harrison could point to at least three "new" types of survey that were emerging: (1) the "neighborhood" survey, limited to a small section of a community; (2) the "pathfinder" survey, limited to an informal exploration of a city's problems and considered as preliminary to a major investigation; and (3) the "specialized survey," limited to a single field of service (at that time the only field that had been studied in this way was public health and sanitation).[65]

These transformations of the survey method proceeded apace. Specialized surveys received a great impetus from the intensive series in Cleveland, starting with the Cleveland School Survey (1915–1917), which began with an investigation of the field of education and took up in turn recreation, hospitals and health, and crime.[66] By 1924 Falk could state that

> There is an increasing tendency to get away from the "'whole field" survey policy. A general survey has a tendency to create a panicky feeling in the community, both among workers, sub-scribers, and the general public. The very magnitude of such an undertaking suggests cause for alarm, otherwise why so much fuss and expense?[67]

Harrison described the change that took place as follows:

> The first surveys covered a broad range of subjects; they were general surveys of entire communities. A tendency set in, how-ever, after a few years toward employing the survey to appraise some major phase of community life, such as health and sanitation, public education, recreation, or delinquency and correction.[68]

The explanation for this trend was later given in the following terms:

> Doubtless one of the chief reasons for the shift toward the more specialized inquiry is the fact that many communities have now passed beyond the "awakening" stage and are ready to deal in a more intensive way with special problems or groups of them, taking them up one by one. Moreover, as the technical equip-ment of surveyors has improved, surveys in single fields have become so intensive and comprehensive that the accumulated findings in a single field often promise to be as much as a com-munity can well assimilate before being diverted to new topics— and in some cases as much as it can be responsible for or finance at a given time.[69]

It is interesting to contrast the primarily positive interpreta-tion of the trend away from the original survey form, given by Harrison here, with some of the negative reactions and criticism expressed by other writers in the field, as noted in the preceding section. For example, Ruth Hill, writing at about the same time, proposed the following as an alternative interpretation: "the expensiveness of these thorough surveys and the effort necessary to make them work . . . may account for the gradual dying down of enthusiasm."[70]

In addition to the shift from "general" to "specialized," a trend toward greater local participation by local agencies and groups was noted, starting with the Springfield Survey.[71] Apparently the invasion of a community by outside "experts" sometimes backfired, and more and more stress was placed on the "self-survey" aspect of such community studies. In a sense this was a somewhat belated adaptation of the core social work principle of "growth from within, rather than from without" to the field of community studies.

Another change, occurring during the later 1920s, was the increasing centralization of surveys in local community chests and councils of social agencies, which were then spreading rapidly as a concomitant of the federated financing movement in social work.[72] Thus the survey found a "natural" sponsoring body in more and more communities in the form of a permanent local planning organization. At the same time, such an auspice provided an opportunity for the conduct of more flexible and continuous types of study and reporting than was previously possible, and gradually developed research functions that assumed some aspects of the role that had heretofore been played by the "one-shot" survey.[73]

A final tendency that may be noted in later surveys is their limitation to more specialized social work needs and services, as these are construed today. Less often did the survey range into the broader areas of community concern such as industrial conditions, political problems, economic factors, crime, or education. In part this was undoubtedly due to a progressive delimitation of the central core of professional social work, as contrasted with the earlier breadth of social welfare. During the "normalcy" of the 1920s professionalization progressed rapidly in social work, and the pendulum of interest swung back from environmental change to individual treatment, this time with an increasingly Freudian slant. Hence, some of the crusading enthusiasm that fired the survey's attack on social conditions began to wane, and the field settled into a more intensive cultivation of practice methods. At the same time, the growing body of services and programs that had evolved within social work during the first quarter of this century provided substantial content and problems for survey inquiry and began to command a growing share of attention.[74] As a result surveys of *social work* needs, of related social work services, and of their organization and coordination were conducted more and more frequently.

In closing this appraisal of the "golden age" of the social survey movement of the early 1900s, it will be well to cite Robert Bremner's handsome tribute to this period of American social welfare history:

> In the United States, as in . . . England, the great outburst of
> interest in social investigation came during a period of political
> liberalism. Conversely, the development of political progressivism
> coincided with the rise of social research. The two movements
> were so closely related that it is almost impossible to separate
> one from the other. . . . Reform could no more be effected by
> platitudinous avowals of righteousness than by generalized de-
> nunciations of evil. Nor could research alone accomplish re-
> form. . . . On the whole, however, the first decade and a half of
> the twentieth century was unusually productive of social reform.
> It was a time when the will to improve conditions was studied
> and strengthened by knowledge carved from factual inquiry,
> when the zeal to do good was matched by eagerness to learn how
> and what to do.[75]

And if the quality of the research fell short, as with hindsight it
did in many respects, it was not because of lack of good faith or
intent. Rather, it was largely because social work research was
then relatively undeveloped and unsophisticated and the movement was consciously more promotional than scientific.

## The Second Pittsburgh Survey

Because it incorporates some of the changes in survey emphasis
described earlier, it is of interest to compare the well-known
second *Social Study of Pittsburgh* (1938) with its monumental
predecessor. The second Pittsburgh survey, conducted during the
period 1934–1938 and directed by Philip Klein, professor at the
New York School of Social Work, differed from the earlier one
primarily in that it focused more specifically on needs and services
now generally considered to fall within the primary province of
social work concern. While Dr. Klein gave considerable attention
to the broader context of economic and political life in this study,
it was mainly to provide a setting and perspective, rather than
a fulcrum for general social action and reform as in the earlier
case. Indeed the first third of Klein's book (the report was published in a single 600-page volume rather than in six bulkier ones
as in the first Pittsburgh Survey) was devoted to filling in this
broader picture, but now this material was explicitly labeled
"Social and Economic Background."[76] The bulk of the report
consisted of an analysis of needs and services in the major fields
of social work in Pittsburgh in the mid-1930s.

Thus in moving from the first to second Pittsburgh surveys
we follow the transition that the field has made from its relatively

"unlimited" social reform and action days at the opening of the century to the more highly specialized and professionalized modern era, in which the central concerns of social work are more closely circumscribed and the wider aspects of social problems tend to be looked upon as significant background and context rather than serving as the major focus of attention. This contrast is affirmed in the opening passage of the report:

> It is not a sequel to the famous Pittsburgh Survey which revealed to that community and to the nation at large the dangers to workers and citizens inherent in a community of rapid and uncontrolled industrial expansion. In prime intention this is a social work survey: an examination of agencies and institutions that provide social and health services, whether under public or voluntary auspices. A substantial part of the report is devoted, however, to an interpretation of the social and economic life of the community—the background and matrix of social work.[77]

The study was initiated by a group of local citizens who felt that the time had come for "a comprehensive study of the needs of the community and the resources already existing to meet them."[78] This committee submitted an application to the Buhl Foundation, and a grant of $75,000 was approved for such a study in April 1934. Philip Klein, of the New York School of Social Work, who was engaged as director, drew together an outstanding staff of some thirty specialists and consultants in various fields of social work, most of them on loan from different national, state, and local agencies, and entered upon what was to be a three-year study. The key question was formulated as follows: "Is there any discrepancy between what is needed and what is supplied: if so, what can be done to eliminate or at least to reduce this discrepancy?"[79]

There is little description of methodology, so one must infer the procedures that must have been followed. These techniques included statistical, demographic, case study, and interview methods, and were primarily of a descriptive nature.[80] In this connection Klein states:

> It would take too long to recite the details of the procedure followed by the study, and such a recital might be of only limited interest to the reader. Time, place, and other peculiarities of the situation, idiosyncrasies of the staff, limitation of the personnel, and unpredictable developments in the course of the study were all factors in determining procedures.[81]

While this decision is understandable and perhaps unavoidable, it obviously limits the scientific usefulness of the findings presented. Frankly enough, the author disclaims any rigorous scientific intentions. "Research in the strict and formal meaning of the word as indicating the original collection of primary material," Klien writes, "was subordinated to selection guided by experience and to the authoritative judgment of expert personnel."[82] The research limitations of the document were thus fully acknowledged by the author.

The aspects of social work that the survey investigated included social work financing, social work personnel, public relief, family casework, child welfare, health, and recreation. For each of the fields of service taken up, a description and evaluation of needs and existing services—largely narrative, sometimes statistical—was given. The standards by which needs were revealed were for the most part unarticulated and only implied by the survey's interpretations and recommendations. In lieu of such criteria, a summary of the background and qualifications of the specialists making the appraisals was presented as "credentials for the authoritativeness of the opinions submitted. In a field where no absolute standards exist and no constituted authority prevails the reader is entitled to that much at least of the supporting evidence."[83] This degree of candor on the part of a survey maker comes perhaps as a welcome change from the invocations to science and objectivity that characterized many earlier research ventures in this field.

A year and a half after the completion of the survey Klein evaluated the changes that had taken place in the community that were believed to have come about largely as a result of the survey. Ten major changes were identified that were in line with its principal recommendations, including steps toward the merging of several agencies.[84] In view of the fact that the principal recommendations of the study occupied over 12 pages of fine print and covered in detail some 2 different fields of service, this would not appear to be a particularly impressive record. This was, however, quite a short period of time as community processes go, and a later evaluation imputed a much wider influence to the undertaking.[85]

In summary, then, the second Pittsburgh survey concentrated primarily on social work needs and services. While aiming at practical results, it did not go to the journalistic and promotional extremes that characterized its forerunner, relying for action primarily on lay committee participation in the study process. Furthermore, Klein made a point of clearly emphasizing the scientific limitations of his data and conclusions. In these respects the *Social Study of Pittsburgh* marked an important transition in the history of the social survey and of social work research.

## The Social Survey Yesterday and Today

In the years immediately following the first Pittsburgh Survey interest in the movement spread rapidly. Then, during World War I, it underwent a temporary eclipse owing to the war effort, only to revive with increased volume thereafter. By the mid-1920s, however, reaction had set in. The movement had changed much of its original character and no longer commanded the enthusiastic following that it once had. During the Depression the number of employment and relief "surveys" conducted throughout the country reached staggering proportions, but this form of study, though often referred to as a survey, actually bore little or no resemblance to its namesake. In 1931 the Department of Surveys and Exhibits of the Russell Sage Foundation was revamped to become the Department of Social Work Interpretation, dropping its earlier survey functions. World War II and the postwar years saw the further decline of the survey movement, with governmental and social agency auspices becoming more prominent.[86] Finally, in 1952, the professional journal that had spawned the survey idea and then taken it as its name was forced to cease publication for lack of support. Paul Kellogg, then 71 years old and ailing, decided it was time to retire.[87] The passing of *Survey* magazine may be taken as a symbol marking the close of this colorful era in social work, which had already long passed its zenith.

Thus the survey movement in its original form passed from the social work scene. In its wake it left a variety of derivative forms, which have become common in social work research and are generally indistinguishable from the broad and varied fare of studies encountered in community organization and planning settings that are referred to loosely as surveys. Typically they involve the determination of "unmet needs" through the relating of "needs" and "services" in a delimited field of social work concern, frequently within a segment of the larger community. To a considerable degree they are still subject to the same strengths and weaknesses as their more elaborate forebears. While they sometimes draw upon newer research techniques borrowed from the social sciences, in general they adhere to relatively traditional descriptive lines, leaning heavily on straightforward statistical data, on which base considerable qualitative interpretation and recommendations may be built. Certainly not all such studies, which figure prominently in community welfare council research today, can be considered to be descendants of the survey movement, for as has been seen, studies of social needs in social work preceded this movement and continued to evolve outside of it. Nevertheless the impact of the survey idea and approach undoubtedly premeated and conditioned much of what followed along these lines. Not only in name but also in methods (descriptive-statistical), concepts ("unmet needs," "service standards," etc.), and process (involvement of local groups, lay-professional collaboration), the movement has left its impress on social work research and community organization practice.

Illustrative of the extent to which the survey has been extended to quite different types of studies is the breakdown of survey types given by the National Social Welfare Assembly in its 1949 pamphlet *Shall We Make a Survey?*

1. General survey of community needs and services.
2. Survey of social agencies.
3. Survey in one particular field.
4. Survey of administrative set-up and relationships.
5. Survey of community planning structure.
6. Survey of special problems.[88]

When the term *survey* is applied to such a broad range of study types it ceases to have much specific denotation and becomes a generic title that can be applied to almost any kind of study. Thus one now encounters "attitude surveys," "need surveys," "agency surveys," "caseload surveys," "surveys of the literature," and so on ad infinitum. In this way the social survey movement came to an end, willing its name and title to many heirs, some of which were closely related and some of which were not.*

# The Pittsburgh Survey
## PAUL U. KELLOGG

The plan and procedure of the Pittsburgh Survey were set forth in Volume I, Appendix E (pp. 494–515), which is quoted in part in the following pages after a brief introduction.

From Paul U. Kellogg, *The Pittsburgh Survey* vol. I, *The Pittsburgh District— Civic Frontage* (New York: Survey Associates, 1914), © 1914 by the Russell Sage Foundation, New York.

* Occasional city-wide surveys covering several fields of health and welfare are still being conducted, but these are usually much more restricted in scope, style, and method than their classic prototypes.

## INTRODUCTORY NOTE

The gist of the Pittsburgh Survey was brought out in thirty-five magazine articles in the six months following completion of the investigation. The succeeding year the findings of four major lines of inquiry were published under separate covers.

In binding up the minor reports at this date in permanent form, only those are included which as transcripts of the human consequences of some phase of our civic or economic order, as cross sections of the community life, or as exhibits of either retrograde or nascent social institutions, will be of service generally to those at work upon the fabric of the common welfare.

Booth compressed into a single masterful phrase the scope of his panoramic analysis of the People of London. He dealt with their life and labor. We fell into the same great division in our much less exhaustive study of the wage-earning population of Pittsburgh, taking up both the civic conditions which bore especially upon them, and their industrial relations. It has been natural to employ the same division in bringing out these final monographs under two titles: The Pittsburgh District and Wage-earning Pittsburgh.

Certain writings are included which give the inter-relation of the various studies and their Pittsburgh setting. As the set stands on a shelf, therefore, these concluding volumes may well become the first of the six; and it is appropriate to incorporate as Appendix E a brief statement of the whole working scheme.

## FIELD WORK OF THE PITTSBURGH SURVEY (APPENDIX E)

The Pittsburgh Survey was a rapid close range investigation of the ranks of wage-earners in the American steel district. The staff included not only trained investigators—housing inspectors, sanitarians, lawyers, engineers, labor experts, and the like—but members of the immigrant races who make up so large a share of the working population. Our field work was done in railroad yards and mill towns, sweatshops, and great manufacturing plants; in courts, hospitals, and settlements. The investigators talked with priests and labor leaders, superintendents, claim agents and labor bosses, landlords, housewives, butchers and bakers—the workers themselves and those who live close to them.

The work was carried on by a special staff, organized for the purpose by the editors of *Charities and The Commons,* since become *The Survey* magazine. It was financed chiefly by three grants, of moderate amount, from the Russell Sage Foundation for the improvement of social and living conditions. It was made practicable by co-operation from two quarters: from a remarkable group of leaders and organizations in social and sanitary movements in different parts of the United States, who entered upon the field work as a piece of national good citizenship; and from men, women, and organizations in Pittsburgh, who were large minded enough to regard their local situation as not private and peculiar but as part of the American problem of city-building.

Without either funds or time to adopt census methods, we made use of case investigations and statistical studies, both in exploring for a basic understanding of the situation and in clamping our facts in. In the words of one of the collaborators in the field work, the end was "piled up actualities." More than in investigations hitherto carried on, we made use of graphic methods for interpreting those facts by maps, charts, diagrams, photographs, drawings in pastel and charcoal, and the large frames for an exhibit in Carnegie Institute. This exhibit was part of a general civic exhibit, arranged by a local committee in conjunction with the annual conventions in Pittsburgh in November, 1908, of the National Municipal League and the American Civic Association.* Our reports were interpreted in their civic relations at these meetings, and in their economic bearings at Atlantic City in December at joint meetings of the American Economic Association, the American Sociological Society, and the American Association for Labor Legislation.†

The gist of them was originally published by *Charities and The Commons* in the winter of 1909, in three special numbers:

January:     The People
February:    The Place
March:       The Work

The Pittsburgh Chamber of Commerce sent out copies to its entire membership, and budgets of advance matter were published by the Pittsburgh newspapers. Wider audiences were acquainted with the Survey and its finding by articles in the *World Work*, the *Outlook*, the *Independent*, *Collier's Weekly*, the *American Magazine*, and the *Review of Reviews*; by the labor press and by such trade journals as the *Iron Age*, *Engineering News*, and the *Iron Trade Review*. Editors, ministers, and public speakers throughout the country drew on them to such extent that Jacob A. Riis, then on a Pacific Coast lecture tour, said that he had never known the results of an investigation to have such widespread and practical currency.

**The Problem Stated**

In a sense the Pittsburgh Survey was a demonstration in social economy made graphic against the background of a single city—a city set as it were on the hill of our material development. Hundreds of industrial towns, a score of great industrial centers, are growing up in this country. Of their technical and commercial success we have evidence in plenty. What of their human prosperity? Pittsburgh itself is the social expression of one of the master industries of the country, iron and steel, yet in so far as work-accidents are the crudest exponents of human waste in industry, the Pittsburgh District had been spendthrift of

* Speakers: Robert W. de Forest, chairman Charities Publication Committee, Robert A. Woods, Grosvenor Atterbury, Paul U. Kellogg; and in response, H. D. W. English.

† Speakers: Edward T. Devine, Crystal Eastman, Margaret F. Byington, and Paul U. Kellogg.

its own life blood. Here, as nowhere else, was a district conditioned by a tariff policy which for a generation had obstructed competing European goods and by an immigration policy which had opened wide the doors to let in Slavs, Huns, and Italians to compete with resident labor. What had been the outcome of these two great national policies in the everyday welfare of the workers of Pittsburgh? Again, here in the master industry in the District, employers had the upper hand. What had they done with it? Here, as in growing numbers of industrial communities, outside investors owned the mills and the railroads on which the work of the District depended. Was absentee capitalism working out any better for an industrial democracy than the absentee landlordism of England and Ireland; or the absentee political rule of colonial America? The Survey was an attempt to throw light on these and kindred economic forces not by theoretical discussion of them, but by spreading forth the objective facts of life and labor which should help in forming judgment as to their results. We did not turn to Pittsburgh as a scapegoat city; progressive manufacturers have here as elsewhere done noteworthy things for their employes, and for the community. Yet at bottom the District exhibits national tendencies; and if the great industries of the country are to be owned by great bodies of stockholders scattered all over the country—or if we are to change that system of ownership and control—then on the shoulders of a national public opinion must rest the responsibility for sanctioning, or for changing, the terms of work and livelihood which accompany industry. As a basis for that national public opinion, facts are needed; such facts at the Pittsburgh Survey endeavored to bring to the surface.

As a collection of human beings, and equally so as an industrial center, Pittsburgh was an exceptionally interesting phenomenon. Half a million people were living and working at the headwaters of the Ohio; as many as Baltimore, Boston, Chicago, Philadelphia, and St. Louis combined had in 1850. Not in numbers alone was the city and example of the dynamic urban growth which has characterized the past century. In libraries, institutes, conservatories, universities, great parks, and in other ways, this growth expressed itself. The Survey set out to get at certain underlying factors in this growth as the affected the wage-earning population. The present volume reveals a community struggling for the things which primitive men have ready to hand—clear air, clean water, pure foods, shelter, and a foothold of earth. We found in Pittsburgh a smoke campaign, a typhoid movement, and the administrative problems of the bureau of health in milk and meat inspection; thus there was bitter evidence of the necessity for sanitary regulation of housing wherever people lived, dense or deep, and the necessity further for increased numbers of low-cost dwellings. Similarly, the agitations for flood prevention, traction development, bridge building, and the like have been so many efforts to expand, or conquer the difficulties of the town's corrugated floor. With the moving into Pittsburgh of new and immigrant peoples, the spirit of the frontier and of the mining camp has possessed the wage-earning population. This spirit has also characterized civic development. Wherever there has been profit in public service, private enterprises have staked their claims to perform in. While the biggest men of the community made steel, other men built water companies, threw bridges across the rivers, erected inclines, and laid sectional car lines. To bring system and larger public utility out of these heterogeneous units threfore became the city's governmental problem in the new century. In a sense, this situation is repeated with respect to the institutions transplanted into Pittsburgh, or initiated there, to meet the cultural and social needs of the community. Thus we found local aldermen's courts, uncoördinated charitable enterprises, and a ward system of schools. Yet the trend here, too, was obviously toward system— toward a municipalization of lower courts, an expansion of the health service, an association of charities, a city system as against a vestry system of schools, the coördination of public sentiment in movements for municipal improvement.

To make inventory of such an American community was in the large the commission undertaken by the Pittsburgh Survey.

**Origin of the Work**

The Survey was in its origin a journalistic project. In 1905 the Central Council of the Charity Organization Society of New York appointed a Publication Committee to give national breadth and effect to its weekly magazine, *Charities*, with which that year was merged *The Commons*, brought out by the Chicago settlement of the same name. The stated purpose of this national committee was "to get at the facts of social conditions and to put those facts before the public in ways that will count."

Five of the specific methods proposed were these:

> 1. The undertaking of important pieces of social investigation not undertaken by any existing organization.
> 2. The issuing of special numbers, putting into comprehensive and concrete form groups of facts entering into some one social problem.
> 4. The extension of the spirit of organized philanthropy to smaller cities and the re-kindling of existing agencies to more progressive ways.
> 6. The promotion of movements already under way, co-operating with communities or national bodies, to give general application to reforms wrought painfully in one locality.
> 10. The education of public opinion through connection with newspapers, speakers, and other agencies of publicity.

These methods were successfully combined in a piece of journalistic research carried on the year following at Washington. Grave abuses in the hospitals and charities supported in part by federal funds, came to the attention of the editor, Edward T. Devine, and he conceived the idea of bringing national public opinion to bear upon them through *Charities and the Commons.* As developed by the staff in co-operation with various local organizations, the plan broadened into a special number on the national capital as a model city. The Washington monument has a stone for every state in the Union, and the civic neglect which crushed down upon the District of Columbia has come from the same quarries. United States senators and representatives as a body make up the common council of the District, and year after year they had administered defeat to measures to restrict child labor and lower an excessive infant mortality; to require compulsory education for Washington children at the hands of the same authority which was building school houses for the Tagalogs; and to raze alley shacks, fairly under the eaves of the Capitol, which, in the words of western senators, were "not fit for cow stables." The late Justice Brewer of the United States Supreme Court, S. W. Woodward, and others backed the enterprise, and Charles F. Weller, then general secretary of the Washington Associated Charities, spent ten months in investigating housing conditions. Two thousand copies of the issue, Next Door to Congress, were distributed in Washington itself; other copies and special letters over the signatures of the committee were sent to all members of Congress, to five hundred newspapers and magazine editors, and to one thousand child labor committees, civic leagues, tuberculosis associations, women's clubs, charity organization societies, and so forth, throughout the Union. They were asked to help, and they did, sending scores of letters to congressmen and senators. Newspapers everywhere added their urgency to the appeal of the Washington organizations which used the number as a weapon in their campaigns for the improvement of conditions. A wife-desertion law was passed at this session, a juvenile court law enacted and a judge appointed; two blind alleys were opened at once into a minor street; and a bill for the condemnation of insanitary dwellings, which had hung fire for nine years, was passed. Mr. Weller continued his housing investigations, bringing them out in book form—Our Neglected Neighbors. The President's Homes Commission, later appointed by Mr. Roosevelt, carried on further investigations into the general social and sanitary conditions in the District. Now, as then, much remains before the national capital will set the standard for the cities of the country as a whole; but this special number helped carry the slow process forward by another stage.

### The Pittsburgh Investigations

Thereafter an invitation came to us from Mrs. Aice B. Montgomery, then chief probation officer of the Allegheny Juvenile Court to undertake a similar venture in Pittsburgh. We felt that Pittsburgh had somewhat the same relation industrially to the country at large that Washington did politically. It was not until the early winter following that Charities Publication Committee entered upon the work. The impulse that actually set it under way came through Frank Tucker, a member of the Committee, who, as a former journalist, visualized the possibilities of Pittsburgh in public opinion. The idea met with hearty response from

William H. Matthews, head worker at Kingsley House, Pittsburgh, through whose co-operation Mr. Devine put the plans before a group of forward-looking Pittsburghers who gave it their encouragement and co-operation. Mayor Guthrie, President English of the Pittsburgh Chamber of Commerce, and Judge Buffington of the United States Circuit Court consented to be our references—a part which at times required no little courage. The initial plan, to quote from the original prospectus, was to get at

> the facts of underlying needs through investigation by experts in sanitary and civic work; to supply unbiased reports in each field as a basis for local action; and to publish a special Pittsburgh number for distribution locally so as to reach public opinion and for use nationally in movements for civic advance in other American cities.

The work was begun on an appropriation of $1,000 from Charities Publication Committee, in addition to the following Pittsburgh contributions:

| | |
|---|---|
| Civic Club of Allegheny County | $ 50.00 |
| H. J. Heinz | 100.00 |
| Wallace H. Rowe | 100.00 |
| Benjamin Thaw | 50.00 |
| Mrs. William R. Thompson | 50.00 |

The late Robert C. Hall gave us the use of offices, but little further money was forthcoming from Pittsburgh sources for what seemed a rather vague and not altogether pleasant enterprise. On our limited funds, the work would have been handicapped from the start had not new and unexpected reinforcement come in the spring of 1907. The Russell Sage Foundation was created by the gift of $10,000,000 from Mrs. Sage, and one of its first grants was $7,000 to develop the Pittsburgh Survey. We secured the co-operation of several national organizations; such as the Industrial Committee of the International Committee of the Young Men's Christian Association, the National Consumers' League, the Association for Labor Legislation, Seybert Institute (Philadelphia), and the Department for the Improvement of Social Conditions of the New York Charity Organization Society.

After some exploring during the spring and summer, we injected into Pittsburgh in September, 1907, what might be called a flying wedge of investigators who were on the ground for from six weeks to two months. Each was a specialist in a given line and the commission of each was to make a diagnosis of the situation in his field. The returns from this exploring process was such that we felt it would be ignoring a wonderful opportunity for constructive research to limit the work to the quick journalistic diagnoses originally planned. Following a visit to Pittsburgh by John M. Glenn, director of the Russell Sage Foundation, a second grant, of $12,000, was made, which, together with a third grant in February of $7,500, enabled us to round out a full year's work. The staff had the advantage of being a flexible one, and some of its most notable service was performed on practically a volunteer basis. It had the disadvantage that comes of demonstrating a piece of work as it goes along without surety of engagement or funds. In certain further instances the plan of getting specialists to diagnose particular problems was carried out, and in this way we covered in brief reports the immigrants and Negroes, among the racial groups; housing, health and police departments, aldermen's courts, playgrounds, children's institutions, and schools, among social institutions; factory inspection, child labor, industrial education, and general labor conditions in the economic field.

The more sustained inquiries were carried out by six responsible investigators, who put in the working months of the year on their inquiries, assisted by visitors.

The sustained investigators were:

> 1. An inquiry into hours, wages, and labor organization in the dominant industry in the District. [Mr. Fitch]
> 2. An interpretation of household life and costs of living in a typical American mill town—the first to be studied with an accuracy comparable to that which has characterized studies of city tenement neighborhoods. [Miss Byington]
> 3. A study of the 500 cases of workmen killed in Allegheny County in one year (together with the injury cases treated in the hospitals for three months) to determine the prevalent causes, and to see where, under the existing liability laws, the income loss was borne. No such concrete body of facts had been gathered in this field in America. [Miss Eastman]
> 4. The first general survey of the women-employing trades in an American city. [Miss Butler]
> 5. A study of the economic cost of typhoid fever in six representative wards, the first house to house investigation of this sort made in this country. [Mr. Wing]
> 6. A survey of the child-helping institutions and agencies of Pittsburgh. [Miss Lattimore]

These investigations closed in June, 1908. Mapping, diagramming, and statistical work were carried on by a special staff during the summer, and there was a final foregathering of responsible investigators in Pittsburgh in September, 1908, in advance of civic exhibit and magazine presentation. At the end of the field work, the director recommended certain further lines of inquiry, opportunity for which the first year's investigations had laid bare. These included a study of the structural, sanitary, and financial aspects of housing in industrial towns; of occupational diseases, carrying the study of accidents over into the more intricate field of health; of criminal and civil courts as they affect the poor; of the state subsidy system to philanthropic institutions; of public service as it affects the wage-earner of municipal accounting, and of outdoor relief.

It was felt, however, that the Survey's work had best end when it has inequivocally interpreted the ingestigations of the year, and carried its findings flush with that line where local initiative could be hopefully challenged to shoulder the responsibilities which the facts showed to be obvious; and to explore other needs.

One line of investigation, however—a case-work inquiry of institutional children—was carried out by a special staff of the Russell Sage Foundation the succeeding year; and in the summer of 1910 two further diagnoses were undertaken to fill what were felt to be important gaps in the work—a study of the land and school tax system, and a study of the social aspects of factory administration.

There follows a couple of pages of staff listings, together with references to prior magazine publication of portions of the Survey. Our excerpts continue with the plan of presentation of the Survey volumes.

## Volume Presentation

The four special volumes: Women and the Trades; the Steel Workers; Homestead: The Households of a Mill Town; and Work-Accidents and the Law, were brought to press in the ensuing year, and in the summer of 1910 an attempt was made to round out several important gaps which the magazine presentation had indicated; and to bring the minor reports to date for the succeeding volumes. The flexibility of publication plan, like that of staff, had both advantages and disadvantages. Where any report was of immediate service, it was brought to bear at once: thus, preliminary reports on housing conditions, and the law of master and servant were published in *Charities and The Commons,* while the field work was in process in 1908, and a report on the Morganza reform school was placed in the hands of the trustees, and so forth. The pith of the sustained investigations, no less than the short ones, was compressed into the magazine presentation, January–March, 1909. On the other hand, the changing situation which made this treatment of material opportune, made it difficult subsequently to gather up threads of evidence dealing with a situation as volatile as that in Pittsburgh, and involving so many fields of social concern. The staff was a temporary one whose members scattered following the investigation and became engrossed in new and emergent tasks, not a few of which were a natural outgrowth of the Survey. The lure of doing the thing rather than recapitulating it has been ever present. Repeated delays, for which the editor more than any other person is responsible, led to a shift in the final plan of publication at this date. Instead of an inclusive symposium, covering the same ground as the magazine publication, together with a general résumé by the director, we are publishing in extenso in two volumes those monograph reports which are thought to have permanent significance. This has meant the omission of certain reports which in the process of the work were important, such as Christopher

Easton's initial inquiry into occupations and health, which paved the way for our study of industrial accidents, and showed that we could not look to the records of public authorities, or hospitals, or medical agencies for accurate facts as to the human waste caused by preventable injury and disease, but must carry our inquiry back into shops and homes—to the individual cases themselves. The change has meant leaving out reports which were valuable in their local bearings. Thus, our magazine publication carried Miss Tucker's survey of the Negroes of Pittsburgh as a challenge to local action; the volumes present Mr. Wright's case-study of one hundred Negro steel workers as a commentary on the general northward movement of Negro farm hands to industry.

We omit here a page or so of specific inclusions and exclusions from the published volumes, together with further acknowledgments, picking up again on the following plan of organization of the six volumes.

## THE PITTSBURGH DISTRICT (Civic Conditions)

The Pittsburgh Survey brought onto the ground for short periods a group of experts who applied the experience of a score of industrial cities in learning about this one. Their findings are turned back to the larger service of the cities from which they came—and of American cities generally.

Contents

I. *The Community:* Pittsburgh the Year of the Survey, by Edward T. Devine. Pittsburgh: An Interpretation of Its Growth, by Robert a Woods Coalition of Pittsburgh Civic Forces, by Allen T. Burns. Civic Improvement Possibilities in Pittsburgh, by Charles Mulford Robinson.

II. *Civic Conditions:* Thirty-five Years of Typhoid, by Frank E. Wing. The Housing of Pittsburgh's Workers, by Emily Wayland Dinwiddie and by F. Elisabeth Crowell. Three Studies in Housing and Responsibility: Skunk Hollow, the Squatter, by Florence Larrabee Lattimore; Painter's Row, the Company House, by F. Elisabeth Crowell; Tammany Hall: A Common Rookery, by F. Elisabeth Crowell. The Aldermen and Their Courts, by H. V. Blaxter and by Allen H. Kerr. The Disproportion of Taxation in Pittsburgh, by Shelby M. Harrison.

III. *Children and the City:* Pittsburgh Schools, by Lila Ver Planck North. Pittsburgh Playgrounds, by Beulah Kennard. The Public Library, by Frances Jenkins Olcott. Pittsburgh as a Foster Mother, by Florence Larrabee Lattimore.

*Appendices:* (a) Facsimile of Card Used in Typhoid Fever Investigation; (b) Tax Laws, Rates, and Exemptions; (c) The New Pittsburgh School System, by Beulah Kennard; (d) Report on City Planning; (e) Field Work of the Pittsburgh Survey.

## WAGE-EARNING PITTSBURGH

Here the emphasis is transferred from civic to industrial well-being—the vital, irrepressible issues of hours and wages, of organization among the workers, administration by the managers, and factory inspection by the state. Interpretations of the immigrants who flood the district and of human seepage to the life of the underworld afford stark contrasts; while the meaning of life to the new generation is put in terms of childhood in an industrial town.

Contents
Community and Workshop, Paul U. Kellogg. Immigrant Studies; The New Pittsburghers, Peter Roberts; The Slav's a Man for a' That, Alois B. Kozkok; Old Believers, Alexis Sokoloff; One Hundred Negro Steel Workers, R. R. Wright; Factory Inspection, Florence Kelley. Industrial Management, H. F. J. Porter. The Reverse Side, James Forbes. Sharpsburgh: Child Life of an Industrial Town, Elizabeth Beardsley Butler.
*Appendices:* (a) Letter from State Factory Inspector; (b) The Pittsburgh Morals Efficiency Commission.

## WOMEN AND THE TRADES

ELIZABETH BEARDSLEY BUTLER

Miss Butler's investigation is the first general survey of the women-employing trades in an American city. It deals with 22,000 women who are on the payrolls of Pittsburgh's establishments. For Pittsburgh is not only a great workshop; it is many workshops; and in many of these workshops women stand beside the men.

Not only are they to be found in laundries, garment factories, canneries, cracker bakeries, and other occupations which have their roots in old-time housework, but they help finish the tumblers that the men of the glass-house blow; they make cores for the foundry men; they are among the sharpers of metals for lamps and hinges and bolts and screws. They make up a new labor force.

They complicate every industrial question; and the conditions and tendencies affecting their employment can not adequately be dealt with apart from the general problems of the community. This general view of the women wage-earners of a typical city is valuable to every one who would know of not the worst sweat-shop nor the best model factory, but the possibilities which work at wage's opens up to the great mass of working girls of this generation.

Contents
Workers and Workrooms. The Stogy Industry. Needle Trades. Cleaning Industries. Metals, Lamps, and Glass. Miscellaneous Trades. Commercial Trades. Social Life of Working Women. Summary of Industrial Conditions.

Appendices: Plan and Methods of Study. Tables and Charts. Margaret Morison Carnegie School for Women. Legal Restrictions of Work Hours for Women.

## HOMESTEAD: THE HOUSEHOLD OF A MILL TOWN

MARGARET F. BYINGTON

Miss Byington's study is an inquiry into our two oldest social institutions, the family and the town, as they are brought into contact with a new and insurgent third, the factory. It raises searchingly the questions: Have home and town held their own against the mill? Has local self-government kept abreast of a nationalized industry? What has prosperity brought to the rank and file of the wage-earners?

The answers are drawn from the household budgets of 90 mill-town families, and from the author's experience of a year spent among the people who earned the money and ate the food, and lived in the houses of Homestead.

And they are answers set down with all the warmth, simplicity, and intimate color of an old-fashioned 16-page letter.

This volume, perhaps more than the others of the set, tells in human values—of men as breadwinners, of women in their homes, and children in their growth—the story of life and labor which the Pittsburgh Survey has unfolded. It is not a story for student and social worker alone, but for every reader who would know what underlines the drive and clang of our industrial progress.

Contents
I. *The Mill and the Town:* Homestead and the Great Strike. The Makeup of the Town.
II. *The English-speaking Households:* Work, Wages, and the Cost of Living. Rent in the Household Budget. Table and Dinner Pail. The Budget as a Whole, Human Relationships. Children of Homestead.
III. *The Slav as a Homesteader:* Life at $1.65 a Day. Family Life of the Slavs. The Slav Organized.
IV. *The Mill and the Household:* The Mill and the Household.
*Appendices:* Cost of Living in Pittsburgh; Carnegie Relief Fund; Slavic Organizations in Homestead, and twelve other sections.

## WORK-ACCIDENTS AND THE LAW

CRYSTAL EASTMAN

The first systematic investigation of work-accidents in America—a book of broken lives as well as of machines gone wrong. It is the story of 500 wage-earners killed at their work in Allegheny County, Pa., in 1908, and an equal number of injury cases cared for by the hospitals of the District in three months. This steady march of injury and death means an enormous economic loss.

The purpose of the study was twofold: to see what indications there are that such accidents can be prevented, and to see if the burden of them falls where in justice it should. Here the master and servant law, court interpretations, employers' liability companies, relief associations, and charitable societies enter into the problem. The hazards of work are clearly stated, and the responsibility put up to the public to safeguard the workers against preventable accidents and to spread out the burden of the unpreventable as a charge on production. Since this report was first published compensation laws have been enacted in 23 states. The book is an arsenal of human facts.

Contents
I. *The Causes of Work-Accidents:* Pittsburgh's Yearly Loss in Killed and Injured. The Railroaders. The Soft-coal Miners. The Steel Workers. Machine Shops; Building Trades, and so forth. Personal Factor in Industrial Accidents. Suggestions for Prevention.

II. *Economic Cost of Work-Accidents:* Distribution of the Burden of Income Loss. Effect of Industrial Fatalities Upon the Home. Problems of the Injured Workman. Policy of Certain Companies.

III. *Employers' Liability:* The Law. By-product of Employers' Liability Legislation.

*With Appendices Including:* The Process of Steel Making; The Accident Prevention of the U. S. Steel Corporation, and eleven other sections.

## THE STEEL WORKERS

JOHN A. FITCH

Mr. Fitch portrays the human element that goes into tonnage. Steel making in its various processes is illustrated by personal studies of the workmen, the blast furnace crews, the puddlers and roll hands. Previous to this investigation little was known of the 70,000 men who are employed in the steel mills—of the social unrest developing under the twelve-hour day, the seven-day week, through speeding up and the bonus system, through repression of democracy. The reaction of mill conditions upon the lives of men is demonstrated. And, as a hopeful element, the advances of the last five years in safety and accident relief are outlined. The book traces the rise and fall of unionism and shows the consequences of unrestrained industrial power now in the hands of the corporations secured by their policies of surveillance and coercion. The work constitutes a graphic, authentic study of the industrial situation under the largest employer of labor in America today.

Contents
I. *The Men and the Tools:* The Workmen. The Blast Furnace Crews. Puddlers and Iron Rollers. The Steel Makers. The Men of the Rolling Mills. Health and Accidents in Steel Making.

II. *The Struggle for Control:* Unionism and the Union Movement. Policies of the Amalgamated Association: The Great Strikes.

III. *The Employer in the Saddle:* Industrial Organization under Non-union Regime. Wages and the Cost of Living. The Working Day and the Working Week. Speeding Up and the Bonus System. The Labor Policy of Unrestricted Capital. Repression.

IV. *The Steel Workers and Democracy:* Citizenship in the Mill Towns. The Spirit of the Workers.

## Working Factors

The term *survey* is a new one in social investigation, although curiously enough it was the name applied by the Normans to their census of Saxon land and folk which was written up in the Doomsday Book.

The work in Pittsburgh was new in more than name; it was experimental, making repeated draughts on fresh sources of information, holding to a flexibility of front that admitted of a following up of clues such as the investigation itself uncovered, and only could uncover.

### Focusing Many Cities on One

In bringing experts to gauge the life and labor of Pittsburgh, we had to begin at the beginning in some fields, but in many we could rapidly apply standards which had been worked out by slow processes of reform elsewhere—measure Pittsburgh against the composite community made of the nation's best. The Survey, thus, was a spirited piece of inter-city co-operation in getting at the urban fact in a new way. For consider what has been done in this field in America. We have counted our city populations regularly every ten years—in some states every five. We have known the country has grown and spread out stupendously within the century, and that within that period our cities have spread out and filled up with even greater resistlessness. We have profited by incisive analysis of one factor or another which enters into social well-being—tuberculosis, infant mortality, factory legislation, public education, to name examples; and we have had the needs of neighborhoods put forth by those who know them well. But there is something further, synthetic and clarifying, to be gained by a sizing-up process that reckons at once with many factors in the life of a great civic area, not going deeply into all subjects, but offering a structural exhibit of the community as a going concern.

### Structural Relations

The engineer has to do with levers, eccentrics, and axles, with chemical reagents, and dynamos; but when it comes to making steel, it is with the organic whole of which these are but so many parts, and with the interplay of those parts, that he has his real business. So with the factors which condition a working population. Thus, for example, the problem of industrial accidents ramifies in a score of directions. Practically every member of the staff was faced with one phase or another of it. It was found to bear upon the relief funds of the labor unions, the multitudinous benefit societies of the immigrant races, and the relief plans of corporations; with employers' liability associations and with employes' liability associations; it was bringing pensions to the charitable societies and inmates to the children's institutions; it was a dominating factor in the local hospital situation and involved at this point the whole state subsidy system; it was the concern of the coroner's office, the office of foreign consuls and the health bureau where it was one of the two causes which gave Pittsburgh its high general death rate; it had to do in a minute degree with the discipline, intelligence, grit, and moral backbone of the working force in the mills; in the courts it harked back to the fundamental issues of public policy and freedom of contract; and in its effect on income and the standard of living of workingmen's families it set its stamp on the next generation.

In the spread of the Survey movement throughout the country in the last five years we have an indication of what this method of gauging the interrelations of social problems may come to mean. In the midst of the field work we had some glimpse of its possibilities as it molded under our hands. To quote from a report issued midway in the investigation:

> How significant this may prove is only a matter for speculation at this stage. But there is to be remembered the fiber which was put into philanthropy with the beginning of the charity organization movement, which for the first time in charitable effort treated not only the sick, or the aged, or the orphaned, or the homeless, or the poverty stricken, but the family in all its relations; and again, the quickening spirit which was infused into social work with the opening of the settlement movement which, holding to the same personal relations, widened the group whose wants they sought to interpret from the family to the neighborhood. In the Survey there is, perhaps, suggestion of a third phase of collective effort, more intimate in its relation to the concrete needs of people than are civic bodies, but like them, town-wide in scope.

Human Measure

Our effort to grasp social conditions, problems, and institutions in terms of a town had its counterpart in our effort to put these things to the test of a distinctly human measure. This was a second benchmark in the works of the Survey.

The case records of charitable societies, especially during the past ten or fifteen years, have been rich in social information as to the dependent segment of the population and as to self-dependent families whom untoward events or conditions have rendered in need. But few attempts have been made to study the great body of the working population on such an individual basis. The very fact that Pittsburgh had not had any large poverty stricken body of people and had no collected social data forced upon us, even in arriving at a preliminary estimate of the local situation, the necessity for working out units and methods of gauging these other groups.

In dealing with the wage-earning population we took a leaf out of the budget studies of Rowntree, Chapin, and others, and tried to put our investigation on an individual and family basis; that is, instead of relying on abstract categories, such as death rates, or telling pathetic stories of tragic individual figures such as the novelists use, we tried to draw upon the common experience. By systems of accounting and units of time and material, the modern manufacturer knows what the costs are that go into a finished shoe, or steel plate, or iron bedstead. So, too, the propaganda of the Bureau of Municipal Research demands such an ordering of municipal budgets and accounting as will get at just what the tax payers' money goes for, where the wastes are, and what, for example, is the actual educational product of the twelve months' business of a public school. So we sought to get at those drains upon the means and life of a wage-earning population which the year brings round. Our investigation of industrial accidents and typhoid fever well illustrate this method.

## Graphic Interpretation

We wanted to make the town real—to itself; not in goody-goody preachment of what it ought to be; not in sensational discoloration; not merely in a formidable array of rigid facts. There was the census at one pole, and yellow journalism at the other; and we were on the high seas between with the chartings of such dauntless explorers as Jacob Riis and Lincoln Steffens before us.

This is why we tried to tell our findings through the eye as well as through the written word. This is why we collected industrial biographies as well as wage schedules; why we got the group picture of child life in a glass town, as well as analyzed the provisions of labor legislation and compulsory education laws; why we were concerned with the margins of leisure, and culture, and home life which are possible when a man works on a twelve-hour shift, as well as the free surplus which high wages may leave over a high cost of living.

## Co-operation with Local Agencies

Our further purpose was to make the Survey not merely a criticism or an inventory, but a means for establishing relations which would project its work into the future. We were studying the community at a time when nascent social forces were exerting themselves toward throwing off the meshwork of crude village conditions, toward standing out against the indirect taxation—levied in the last analysis upon every inhabitant of the city—of bad water, bad houses, bad air, and bad hours; and toward asserting aggrressive movements for the advancement of civil well-being.

Mr. Woods* shows how many forms of progressive social service had gained a foothold, and with an essentially sound moral foundation to its life, the city was not altogether unprepared to rise to the call of

* Woods, Robert A.: Pittsburgh, an Interpretation of its Growth, pp. 1 ff.

the great new issues which its growth had precipitated. What, above all, was needed, we felt, was a comprehensive knowledge of the underlying facts which could be made the basis for united effort, if those Pittsburgh men and women who, single-handed or in thin groups, had long stood out for civic righteousness in one or another of its phases, could but get the whole town back of them.

That the Survey was alive to the new, quickening public spirit in Pittsburgh, as well as to the untoward conditions of the city, was evidenced by services it was our good fortune to render during the year.

Thus, the first fortnight we were on the ground, we were instrumental in closing up four abdominal lodging houses which were nests of disease. Our preliminary housing report was circulated by the Chamber of Commerce in midwinter, in the local campaign which resulted in doubling the municipal inspection force, in a complete tenement house census, and in tearing down some of the worst structures. Pittsburgh was the last great American city without a central organization of its charities. Movements to this end had been blocked for ten years, and through a committee of the Civic Club, the secretary of the Field Department of Charities Publication Committee brought them to a head. Through the co-operation of Columbian Settlement, Superintendent Edwards of the bureau of health, and Superintendent Morris Knowles of the bureau of filtration, we were able to carry out our economic study of typhoid fever; and, turning the tables, when local appropriations to carry on a technical study of typhoid were not forthcoming in line with recommendations made by these superintendents, we were instrumental in promoting the Pittsburgh Typhoid Fever Commission. The Survey as a whole paved the way for the Pittsburgh Civic Commission which, under the chairmanship of H. D. English, in its first year organized committees on city planning, sanitation, housing construction, industrial accidents and over-strain, minor courts, schools, and so forth, championed a bond issue of $7,000,000 for water front and street improvement, a tuberculosis hospital and other municipal enterprises, and called in three of the foremost municipal engineers and city planners of the country to make a preliminary report on methods of approaching the large problems of city construction. The developments of the succeeding five years are set forth by Mr. Burns.*

In the fields reviewed by our reports perhaps the most notable reforms have been the revolution in the school administration; the overthrow of the unjust tax system; the creation of a department of health; the enactment of adequate housing laws; the creation of an efficient minor court of justice for civil cases; the work of the Morals Efficiency Commission; the adoption of a comprehensive relief plan by the United States Steel Corporation; and the rapid development of safety engineering.

In enumerating these advances, and noting that the work of investi-

* Burns, Allen T., Coalition of Pittsburgh's Civic Forces, pp. 44 ff.

gation was of appreciable service with respect to some of them, it should be borne clearly in mind that the Survey has never made pretensions to being the founder, originator, or discoverer of civic progress in Pittsburgh. Its reports afforded a general view of conditions in a given year. With a few exceptions the intensive work in each field had still to be done. Setbacks and encroachments upon the public well-being, as well as civic advances, could be cited. In the future, as in the past, the brunt of change must be borne by local organizations. The Survey's chief service to Pittsburgh lay in making a fearless statement of a range of current needs. Opinion may differ as to whether we overstated the forces which in Pittsburgh and elsewhere tend to perpetuate those conditions. Even our most enthusiastic social movements have encroached but a little way upon the fastnesses of selfishness and inertia, ignorance and privilege.

In Pittsburgh, for example, it has been only within the last few months (1914) that the last wards of the North Side have had filtered water. The subsidy system still perverts the normal development of public and private charities of Pennsylvania. The insane, feeble-minded, and children are still housed in the almshouses of Allegheny and the other counties of the state; aldermen's courts still mete out injustice to immigrants. There is in Pittsburgh still no adequate system of probation work for adults or an inclusive system of placing-out work for children. Bad housing persists, in the city as well as in the mill towns, and Mr. Burns' review shows how the new bottles of municipal government need today as yesterday the new wine of disinterested public spirit. The twelve-hour day still weighs down household life and citizenship, children still work in the glass-houses at night. Pennsylvania remains the last of our great industrial commonwealths to pass a workmen's compensation law, and the situation with respect to the choking out of democratic organization among the men of the steel industry is if anything more tense than five years ago.

Testy as have been criticisms of the Survey in certain quarters in Pittsburgh, we were not amiss in expecting that private interests would not for long shunt local pride into a barrier between evil conditions and an aroused citizenship. The loyalty which Pittsburghers bear their city is of finer metal. "The truth is beginning to reach home," wrote a leading minister. "However much they damn you, there never was anything which stirred this town into action like the Survey," said a professional man. "I stand by everything you said about conditions," said a steel superintendent; "the solid body of the people are with you." For the progressive men and women, broad-minded enough to put up with the easy jibes of rival cities which had undergone no such diagnosis, and courageous enough to face daily the exacting work of municipal upbuilding, the staff on leaving the field here bore with them a feeling of sincere respect. But the Survey has not given Pittsburgh a black eye. Rather, Pittsburgh is pointed out as a city which at the present time of deficit in urban well-being has had the civic grit to take an inventory and publish a statement.

National Bearing

In judging of these objective facts we can distinguish between those conditions which are subject directly to local determination through civic and political action and those elements in the industrial situation which will respond when public opinion is aroused nationally. The Pittsburgh investigations were in fields where they could be of appreciable service to national movements. For example, Dr. Roberts' study in the mill neighborhoods was the first experimental work for immigration which has since been developed so adequately under his leadership by the International Youth Men's Christian Association. Our housing investigations were one of the first pieces of interstate field work by the group which, under Mr. Veiller, has created the National Housing Association. Our responsible investigator in the field of industrial accidents became the secretary of the Employers' Liability Commission of New York—the first of the group of state commissions which in the last five years have written compensation laws in twenty-three states.

The inquiry into industrial accidents came as a strategic time in the inception of the safety movement. Under the Cabot Fund, Mr. Fitch carried his investigations of labor conditions in the steel industry to Gary, Pueblo, Birmingham, Lackawanna, and the other steel centers. *The Survey's* wide-spread publicity of the seven-day week, coupled with the courageous initiative of men inside the steel industry, led to the adoption of one day of rest in seven by the American Irion and Steel Institute. Miss Butler's findings as to women's work have been quoted in the remarkable series of briefs prepared by Louis D. Brandeis and Josephine Goldmark in the test cases on which has hung the constitutionality of labor legislation limiting the hours of women's work. In 1910 the Federal Council of Churches of Christ in America sent out a broadside to its congregations and churches numbering 18,000,000 members. Using the Pittsburgh Survey findings as a text as to conditions in American industrial centers generally—"true to a greater or less extent, often to the same extent"—the Council's Commission on Church and Social Service recommends that the official bodies of Christian churches, "standardize, as it were, the simplest Christian obligations in the industrial field," by adopting resolutions

> calling upon employers of labor within those churches to conform, in their industrial operations to these three simple rules:
> One day's rest in each seven.
> Reasonable hours of labor.
> A living wage based on these reasonable hours of labor.

Mr. Devine acted as chairman of the committee which promoted the creation of a federal Industrial Relations Commission; Mr. Burns was granted leave of absence by the Pittsburgh Civic Commission to act as Washington representative in securing its enactment, and Professor Commons is one of its members.

More particularly, the Pittsburgh Survey crystallized the standards and spirit of the magazine which took over its name, and which in a staff of investigational reporters is developing a range of work midway between scientific research on the one hand, and newspaper and magazine journalism on the other.

It led to the creation of a Department of Surveys by the Russell Sage Foundation under the directorship of Shelby M. Harrison, who was in charge of our map and statistical work in Pittsburgh. The survey movement has been slow of development, but it has been cumulative. A survey of the Polish district in Buffalo the following year, carried on by local agencies; a Syracuse survey, directed by Mr. Harrison, in which the Chamber of Commerce, Associated Charities, Ministerial Union, and central federated labor body co-operated; a quick journalistic survey of Birmingham, as type of the new industrialism of the south, by *The Survey* magazine, were early examples. Surveys of various sorts have been carried out in over twenty cities, the two most comprehensive operations of the present year being a survey of health, delinquency, and correction, industry and municipal efficiency in Topeka, and a general survey of Springfield, Illinois, in which twelve national agencies have co-operated under the leadership of the Survey Department. Surveys are under consideration in Baltimore and Cleveland, which promise not only to match the Pittsburgh Survey in scale, but to eclipse it, extending the work over a five-year period, with expenditures of time and money in proportion.

The Scheme of Work

In its combination of spirit, scope, and technique, the Pittsburgh Survey was the first of its kind. If one were searching for great precedents for what was after all a modest understanding, it would be the knot of scientists gathered by Pasteur in starting his institution in Paris; the group of Oxford men who took up their residence with Arnold Toynbee in London's East End; or the group who, under the leadership of Jane Addams, founded Hull House in Chicago's South Side. On the other hand, the Survey was distinctly in line with progressive methods in business and in the professions. It was kindred to what the examining physician demands before he accepts us as insurance risks, what a modern farmer puts his soil and stocks through before he plants his crops, what the consulting engineer performs as his first work when he is called to overhaul a manufacturing plant. The wonder is not as to the nature of the undertaking, but that the plan had never been tried by a city before.

Not a little expert work for the Survey was done in brief periods, practically without pay—a contribution on the part of leaders in social work to what they looked upon as the demonstration of a way for social advance. We can only speculate as to the results which would accrue to any one city were it able to call to its service permanently men and women each of whom had been able to give to his own city a position of leadership in some given field of civic well-being, and each of whom would be commissioned to map out the way to bring this super-city abreast of the foremost. The Pittsburgh Survey broke new ground.

Against such a comprehensive scheme it is seen to be fragmentary, if prophetic.

If we were to reduce to six in number the methods which in their combination made the Pittsburgh Survey a distinctive enterprise, they would be these:

1. To bring a group of experts together to co-operate with local leaders in gauging the needs of one city in several lines.
2. To study these needs in relation to each other, to the whole area of the city, and to the civil responsibilities of democracy.
3. To consider at the same time both civic and industrial conditions, and to consider them for the most part in their bearings upon the wage-earning population.
4. To reduce conditions to terms of household experience and human life.
5. To devise graphic methods for making these findings challenging, and unmistakable.
6. To establish natural relations with local agencies, to project the work into the future.

The "second" Pittsburgh Survey, undertaken a quarter of a century after the first, aptly illustrates some of the changes that the social survey movement had undergone since its initial inception. We excerpt here portions of the Preface (pp. xi–xii and xiv–xvi) and the full Epilogue (pp. 877–884). Professional and community trends may also be noted in this juxtaposition of selections from the two studies.

# A Social Study of Pittsburgh

## PHILIP KLEIN

### PREFACE

The contents of this volume represents a type of enterprise that has come to be known as a social survey. It is not a sociological survey, such as Charles Booth's *Life and Labor in London* or its sequel, the *New Survey*, and the contemporary studies of Liverpool and Southampton. It is not a sequel to the famous Pittsburgh Survey which revealed to that community and to the nation at large the dangers to worker and citizens inherent in a community of rapid and uncontrolled industrial expansion. In prime intention this is a social work survey: an examination of agencies and institutions that provide social and health services, whether under public or voluntary auspices. A substantial part of the report is devoted, however, to an interpretation of the social and

From Philip Klein et al., *A Social Study of Pittsburgh: Community and Social Services of Allegheny County* (New York: Columbia University Press, 1938). Reprinted by permission of publisher and author.

economic life of the community—the background and matrix of social work. The amount of space given to this phase of the subject might appear, in comparison to the space usually allowed in social surveys, out of proportion within the proper limits of a social work report. The reason for this emphasis lies partly in the history of recent years. The social worker himself has lifted his eyes to the larger scene and improved his perspective, recognizing social work as part of the vital forces of community life, embraced by them, modified, enlarged, and diminished by them, the property of all men, not the domain of specialists alone. The lay mind, on the other hand, has also recognized that for these same reasons social work has come to be a major instrument of social adjustment and development along with education, civic reform, and evolution of government.

The study was proposed by a group of citizens of Pittsburgh and Allegheny County in the form of an application for funds to the Buhl Foundation. In that document the dual interest—interest in the technical improvement of service and in the adaptation of the entire hierarchy of services to the evolving social structure—was made manifest. To quote:

> The pressing need for such a survey appears from a number of considerations. Foremost among them is the necessity of seeing how far a study of the work of individual agencies and their relation to each other would reveal on the one hand large geographical areas where the need is not being met and, on the other hand, instances, doubtless numerous, of overlapping and of duplication.
>
> In addition . . . this community ought to re-examine its program of social work in light of changed conditions. The welfare organizations of Allegheny County, both public and private, are today facing new conditions and new needs which they cannot meet successfully without a thorough readjustment of their services. Such a readjustment, if it is to be made intelligently and with impartial disregard of possible effect on existing organizations, can be undertaken only after a careful study of our whole field of social service. . . .
>
> Social agencies have been established and have grown and expanded with relatively little consideration given to the needs of the community as a whole or to the most effective organization necessary to meet them. The present time is especially opportune for the development of a coordinated, effective and adequate program of social work in Allegheny County. The first step toward the development of such a program of social welfare is a comprehensive study of the needs of the community and the resources already existing to meet them.

The focus of the study, it is clear, is on the work of social agencies, but its orientation is to the community needs in so far as they may be ascertainable. The application for funds was made on February 13, 1934, by a committee consisting of persons appointed in equal numbers by the Federation of Social Agencies and the Community Fund. The grant, as authorized, was announced in a letter dated April 14, 1934, in which only two specific conditions were stipulated:

1. That a personnel acceptable to and approved by the Foundation be engaged.

2. That a budget be drawn within the total amount herein set forth, acceptable to and approved by the Foundation.

The plan for the study as submitted by the director and incorporated in a tentative budget contemplated a field study of eighteen months, extending from August, 1934, to January, 1936. A staff was engaged for varying periods of time depending upon the nature of the tasks to be performed within the available budget. A simple organization was devised. Wide leeway was left for the judgment and preferences of divisional experts in charge. Research in the strict and formal meaning of the word as indicating the original collection of primary material was subordinated to selection guided by experience and to the authoritative integrated picture and to build up a comprehensive plan, was kept in mind, the attempt was made to put into effect whatever recommendations might be made in the course of the study that seemed both acceptable and practicable to the Citizens' Committee. To this extent the study was allowed to partake of the nature of expert "guidance" and "community organization." It was agreed, however, that the chief responsibility for carrying out the findings of the study remained with the local community through its Citizens' Committee, the established agencies, and the public that stands behind them. Much was actually effected by way of changes or acceptance of plans prior to the expiration of the field study, and the supreme importance of practical results, ultimate if not immediate, was never lost sight of.

The Preface continues with a couple of pages of detail concerning Committee structure and staffing. It then picks up with the study procedure and organization of the report.

As already stated, the present study was proposed by a group of citizens constituting a committee for planning, and then sponsoring, the study. By what right—the reader might ask—did this committee set itself up to represent the public's interest in social work? Who wanted the study? Was it a legitimate expression of responsible public concern? The membership of the committee was at first composed of individuals appointed in equal numbers by the Community Fund and the Federation of Social Agencies, and later it was expanded by accessions added by the committee itself. Its representativeness is measured on the whole by that of these two organizations, by the extent to which they stand for the social work interests of the public and of their member agencies. Both are federative organizations, both submitted the proposal for a study to their constituent agencies, and the records show approval without dissenting opinion. It gives us extraordinary pleasure to be able to testify that any disapproval that may nevertheless have existed of the study as a whole was in no instance permitted to interfere with the giving of full and unconditional assistance to the staff at every point and throughout the duration of the study. There can be recorded only one actual refusal to coöperate and that was made by an agency that is not a member either of the Community Fund or of the Federation of Social Agencies.

It would take too long to recite the details of the procedure followed by the study, and such a recital might be of only limited interest to the reader. Time, place, and other peculiarities of the situation, idiosyncrasies of the staff, limitation of the personnel, and unpredictable developments in the course of the study were all factors in determining procedure.

The contents of the present volume are divided into two major parts: the first devoted to an attempt at sketching the social and economic background of the community life in and for which the social services operate; the second given to the specific problems of the organization of social and health work. The essential unity of the two, obivious to the student, unavoidable in practice, is carried into the text so far as clarity of exposition permits. Naturally, Part I is less exhaustive than Part II. A scientifically defensible presentation of social and economic life of such a metropolis as Pittsburgh is a large undertaking, which has never yet been attempted in this country, though aided by American funds when carried on abroad, as in Liverpool and London. What social and economic data could be garnered under the limitations of the study are presented in the first eight chapters and consciously woven into the fabric of the report as a whole by the author and collaborators. Specifically, Part I sketches the nature of Allegheny County and its constituent communities (Chapter II); attempts an estimate of the chances for making a living as they bear on the large mass of the population and measures the needs to be met by social work (Chapter III); summarizes the progress in social legislation and labor organization (Chapter IV); describes the general physical conditions under which the masses, especially of the poor, live (Chapter V); and the peculiar characteristics of the county because of its racial and ethnic problems (Chapter VI). General attitudes and public opinion are then touched upon (Chapter VII), followed by a brief recital of improvements in the public school system of Pittsburgh in the past quarter of a century (Chapter VIII).

Part II, though given the chief emphasis in the report, is itself subject to a number of limitations. First, the scope of the study had to be limited by budget, time, and practical considerations. Thus, sizable areas of social work were arbitrarily omitted, including, for example, courts (except the Juvenile Court), penal institutions (except certain ones for children), employment services, the problem of the handicapped, the technical aspects of mental hygiene, and the pastoral work of churches. Within the field under scrutiny the orientation was toward future planning rather than present evaluation or past performance. Much therefore is omitted that is historically significant and creditable to individual agencies. No report is made agency by agency even though the material collected might easily fall into such a frame work. The arrangement as presented provides for a panoramic view of social work in Allegheny

County (Chapter IX), then is focused on financial support (Chapter X); on social planning (Chapter XI); on problems of personnel and training (Chapter XII); on the intricate and related problems of relief and social case work (Chapters XIII–XVII); on public health and medical care (Chapters XVIII–XIX), and on the leisure time problem (Chapter XX). A final chapter summarizes the more obvious results of the study up to the time of the writing of the report.

One objective of the study and of the present report, which is not contained in any document but which underlies the thought of the Citizens' Committee, of the staff, and of the Buhl Foundation is to extend the benefits of the task, if any, to the field of social work as a whole beyond the corporate limits of Pittsburgh and Allegheny County or the institutional interests of the local agencies. It was hoped that the study would have some national significance for public and profession, for taxpayer, philanthropist, and client. This objective has pervaded the minds of author and collaborators and may explain some of the discussions and expositions that might otherwise seem beyond the scope of a purely local social survey.

**EPILOGUE**

One and one-half years have elapsed since the completion of the field work from which the data for this volume have been secured. Three years have elapsed since the launching of the study. During these three years the possibility of "achieving practical results" has been steadily kept in mind. Direct results, as well as the evaluation of needs and the formulation of permanent plans, were within the scope of the study.

What has been achieved in these three years? What is reasonable to expect? From the outlook of the cynical pessimist who sees all surveys as mere dust gatherers on forgotten shelves, to that of the placid optimist, to whom, as to the Lord, a thousand years are but a day, the rate of expectation and degree of disappointment may cover a wide range. The experienced observer of civic and communal life will not expect rapid changes nor a great number of them. He will gauge the reasonable expectations in the light of two separate sets of factors: those that are inherent in any far-reaching evaluation and the fundamental changes that may be suggested by them; and those that arise from the characteristics of a particular community and its capacity for change, for self-criticism, for coöperation, for decision.

Certain retarding factors inherent in such a study should be given full recognition before pessimistic judgment is passed on the community's capacity to profit from the enterprise. First, facts and observations must be obtained by the staff. These data must be compared, their significance pondered and discussed, and some staff judgment arrived at; findings must be formulated; plans and recommendations crystallized.

The next step is promulgation, seeking to carry the process through to achievement. Granted that the staff is reasonably certain of its interpretation, that among possible recommendations those agreed upon are the best or the most nearly feasible, there are groups, interests, and wills which must understand what has been discovered; if changes are proposed, they must know why they are advisable and why they should be adopted. The groups which confronted the staff in its attempt to secure immediate action comprised in this instance at least the following:

1. The Citizens' Committee on the Social Study, which had the right to approve or disapprove particular recommendations, the manner of their promulgation, their release to the agencies or to the public—though not the ultimate publication or the nature of published recommendations, which were reserved as a right of the director of the study.

2. The agency specifically affected by plans proposed or changes suggested. Within the agency several factors are involved: board, executive, staff—and, in a sense, client.

3. The financial backers of social work: public bodies, state, county, and local, with their political affiliations and implied public policy; wealthy contributors, individual and corporate, and other contributors; the Community Fund as a financing agency.

4. Public opinion in all its varieties and attitudes: the Church; the dominant minority; the inarticulate majority; the militant opposition minority; lay and professional opinion; civic pride and civic conscience; the actual and potential client.

Theoretically, all promulgation should, in the military phrase, proceed "through channels"; from staff to Citizens' Committee, from Committee to agency, and from agency to the public. In this process the staff members would serve as interpreters, reporters, expert advisors, guides in compromise and modification, reservoirs of evidence. Yet, as we shall see, this orderly procedure through channels was not always practicable, and may actually have been sterile or self-defeating; for time is always a factor, and often there is a right moment that may determine the effectiveness of action (as, for example, appearing before appropriation hearings).

A deep-seated series of paradoxes complicates the logical process from fact to conclusion and thence to recommendation and acceptance. Facts do not always lead to one conclusion alone; recommendations are compounded of opinion, as well as of facts, and opinions may differ; expertness of opinion is conditioned not only by the specialist's previous experience but also by the acceptability of his recommendations to the interested party. Facts and conclusions may be distasteful, disturbing, in conflict with fundamental attitudes, and their expression—a primary obligation of the survey—may endanger any acceptance or action, and action is the ultimate purpose of this study. The "Truth shall set you free" applies to the individual when his own conscience is his judge; it does not necessarily follow when his fellow man is in the judgment seat. The practical incompatibility of findings, promulgation, and acceptance is too frequent a phenomenon to make the sequence assured.

In the light of these considerations and of the necessary delay that all action involving large and settled bodies must encounter, what may, nevertheless, be regarded as progress along the paths proposed by the study? What are the particular characteristics or facts in the community that would seem to favor or to retard changes as proposed by the study staff?

The first important fact relates to the Citizens' Committee. The members of that body are representative not only of the community at large but also, though informally, of important organizations: the Federation of Social Agencies and the Community Fund. While approval by this sponsoring body does not insure the immediate realization of proposed plans, disapproval by the committee would certainly interpose an almost unsurmountable obstacle in the path of their execution. With one exception, which related to the follow-up organization of the committee itself, every recommendation submitted by the staff of this study was accepted and approved by the committee, and practicable steps were devised by it for promulgating them and carrying them into effect. This fact is important beyond possible exaggeration. It means that a body of men and women—all but three representing lay opinion, industrial, financial, and social leaders of the community, some with long and varied experience on boards of agencies, some with public service of long standing in city or county, representatives of the principal religious faiths, and all loyal to the good name of the community—say in the proposals of this study opportunities for effecting valuable changes and progress for Pittsburgh and Allegheny County. If, then, substantial opposition, direct or passive, should be encountered, it would be difficult to believe that it could be attributed to subversive ideas, to over-professional notions, or to incompatibility of the proposals with the basic phrases of the community's life and ways.

The second medium for carrying out recommendations of the study consists of the agencies and institutions through which the social work of the community is practiced, their managing boards, and the executives who guide their policies. Many of the proposed plans affect these agencies, suggest changes of policy, modification of program, new orientations, elimination of one function and assumption of another; in some cases, indeed, mergers of agencies and even the discontinuance of some have been recommended. How ready have agencies been to respond to proposals of this character when submitted by staff and approved by leading citizens that constitute the sponsoring citizens' committee?

Pittsburgh social workers have never been noted for their coöperative habits and unanimity of action. Agency competition—sometimes embracing boards, at other times only executives or scattering board members—has been frequent. Many exemplars of such competitive attitudes might be mentioned, but those that have been most conspicuously retarding constructive coöperation and progress in the community's social work include: rivalry between the two schools of social work, between the Community Fund and the Federation of Social Agencies, between the Children's Aid Society and the Children's Service Bureau, between the Family Society (originally the coördinative body) and the Federation of Social Agencies. We shall see below some of the points at which the importance of agencies to the recommendations of the study staff and sponsoring committee has become pronounced.

How the financial supporters of social work and public opinion which is interwoven with it will respond to the appeal presented in the study recommendations depends in large part on the way in which their significance reaches them and on the extent to which the agencies and the sponsoring committee of the study may be able to adjust and integrate their viewpoints. Up to this time contributors and taxpayers have had no opportunity for a clear choice on the merits and acceptability of the proposals.

Acceptance of recommendations by the agencies affected, and decisive steps for putting them into effect may be reported for the following district items:

1. The new plan of budgeting in association with social planning for agencies in the Community Fund was tentatively put into effect in the spring of 1935. The new committee is composed of representatives in equal numbers from the Community Fund and the Federation of Social Agencies, gives year-round service instead of the previous pre-campaign budgeting and is assisted in its labors by the budget specialist on the staff of the Federation. The full working out of the purposes underlying this proposal will take several years, during which the maximum effort on the part of the personnel of both the Fund and Federation will be required to make this task as successful as it can be. The beginnings, however, have been made.

2. The proposed consolidation of case work agencies within the Federation of Jewish Philanthropies was accepted and put into effect shortly after the termination of the field study. A new organization, entitled the Jewish Social Service Bureau, succeeds the following previously separate organizations: The Jewish Family Welfare Association, The Jewish Big Brothers Association, The Girls' Bureau, The Pittsburgh Bureau for Jewish Children, and Service to the Foreign-born. The inclusion of the last-mentioned agency represents the extension of the principle proposed by the study beyond its specific recommendations and indicates a determination by the Jewish communal body to go beyond the letter into the spirit of the recommendations.

3. Basic improvements in the quality and point of view of the work of the Juvenile Court preceded the organization of the Social Study. It was possible, however, to assist the progress of the court substantially through the continuous advice provided by

members of the staff and rendered possible by the interest and coöperation of the incumbent judge. The particular recommendations on fundamental reorganization of the administrative structure and programs of the court were not involved in this coöperative relationship, but represent a later stage of the study.

4. The Conference of Catholic Charities had already, previous to the inauguration of the study, undertaken to some degree amalgamation of family and child welfare, which placed it in line with modern developments in that field. Such recommendations as were made in the further development and qualitative improvement of this amalgamation have taken place in consequence of advice given by the study staff during the field-work period, and a greater integration of these services has been effected.

5. In the hospital field, the idea of group insurance, recommended by this study, met a sympathetic response by many of the interested hospital executives who had previously seen the possibility of increasing financial stability through this system. Largely as a result of this readiness, the program has been put into effect within the last year, and Pittsburgh's private hospitals have now joined the growing list of medical institutions in American communities which take advantage of this plan of auxiliary hospital financing.

6. The Hospital Conference, which had existed prior to the study, with membership limited to executives and a strictly circumscribed program, has in pursuance of recommendations of the study been transformed into the Hospital Council of Allegheny County with a more inclusive membership along lines suggested by the study and with a more comprehensive program in keeping with the recommendations.

7. Some progress has been made in expanding the concept and improving the content of social interpretation. Actual achievements in this direction were unfortunately retarded by the untimely death of one of the leading spirits of the group, but the first steps toward a larger conception of publicity and toward a suitable organization for that purpose may be recorded.

8. In keeping with recommendations on Public Health Administration, the Nurses' Council has been organized within the Federation of Social Agencies, and a somewhat greater integration of policies and activities has taken place between the General Health Council and the Federation of Social Agencies, of which the former has become a member.

9. Despite some early hesitation, decided steps have been taken in recent months to carry through the spirit of the recommendations with respect to the organizations serving new Americans. There is possibility of merging the programs of the American Citizenship League and the International Institute of Pittsburgh, and a revision of the program of the International Institute in the light of the findings of the study is reported as being under way.

10. Committee appointments which may be regarded as steps toward the realization of objectives assigned to them may be mentioned as follows: Committee on City Community Councils and Training Committee of the Federation of Social Agencies; Capital Account Committee of the Community Fund.

These represent, roughly speaking, the visible results of the study recommendations up to this time. They do not include a certain indefinable amount of change that has taken place as a result of personal contacts, consultations, and incidental advice to agencies given by the study staff, but not in the form of formal recommendations. In view of the brief time that has elapsed since the completion of the study, it would be unfair to charge the community with disregarding the proposals of the study merely because changes suggested have not been put into action. Not only the specific retarding influences mentioned above should be taken into consideration but also the inevitable fact that under the best circumstances it takes time to carry through important changes. This is particularly true of proposals that require legislative action on the part of public bodies. Thus, the fact that a county department of public assistance, a hospital department, a county recreation department have not been created cannot be regarded as a rejection of proposals for creating them.[1] They have, in fact, received practically universal acceptance. Perhaps, if after another five or ten years progress toward the realization of these recommendations has not been made, either the public authorities or the interest and initiative of private citizens may be charged with failure to produce results. Even then, however, any such judgment would be valid only in view of the general acceptance of these basic recommendations as important fundamental proposals.

With respect to a few of the recommendations, less responsibility may be placed upon time and tide and more upon the resistive interests of entrenched agencies. No progress can be reported, for example, on coöperation between the two professional schools in arriving at an integrated and coördinated program. Nor does it seem that effective efforts have been made by the Social Work Division of the University of Pittsburgh to carry through the recommendations of the study, despite the fact that no theoretical objections have been raised by that organization with the Citizens' Committee. It may be too early to judge whether the reconsideration of programs and the management of Community Councils might have progressed farther. Some of the suggestions in relation to this very important social program had, however, been made and accepted during the course of the field inquiry, and without undue optimism more advance might have been expected. This is true also of the organization of a family and child welfare division in the Federation of Social Agencies.

[1] As this goes to press the passage of legislation creating a public assistance board for Allegheny County is reported—making further progress in the direction favored by the study recommendations.

To some members of the community it seems that the least excusable delay has occurred in connection with the proposal for the creation of a new case work agency which would replace the Children's Aid Society, the Children's Service Bureau, and the Family Society and would replan their work as to both content and geographic service. This, indeed, has been a proposal of far-reaching importance, though of less ultimate significance than that of the establishment of certain public departments, particularly a county health department and a department of public assistance. It looms larger because in a sense it tests the capacity of the lay and professional leadership of the community to subordinate vested agency interests to the good of the community and of the potential clientele which would ultimately profit from this proposal. The objections may seem even less tenable in view of the fact that within the Catholic denominational work the ideas underlying this proposal had been in operation for some time and that within the Federation of Jewish Philanthropies a large-scale merger of agencies was undertaken to carry these recommendations into effect. It would be unjust, however, to sit in judgment on these agencies alone for resisting that particular recommendation without bearing in mind that similar resistance, some of which has been mentioned, has been shown by other bodies.

These are the principal points in a progress report on some of the more important recommendations of the study. Other events that have affected the life of the community have occurred during this period and will undoubtedly affect, sooner or later, the entire social work panorama of Pittsburgh and Allegheny County. Within the field of better government there are activities that directly and significantly affect social work and reflect the new bent of public interest in fundamental measures for the public welfare. The Goodrich Commission, appointed by the governor to submit a sound permanent system of relief administration for the state of Pennsylvania, has made its report and proved that the best experience of voluntary social work which was represented on the personnel of its staff and the new recognition of government responsibility for the economic welfare of its less favored members can together devise suitable machinery for conserving traditional values, while recognizing realities of the day. The chief characteristics of the commission's proposals are: the clear-cut acceptance of responsibility for standards, administration, and fiscal efficiency; the coördination of administrative centralization with local responsibility and public approval of pensions and insurance systems; interdependence of trained personnel and lay leadership. If the recommendations of that commission should be carried into effect, the chances of realizing the advantages of the plans recommended for Allegheny County will be increased beyond any expectation.

Civic interest continues to bring together government and private citizens in the work of bodies such as the Efficiency Commission, the City Planning Commission, the various groups interested in some form of metropolitan consolidation, and committees working in coöperation with Federal housing authorities, the Public Works Administration, and the Federal works program. The possibilities of direct benefit to the field of social work from these civic and governmental movements may depend in large part on the extent to which the sponsors and executives of social agencies, especially those under voluntary management, can align themselves with the objectives and activities of these public groups.

The possibility of far-reaching effects upon the social attitudes which underlie social work is represented by occurrences in the field of labor relations in Allegheny County in recent months. The recognition of collective bargaining as a necessary part of industrial organization, the particular alignment of organized labor in the steel and coal industries with the C.I.O., that is, the more radical wing of organized labor, and the established constitutionality of the functions of the National Labor Relations Board may have an incommensurable effect upon public opinion and upon the division of power between dominant interests and mass opinion. There may be substantial influence upon the earnings of the laboring population which, combined with a generally changing attitude of government and politics, may draw into the management of voluntary and public social agencies a larger citizen interest inclusive of labor and of the professions as well as of industry and finance.

Whether the cleavages among the different sections of the people of this community (which are so distinctive and which account for so much of the anxiety of the present day) will shrink; whether employer and employee, Anglo-Saxon American and Central European peasant, Negro and white, adherent of this church and that, Republican and Democrat, majority party member and Socialist or Communist will, within this generation, see in each other differences of opinion rather than hostile interests may well be doubted. It is, however, not beyond hope that through an enlightened school system, a press which has been increasingly liberal and fair, and, possibly, through a more realistic and courageous social work leadership the new generation will record sufficient progress so that Pittsburgh and Allegheny County may be as proud of the achievements of the next quarter century as the present generation has cause to be of the tremendous strides toward a better life which the people of that community have made in the quarter century just past.

## Chapter Summary

The social survey movement in social work emerged at the turn of the century with the swing in professional emphasis that was then taking place in the direction of environmental reform. Posing as a comprehensive attack on the evils of urban society, it struck a responsive chord throughout much of the profession (and the surrounding society as well), which was reacting against the individual-moralistic approach of the charity organization movement. As compared with such "retail" measures, the "wholesale" survey approach—with its sweeping scope, research trappings, and moving rhetoric—had an irresistible appeal.

The immediate forerunners of the social survey movement were the muckraking novelists and journalists of the late nineteenth century, and the first surveys acknowledged their close affinity with such journalistic motives and methods. The pioneering Pittsburgh Survey of 1907 was launched under the auspices of the leading professional journal of the day, *Charities and The Commons,* which soon changed its name to *Survey,* thus symbolizing the ascendancy of the movement within the field.

In terms of results, it seems likely that in the short run at least these surveys put a variety of forces in motion in the communities involved, and that a number of their recommendations were put into effect sooner than might otherwise have been the case. Whether the results were commensurate with the energies and resources invested, or whether in the long run the surveys put the communities ahead in their welfare development as compared with communities not participating in surveys, cannot be answered with any certainty.

In any case, the quality of an allegedly research-related activity must ultimately be measured by criteria other than practical consequences, even in an applied field such as social work research. For otherwise we might find that direct social action ranks as better "research" than a model experiment that draws negative results. Weighed in this balance, the social survey movement is found wanting. Its overriding concern was to move and to convince, and its selection of facts was frequently guided by such considerations rather than by a disciplined, balance effort to answer explicit questions or hypotheses. Hence, while its individual facts may have been correct, its overall selection of them gave the impression of a partisan attempt to "make a case," which might not correspond to the perceptions of other observers going over the same ground.

Furthermore, the interpretation of the data gathered was based on largely implicit criteria and standards of need, which were not fully recognized or articulated. Hence, the conclusions arrived at cannot be considered as verifiable in a systematic sense; they represent the personal judgments of the survey makers rather than demonstrable propositions. In the final analysis, we have maintained, such standards must be subjective and value based; but it seems clear that for research purposes they should be explicitly operationalized so that others may review their appropriateness to the subject matter and either accept or reject them.

For these and other reasons the social survey in its classic form came under increasing attack, first from outside the profession and then from within. As a result of such criticisms, and also on the basis of experience gained in the widespread application of the survey method, a number of significant modifications took place that eventually led to the diffusion and dilution of the survey idea to a point at which it no longer represented a distinct entity within social work research. Quite early in the survey movement the scope of the survey began to be increasingly restricted to specialized fields of health and welfare, concentrating on selected *social work* problems and needs rather than attempting to encompass the broad gamut of urban ills. The contrast between the first and second Pittsburgh Surveys (begun in 1907 and 1934, respectively) reflects this shift in emphasis. Another change that took place was the increasing responsibility that was placed on local groups and organizations, first for "lay" participation in aspects of the survey process and then for the actual planning and direction of the entire undertaking. This trend was accelerated by the growth of community chests and councils in social work, which provided a logical setting for the conduct of such periodic "self-surveys" as well as for other types of special studies and reporting systems (see next chapter).

Today social surveys of the classic mold are rarely if ever seen. The movement in its original form apparently oversold itself. While city-wide surveys are still undertaken from time to time, these are now largely limited to selected social work content, involving mainly the social work lay and professional community. The elaborate journalistic and promotional emphasis that marked the early surveys, flooding the communities involved with dramatic publicity, have passed from the scene. Some of the skills and methods developed in the survey movement have been incorporated into the general "know-how" of the modern community organizer—for example, its educational and interpretive potential, its use of publicity media, and its involvement of the public in the study process. Other aspects of the survey movement have been added to the array of research techniques and methods within the field. Thus the many local social work studies of needs and services in various fields of practice are frequently indebted to the survey model for their general form and method, as well as their name.

The chapter ended with selections from the original texts of the first and second Pittsburgh Surveys (1914 and 1938, respectively).

## NOTES

[1] For example, see Clark A. Chambers, *Paul U. Kellogg and the Survey: Voices for Social Welfare and Social Justice* (Minneapolis: University of Minnesota Press, 1971); Robert H. Bremner, *From the Depths: The Discovery of Poverty in the United States* (New York: New York University Press, 1956), pp. 140–164; Pauline V. Young, *Scientific Social Surveys and Research* (New York: Prentice-Hall, Inc., 1949), 2d ed., pp. 1–55; Allen Eaton and Shelby M. Harrison, *A Bibliography of Social Surveys* (New York: Russell Sage Foundation, 1930), Preface; Paul U. Kellogg, "The Story of the Survey," *The Survey,* March 1920, pp. 791–794; Shelby M. Harrison, "The Development of Social Surveys," *Proceedings of the National Conference of Charities and Corrections,* 1913, pp. 345–353; Shelby M. Harrison, "Social Survey," *Social Work Year Book,* 1929, pp. 431–434.

[2] Corinne A. Sherman, "The Case Worker and Social Research," *The Family,* June 1925, p. 100.

[3] Bremner, pp. 67–70, 123–184; also, Chambers, pp. 46–61.

[4] Harrison, "The Development of Social Surveys," p. 345.

[5] Frank J. Bruno, *Trends in Social Work* (New York: Columbia University Press, 1948), p. 111.

[6] Jane Addams et al., *Hull House Maps and Papers* (New York: Crowell, 1895).

[7] Young, p. 22.

[8] Bruno, p. 117.

[9] Philip Klein, *From Philanthropy to Social Welfare: An American Cultural Perspective* (San Francisco: Jossey-Bass, 1968), p. 256.

[10] Kate Holladay Claghorn, "The Use and Misuse of Statistics in Social Work", *Proceedings of the National Conference of Charities and Corrections, 1908,* p. 235.

[11] John Daniels, "The Social Survey: Its Reasons, Methods, and Results," *Proceedings of the National Conference of Charities and Corrections,* 1910.

[12] John Koren, "Report of the Committee on Statistics," *Proceedings of the National Conference of Charities and Corrections,* 1908, p. 215.

[13] Chambers, pp. 3–11.

[14] Bremner, p. 154.

[15] Chambers, pp. 12–34.

[16] Ibid., p. 34.

[17] Eaton and Harrison, p. x.

[18] Paul U. Kellogg, ed., *Pittsburgh District: Civic Frontage* (New York: Russell Sage Foundation, 1914), p. 497.

[19] Ibid., p. 495.

[20] Ibid., p. 498.

[21] Ibid., p. 497.

[22] John A. Fitch, *The Steel Workers* (New York: Russell Sage Foundation, 1910).

[23] Margaret F. Byington, *Homestead: The Households of a Mill Town* (New York: Russell Sage Foundation, 1910).

[24] Crystal Eastman, *Work Accidents and the Law* (New York: Russell Sage Foundation, 1910).

[25] E. B. Butler, *Women and the Trades* (New York: Russell Sage Foundation, 1910).

[26] Frank E. Wing, "Thirty-five Years of Typhoid," in Kellogg, *Pittsburgh District,* pp. 63–87.

[27] Florence Larabee Lattimore, "Pittsburgh as Foster Mother," in Kellogg, *Pittsburgh District,* pp. 337–453.

[28] Eastman, p. 120.

[29] Ibid., p. 129.

[30] Ibid., p. 36.

[31] Ibid., p. 119.

[32] Mary Van Kleeck, "Social Research in Industry," *Social Work Year Book,* 1929, p. 422.

[33] Lattimore, p. 378.

[34] Ibid., p. 431.

[35] Ibid., p. 438.

[36] Ibid., p. 384.

[37] Ibid., p. 442.

[38] Ibid., p. 357.

[39] Ibid., pp. 441–449.

[40] Kellogg, *Pittsburgh District,* p. 509.

[41] "The Common Welfare: Preliminary Social Survey of Syracuse," *The Survey,* 27 (October 1911): 921.

[42] Eaton and Harrison, p. xx.

[43] "The Common Welfare: Spread of the Survey Idea," *The Survey,* 30 (May 1913): 157.

[44] Ibid.

[45] Charles A. Ellwood, "Social Facts and Scientific Social Work," *Proceedings of the National Conference of Social Work,* 1918, p. 689.

[46] Young, p. 34.

[47] Daniels, p. 237.

[48] Shelby M. Harrison, "Social Surveyor," *The Family,* 27 (March 1946): 29.

[49] Shelby M. Harrison, "Social Survey," *Social Work Year Book,* 1929, p. 431.

[50] Kate Holladay Claghorn, "Social Surveys to Date," *The Survey,* July 1934, p. 218.

[51] Kellogg, *Pittsburgh District,* p. 508.

[52] Claghorn, "Social Surveys to Date," p. 217.

[53] Ibid., p. 218.

[54] Kellogg, *Pittsburgh District,* p. 508.

[55] See, for example, Young, p. 20; Eaton and Harrison, p. xxiv; Niles Carpenter, "Social Surveys," *Encyclopedia of the Social Sciences,* 1934, XIII-XIV, 162; *Shall We Make a Survey?* (New York: National Social Welfare Assembly, 1949), p. 9; Claghorn, "Social Surveys to Date," p. 217.

[56] Kellogg, *Pittsburgh District,* p. 515.

[57] J. L. Gillin, "Social Survey and Its Further Development," *American Statistical Association Publications,* XIV, n.s. 111 (September 1915): 607–608.

[58] George H. von Tungeln, "Rural Social Research—Methods and Results," *Proceedings of the National Conference of Social Work,* 1927, p. 338.

[59] A. Mandel, "How Much Can or Should Be Made of the Survey Methods," *Proceedings of the National Conference of Social Work,* 1924, pp. 492–496.

[60] See Ruth Hill, "Some Community Values in Social Survey," *Proceedings of the National Conference of Social Work,* 1930, p. 424; Irving Weissman, "Organizing Research for Community Planning," *Jewish Social Service Quarterly,* XIV (September 1937): 95; *Shall We Make a Survey?,* p. 11.

[61] J. Howard T. Falk, "How Much Use Can or Should Be Made of the

Survey Method: For the Revamping of Existing Organizations," *Proceedings of the National Conference of Social Work,* 1924, p. 502.

[62] Ibid., p. 504.

[63] Sherman, p. 100.

[64] Cited in Hill, p. 423.

[65] Harrison, "The Development of Social Surveys," p. 349.

[66] Young, p. 30.

[67] Falk, p. 503.

[68] Harrison, "Social Survey," p. 432.

[69] Eaton and Harrison, p. xxvii.

[70] Hill, p. 421.

[71] Eaton and Harrison, p. xlvi.

[72] Hill, p. 421.

[73] Young, pp. 50–51.

[74] Edward E. Schwartz, "Social Work Research" *Social Work Year Book,* 1951, p. 501.

[75] Bremner, pp. 162–163.

[76] Philip Klein et al., *A Social Study of Pittsburgh: Community Problems and Social Services of Allegheny County* (New York: Columbia University Press, 1938).

[77] Ibid., p. xi.

[78] Ibid., p. 13.

[79] Ibid., p. 3.

[80] Ibid., p. 48.

[81] Ibid., pp. xiv–xv.

[82] Ibid., p. xii.

[83] Ibid., p. xiii.

[84] Ibid., pp. 880–881.

[85] Young, p. 49.

[86] Ibid., p. 50.

[87] Chambers, pp. 188–212.

[88] *Shall We Make a Survey?* p. 9.

# Chapter 6
# Statistics and Index
# Making in Social Work

————— • —————

### The Long Struggle for Uniform Statistics

For over a century the need for adequate, standardized social welfare statistics has been widely recognized in the field. The early meetings of the National Conference of Charities and Corrections witnessed frequent pleas for improved reporting methods, and steps were taken in this direction beginning with the very first Conference in 1874. While these seeds did not come to early fruition, there was recurrent interest in and experimentation with statistical reporting plans and procedures. These developments were frequently eclipsed by the more ambitious and dramatic research fashions previously reported, but a hard core of interest in the development of basic social work statistics persevered and was at times rewarded with progress. We noted such efforts in Chapter III with Warner's statistical compilations of Charity Organization Society services in the late 1800s. The "measurement of poverty" (see Chapter IV) may also be seen as a major example of this early impetus.

This quantitative thrust has persisted and has pervaded many facets of social welfare over the decades with fluctuating emphasis and success. In part, the drive for uniform statistics was stimulated by the pressing need of the emerging profession for "intelligence" regarding the nature of the problems being addressed and the scale of the programs mounted to deal with them; it thus represented an earnest desire to chart the murky terrain social workers were exploring and settling. In part, too, it reflected a demand by the sponsors of social services for documentation of their investment. Moreover, the positive example of neighboring disciplines—such as public health, medicine, and economics—spurred efforts to emulate their statistical progress.

Under the broad label "social welfare statistics" a distinction should be made among statistics of social services, statistics of clients, and statistics of need. By "social service statistics" is meant the quantification—through counting or measuring—of program activities (e.g., number of casework interviews, amount of public assistance grants disbursed, etc.) for a specified period or point in time. By "client statistics" is meant that counting or measuring of the recipients of social service and their characteristics (e.g., total number of service recipients, their socioeconomic status, age, etc.). There is obviously a close connection and overlap between these two types of social work statistics, since a key criterion of a social service is contact of some sort with a recipient. In a sense these measures are two sides of the same coin.

However, a sharp line should be drawn between the preceding two types of statistics and statistics of social *need*. (The reader is referred to Chapter 4, pp. 76–77, for a discussion of this concept.) The point to be made here is that there is no necessary relationship between the measure of a service, or a count of the recipents of a service, on the one hand, and the measure of the *need* for that service on the other. Statistics of need for a given service (e.g., welfare payments to the poor) would encompass those in need who are currently receiving the service as well as those in need who are not, that is, the count of *actual* recipients as well as the count of *potential* recipients. This basic differentiation was, as we shall see, often lost sight of in the interpretation of social welfare statistics.

In the following pages dealing with the federal census our discussion will focus mainly on statistics of social need. The sections that follow thereafter will deal primarily with the evolution of statistics of services and clients. The second half of the chapter will address itself to a special hybrid type of quantification—the "social welfare index," which emerged in this field at a later point.

## The Federal Census as a Source
## of Social Welfare Statistics

The earliest source of "social need" statistics was the U.S. census. In view of the national scope and implications of data on "dependent, delinquent, and defective classes," it is not surprising that the federal government early interested itself in such measurement. The decennial census presented itself as a logical medium, and certain beginnings in this direction were made as early as 1830, when the numbers of blind and deaf people were sought during the regular enumeration. In 1840 a count of insane and feebleminded people was included, and in 1850 the first attempt at enumerating paupers was made.[1] In each case the census enumerator would ask as a part of his interview whether or not any people with the specified defects were in the family. As might be expected, the resulting counts of these classes were notoriously inaccurate, providing in each case an appreciable underestimate of the numbers involved. The problem is nicely expressed in this early comment: "I hope you will not put too much stress on [census] statistics. . . . When the enumerator came to our house and enquired for idiots, he put on such a melancholy tone that if there had been any we wouldn't have told him."[2] With statistics obtained in this way, comparisons made from state to state or year to year were of little value. In 1880, when a more intensive effort to obtain accurate information was made, the number of "idiots" reported was over three times that obtained in 1870, and the count was still considered to be far from complete.[3] It is not surprising that by the 1900 census this approach to the estimation of such "problem" classes was abandoned.

The counting of the pauper population was of special interest to the field, and as we have seen, an item on paupers was added to the census in 1850. As might be expected, asking whether there were any paupers in the family proved equally dubious, and in 1860 the enumeration of inmates of almshouses was added to the census in the attempt to obtain additional information on the incidence of dependency. In 1880 a special, intensive effort was made to improve the count of dependents, as well as that of the other categories mentioned earlier. In this undertaking the newly formed National Conference of Charities and Corrections took an active part, and some of its leaders were responsibly involved in its planning and execution.

Prominent among these was Frederick H. Wines, who became Conference president in 1883. Wines had been active for many years in the general area of welfare statistics and as a result was placed in charge of the portion of the 1880 decennial census dealing with "dependent, delinquent, and defective classes."[4] This census introduced many improvements over previous enumerations, including the following: (1) A special supplementary schedule was provided whereby detailed information regarding paupers and other groups could be sought; (2) special compensation was provided to census takers for filling out these supplementary schedules; (3) an intensive search was made through institutions and physicians for additional cases. Questionnaires were sent to approximately 150,000 physicians, and replies were received from about two-thirds of this number. As a result of these innovations "a very much more complete enumeration than ever before" was achieved.[5]

Despite the considerable improvement in coverage thus attained, results were still considered far from satisfactory for the extrainstitutional poor. After the 1890 census the following conclusion was arrived at:

> It is almost, if not quite impossible, to obtain the statistics of pauperism. The first question to be decided is, Who are paupers? . . . The indoor poor can be found and counted with comparable ease; but how are we to know when we have succeeded in finding the outdoor poor?[6]

Accordingly, in 1900 the attempt to obtain overall figures of these classes was abandoned by the census, and efforts were restricted to coverage of institutional populations only. Thus, after a half-century of experimentation, it was finally recognized that information stigmatized by society cannot readily be obtained merely "for the asking."

Thereafter the federal census limited its efforts to populations of institutions of various types, thus shifting to a more accessible "service" statistic. Institutional censuses were made of paupers and other special groups in 1904, 1910, and 1923. In 1933 another institutional census was made, omitting many of the groups previously covered.[7] In 1926, with the active cooperation of social agencies, the Bureau of the Census began a series of annual reports on inmates of institutions for mental disease, institutions for mental deficiency, and prisons. The last intercensus count of almshouse populations by the Bureau of the Census was made in the special census of 1923.[8] The Bureau of Labor Statistics made occasional surveys of almshouses and homes for the aged after that time.

Subsequently the U.S. Department of Public Health took over the reporting of inmates of public mental institutions on an annual basis and the Bureau of the Census retained responsibility only for reports on institutions for the mentally defective and institutions of correction. Later such data were centralized in the National Institute of Mental Health of the U.S. Department of Health, Education and Welfare and in the Federal Bureau of Investigation of the U.S. Department of Justice, respectively.

It should be noted that the decennial census method of obtaining institutional "service" statistics provides a "cross-sectional" or periodic enumeration as of a particular point in time; statistics in social work may also be maintained on a "longitudinal" or "continuous" basis in the sense that data are reported regularly over an extended period. According to most authorities, the continuous reporting method tends to yield more consistent and reliable data.[9]

After this early, largely unsuccessful foray into social statistics, the U.S. census withdrew in favor of "straight" demography until the census of 1970. Then, with the impact of the Great Society priorities of the 1960s, renewed emphasis was given to the counting of socially relevant factors such as poverty and associated conditions, characteristics of working mothers (with potential need for child care), and the specific circumstances of the aged (detailing their many social deficits). Thus, after an abortive start and a long retreat, the great resources of the decennial census are finally beginning to be applied to welfare-related issues.

### Statewide Welfare Statistics

It will be recalled that the early National Conference of Charities and Corrections was primarily an assembly of representatives of the recently developed state boards of charities and, hence, concerned itself largely with problems at the level of state programs.[10] Prominent among these problems, as we have noted, was that of establishing a basis of comparison among the different states and their constituent municipalities regarding the incidence of pauperism and other social ills.

An intriguing example of the limitations of the statistics then available was related before the 1877 Conference by one of its founders, Franklin B. Sanborn:

> I refer to the duplication of the same person, on account of the mode of keeping records, and the great number of municipalities making the return. There are 342 towns and cities in Massachusetts, and each one may return the same vagrant five times a year. Here would be 1710 tramps manufactured out of one. The number of vagrants reported in 1875–6 was 209,739—the actual

number found by counting on the night of March 1, 1876 was only 1,081—or 1/200 part as many.[11]

The mistaken comparisons resulting from such record keeping were numerous.[12]

In his presidential address before the 1891 Conference Oscar McCulloch deplored these shortcomings in the field: "1st, that no State keeps complete statistical records, 2nd, that there is no uniformity among States as to the few and fragmentary records that are kept, 3rd that there is an absence of scientific method."[13] Certainly, in terms of top-level attention within the field, the problem of uniform statistics in social work enjoyed a very high priority in the early meetings of the National Conference (higher indeed than it has often been given since!).

The early case for better statistics was summarized in a paper before the 1894 Conference by Charles R. Henderson as follows: "We cannot measure social facts without statistics. . . . We do not know whether pauperism is increasing or decreasing, whether our methods are promoting thrift or degrading the poor, whether our benevolence is beneficent or maleficent."[14] This quotation also illustrates a rather naive hope that was often voiced during this early period, namely, that with the advent of standard statistical reporting in social work such a flood of light would be cast upon the topic that many perplexing problems of practice would be readily solved. Thus statistics were seen not only as a planning and administrative tool but also as a means for evaluation of the effectiveness of existing techniques and programs. It was also hoped that improved statistics would give answers to the urgent questions of causation that were then pressing the field. In short, the situation was one in which charity workers who were grouping "in the dark" looked to the development of uniform statistics as the panacea for the many riddles and unknowns that plagued them in their work. Only later, when some progress had been made toward uniform reporting, was it recognized that service statistics, helpful as they may be for administrative and planning purposes, do not in themselves provide the answer to such complex questions.

The interest of the early Conference in this subject did not stop with talk about it; a number of efforts were made to mobilize comparable welfare reporting systems in the several states.[15] Unfortunately, the Conference was necessarily handicapped in its efforts by its lack of authority to enforce its recommendations upon the states. In addition, there was no machinery available for collecting and compiling the material on an ongoing basis. The lesson is an important one, for the problem of maintaining adequate statistics without sufficient resources for central supervision and compilation is still with us in many sectors of the field.

These difficulties were not resolved, and as late as 1906 it could be stated that "no two states use the same system and it may be questioned whether some use any system at all."[16] Nevertheless interest in the problem remained strong, and continuing efforts at improvement were made under Conference auspices. Perhaps the most active period was during John Koren's chairmanship of the Committee on Statistics, from 1904 to 1911, when a section on statistics was held annually at each Conference and a number of papers and discussions were devoted to different aspects of the subject each year.

Thus the initial push in statistical activity in the profession was at the level of state reporting, corresponding to the administrative jurisdiction of the newly established state boards of charity. Some semblance of statistical order had been achieved before 1900 within several states under the supervision of the state boards, but the attempt to project this modest degree of standardization on an interstate basis did not succeed. Unfortunately there was then no federal authority to assume the repsonsibility for collection and control, and the National Conference of Charities and Corrections was not strong enough to fill the gap.

It was not until the passage of the Social Security Act in 1935, with its provision for federal participation in state welfare programs, that machinery was available for implementing standardized, periodic reporting on a nationwide basis. Indeed the passage of this act was perhaps the most significant event in the history of social work statistics. With this act the federal government entered into formal participation with the states in the financing and administration of the various categorical assistance programs and other services, thus opening an official national wedge for standardized reporting in all of the public welfare programs involved. In fact this federal authority over state reporting was written into the Social Security Act as one of the conditons of receiving allocations.[17] As a result a veritable revolution occurred almost overnight in the quantity and quality of social work statistics being produced in this portion of the field. Statistics of services and expenditure in the various assistance programs in nearly all of the states and territories were available shortly thereafter in the monthly publications of the *Social Security Bulletin*.

By the end of the decade the transformation that had taken place in the nation's public welfare statistics impressed itself upon many observers. Helen Jeter hailed it as "one of the most noteworthy developments of the past decade" in this field. In 1938 Ralph Hurlin commented:

The impressive present development of statistics of welfare administration has been primarily the result of emphasis, or pressure, exerted by the federal agencies. But it would be a mistake to overlook the fact that the cause of the development has not been academic interest, but a direct administrative need for statistics.[18]

Apparently a combination of administrative need, central authority, and adequate resources was required in order to bring about the improvement in public welfare statistics for which the field had looked for so many decades.

## The Growth of National Private Agency Statistics

In the field of private charity progress at first was even slower. With the establishment of national professional organizations in different fields of service, such as the Family Service Association of America in 1911 and the American Association of Medical Social Workers in 1918, some important steps toward uniform reporting in those fields were taken. In these developments the Russell Sage Foundation lent important help.

Progress was halting and piecemeal, however, until a new movement made its presence felt on the social work scene, namely, the rapid development of community chests and councils during the 1920s. Such a central organization provided a needed structure for the coordination and supervision of social work statistics on a community-wide basis. Thus the way was paved for the establishment of the Registration of Social Statistics Project. In the field of child welfare the U.S. Children's Bureau stimulated national reporting along several lines. These developments will be traced later in this chapter.

In 1907 John Koren, chairman of the Committee on Statistics of the National Conference of Charities and Corrections, presented a plan for uniform statistics in private family casework agencies. Apparently little came of this proposal or of the one put forward by a later Conference committee under the chairmanship of Margaret F. Bergen on the same subject.[19]

With the establishment of the American Association of Societies for Organizing Charity (now the Family Service Association of America) in 1911, more intensive efforts in this direction were begun. In 1915 and 1918 committees of this association published recommendations for standardizing statistics of family welfare societies.[20]

The major purposes of family welfare statistics, according to these early reports, were "publicity" and "case supervision."[21] Note that this was before the day of federated financing and central planning councils in private social work, and therefore nothing was said of the potential usefulness of such data for allocating funds or for community welfare planning. These recommendations were adopted by a number of agencies, but central collection and tabulation of figures from participating agencies did not begin until 1926, when this responsibility was assumed by Ralph G. Hurlin, head of the Department of Statistics of the Russell Sage Foundation.

Within the first year of the project's operation a total of 42 family agencies were submitting reports, and the number has multiplied over the years.[22] In 1947 the Foundation transferred its 21-year series of family agency statistics to the Family Service Association of America. The general usefulness of this series led to the establishment of several others under Dr. Hurlin's supervision. These developments helped pave the way for the next major step, namely, the highly influential Registration of Social Statistics Project* under the direction of A. Wayne McMillen, which was formally launched in 1928 under the auspices of a joint committee of the Association of Community Chests and Councils (now the United Way of America, Inc.) and the Local Community Research Committee of the University of Chicago. Among the many factors that led to its inception, one of the most immediate was a related pilot project in the collection of social work statistics published by Raymond Clapp of the Cleveland Welfare Federation in 1924 under the title *Study of Volume and Cost of Social Work in 19 American Cities.*

The Cleveland Welfare Federation was faced with a number of vexing problems in the early 1920s concerning needs and standards in the local health and welfare field. For example, questions were being raised regarding the number of hospital beds needed in the Cleveland area and similar planning problems.[23] In order to obtain fuller data than were currently available concerning such services in other cities, a reporting plan was set up under the joint sponsorship of the Cleveland Welfare Federation and the Association of Community Chests and Councils whereby agencies in the various fields of health and welfare in some 30 communities were requested to submit annual totals of volume and cost of service. Returns from 19 cities were considered suf-

---

* This project was not limited to private agencies, but it had its greatest impact in this area of statistical reporting.

ficiently complete to be utilized, and were collated in tabular and graphic form to facilitate comparison and interpretation.[24]

The Clapp study was repeated in 1926. Some of the results were so unsatisfactory that the figures were never published.[25] As a result of these experiences it was decided that in future attempts of this type the data would not be collected from the agencies at the *end* of the reporting year, since in this way it was difficult to establish adequate control and supervision over the reporting procedures. Hence, the approach arrived at was that of requiring the submission of monthly reports according to a defined listing of items, with detailed instructions, so that the resulting totals would be based on data properly standardized and regularly maintained. In effect this was a recognition of the principle mentioned earlier, namely, that continuous record keeping tends to result in more reliable data than periodic census taking.

Following up on these studies of 1924 and 1926, the Association of Community Chests and Councils enlisted the cooperation of the Local Community Research Committee of the University of Chicago in the summer of 1927, and a Joint Committee for the Registration of Social Statistics was set up.[26] In addition to the significant change from an annual "census" to regular monthly reporting procedures, other modifications in the plan of study included the dropping of several fields of reporting (recreation, planning and coordination, etc.) because of difficulties involved in standardizing units of count; the division of the reports into twenty-four fields of service rather than the three broad fields of health, dependency, and delinquency as in the Clapp study; the designation of local agents, usually staff members of chests and councils, to supervise the local collection and compilation of the monthly agency reports; the provision of more detailed items and fuller instructions; and so on. All in all, it represented the most systematic and intensive approach to the production of reliable statistics in social work to date. Each city had to report a minimum of 15 out of the 24 fields; moreover, each field of service reported on was to be at least 80 percent complete in coverage; that is, the reports submitted within the field had to represent 80 percent of all the service rendered in that field within the urban area. In this regard the project was taking a leaf from the book of birth and death statistics by adopting the concept of a "registration area" within which a given standard of reporting was to be maintained.[27] Indeed the term *registration* in the title of the project reflects this relationship.

The project began formal operation in 1928 with Professor A. Wayne McMillen of the School of Social Service Administration of the University of Chicago as project director. At that time some

300 cities were invited to participate; of these, a total of 29 accepted and submitted service statistics reports within the requirements just described. A related study of gross welfare expenditures, known as the "Z" study,* was conducted at the same time; thus at the outset there was an effort to relate the service and expenditure data in such a way as to determine unit costs within each field.[28] Difficulties were encountered in this attempt, however, and this original intention was never fully realized.

Despite some early problems, the reception of the project by the field as a whole was encouraging, and the results were found to be sufficiently useful to warrant the continuation and extension of the project. Accordingly, in 1930 the operation was transfered to the U.S. Children's Bureau, which accepted responsibility for its supervision until 1945, at which time control was again assumed by the Community Chests and Councils of America.[29]

In 1948 forty-nine urban areas were participating in the Registration of Social Statistics Project. The data appear to have been used primarily for local planning and budgeting purposes, with little emphasis placed on the intended intercity comparisons or trends.[30]

The project increased in coverage with the passage of years and for a time appeared to be rather stabilized in scope and function. However, many technical and administrative problems remained to be solved. A heavy supervisory load fell upon the shoulders of the local agent, particularly in the larger cities, and a question may well be raised as to the competency of the typical research department in a chest or council to exercise adequate supervisory control over reports from the great range of agencies and fields of service to be found within a modern metropolitan area. Since reporting was largely voluntary, agencies had to be worked with closely and persuaded to conform to the detailed instructions, which often required special internal record systems and the careful observance of fine distinctions.

Thus many observers questioned the feasibility of an all-inclusive citywide collection of reports by a single supervisory body. Could one small staff be sufficiently expert in all the fields of service to exercise the close and knowledgeable vigilance that is necessary to ensure accuracy of reporting? This school of thought supported an approach to uniform statistics by way of the

---

* The "Z" study has since been conducted biennially on a separate basis; at its peak it was carried out in 31 urban areas. However, by 1950 this number had dropped to 15 owing to the great burden of detail that the study entails. The project is now being conducted every five years rather than every two by the dwindling number of cities that still continue it.

national professional organizations operating in the various fields of service, such as the Family Service Association of America, the Child Welfare League of America, the American Association of Medical Social Workers, and so on, each taking responsibility for reporting within its own field.

On the other hand, as it was pointed out, one limitation to the utilization of the national associations for this purpose is their lack of local agents to provide on-the-spot supervision and interpretation. And so the problem of comprehensive statistical reporting in social work stands. The ultimate solution, in the prescient opinion of the project's first director, lies in federal operation of the entire reporting system. In 1930 McMillen stated:

> While a cooperative arrangement between the various national societies and the association of councils is from some points of view the most desirable way to carry on a central statistical service, it is doubtful that such a combination should direct the work indefinitely. . . . If a central statistical service for social work proves its utility, it should, before the lapse of many years, attain proportions that strain the resources of any but a federal bureau.[31]

As has been noted, the project actually was under federal auspices from 1930 to 1945, during which period the Children's Bureau assumed responsibility for national collection and compilation. Local supervision, however, remained in the hands of chests and councils. In 1945 the Children's Bureau returned control of the project to one of its initiators, the Community Chests and Councils of America. Behind this transfer appears to have been the understandable need of the Bureau to give priority to the research and statistics bearing directly upon children, and it, therefore, limited its statistical role to that area.

The Community Chests and Councils of America—later the United Community Funds and Councils of America and more recently the United Way, Inc.—carried the program until 1956, when it was finally terminated owing to the serious operational and comparability problems noted earlier and the changing priorities of the national voluntary movement. A number of cities have since independently continued local community-wide collection and compilation of agency service statistics by welfare councils or community funds for planning and budgeting purposes, but national coordination and intercity compilations of volume of service have been given up.

So ended a heroic effort by the private sector of the field to organize national social service statistics on a comprehensive basis.

There remains specialized national coverage of selected programs, such as family casework by the Family Service Association of America and child care by the Child Welfare League of America. But the emphasis and potentialities of uniform national statistics in social work have for many years been centered in the public sector at the federal level. These potentialities are yet to be realized, though in a few areas, such as public assistance and social security programs, high standards of coverage and consistency have been achieved. As foreseen by McMillen at the launching of the Registration of Social Statistics Project almost half a century ago, only the federal government has the resources and authority in the last analysis to implement such complex and demanding information systems. It appears, too, that when program funding responsibility is combined with service data responsibility (as in the case of the public assistance categories), the prospects of achieving the essential compliance and conformity are greater. Unfortunately, in view of the discipline required for effective statistical programs, "voluntarism" obviously has its limits.

## The Special Role of the
## U.S. Children's Bureau

The needs of "dependent and neglected" children, and the provision of child care services for them, have always held a high priority in social work. From 1912 until its split-up in 1969 the U.S. Children's Bureau was a key instrument on this crucial professional front, and one of its many contributions lay in the area of research and statistical leadership. Indeed the agency was established in 1912—the first of its kind in the world—in order to "investigate and report . . . upon all matters pertaining to the welfare of children and child life among all classes of our people."[32]

One of the first problems tackled by the Children's Bureau was infant mortality, and in its attempt to establish the extent and seriousness of this phenomenon it found itself hampered by the lack of adequate birth records and statistics. In 1912 the "birth registration area" had not yet been established by the Bureau of the Census, and hence "it was impossible to discover how many babies were born in a year in the United States, or how many of these died in the first year of life."[33] The Children's Bureau therefore took an active interest in the development of such statistics and played an important part in hastening the day of regular reporting in these areas.

Another early concern of the Bureau was the problem of child labor, and one of its accomplishments along this line was the establishment of a statistical series on the number of children in gainful employment. This information was obtained through arrangements with state departments of labor and was maintained from 1920 until the series was taken over by the Department of Labor when the Children's Bureau was transfered to the Federal Security Agency in 1946. It provided an index of the scope of the problem and gave an objective measure of the decline in child labor in this country since the early 1920s.[34]

A series of annual statistical reports on juvenile delinquency was also set up by the Bureau, based on reports received from courts and state welfare departments, starting in 1927. These compilations have been extended over the years and have been widely utilized, though they are recognized to have serious limitations as a reliable measure of delinquency.[35]

Much has been written regarding the crucial role played by the White House Conferences on Children and Youth in the development of interest in child care statistics and child welfare research in general. Beginning with the first Conference in 1909, they served as a stimulus to the scientific development of the entire field. Out of the first Conference, on the care of dependent children, came recommendations pointing toward such major later developments as mothers' pension programs and the establishment of the Child Welfare League of America, as well as the launching of the U.S. Children's Bureau itself in 1912.[36] Since then the Children's Bureau has taken responsibility for the decennial Conferences.

The second White House Conference, on child welfare standards, was held in 1919; and the third, on child health and protection, convened in 1930. Since then they have met each decade, the last being held in 1971. These conferences, and the various committees and sections set up to carry forward their work, resulted in marked research interest and statistical activity. The third Conference (1930) was representative of this emphasis and may be taken as illustrative. One of its committee publications expressed concern over the inadequacy of juvenile delinquency statistics in the following terms:

> No one can state with certainty whether juvenile delinquency as known to police and courts is increasing or decreasing, because of the absence of reliable and comprehensive data over a period of years for the United States, the states (with two or three exceptions) or local communities. With practically no foundation of factual material, there is perennial agitation in the United States about "youth and the crime wave."[37]

It found the situation in reporting other areas of service to children equally disappointing and concluded that there "is little real recognition of the value and province of social statistics" in this area of welfare work.[38] An attempt was made to improve the statistical picture through an experimental census of dependent and delinquent children under the care or supervision of agencies in the United States. This survey was made in conjunction with the 1930 Conference by Emma O. Lundberg and provided a demonstration of a model nationwide census of its kind. As a further contribution to research and statistics in this field, a vast array of qualitative and quantitative data concerning child welfare needs and services throughout the country was gathered together over a period of 16 months by some 1200 members of nearly 150 committees.[39] Most of this material was collected by means of questionnaires and was of a primarily descriptive nature.

While not all of its recommendations were put into practice, the 1930 Conference had a strong impact on the field, and it seems likely that a significant portion of the improvement in child welfare and delinquency reporting in the following years stemmed from the statistical zeal it displayed. Later White House Conferences, stressing different aspects of child care, provided additional child advocacy and research stimulus along many vital lines.

Finally, during the Nixon administration, the U.S. Children's Bureau was split up, many of its functions being absorbed by a new Office of Child Development in H.E.W.

## Index Making in Social Work

As a special approach to quantification in social work, there have been intermittent efforts over the past several decades to develop various types of statistical indexes* as a means of measuring the

---

* It may be helpful to define some key terms here in order to establish the ground on which the presentation will be based.

*Rate:* The number of actual events of a specified type, expressed as a portion of the total number of events of this type that could possibly have occurred and multiplied by a power of 10 (e.g., 1000; 10,000; 100,000; etc.).

*Relative Number:* A rate or quantity that is expressed as a ratio to a standard" rate or quantity and then multiplied by 100.

*Index:* A composite of two or more series of measures, rates, or relative numbers, which may be assigned either equal or unequal "weights" according to their importance in relation to the phenomenon being studied. They are used as indirect measures of concepts or characteristics that do not admit of simple counting or other direct quantification. Index numbers were first developed in economics as indirect composites approximating generalized concepts, e.g., the Consumer Price Index. In social work indexes have been used to reflect general levels of "social need," "social problems," "social service provision," etc.

incidence of social needs and problems. The potential value such indexes is readily apparent in a field that is continually confronted with the problems of establishing the relative need for services in different areas and planning on a priority basis for the meeting of these needs. Without an appropriate measure of relative need, the distribution of social services must be made on a more or less arbitrary basis. Analogy with the construction of rates and indexes in neighboring disciplines, such as economics and public health, led early to the hope that suitable indexes would throw light on the causal factors associated with trends and differences in social conditions, and on the effectiveness of the services provided to deal with them. As a result of these several decades of experimentation with rates and indexes in social work, many of their strengths and weaknesses became recognized, and there emerged a more realistic appraisal of their potentialities.

### An Early "Dependency" Index

The pioneer in social work index making was I. M. Rubinow, who devised the first major index of dependency in New York City in 1917.[40] Basing his experiment on precedents from the field of economics (where the concept of "index numbers" had evolved), Dr. Rubinow set up a composite measure encompassing several different forms of social dependency in the effort to gauge the total "force" of dependency in the area. He intended to use this measure as an indicator of overall trends in dependency, as well as a source of insight into the causes of the phenomenon.[41]

The method of construction was quite elaborate. Rubinow had available the resources of the privately financed Bureau of Statistics of the Department of Public Welfare of New York City, with the aid of which he collected monthly statistics from a variety of agencies for the period 1914–1917.[42] Nine different statistical series were brought together in this way, consisting of the following:[43]

1. The general casework of relief organizations
2. Care of homeless men and women
3. Operations of the municipal lodging house
4. Free burials
5. Commitment of childen to institutions
6. Payment to private hospitals with public funds for care of indigent patients
7. Free medical work of dispensaries
8. Chattel loans
9. Free loans

These data were selected on the basis of their having in common a presumed relationship to the general concept of "social dependency," by which was meant community support of needy people, whether in cash or in kind. While these selected services did not cover all forms of dependency in New York City at that time, and not all of what was counted under these services actually constituted dependency, the assumption was made—and every index contains some such premise—that a combination of the nine types of information listed would provide a useful barometer of the overall welfare load borne by the community. Whether or not this assumption was justified is open to question; the burden of proof, it would seem, rests on the index maker to demonstrate the adequacy of his index.

For each of these nine series of data relative numbers were computed, with the year 1916 taken as the "standard." For each month of the period 1914–1917, then, the nine relative numbers were combined and averaged, thus yielding an "index of dependency" with nine components.[44] In technical parlance, each of these components was "unweighted," being combined into the resulting index on an equal basis with the others. And herein lies a crucial difficulty in the construction of indexes in so complex a field as social work, where objective means of determining the proportions of components are not readily available. One cannot avoid the problem through recourse to an "unweighted" index, for this involves the assumption that the various elements entering into the index have *equal* importance in determining its value. What justification is there in giving, for example, "free burials" and "free loans" equal weight in the computation of an index that is supposed to reflect the overall level of social dependency in a community? The basis is obviously an arbitrary one, depending entirely on what items are selected to enter into an index and on how these items are defined. While the final computations may be objective and quantitative, the initial planning and design of such an index is very largely a subjective process, depending on the judgment of the researcher and the availability of data.

This is not to say that indexes thus derived may not be of considerable pragmatic value; it is, rather, to caution any who would look upon the final formulas and figures as "scientifically" determined. Indexes in social work represent in a sense the rough quantification of qualitative judgments, rather than any substitute or automatic improvement on them. However, they have the advantage (and disadvantage) that once the initial decisions and assumptions are made, the remaining steps are fairly systematic and objective.

It should be emphasized, moreover, that frequently the basic data that are entered into the index are far from adequate. In setting up his index, as we have seen, Rubinow instituted a temporary system of monthly statistical reporting for New York agencies in order to obtain the raw figures for his index.[45] Looking back over the diverse items listed earlier that were included in his index, one might well question the reliability of a number of them.

But perhaps the gravest weakness in such attempts to establish a measure of the incidence of needs or problems is the common error of equating statistics of *service* with statistics of *need;* this hazard is illustrated in Rubinow's index. It will be noted that the items making up this index are all *services* of one type or other, and so long as one limits the meaning of the term *dependency* to actual community support through the rendering of such services, then one is on tenable ground. The temptation is great, however—and neither Rubinow nor many of his successors have resisted it—to interpret such service measures as gauges of the *need* for service and to draw conclusions as to trends in social need and the factors associated therewith. Thus Rubinow states: "Considerable light is thrown by the facts brought together in this index upon the problem of causation of dependency and destitution."[46] In point of fact, an index based on services alone reflects the quantity and quality of existing welfare programs as much as the need for them. It is therefore difficult to see how such an index of dependency services can throw light on the extent or causes of "dependency and destitution," except in a very indirect and nebulous fashion. Only where *all* cases of dependency and destitution were known to the agencies included in the index, or at least a constant portion thereof—both quite unlikely eventualities—might one be justified in projecting from welfare services to welfare needs.

Despite such pitfalls, the development of Rubinow's dependency index gave important momentum to better quantification in the field. Thus in 1926 the American Statistical Association set up a Committee on Social Statistics, with Ralph G. Hurlin of the Russell Sage Foundation as chairman, in order to "consider the problem of a dependency index, to study statistics of social work and to keep informed in statistical work in progress in that field."[47] Shortly thereafter, as we have seen, the Russell Sage Foundation initiated collection of family agency statistics on a uniform basis. Also, the planning of the previously discussed Registration of Social Statistics Project included an effort to utilize the data collected to set up an "index of dependency" and other composite measures of services, a hope that was soon abandoned.[48]

Today the field does not hear much about dependency indexes of this type. The attempt started by Rubinow in 1917 seems to have succumbed to intrinsic weaknesses. Similarly, the intent to read causes of dependency into such measures, or to evaluate the effectiveness of social service with their aid, have come to naught. Based as they were on a conglomeration of statistics of service, they were limited not only by the inadequacy of the data that went into them but also by the fact that in the social work field statistics of service do not necessarily reflect need.

### The Social Breakdown Index

In 1939 Community Chests and Councils, Incorporated, published a pamphlet entitled *Social Breakdown: A Plan for Measurement and Control* in which the results of a study in Stamford, Connecticut, were presented.[49] The plan proposed therein was perhaps the most ambitious of the index-making attempts in social work, and certainly stirred up as much reaction, both positive and negative, as any.

The purpose of the new index, whose leading architect was Bradley Buell, was to provide "a basis for measuring the volume and trend of social breakdown in the community."[50] As a measure of "social breakdown," a composite index consisting of seven different categories of data was devised, each category corresponding to a type of social maladjustment officially registered in the public records of the community. It was assumed that such an index "should provide a more concrete point of departure than has so far been available from which to analyze and evaluate the overall relationships of social services to significant social trends."[51] Thus fluctuations in the social breakdown index were interpreted as reflecting not only the trends in social needs and problems of the type included in the index but also the effectiveness of the social services in preventing or reducing the incidence of such problems. Moreover, it was assumed that this measure, though limited to official breakdown categories, could also be used to infer trends in the broader gamut of social problems not coming to the attention of public authorities. Thus it was stated that the "rate of social breakdown can be used as an index to the trend of this broader area of the community's social difficulties."[52]

The Social Breakdown Index, which was to accomplish these several objectives, was arrived at in the following way. Information was obtained as to the number of cases falling into the following seven categories:

1. Mental disease (from probate courts and state mental disease hospitals)
2. Mental deficiency (from probate courts and state training schools)
3. Crime (from the city courts)
4. Delinquency (juvenile courts)
5. Neglect (juvenile courts)
6. Divorce (superior courts)
7. Unemployability (from the local public welfare department)[53]

After the number of cases within these classifications has been determined for a given year, the rate for each was determined per 1000 population for the geographic area under consideration. Then the resulting seven rates were added together, yielding a composite index based on the "unweighted" total of the seven constituent rates. In other words, divorce rate was counted as of equal weight with the rate of mental disease, juvenile delinquency rate, and so on.

After the publication of this manual the index was applied in a number of other communities, including Akron, Ohio; Galveston, Texas; Hartford, Connecticut; and Memphis, Tennessee.[54] For a time it appeared that "social breakdown"—like the earlier "social survey"—was going to sweep the field. A reaction soon set in, however, in which the shortcomings of the method were effectively exposed.

One of the first—and most telling—of these critiques was delivered the following year by Kenneth L. M. Pray before the 1940 National Conference of Social Work. He questioned not only the quality of the data on which the index was based but its underlying assumptions. Since the index makes use of official statistics only, the limitations of such public records should be clearly recognized, he emphasized.[55] These include their dependence on the state of the law in the locality under consideration, the quality of the personnel, the availability of facilities, and so on. Reporting may depend as much on the characteristics of the community and agencies involved as on the incidence of particular behaviors. Moreover, many of the problems and limitations in achieving uniform statistical reporting discussed at length earlier apply with full force to the data utilized in the index.

Dr. Pray took particular issue with the assumption of the report that "the whole range of social difficulties which represent

the community's total need for social services" is reflected in its official categories of breakdown.[56] There is no necessary connection between the number of cases that come to the attention of public authorities and the number of cases that do not. "The fact is," he stated, "that these extreme forms of behavior [that is, the official breakdown categories] . . . compose what amounts to a separate problem."[57] The belief that these extreme manifestations of social maladjustment can be interpreted as an index to the greater volume of less acute disorders is an instance of the application of the false analogy between social and physical "disease." Hence, any generalization regarding the sum total of "social maladjustment" in a community based on the incidence of such official categories must be looked upon as an untested hypothesis rather than a conclusion.

Finally, Pray declared himself strongly opposed to the premise of the report that such an index could provide a "simple method of determining the relationship of social agency services to the prevention and control of social breakdown."[58] In the first place, the categories themselves cannot be uniformly interpreted as "breakdown" in the sense implied in the report, as an inspection of its components revealed. At one point the report defines "social breakdown" as occurring when "people are unable to make for themselves the adjustments essential for self-sufficiency"; at another point it is defined as "behavior that does not conform to currently accepted concepts of satisfactory social adjustments."[59] But does an act such as divorce necessarily imply any such inability or non-conformance? And may not the commitment of an individual to a mental institution in some instances be a sign of strength and progress rather than "breakdown," as for instance in a case in which the need for such care has been resisted and denied for a long time? Therefore the units being counted may in some cases be as much a measure of social "progress" as of social "breakdown." In addition, the existing social services within a community are but one of the many forces making for social weal or woe, and it is illogical—as well as dangerous—for social workers to allow themselves to be held accountable for trends revealed by this measure. Unless all other factors are controlled or properly taken into account—and these include economic trends, legal and administrative changes, social and cultural forces, public knowledge and attitudes, and so on—there is no sure basis for inferring any causal connection between fluctuations in "social breakdown" and the adequacy of a community's social services.[60] The report acknowledges this limitation but apparently considers it surmountable through "common-sense interpretation." Referring to the qualifying influence of the uncontrolled variables contributing to social maladjustment, Buell states:

> In general, what is required is not additional statistical tabulation but rather a critical, common sense interpretation in the light of known facts about the community. Among such qualifying factors are:
>
> 1. Changes in administration and policy.
> 2. Basic economic changes.
> 3. Long-time trends.
> 4. Statistical safeguards.[61]

However, the extent to which such "qualifying factors" can be properly weighted by means of "known facts" and "common sense" is an open question. Certainly the conservative research approach here would appear to have been to withhold judgment regarding relationships or causation until much more was known regarding the behavior of the "social breakdown" variable and its correlates.

A further effective attack on "social breakdown" was delivered in *The Family* (1941) in a symposium on the subject in which Hurlin and others participated.[62] But despite such cautions the Social Breakdown Index continued to be promoted by the Community Chest and Council movement for a time, and was applied in several additional cities. The balloon had been pricked, however, and by the end of the 1940s the fad had collapsed.

In retrospect the social breakdown episode may be described as a bold though premature attempt to measure community pathology and to relate such a yardstick to the adequacy of community programs for the control and prevention of social problems. Its early exposure by social work critics, and its subsequent demise, demonstrated the growing capacity of the profession to control its own research excesses.

### Geographic Indexes of Need

Despite the lack of success of the early attempts at index making in social work, the device has been retained and refined over the years. A later impetus came from community social welfare planning in the major urban centers, where the pressures for services from the different sections of the city and suburbs are likely to be many and conflicting. Here any measure that purports to assess the level of relative need in different subareas of the community is of great potential value in planning and setting priorities for services. It is not surprising, therefore, that the idea should take root and grow despite methodological and conceptual difficulties.

Since the 1940s indexes of "social need" have been constructed and applied in such major cities as New York, Los Angeles, Boston, and Cleveland.[63] Refinements have been introduced in some of these studies that represent major improvements over the cruder dependency and "breakdown" measures of the past. These developments include (1) the substitution of standard scores for raw scores, (2) the emergence of specialized indexes in addition to generalized yardsticks of need, and (3) the factor analysis of index components.

The use of "standard scores" is a technical refinement in which both the mean and the variability of frequency distributions are expressed in comparable relative terms; that is, the means are expressed as 100.0 (as in the case of relative numbers) and the variability is expressed as a fraction of the standard deviation. This avoids the hazard of one series of data overbalancing another by virtue of unequal average size or dispersion. The standard score technique was first applied to a social work index, insofar as the writer has been able to determine, by Walter I. Wardell as part of the Greater Boston Community Survey[64] of 1948. It was also utilized in perhaps the most extensive and thoroughgoing index of community social need—that developed over a period of years at the Cleveland Welfare Federation by Virginia Kann White.[65]

The second major improvement was the "specialized index," which represented an important advance over the "general" geographic indexes of social need referred to earlier. The "general" index aspires in one measure to encompass a multitude of health, welfare, and recreation needs. It is common experience, however, that not all needs are present in the same degree in a given area, though there may be a tendency for some types to occur together. The need for day care centers may be greater in middle-class residential neighborhoods with many families with young children than in "skid row" areas where there are few such families; on the other hand, the need for alcoholic treatment clinics will probably be greater in the latter. To attempt to straddle such disparate types of need in one general measure might well obscure the need for the specific type of program under consideration. The first specialized index was prepared by the Research Department of the Welfare Council of Metropolitan Los Angeles under the direction of Genevieve Carter and Elizabeth Frank. Its "Youth Project Yardstick," completed in 1953, was a specialized index aimed at reflecting the need for intensive services to "hard-to-reach" youth groups in the Los Angeles area. A number of innovations were made in the construction of this index that warrant mention. In addition to the specialized nature of the index, it made use of percentiles in place of standard scores to equate variability. In addition, for the first time there was a *differential* weighting of component factors according to the "pooled judgment of Youth Project Committee and staff." Finally, census tracts were used in place of broader neighborhoods in order to permit finer discrimination between subareas.[66] A later revision of White's Cleveland index provided for two specialized measures of leisure needs—an "index of area characteristics," intended to reflect "normal" recreational needs, and an "index of social problems," aimed at gauging the need for more intensive and aggressive youth services.[67]

Finally, factor analysis has been applied to the study of small-area characteristics with promising results. In essence, this sophisticated statistical technique (first developed in psychology by Charles Spearman for the study of the components of intelligence) seeks to group the various constituent factors utilized in constructing an index into two or more distinguishable sets corresponding to underlying "factors" or dimensions of the data. Factor analysis was applied to the study of social areas by sociologist Eshref Shevsky[68] and adapted by Elisabeth Frank at the Los Angeles Welfare Council to the "two-dimensional" representation of neighborhood types for social planning purposes.[69] The traditional index ranked or measured geographic areas along a single continuum; the introduction of multiple dimensions or "factors" obviously permits richer delineation of the geographic areas of a city and makes possible more adequate differentiation for need assessment and planning purposes. The two dimensions utilized in the Los Angeles index were "social rank" and "urbanization," originally identified by Shevsky.

## Limitations of Indexes as Measures of Social Need

It may be helpful to review here the major limitations of these measures, most of which have been touched upon in the preceding pages. These limitations may be summarized as follows:

1. The *selection* of the items to be included in the index is arbitrary. Their utilization is based in part on the availability of data and in part on the judgment of those constructing the instrument. No objective basis of selection has been developed thus far.

2. The *weighting* of the items included in the index is arbitrary. In some instances the different factors influence the composite haphazardly, depending on their respective means and variability. With proper refinements (for example, standard scores, percentiles), this disproportionate influence of a particular components can be controlled, but the question of what the proper weighting of the items selected should be remains unanswered. There is as yet no objective basis of allocating weights to the various components, though the "pooling" of judgments may help.

3. The *raw data* entering into the index are frequently of limited reliability or adequacy. Where census data are used, they are often out of date; where public or private agency records are used, their accuracy and completeness are frequently questionable. The various limitations noted on obtaining uniform statistics in social work apply with full force here (for example, the inadequacy of juvenile delinquency statistics has been noted).

4. The *areas* for which rates are computed may be too heterogeneous to permit any meaningful interpretation or comparison. An area rate or index is an *average* measure and, hence, would cover any internal variation that may obtain within the area. Thus an area rate or index may mask the fact that there may be one sector with an extremely high rate balanced by another with an extremely low rate, and hence planning on the basis of the average rate may miss the needs of both. This problem may be lessened through the choice of smaller, more homogenous geographic units, though these may have other shortcomings.

5. The *differences* observed between area rates and indexes may not be statistically significant, and therefore interpretations based on such differences may be unwarranted.

6. Indexes can at best reflect only *relative* need. Their interpretation in terms of absolute needs for service depends on the application of the explicit or implicit standards of those making use of the index. Thus they may tell us whether according to the index there is more or less "need" in one area than another, but the question of how much need, requiring how much service, is left unanswered.

Underlying these specific limitations of the need index is a more general one discussed earlier, namely, the clouded scientific status of the concept of social need (see Chapter 4, pp. 76–77), which hampers the development of other research approaches to the assessment of social work need as well.

Within the past 10–15 years there appears to have been a decline in emphasis on indexes in social work as such, due either to their inherent shortcomings or to external factors such as the diminishing role of community welfare councils (a major site for such efforts in the past) in social planning and research. Concomitantly, increased index construction activity of an *interdisciplinary* nature may be discerned at the state and national governmental levels. At the state level, departments of public health, mental health, public welfare, and the like have employed social indexes as tools in statewide planning and allocation of resources on a priority need basis (e.g., ranking counties or regions on the basis of social need).

On the national level, federal agencies and some congressional acts have utilized indexes and index-like formulas as guides in allocating resources to various geographic districts on the basis of "need" (e.g., special revenue sharing, "impacted area" funds, compensatory education programs, and some child welfare programs). Whatever their technical weaknesses, the index idea seems to be pragmatically useful in large-scale program planning and priority determination—hence their continued application and evolution over the past half-century. Their future development and further improvement seems likely for these reasons.

## Social Indicators

As the most recent development in the checkered history of quantification and indexes in social welfare, reference should be made to the emergence of "social indicators" as a goal of social measurement. While the weight of this movement has fallen largely outside of social work—in sociology and other social sciences—social work researchers and planners have been actively involved and strongly supportive of the cause. Thus effective impetus to the development of social indicators was given by Wilbur J. Cohen, secretary of the U.S. Department of Health, Education and Welfare at the end of the Johnson administration. Secretary Cohen—a prominent social work leader since the New Deal of the 1930s—had convened a commission composed of citizen and professional representatives to consider the potentialities of social indicators as objective benchmarks of progress in the "social health" of the nation, and the result was the influential publication *Toward a Social Report* (1969),[70] transmitted just before he left office. In the 1971 *Encyclopedia of Social Work* an article was included for the first time on "Social Indicators," written by Howard E. Freeman and Eleanor B. Sheldon.[71]

For our purposes a "social indicator" may be defined (as in *Toward a Social Report*) as a "statistic of direct, normative interest which facilitates concise, comprehensive and balanced judgments about the condition of major aspects of a society."[72] For example, the portion of the total population under the "poverty line" for a period of years might be a social indicator of poverty trends. Interestingly enough, the bulk of the 1971 *Encyclopedia of Social Work* was devoted to a critique of the social indicator concept and to cautions regarding its abuse. Thus strictures were placed against the interpretation of social indicators as goal-setting or priority-determination devices, or as evaluative measures.[73]

The conclusion reached was that social indicators are an "elusive concept" that must await the development of "better-conceptualized" social statistics and "improved analytical studies" for successful realization.[74] In view of the well-documented propensity of the field to overestimate the prospects of a new research fashion, this conservatism must be viewed as a healthy change, reflecting a growing research sophistication in the profession.

In 1973 the Office of Management and Budget's Statistical Policy Division issued the first *Social Indicators* report to be published by the federal government.[75] From the standpoint of social welfare yardsticks, the content must be viewed as disappointing. While major sections of the dozens of charts and tables deal with health, public safety, education, employment, income, housing, leisure and recreation, and population, there are none devoted to public welfare programs or to social service needs as such. Whether this is due to the selectivity of the sponsors of the report (the Executive Office of the President—under the Nixon administration—and the U.S. Department of Commerce) or to the lack of usable data series in this area is not known. Perhaps the most pertinent "social work data" in the report are the trends in numbers and characteristics of the poor—euphemistically referred to in these official pages as "low-income" population.[76] In any case, much of the promise of significant social welfare measures contained in the earlier *Toward a Social Report* is yet to be fulfilled. Moreover, unlike the latter publication, *Social Indicators: 1973* completely avoids any interpretive commentary.

It may therefore be suggested that for this field "social indicators" is a new term for a venerable goal—the quantification of social needs and services in reliable, illuminating, meaningful terms. While the concepts, technology, and aspirations of this current "movement" are more advanced than those of earlier attempts, substantial breakthroughs are yet to be achieved, and the historic hurdles noted earlier are still to be surmounted. At the same time, the objectives are of overriding importance to the nation, as well as to the social disciplines involved, and the groping efforts to make headway should be well worth the risks.

The most recent effort related to social work in this area is a project directed by Leonard S. Kogan and Shirley Jenkins aimed at the development of state and regional child health and welfare indicators. The study, funded by the U.S. Office of Child Development, identified "disorganized poverty" (DIPOV) as a major demographic dimension differentiating one geographic area from another.[77]

# Measurement in Social Work

## A. W. McMILLEN

We present here the first two chapters of this highly influential report on a major experiment in national social service measurement. (pp. 1–21.)

### INTRODUCTION (Chapter 1)

The attempt to establish uniform central reporting of statistics by social agencies has been prompted by a desire for accurate and current knowledge of social needs and resources and by a demand for appraisal of present methods of utilizing resources to meet needs. The effort may be regarded, on the one hand, as merely an extension of the social measurements of the census, which counts the numbers of the population, the amount and value of the products of agriculture and manufacturing, compares the death-rate for community to community, and supplies other details with regard to the social and economic status of the population. On the other hand, it may be regarded as the converse of attempts to measure periodic changes in prosperity. Although the problems that confront social agencies are not all problems of dependency, many of them do represent phases of contemporary life that are the antitheses of prosperity and others may be regarded as direct by-products of industrial progress. Among the latter are ill health,

From A. W. McMillen, *Measurement in Social Work: A Statistical Problem in Family and Child Welfare and Allied Fields* (Chicago: University of Chicago Press, 1930). Reprinted with permission of publisher.

mental strain, industrial accident, unemployment—in short, situations in which the individual or family finds it impossible to adjust to some stress of social life without assistance from the community. Since these adjustments cost something to the community, both in human efficiency and in material wealth, they cannot be overlooked in any development of a comprehensive accounting of the economic situation of the community.

Among the many questions to be answered by this social accounting are the following: How many individuals and families were unable to carry on their economic and social life during 1928 without the assistance of a social agency? How many of these were adults, how many were children, how many were aged persons? How were these persons served—by material relief in their own homes, by service without relief, by institutional care? How much did their care cost the community in human service and in dollars and cents?

The need for such an accounting challenges the statistician to devise methods of measuring a very complex problem. It is perhaps no more complex, however, than the business cycle appeared to be before statistical methods were turned toward its analysis. Moreover, just as an understanding of the business cycle contributes toward a leveling of peaks and depressions, so, it may be hoped, will a knowledge of the extent and character of the problems faced by modern social work contribute toward an improved control of those problems.

The task, which appears insuperable when viewed in its general significance, becomes more manageable when viewed in its practical and local aspects. First of all, the problem of measurement is not a remote academic question. On the contrary, it is, in the minds of executives of national social agencies and directors of local community chests and councils, an immediate practical consideration, and as such enlists their interest and their co-operation. These persons are charged with a public responsibility and they are required from time to time to render an account of their trust. If this account can be rendered in accurate terms that may be compared from period to period, their task of interpretation is greatly simplified. They are interested, moreover, in improving the technique of social work. They believe that the exchange of experience, that comparison from agency to agency and from city to city may provoke discussion that will tend to elevate both standards and practice. For these reasons a co-operative attitude toward central reporting already exists in many cities and facilitates immeasurably the approach to the problem.

To the eager and uninitiated inquirer who wishes to know how many separate individuals were served during the year and how many units of service of various kinds were rendered, the answer must prove disappointing. The technique of social work has not yet advanced to a point where there is no duplication in service. In fact, improving technique, while reducing duplication in real service, increases duplication from a statistical point of view. Is the homeless man who receives temporary shelter in an institution, medical treatment from a free clinic, and assistance in getting a job from a free employment agency to be considered as three persons or one? Existing statistical systems must count him as three. Moreover, the tendency toward specialization in social work—psychiatric social service, medical social service, institutional care for selected groups, and the like—makes a large degree of duplication inevitable. Hence, statistics of social work must be presented now—and probably for a long time to come—for broad classes of agencies or fields of work, and no attempt should be made to add together the numbers of persons or cases served in the several groups.

Statistical reporting by local social agencies is not new, of course. Monthly, quarterly, or annual reports have been made to boards of directors of private agencies and to the city council or county board by public agencies for many years. Many of these reports have been printed and may be found in libraries and in the files of social agencies. The persons preparing these reports, however, have often felt very little responsibility for preserving comparability of data from year to year. Moreover, each agency has prepared its reports without regard to the types of data presented by similar agencies. Hence, the statistics of social agencies cannot be compared with confidence over a period of years within a given field or even within a given city.

Significant efforts toward definition and standardization have been made by certain national social agencies. The work of the American Association for Organizing Family Social Work, the National Association of Legal Aid Organizations, the National Association of Travelers Aid Societies, and the Child Welfare League of America will be discussed in subsequent chapters. These national organizations have conceived it to be their function to devise case record blanks and statistical cards and to define the terms used. A few have asked for reports from member societies and have used the reports as a basis for comparative analysis of the technique of the several societies. In general, however, the national agencies have not gone beyond suggestion and mild persuasion toward uniform statistics since they exercise no actual control over member organizations.

Local groups of agencies organized along functional lines, such as the federations of health agencies in New York,[1] have made considerable progress in standardization of statistics by the establishment of central monthly reporting systems which include the publication of monthly reports to member agencies. The first of these central reporting systems in New York was established by the Association of Tuberculosis Clinics in 1918. Four other health organizations[2] have adopted similar plans.

---

[1] See Wilford I. King, "Central Collection of Social Statistics," *Journal of the American Statistical Association,* June, 1929, p. 178.

[2] These are the Tuberculosis Sanatorium Conference of Metropolitan New York, the Heart Committee of the New York Tuberculosis and Health Association, the Convalescent Homes for Cardiac Children, and the Bellevue-Yorkville Health Demonstration.

With the development of councils of social agencies and community chests has come an effort toward the collection of reports from all social agencies on a city-wide basis. Since it is impossible to apportion the parts of a common fund to a considerable number of agencies intelligently without accurate knowledge of the problems to be met by each agency, current reports have become an extremely useful tool in community planning. In certain cities the federation has accepted from the agencies whatever types of report they were already in the habit of preparing, but in a few cities a successful system of uniform reporting has been established.

In addition to these efforts toward standardization from within the profession by national agencies and local councils, certain contributions have been made by the states and by the national government. In a few states, departments of public welfare have been vested with the power to require reports from private as well as from public social agencies and institutions. In other states statistics are available for at least the public institutions. This method of standardization by state departments, while it may achieve important objectives within the several states, raises a further problem of making statistics comparable from state to state.

The federal census bureau has for several decades issued statistics with regard to the numbers of certain dependent, delinquent, and defective persons with whom the field of social work is concerned, including prisoners in jails, workhouses, prisons, and reformatories, feeble-minded and epileptics in institutions, patients in hospitals for mental diseases, dependent and neglected children cared for by institutions and child-placing agencies, children in day nurseries, juvenile delinquents in institutions, and adults in homes for the aged, convalescent, and incurable.

One attempt on the part of the national government to collect statistics from social agencies more frequently than once in a decade has been made by the United States Children's Bureau. This bureau has developed a plan for uniform statistics collected at least once a year from juvenile courts. The plan was put into operation in July, 1926, and a report of the first year's work has recently been published.[3] The Children's Bureau in this project has adopted the registration method of the Bureau of Vital Statistics. In other words, the juvenile court is asked to fill out a separate card for each case disposed of at any time during the year. The cards are forwarded to Washington at least once a year, and the Children's Bureau itself makes all compilations.

In another field, also, the federal government has embarked upon the collection of frequent reports from local agencies. The Federal Employment Service in the United States Department of Labor publishes the monthly reports of public employment bureaus.

Interest in uniform social statistics has also aroused the attention of research organizations that are not actively engaged in social work

[3] *Juvenile Court Statistics, 1927,* Children's Bureau Publication No. 195.

and that are not government research bureaus. In 1917 Dr. I. M. Rubinow, head of a privately supported bureau of social statistics in the Department of Public Charities of New York City, made the first attempt to record changes in dependency by means of statistical indices.[4] In 1924 Ferris F. Laune, of the Wieboldt Foundation, published a suggested plan for attaining uniform financial statistics in social agencies and institutions.[5] In January, 1926, Ralph G. Hurlin, of the Russell Sage Foundation, began collecting monthly reports from twenty-nine family welfare agencies.[6] The societies selected for this experiment included several Jewish agencies and 3 public departments. The group, as a whole, was representative of the best organized family welfare societies in the United States and Canada. The work of the Russell Sage Foundation was extended in 1928 to the fields of medical social service and child welfare, and in 1929 to the field of temporary shelter for homeless persons.

Thus, the present effort of the Joint Committee of the Association of Community Chests and Councils and the Local Community Research Committee of the University of Chicago is not an isolated venture into an entirely unexplored field. In fact, there seems to be considerable danger that the patience of a local social agency may be sorely tried by the demand of a national society, a local council, a state department, a federal bureau, and a private research foundation, each for a report of a slightly different nature. Discussion of this problem of duplication of effort, however, will be postponed to a later chapter, though it may perhaps be said here in justification of this apparent waste that it has been occasioned by the discovery that preparation of a plan for uniform statistics accomplishes little unless accompanied by the actual collection of figures.

The interest of the Association of Community Chests and Councils in comparable statistics is an outgrowth of the statistical efforts of certain local councils. The results of comparing case loads and budgets from agency to agency within one city suggested the advantages that might be derived from camparison between cities. In 1924, Raymond Clapp, of the Cleveland Welfare Federation, undertook, with the co-operation of the Association of Community Chests and Councils[7] and representatives of local councils, a study of the income, expenditure, and service of the social agencies in 40 cities of more than 100,000 population. Nineteen of these cities succeeded in collecting the required data with sufficient promptness and accuracy to be included in the tabu-

[4] Indexes were published for family case work, care of homeless men and women, free funerals, commitment of dependent children, hospital cases paid for out of public funds, dispensary services, and small loans. See I. M. Rubinow, "A Dependency Index for New York City, 1914–1917," *American Economic Review*, VIII (December, 1918), 713–40.

[5] Published by the Wieboldt Foundation, Chicago.

[6] In May, 1929, the number had been increased to 53.

[7] Then known as the American Association for Community Organization.

lations.[8] The results were published in two volumes,[9] one presenting figures on income and expenditure, the other, statistics of services rendered by social agencies. The figures given are totals for the year 1924 and were collected at the end of the year without any previous attempt to establish uniform statistical systems or comparable definitions of terms. As was to be expected, many cities were unable to report completely because existing statistical systems were not designed to yield the particular items requested.

This experiment was repeated at the end of the year 1926 by the New York office of the Association of Community chests and Councils. Representatives of local community chests and councils in 40 cities collected reports from their agencies at the end of the year. These reports included total income and expenditure for the year and statistics of services for each of the twelve months of the year. This request for monthly service figures increased the difficulty of the undertaking. Many agencies that could make an annual report had not yet established a plan for the monthly compilation of figures. The results of this study were unsatisfactory to its sponsors that the figures were never published.

These studies made under the guidance of the Association of Community Chests and Councils differ in one important respect from the others that have been mentioned. The other efforts have in the main either tried to show periodic fluctuations from a given base or have aimed at the fundamental objective of teaching agencies the principles of statistical reporting. In either case it has been possible to select arbitrarily any desired group of agencies and to disregard those in which standards were low or co-operation difficult to secure. One of the major objectives of the Association of Community Chests and Councils, however, has been to present comparisons of the volume of various types of social work in different cities. This could be done only by seeking figures on the total amount of work carried on in a given field irrespective of the standards of the agencies and of the auspices under which the programs were directed.[10]

As a result of its experiences in 1924 and 1926, the Association of

[8] The nineteen cities included were: Akron, Buffalo, Canton, Chicago: Cleveland, Dayton, Des Moines, Detroit, Duluth, Grand Rapids, Indianapolis, Kansas City, Milwaukee, Minneapolis, Omaha, Rochester, St. Paul, Toledo, and Wilkes-Barre.

[9] Raymond Clapp, *Study of Volume and Cost of Social Work (1924)*: Vol. I, *Tabulation of Income for Nineteen Cities;* Vol. II, *Service Supplement, Tabulation of Service for Nineteen Cities.* Published by Welfare Federation of Cleveland. Mimeographed.

[10] The reporting system for juvenile courts devised by the United States Children's Bureau also contemplated intercity comparisons, but here the problem was simpler owing to the fact that it was usually necessary to secure the co-operation of only one court in each city in order to present total figures for the community.

Community Chests and Councils has modified its point of view. While it retains the hope of achieving total figures by means of which reliable intercity comparison may be made, it recognizes also the impossibility of omitting the preliminary step of developing sound methods of record-keeping within the agencies. It realized as a result of the work done in 1924 and 1926 the need for a more permanent research organization. It was obvious that statistics could not be compiled at the end of the year if proper records had not been kept of the units that were to be counted month by month. The Association, therefore, in the summer of 1927, enlisted the co-operation of the Local Community Research Committee of the University of Chicago, and a Joint Committee for the Registration of Social Statistics were organized in September, 1927. This Committee proceeded immediately to make plans for the collection of monthly reports from social agencies during the year 1928.

## THE REGISTRATION OF SOCIAL STATISTICS—1928 (Chapter 2)

The Joint Committee, soon after its organization, outlined the specific aims it desired to achieve in 1928. The primary objectives were, first, to obtain statistical measurements of the total volume of social service in a representative group of cities and, second, to relate this service, if possible, to the income and expenditure of the agencies providing it. Back of these objectives lay a desire to encourage agencies to develop better records and statistics and to stimulate communities to collect as a routine function accurate data pertaining to social work.

From the outset of the plan was considered the nucleus of a possible national scheme which might be extended to other cities as they became able and willing to co-operate. For that reason the study was called the "Registration of Social Statistics," and the first cities included were thought of as a "registration area," similar to the registration area for vital statistics,[1] that is, an area within which certain statistical requirements could be met.

The first concrete task was to define the field of social work to be covered by the registration. Since few efforts have been made to define "social work," the legal definitions of the term "charity" were consulted to determine whether any one of them could be adapted to the present need. The definition formulated by Justice Horace Gray in a famous charity case[2] that came before the Massachusetts Supreme Court in 1867, which, according to Zollman,[3] is the most satisfactory of the series, reads as follows:

[1] The plan does not, of course, follow the registration method of requiring a report to be forwarded to the central office for each case. The reports received are really monthly tabulations of cases handled by the local agencies.

[2] *Jackson* vs. *Phillips*, 96 Mass. (14 Allen), 539–99.

[3] Carl Zollman, *The Law of Charitable Trusts*, chap. iv.

> A charity, in the legal sense, may be more fully defined as a gift, to be applied consistent with existing laws, for the benefit of an indefinite number of persons, either by bringing their minds or hearts under the influence of education or religion, by relieving buildings or works, or otherwise lessening the burden of government.

It was clear that this definition, which sought to limit the area within which charitable trusts might operate, was too broad to apply to the field of social work. Such trusts could properly be turned to the creation and maintenance of museums, art galleries, and similar establishments with which social work does not concern itself. In other words, social work was clearly only one of the activities to which charitable trusts and the legal definition of such trusts could be applied.

The longer it was considered, the more questionable appeared the advisability of attempting to define the field. Much may be said against reducing the concept of social work to a narrow formula. New discoveries in science, new avenues into which energy may be turned, the flux and change in human needs and wants—all these must inevitably enlarge the scope of social work, which, first and last, must concern itself with the stresses and strains occasioned by the lack of, or the imperfect operation of, the machinery for living which society has created. It will perhaps always be a sort of marginal field, free to push forward its boundaries and to alter its purposes as need suggests. Quite apart, then, from the practical difficulties involved, there is valid ground for asserting that social work may, with greater fairness to its aims, be defined, not in rigid and general terms, but rather by means of a description of some of the more specific functions which may fall within the general field of philanthropy at any given time.

The problem thus became one of modifying the analyses of the field that had been made in the studies of 1924 and 1926. In these two studies the field had been divided into the four categories of dependency, delinquency, health, and character-building. The task of gathering accurate data from the organizations commonly classified as "character-building agencies," however (that is, agencies concerned with education, recreation, and similar leisure-time activities) provide exceptionally difficult. Accordingly it seemed wisest to exclude that field from the outset and to concentrate upon fields in which more rapid progress could probably be expected.

The elimination of the character-building agencies limited the scope of the study to organizations concerned with problems of dependency, delinquency, and illness. These fields overlap at points, and all of them shade off into activities that probably do not belong within the field of social work. The first step toward definition consisted in the preparation of a list of all activities, both institutional and non-institutional, that appeared to be within the field of social work and that were concerned with the individualized treatment of cases of dependency, delinquency, or illness. Agencies such as the social reform groups that are interested in these fields, but concerned with the broad aspects of the problem rather than with treatment of specific cases, were excluded.

If any given function in the completed list had habitually relied upon altruistic considerations for its support and if it had commonly been accorded a place in the programs of the National Conference of Social Work, it was accepted as one of the fields with which the present study should be concerned. By this process a list of twenty-four functions was worked out, all of which could be described as social work.[4] In lieu of a verbal definition, this list of functions was accepted as delimitation of the field with which the 1928 study should be concerned.

The delimitation of the field of study was followed by an effort to define each of the twenty-four functions. This problem could not be resolved simply by listing the activities peculiar to each function. An activity that lies within the province of a function in one city may lie outside it in another. Thus in some communities family welfare agencies place unemployed workmen in jobs as a part of social treatment though they do not operate an employment bureau, while in other cities the family welfare societies simply refer unemployed workers to special bureaus created to serve them. The function of institutions yield readily to definition. The difficulties arise chiefly in the cases of non-institutional agencies. The attempts made to meet this problem in each field will be discussed in the chapter relating to that field.

An effort was also made to group the functions so that each of them would fall under one or another of the three main classifications, dependency, delinquency, or illness. This arrangement was attempted, not only because it had been the method used in the studies of 1924 and 1926, but also because there was the hope of effecting combinations in the final tables that would give indices for each of the three major divisions. An examination of the items to be reported in the various fields of work soon proved that it would be hazardous at this stage of development to try to combine the service units of different types of agencies even though they might be operating in the same general field. While it is true that statistical indices may be constructed by combining

[4] The twenty-four functions were: (1) family welfare and relief; (2) non-institutional aid to service and ex-service men and their families; (3) legal aid; (4) non-institutional service for travelers; (5) court work for delinquent and dependent or neglected children; (6) child placing and the institutional care of dependent children; (7) institutional care of delinquent children; (8) institutional care of delinquent young people and adults; (9) care of children in day institutions; (10) non-institutional protective work for delinquent and neglected children or young people; (11) adult probation; (12) free employment service; (13) salvage industries and sheltered employment; (14) temporary shelter for homeless or transient persons; (15) institutional care for aged persons, indigent adults, and chronic invalids; (16) maternity homes; (17) hospital in-patient service; (18) clinic and dispensary out-patient services; (19) city or county non-institutional medical care of the sick poor; (20) medical social service; (21) psychiatric social service; (22) public health nursing; (23) school nursing and school medical inspection; (24) visiting teacher social service.

very unlike units, such as tons of coal and yards of cloth, these measurements both have meanings much more concrete than those prevalent in social work. It seemed doubtful whether there would be real significance, for example, in combining the units of service reported by mothers' aid departments and those rendered by day nurseries, even though both groups are in the last analysis concerned with the relief of dependency. The further difficulty was encountered that certain fields of work cannot be placed in one single category without seriously straining the facts. Thus case work service provided for travelers has often been classified under dependency, though in actual practice Travelers Aid Societies are also concerned with many cases of delinquency. The ultimate decision, therefore, was to develop schedules that would apply to the various functions performed by social agencies and to make no attempt to fit these functions arbitrarily under a general heading such as delinquency or dependency. Each schedule, it was decided, should attempt to cover only clearly defined activity. Thus a blank was developed for juvenile courts that would enable them to report on one form all the work they did both for delinquency and dependents.

On the basis of this policy twenty-four report blanks were prepared which seemed to cover the activities with which the 1928 study was concerned. Some of these fields had been covered in the 1924 and 1926 compilations and others, such as psychiatric social service and visiting teacher work, were now introduced for the first time. Considered as a group, the complete set of schedules seemed to cover, with a few exceptions, the entire range of effort made by social workers in the individualized treatment of dependency, delinquency, and illness.

The preparation of report blanks for these twenty-four fields involved the examination of a considerable body of material that had already been published by national agencies. The advice of statisticians retained by these national bodies was sought and conferences with them were arranged if possible. Some organizations were able to recommend reporting schemes that were likely to fit the needs of their particular fields and others declared that comparatively little uniformity in reporting methods had been achieved within their group. The general policy was to follow closely the reporting systems recommended by the national agencies in fields in which such systems had been developed. In practically every instance the national agency's statistical plan was much more detailed that the needs of the registration required, and the problem was accordingly one of selecting from the scheme those portions that could be reduced to simpler proportions and that would give a measure of volume. Number of days' care given, number of visits made, and other elementary units of similar character were the types of measuring-sticks chosen in each field. In each case the number of items selected was small, and in the end it proved possible to reduce the monthly report form for each type of activity to the dimensions of a convenient card 5 by 8 inches in size. The fact that agencies co-operated in submitting reports much more readily than had been anticipated may have been due to the simple, concise character of the blanks.

The selection of suitable items for the schedules was simpler, however, than the formulating of adequate definitions of terms. The difficulties encountered were of two general types: (1) in some fields units of measurement are in current use which appear to be incapable of verbal definition; (2) in other fields rival definitions of certain terms were found between which a choice had to be made. The first of these problems seemed in some fields practically insoluble on any basis that was statistically sound. Family welfare agencies in all sections of the country, for example, are accustomed to use the terms "major care case" and "minor care case." Both expressions, in spite of numerous efforts to define them, connote different meanings, not only to different agencies but even to different workers within a single agency. Their variability as units of measurement became startlingly apparent in an experiment conducted in the opening months of the registration. Similar discrepancies between definition and interpretation were discovered in medical-social service, in psychiatric social service, and in several other case-working fields. In institutions providing domiciliary care, the basic unit "days' care" has long been accepted and defined. Report blanks for institutions were therefore comparatively easy to construct. The efforts made to define terms in the non-institutional fields will be described in subsequent chapters.

The second problem involved making decisions in questions of a controversial nature. In the field of hospital in-patient service, to cite an instance, there are rival definitions of the terms "pay" and "part-pay." One of these appears to be much sounder than the other, but it also is less widely used and is more difficult to put into operation. In such case the problem was one of determining whether it was better to fall in line with the practice of a majority of the hospitals or to stand with the minority group for a method that in the long run should produce data of superior significance. Wrong decisions were perhaps made on some of these issues. Few, if any, of the definitions were regarded as final, however, and any item remained subject to redefinition if new light could be thrown upon it.

The next step was to formulate a plan for selecting the cities in which to launch the study. It seemed probable that many communities would be interested in entering the registration. An attempt was therefore made to formulate requirements for admission that would not only assure a reasonable standard of performance but that would also limit the area to manageable proportions. The first requirement for admission was that each city agree to appoint a local supervisor who could devote as much time to the local aspects of the undertaking as might be required. Each city was also expected to buy its monthly report blanks from the central office at cost and to use these blanks in assembling the monthly service reports. The most rigorous requirement pertained to the standard of performance that each council would be expected to maintain. Monthly reports covering at least 80 percent of the work done locally in five specified fields and in ten additional fields were required. The five obligatory fields were: (1) family welfare and relief; (2) child-placing and the institutional care of dependent children; (3) hospital in-patient service; (4) clinic and dispensary out-patient service; (5) public health nursing. Some leeway was allowed by permitting a city to count as complete any field in which it had no organized work. Thus a small city with no recognized agency for rendering legal aid was entitled to count the legal aid field as one in which it could meet the requirements. Except in one instance, no city was exempted from trying to report the specified fields.[5]

Some question arose as to what was meant by the expression "80 percent of the work done." Obviously, it would have been disastrous to interpret this requirement as meaning "80 percent of the agencies operating in a particular field," since the organizations included in the missing 20 percent might be the ones that carried the heaviest responsibility. On the other hand, no reliable information was available by which could be determined the proportion of the total amount of work in a city that was handled by an agency that refused to register. It was necessary, in fields in which some agencies refused to co-operate, to reach an estimate of the importance of their work in the total volume of similar activity in the city. Sometimes the local supervisors had information at their disposal by which this percentage could be determined with reasonable accuracy. In other instances information could sometimes be culled from public records or from published reports. Occasionally, when no basis for determining the importance of the program of a non-reporting agency could be established, it was necessary for the local supervisor to decide whether that particular field of work should be entirely omitted or whether sufficient value would accrue to the local council from the assembling of reports to justify asking for them even though no assurance could be given that the figures would be included in the final tables sent out from the central office.

These requirements for participation were outlined in a letter of invitation that was sent out to all cities with federations that are members of the Association of Community Chests and Councils.[6] The cities of the Pacific slope were excluded the first year because budgetary limitations would not permit the travel that would be necessary to institute and supervise the work in those communities.

Responses to the invitation were received from a large number of cities. A majority of the replies indicated a desire to participate, coupled with a realization of inability to do so. Many communities stated frankly that several years' work would probably have to be done before

[5] The one exception was St. Louis which, by arrangement with the Joint Committee, entered the registration under a special plan and agreed to submit reports in only twelve fields.

[6] The number of cities affiliated with the Association of Community Chests and Councils was 300.

their agencies could be relied upon to submit service reports that could be accepted with confidence. Other cities declared that unco-operative agencies in one or more of the obligatory fields made it impossible for them to apply for admission. A considerable number requested permission to buy the standard report forms and declared their intention to put these blanks into operation with a view to qualify-ing later for inclusion in the registration area. This attitude was inter-esting because it indicated a belief that a central bureau for the collection of the statistics of social work was destined to continue as a part of the social structure of the country. In a few cases local councils requested a field visit in order to learn at first hand just what commit-ments they would be making if they identified themselves with the project. When the work finally got under way, 29 cities[7] had affiliated in the registration and several other cities were using the standard forms for their own monthly service reporting. No effort was made by the central office to keep in touch with cities of the latter group either through correspondence or field visits, although all inquiries relative to interpretation of items on the schedules were answered.

It was evident that the success of the study would depend in large measure upon careful field work in the opening months. Accordingly, a visit was made to each city and the items on each schedule were dis-cussed with the local supervisor in the interest of insuring uniform interpretations.[8]

The population of the cities included in the registration area and the numbers of reports expected each month from each city are shown in Chart I. In most cases the local reporting area was not a single legal city but a city with a fringe of suburbs forming a metropolitan area. In a few instances the reporting area was an entire county. The definitions of some of the metropolitan areas raised difficult questions with regard to estimating the population since in certain cases the boundary lines cut across the enumeration districts of the Bureau of the Census. Estimates of the 1920 population of these parts of enumeration districts were reached with the aid of information supplied by local supervisors. Since the latest available census data were eight years old, some doubt may be expressed with regard to the estimated growth between January 1, 1920, and July 1, 1928. The census method of straight line

[7] The cities participating in 1928 were: Akron, Buffalo, Canton, Chicago, Cincinnati, Cleveland, Columbus, Dayton, Denver, Des Moines, Detroit, Grand Rapids, Harrisburg, Indianapolis, Lancaster, Minneapolis, Newark, New Orleans, Omaha, Reading, Richmond, Scranton, Sharon, Sioux City, Springfield (Illinois), Springfield (Ohio), St. Louis, St. Paul, Wichita.

[8] A second opportunity for conference and discussion was provided by the meeting of the National Conference of Social Work which convened in Mem-phis in May. More than twenty of the twenty-nine local supervisors were present at a luncheon meeting and a number of interested workers from non-participating cities also attended. Points that had been causing difficulties in the various cities were brought up for consideration and uniform interpreta-tions were agreed upon.

estimate was used except in the case of a few areas in which sound local opinion agreed that the straight line would yield too large a population figure. Because of the tendency of local groups to overestimate rather than to underestimate population, it seemed safe to accept these modifications. On the other hand, no adjustments were made for some cities which have undoubtedly increased at a faster rate than a straight line increase. Some degree of error must therefore be expected in the case rates per thousand population computed upon these estimates of population.

The total population of the registration area was estimated to be 13,031,000 as of July 1, 1928. For the local reporting areas the populations ranged from 55,000 in Sharon, Pennsylvania, to 3,129,000 in Chicago. The area included 6 cities of less than 100,000, 9 of 100,000 but less than 250,000, 8 of 250,000 but less than 500,000, 3 of 500,000 but less than one million, and 3 of more than one million. The local reporting areas were distributed among six of the nine main geographical divisions of the United States.[9] No local areas were included from the New England, East South Central, and Pacific divisions. The registration area included slightly more than 1 percent of the entire population of the United States.[10] The cities included in the area are believed to be representative of the large manufacturing cities, medium-sized cities with a single dominant industry, such as rubber or iron and steel manufacturing, transportation centers with more diversified industries, and centers of agricultural population.

The number of social agencies, and hence the number of reports due each month, might be expected to vary to a certain extent with the size of the city. That this is true only to a limited degree is shown by Figure 1. The Cincinnati area, with about half the population of the Cleveland area and one-third the population of the Detroit area, had a larger number of reports to submit each month than either of these cities. Likewise, in number of reports expected, Minneapolis exceeded Buffalo and St. Paul exceeded Newark, although their respective populations vary inversely. The number of reports due from a city indicates the number of administrative units among which the various social work functions are distributed. This number, however, may exceed the number of separately incorporated agencies. Thus, a family welfare society operating an institution for the temporary shelter of homeless or transient persons submits two reports, although in a sensus of social agencies it would probably be counted as only one organization. The comparative number of reports expected from these cities indicates either the degree of diversity in the social services offered or else reflects decentralization of certain functions among a number of administrative units.

[9] The geographical divisions referred to are those of the United States Census Bureau.

[10] Comparing the population as reported by the United States Census in 1920.

Figure 1    **Population of Cities in the Registration Area for Social Statistics and Number of Reports Expected Each Month During 1928.**

| Metropolitan area | Population (estimated) July 1, 1928 | Number of reports expected each month | Number of reports expected |
|---|---|---|---|
| Chicago | 3,120,000 | 335 | |
| Cincinnati | 523,000 | 150 | |
| Detroit | 1,688,000 | 138 | |
| Cleveland | 1,174,000 | 138 | |
| Minneapolis | 459,000 | 123 | |
| Buffalo | 727,000 | 111 | |
| New Orleans | 429,000 | 105 | |
| St. Paul | 283,000 | 89 | |
| Newark | 473,000 | 87 | |
| Denver | 294,000 | 73 | |
| Columbus | 339,000 | 70 | |
| Omaha | 215,000 | 69 | |
| Richmond | 245,000 | 67 | |
| Grand Rapids | 150,000 | 60 | |
| Des Moines | 162,000 | 58 | |
| Indianapolis | 385,000 | 54 | |
| St. Louis[1] | 965,000 | 50 | |
| Scranton | 167,000 | 49 | |
| Wichita | 90,000 | 48 | |
| Sioux City | 80,000 | 47 | |
| Canton | 180,000 | 46 | |
| Reading | 148,000 | 44 | |
| Dayton | 219,000 | 41 | |
| Akron | 260,000 | 40 | |
| Springfield, Ill. | 66,000 | 34 | |
| Lancaster | 61,000 | 30 | |
| Harrisburg | 102,000 | 30 | |
| Springfield, O. | 73,000 | 27 | |
| Sharon | 55,000 | 20 | |

The horizontal scale for "Number of reports expected" runs from 0, 100, 200, 300.

[1] St. Louis entered the registration in only 12 fields rather than 24 fields.

A total of 2,231 reports each month, or 26,772 for the year, should have been received. The actual accomplishment is shown in Table 1. Of the 2,231 agencies expected to report, 1,978 reported at least once, and of the 26,772 reports expected for the year, 22,642, or 84.6 percent, were actually received. In addition, estimates that appeared to be reasonably accurate were received for 13 agencies which could not submit reports.

In the following chapters the results of the tabulation of the monthly reports are presented. The figures represent the amount of work done and do not necessarily, of course, measure the extent of the need. Moreover, it is possible that the cities included in the registration are better organized for social work than other cities and may not be typical of the country at large. Conclusions with regard to social work in other cities should therefore be drawn with extreme caution. An effort has been made to present for each field the total number of different cases cared for during the year, and some one unit that could

Table 1 **Percentage Received of Monthly Reports Expected from Cities in the Registration Area for Social Statistics during 1928**

| Metropolitan Area | Number of Reports Expected | Received Percentage |
|---|---|---|
| Total | 26,772 | 84.6 |
| Akron | 480 | 77.1 |
| Buffalo | 1,332 | 99.2 |
| Canton | 552 | 74.8 |
| Chicago | 4,020 | 58.5 |
| Cincinnati | 1,800 | 93.2 |
| Cleveland | 1,656 | 94.2 |
| Columbus | 840 | 87.4 |
| Dayton | 492 | 99.6 |
| Denver | 876 | 84.8 |
| Des Moines | 696 | 69.4 |
| Detroit | 1,656 | 98.0 |
| Grand Rapids | 770 | 91.7 |
| Harrisburg | 360 | 87.5 |
| Indianapolis | 648 | 61.3 |
| Lancaster | 360 | 96.7 |
| Minneapolis | 1,476 | 88.6 |
| Newark | 1,044 | 89.4 |
| New Orleans | 1,236 | 91.1 |
| Omaha | 828 | 99.5 |
| Reading | 528 | 96.8 |
| Richmond | 804 | 73.1 |
| Scranton | 588 | 50.3 |
| Sharon | 240 | 99.6 |
| Sioux City | 564 | 99.1 |
| Springfield, Ill. | 408 | 90.2 |
| Springfield, Ohio | 324 | 78.4 |
| St. Louis | 600 | 89.5 |
| St. Paul | 1,068 | 98.4 |
| Wichita | 576 | 97.7 |

be compared with confidence from city to city. The last consideration mentioned—comparison from city to city—has led to a greater use of monthly averages than would otherwise be desirable. The total number of days' care given during the year, for example, is probably, for a single city, a better measure of service rendered than the average monthly number of days' care. Since in many cases, however, the reports for one month of the year were incomplete, an average for the eleven months reported has been used for the sake of comparison with an average for twelve months reported by another city. Care has been taken to use these averages only when the missing months seemed not to subject to extreme variation. In no case were averages computed for less than six months. An alternative method would have been to estimate the missing figures for each agency. This method, however, would have obscured what seemed to be for the first year's report an important fact—the relative completeness of the data.

## Chapter Summary

This chapter presented a patch-quilt overview of the infrastructure of social welfare statistics—with perhaps more holes than patches. The picture is a spotty one, with many starts and stops along the way, and there is obviously a long way yet to go before an adequate quantitative data base is available for social planning and research purposes.

Three types of social welfare statistics were identified at the outset—statistics of services, statistics of clients, and statistics of need. The first two are closely interrelated, while the third is an essentially separate dimension of measurement independent of the other two. The evolution of each kind of social work data was traced in the preceding pages.

Perhaps the first major attempt to get at statistics of social needs and conditions was made in the decennial federal census, roughly between 1850 and 1900. Information was sought by the official census takers regarding the incidence of pauperism, idiocy, blindness, and so on in the general population. This mass approach to obtaining statistics of social problems was abandoned by 1900, largely because of the reluctance of people to stigmatize themselves or their relatives in this way. Thereafter the U.S. Bureau of the Census has concentrated on special statistics of social services, compiled mainly from institutional populations of various types. More recently, in the 1970 census, a renewed effort was made (more successful this time) to obtain data relevant to welfare concerns, such as poverty, working mothers, and characteristics of the aged.

The "modern era" in statistics of social services did not begin, however, until the rise of central coordinating structures within the field adequate to the task of obtaining some degree of stand-ardization among participating agencies. The first development, before 1900, took place at the state level under the auspices of state boards of charity and corrections. Later the development of national professional associations in social work in the 1910s, of local community chests and councils in the 1920s, and of federal participation in public assistance and social security pro-grams during the 1930s each provided significant impetus to the improvement of statistical reporting within the segment of the field involved. In the private agency field, the major national effort in the standardization of statistics was the Registration of Social Statistics Project, launched in 1927 by the University of Chicago and the Association of Community Chests and Councils. The plan was based on the concept of the "registration area" in vital statistics and required local reporting of 80 percent of services in at least 15 out of 24 defined program fields. At its height several dozen cities were participating on this basis. How-ever, the burdens of local coordination and national supervision proved too great to manage. National collection and coordination of agency service statistics on a community-wide basis by the United Community Funds and Councils of America was finally abandoned in the mid-1950s. At present, community-wide agency service reporting is limited to a few urban areas and continues to be plagued by problems of definition and administration. Nevertheless certain specialized service statistics are effectively centralized by the major national voluntary organizations, such as the Family Service Association of America and the Child Welfare League of America.

In the public welfare field, easily the greatest boost to statistical reporting came with the passage of the Social Security Act in 1935. Before this the states had generally succeeded in obtaining standardization in relief statistics on an intrastate basis. Now, however, an interstate pattern was set up, with the support and sanction of federal authority, whereby monthly reports were col-lected and published, providing uniform data on volume of service and expenditure in the various categories of assistance and other public programs. Thus a major objective that the early National Conferences had long called for was finally realized through the introduction of federal financing and authority into the state welfare picture.

Particular attention was given to the special and influential role of the U.S. Children's Bureau in the strengthening of social work statistics and research pertaining to children.

The second half of the chapter capsuled the uneven develop-ment of indexes in social work. These are composite statistical measures that purport to reflect "social needs," "social problems," or "social welfare provisions." The first index in social work was developed in 1917 by I. M. Rubinow in an attempt to measure the fluctuations in "dependency" in New York City and, it was hoped, to throw light on its causes and consequences. While this short-lived experiment fell short of its goals, it demonstrated the technical potentiality of constructing indexes based on social work data and relevant to social problems. At the same time, it revealed a number of the characteristic limitations of such measures. A major weakness of this early venture, which was to be repeated in some later ones, lay in its attempt to infer "need" from data regarding services. While needs and services are related, to be sure, the connection is much too tenuous and subject to too many extraneous influences to be very useful.

Perhaps the major effort along these lines thus far in social work was the "social breakdown index," which gained some popularity in the late 1930s and early 1940s. The idea here was to provide an instrument for the "measurement and control" of social breakdown, which was defined as "behavior that does not conform to currently accepted concepts of satisfactory social adjustment." The measurement, however, was achieved by combining in arbitrary fashion seven different rates based on official records (such as divorce, delinquency, etc.) and assuming that this composite reflected the broad range of social maladjustment in the community. In addition, the authors of this device went on to advocate that this index be used not only as a measure of social needs, thus confounding needs with services, but also as a gauge of the effectiveness of existing services, apparently on the dubious assumption that social agencies could be held substantially accountable for the amount of official breakdown that occurred in a community. It is to the credit of the field's common sense and growing research maturity that this overly ambitious approach was quickly recognized as deficient in many respects and was subjected to penetrating and effective critique in the literature.

The first experiments with rates and indexes in social work in the 1920s and 1930s was on a community-wide basis in making overall comparisons from year to year and city to city. Later, with the rise of community planning for welfare services, increased emphasis was given to smaller-area rates and indexes, computed for census tracts, neighborhoods, or other subdivisions of an urban area. Along with this shift in emphasis to intracity area indexes of need on a geographic basis, a number of refinements in index construction in social work have been made. The variability of index factors has been subjected to better control through use of standard scores and percentiles. The problem of determining proper weights for the different factors has been tackled, though not fully solved. In addition, the specialized geographic index of need has made its appearance, affording an opportunity for a more specific and meaningful selection of component factors than that offered by the traditional index used to identify clusters of area characteristics along significant dimensions for planning purposes.

A number of technical weaknesses of the social index were noted. These include (1) the arbitrary selection of items entering into the index, (2) the arbitrary weighting of these factors, (3) the limitations of the source materials utilized, (4) the heterogeneity of the demographic areas for which indexes are computed and compared, (5) the questionable statistical significance of some of the differences observed between area rates and indexes, and (6) the necessarily relative nature of the measure they provide. In addition, the primarily subjective nature of the notion of social need itself requires clearer conceptualization.

Despite such shortcomings, social indexes continue to be developed and utilized, increasingly now on the state and national level. The recent interest in "social indicators" as a yardstick of social health and progress is the latest manifestation of the persistent importance of the goal of quantification in social welfare.

In conclusion, it seems that the long-sought ideal of unified, uniform sets of social work statistics for administrative, planning, and research purposes may well have to await sufficient central authority and resources—probably at the federal level, as Wayne McMillen foresaw half a century ago. Only in this way is the necessary support and cooperation up and down the line likely to be obtained. Until that time we should be prepared to accept the limitations and frustrations of a more or less piecemeal, ad hoc pattern of data coverage as one of the necessary costs of our diversified, pluralistic pattern of social services.

The chapter incorporated an extended excerpt from McMillen's comprehensive plan for a multicity program of social service statistics in the late 1920s—the so-called Registration of Social Statistics Project.

### Appendix: Some Current Statistical Sources

Major national social welfare statistics are now published regularly in the federal periodicals—*Social Security Bulletin, Welfare in Review* (now *Human Needs*), and *Health, Education, and Welfare Trends,* in the Council on Social Work Education *Statistics,* and in the NASW *Encyclopedia of Social Work* section on "Statistics."[78]

The National Center for Social Statistics of the Social and Rehabilitation Service of the Department of Health, Education and Welfare was established in 1968 to centralize and coordinate many of the data series related to social welfare (including some of the statistical reports previously compiled by the U.S. Children's Bureau). It may be addressed directly regarding specific data needs and interests of researchers. A parallel National Center for Health Statistics is available. The Bureau of the Census and the Bureau of Labor Statistics are of course also major sources of data relevant to social work. The periodic Current Population Survey samplings of the Bureau of the Census report unemployment data monthly and income data annually, including poverty statistics (series P-60).

## NOTES

[1] Ralph G. Hurlin, "Statistics of Social Work," *Social Work Year Book,* 1929, p. 443.

[2] Thane Miller, "Remarks," *Proceedings of the National Conference of Charities and Corrections,* 1880, p. 319.

[3] Isaac M. Kerlin, "Provision for Idiotic and Feeble-Minded Children," *Proceedings of the National Conference of Charities and Corrections,* 1884, p. 247.

[4] *Dictionary of American Biography,* XX, 386.

[5] Fred H. Wines, "Statistical Report," *Proceedings of the Conference of Charities,* 1881, p. 197.

[6] Charles R. Henderson, "Outdoor Relief: Conditions, Methods, and Statistics," *Proceedings of the National Conference of Charities and Corrections,* 1894, p. 110.

[7] Howard B. Myers, "Research and Statistics in Social Work," *Social Work Year Book,* 1939, p. 378.

[8] Hurlin, p. 443.

[9] Katherine Lenroot, "Government Provision for Social Work Statistics on a National Scale," *Proceedings of the National Conference of Social Work,* 1931, p. 415.

[10] Frank J. Bruno, *Trends in Social Work* (New York: Columbia University Press, 1948), p. 30.

[11] F. B. Sanborn, "Statistics of Pauperism in the United States," *Proceedings of the Conference of Charities,* 1877, p. 28.

[12] Ibid., p. 26.

[13] Oscar M. McCulloch, "Presidential Address," *Proceedings of the National Conference of Charities and Corrections,* 1891, p. 16.

[14] Henderson, p. 108.

[15] Sanborn, p. 21.

[16] Amos W. Butler, "Report of Committee on Statistics," *Proceedings of the National Conference of Charities and Corrections,* 1906, p. 416.

[17] *United States Statutes* 633 (1936), Title V, Part 1.

[18] Ralph G. Hurlin, "Statistics in the Administration of a Public Welfare Program," *Proceedings of the National Conference of Social Work,* 1938, p. 566.

[19] Ralph G. Hurlin, "Some Results of Two Years' Study of Family Case

Work Statistics," *Proceedings of the National Conference of Social Work,* 1928, p. 248.

[20] Hurlin, "Statistics of Social Work," pp. 442–446.

[21] Wayne McMillen and Helen R. Jeter, "Statistical Terminology in the Family Welfare Field," *Social Service Review,* 2 (September 1928): 358.

[22] John Mark Glenn et al., *Russell Sage Foundation 1907–1946* (New York: Russell Sage Foundation, 1947), I, 412.

[23] Raymond F. Clapp, "Research as an Aid in Promoting Scientific Social Work," *Proceedings of the National Conference of Social Work,* 1928, p. 556.

[24] Raymond F. Clapp, "Tax and Contribution Support of Social Work: Facts as Revealed by the Study of Volume and Cost of Social Work," *National Conference of Social Work,* 1926, pp. 449–457.

[25] Wayne A. McMillen, *Measurement in Social Work* (Chicago: University of Chicago Press, 1939), p. 7.

[26] Ibid., p. 8.

[27] Ibid., p. 9.

[28] Ibid., p. 17.

[29] "In the 25th Year of the Social Statistics Project in Chicago, 1928–1952," *Statistics,* 29 (February 1952): 2.

[30] Ibid., p. 3.

[31] McMillen, p. 148.

[32] Grace Abbott, *The Child and the State* (Chicago: University of Chicago Press, 1931), I, 621.

[33] *The Children's Bureau* (Washington, D.C.: GPO, 1929), pamphlet, p. 2.

[34] Hurlin, "Statistics of Social Work," p. 498.

[35] For an early and penetrating challenge to official juvenile delinquency data—which still applies today—see the excellent empirical study by a leading social work researcher, Sophia M. Robison, *Can Delinquency Be Measured?* (New York: Columbia University Press, 1936).

[36] Emma O. Lundberg, "White House Conferences," *Social Work Year Book,* 1941, p. 593.

[37] White House Conference on Child Health and Protection, *The Delinquent Child* (New York: Century, 1932), p. 235.

[38] Emil Frankel, "Government Provision for Social Work Statistics on a National Scale," *Proceedings of the National Conference of Social Work,* 1931, p. 405.

[39] Lundberg, p. 595.

[40] Hurlin, "Statistics of Social Work," p. 444.

[41] I. M. Rubinow, "A National Dependency Index," *The Survey,* April 1919, p. 78.

[42] Hurlin, "Statistics of Social Work," p. 444.

[43] Rubinow, p. 77.

[44] Ibid., p. 78.

[45] Hurlin, "Statistics of Social Work" p. 444.

[46] Rubinow, p. 79.

[47] Glenn et al., II, 411.

[48] McMillen, p. 12.

[49] Bradley Buell, *Social Breakdown: A Plan for Measurement and Control* (New York: Community Chests and Councils, 1939).

[50] Ibid., p. ix.

[51] Ibid., p. 12.

[52] Ibid., p. 11.

[53] Ibid., p. 38.

[54] Ralph Carr Fletcher, "Research and Statistics in Social Work," *Social Work Year Book,* 1947, p. 439.

[55] Kenneth L. M. Pray, "Quantitative Measurement of the Community's Needs and Services," *Proceedings of the National Conference of Social Work,* 1940, p. 443.

[56] Ibid., p. 442.

[57] Ibid., p. 443.

[58] Ibid., p. 438.

[59] Ibid., p. 440.

[60] Ibid., p. 441.

[61] Buell, *Social Breakdown,* p. 20.

[62] Ralph G. Hurlin et al., "Symposium on 'Social Breakdown.' " *The Family,* 21 (January 1941): 288–293.

[63] See, for example, *Recreation for Everybody* (Los Angeles: Welfare Council of Metropolitan Los Angeles, January 1946); Bertram J. Black, *Our Welfare Needs* (New York: Greater New York Fund, 1949); Virginia Kann White, *Measuring Social Needs* (Cleveland: Western Reserve University, 1951); *Greater Boston Community Survey, 1947–1949* (Boston: Committee of Citizens, February 1949); *Youth Project Yardstick: Measuring Youth Service Needs* (Los Angeles: Welfare Council of Metropolitan Los Angeles, 1953).

[64] *Greater Boston Community Survey.*

[65] White, op. cit.

[66] *Youth Project Yardstick,* p. 18.

[67] Virginia Kann White, *Measuring Leisure Time Needs* (Cleveland: Welfare Federation of Cleveland, February 1955), p. 49; see also Shirley Jenkins, *Comparative Recreation Needs and Services in New York Neighborhoods* (New York: Community Service Council of Greater N.Y. City, 1963).

[68] Eshref Shevsky and Marilyn Williams, *The Social Areas of Los Angeles* (Berkeley: University of California Press, 1949).

[69] Elisabeth R. Frank and Herbert R. Larsen, *Differentiating Communities in Los Angeles County* (Los Angeles: Welfare Planning Council, January 1957).

[70] U.S., Department of Health, Education and Welfare, *Toward a Social Report* (Washington, D.C.: GPO, 1969).

[71] Howard E. Freeman and Eleanor Bernert Sheldon, "Social Indicators," in Robert Morris, ed., *Encyclopedia of Social Work: Sixteenth Issue* (New York: NASW, 1971), pp. 1273–1277.

[72] *Toward a Social Report,* p. 97.

[73] Ibid., p. 1276.

[74] Ibid.

[75] Office of Management and Budget, *Social Indicators: 1973* (Washington, D.C.: GPO, 1973).

[76] Ibid., pp. 165–170.

[77] See Leonard S. Kogan and Shirley Jenkins, *Indicators of Child Health and Welfare: Development of the DIPOV Index* (New York: Columbia University Press, 1974).

[78] Paul Schreiber, "Statistics," in Robert Morris, ed., *Encyclopedia of Social Work* (New York: National Association of Social Workers, 1971), 11, 1567–1612. For additional detail and background, see Paul Schreiber, "Statistical Data in Social Work and Social Welfare," in ibid., pp. 1559–1566. See also Ann W. Shyne, "Exploiting Available Information," in Norman A. Polansky, ed., *Social Work Research,* rev. ed. (Chicago: University of Chicago Press, 1975), pp. 109–130.

# Chapter 7
# Evaluative Research in Social Work: The Background

## Introduction

While an entire book might usefully be written on most of the topics to which single chapters are devoted in this text, evaluative research would undoubtedly justify several texts. The burgeoning of evaluative studies in this field—particularly in the 1960s and 1970s—has swamped the research literature and has increasingly dominated professional research interest.[1] A growing number of books on the subject have been published in social work,[2] and many more in closely related social science areas.

As we shall see, this research theme in social work goes back to the early 1900s, but it has veritably exploded in recent years, so that it would be unrealistic to try to do justice to this massive content within the scope of the present volume. Therefore we will endeavor to bring the story up to date through the mid-1960s, when the efforts reached the "takeoff point" with many new directions and developments; we will not attempt any systematic coverage thereafter. A bit of "distance" is important to historical perspective, and in the case of a fast-changing and dynamic specialization such as evaluative research in social work this is especially desirable. In any event, only in this way does the author feel that his task would be manageable within the confines of a textbook chapter.

Thus this chapter should be viewed as a historical backdrop to the "modern era," in which evaluative research has moved to the forefront of the scientific arena in social work. It is hoped that it will add perspective to the student's understanding of the current efforts, in terms of both their roots and their prospects for success.

## Early Interest in the Problem

Implicit in many of the early discussions of research in social work was the idea that with the development of statistical and scientific methods in the field there would emerge knowledge regarding the effectiveness of social work practice. This thought underlay much of the quest for causation in the last century, since it was believed, logically enough, that more adequate knowledge of the etiology of social pathology would point the way to more effective treatment and prevention. As had been noted, the early development of social work statistics owed some of its impetus to the hope that more accurate and comprehensive statistical data would permit the evaluation of practice methods. The purpose of constructing rates and indexes in social work was frequently seen in terms of their potential usefulness in revealing the effectiveness of programs (see Chapter 6). Indeed "scientific charity" and the concern with causation at the birth of social work research was motivated in part, as we have seen, by the hope of thereby finding the Rosetta Stone of cure and prevention (see Chapter 3).

Thus significant interest was attached to the question of social work effectiveness from the very beginnings of research development in the field. However, this concern did not reach expression in the form of productive study until recent decades. It is interesting to speculate on the reasons for the relatively late emergence of evaluative research in social work. (In her influential 1950 article "Obstacles to Evaluative Research in Casework" Margaret Blenkner pointed to a number of likely barriers.[3]) It may not be coincidental that this type of research emerged with the rise of federated financing in social work in the 1920s, with its call for "businesslike" methods and results. Thus it was optimistically stated in 1928 that "the day when a clear and precise evaluation of social work should be available is approaching if it has not already arrived. The extensive adoption of the community fund method of financing social work has apparently precipitated the issue."[4] Prior to this time the more intimate contact between an agency's patrons and its work may have usually provided sufficient confidence in the value of its efforts, whereas now it became necessary to provide more tangible evidence.

## Attitudes Toward Evaluative Research

In a number of areas the history of social work research in the United States reveals an inner dialectic of action and reaction, advance and retreat, optimism and skepticism. In earlier discussions of causal research, social surveys, quantification and elsewhere, it has been observed that along with many of the trends in research in this field there has been a countermovement of doubt and skepticism. In many instances this protest has been based constructively on specific weaknesses and inadequacies of the study approach under consideration; social work has often been its own best critic in this regard, and its research conservatism has frequently served to protect its sensitive subject matter from premature assault by crude, ill-fitting methods. Often, however, the reaction has been an extreme one, questioning the applicability of research methods to major portions of its content. Nowhere is the latter tendency more evident than in the area of evaluative research.[5]

As early as 1908 a discussant of a paper by C. C. Carstens at the National Conference expressed the following opinion regarding a study of results in children's work: "Those are the most intangible and invisible results, and probably never can be classified."[6] This viewpoint was given sanction in an editorial statement by Margaret E. Rich that appeared in *The Family**\* in 1926. She confessed "a doubt whether we can ever even theoretically show any exact data as to the end results of case work, especially where we consider all the other possible community forces and influences."[7] The underlying basis of this doubt was summed up as follows:

> Our fear of statistics—of quantitative evaluation only—is probably partly due to some such feeling as James Stephens voices when he says: "We have labelled these . . . and with the label we have thrown overboard more of the mystery than we could afford to live with."[8]

In the same year, 1926, Frank J. Bruno took up a position on the same general ground, though not committing himself beyond the contemporary status of the research art:

\* *The Family* was the predecessor journal of *Social Casework,* sponsored by the Family Service Association of America.

It seems to me we must candidly face the fact that at present objective data do not help much in estimating the tasks which social case work assumes or in evaluating the results of its efforts. Our means of description are subjective evaluations: the expression of our judgments respecting situations and progress.[9]

His conclusion, read before the National Conference in 1926, was that "the real objective test of case work is an honestly and dramatically described case story."[10]

The much-quoted Presidential Address before the 1931 Conference by Richard C. Cabot, in which he implored the field to apply itself to the evaluation of its methods (see p. 237), did not pass unchallenged. At the same Conference David Holbrook made the following reply:

Dr. Cabot has told us that not to evaluate our work is dangerous. Even more hazardous in my judgment are processes of evaluation expressed in terms of an ultimate professional achievement rather than a social need. . . .

Any hint of setting up a final quantitative goal for evaluating an art increases the hazards of practising the art, whether it be in the field of music, painting, or human relations.[11]

The general viewpoint expressed by these writers, while never more than a minor voice in the literature, explains a good deal of the profession's "passive resistance" to evaluative research over the years. The concern appears to be that the scientific method cannot do justice to the delicate qualitative stuff out of which the fabric of human relations is woven. Margaret Blenkner has interpreted such opposition in terms of psychological, economic, social, and methodological factors.[12] It would appear, further, to be related to the philosophic issue, that is, the proper role of the scientific method in the testing of a social art.

However, the scientific devotees always outweighed the doubters in the mainstream of social work. The prevailing note has been clearly on the side of the scientific approach since the very first National Conference in 1874. The optimistic, rationalistic point of view could be heard on every hand. It was expressed, as we have seen, in the late 1800s in the "philanthropology" of Amos G. Warner; after the turn of the century C. C. Carstens expressed it as follows:

It is only when this work of studying results is given a share of . . . time . . . that we can hope to defend the faith that is in us, or what is more likely to be the case, modify our theories in many important particulars, nay, build a new philosophy in a number of fields upon the sure foundation of facts.[13]

The skeptical attitude was squarely addressed in such statements as "Social case workers cannot indefinitely excuse their lack of accuracy, when asked to state results, by answering that they are dealing with the intangible. Personality is a reality. . . ."[14] and "Those intangibles of personality held but yesterday to be sacred mysteries beyond our ken are now the quantitative materials of the new psychology."[15] But perhaps the best known and most effective of these affirmations of importance and feasibility of evaluative research in social work came from Richard C. Cabot in his Presidential Address before the 1931 National Conference of Social Work, referred to earlier. While not minimizing the difficulties involved, he nevertheless exhorted social agencies "to make more of these fallible judgments, to expose themselves more often to the dangers of statistics, to the risks which come to light when we announce and apply the criteria by which we believe our success or failure may be judged." He then went on to his famous challenge: "I appeal to you—social workers of the country. . . . Measure, evaluate, estimate, appraise your results. . . ."[16]

## A Definition and Framework for Evaluative Research

The term *evaluative research* has been used in a variety of ways in social work. It sometimes refers to the study of the effectiveness of practice in accomplishing its "outcome" objectives; sometimes to the adequacy of program facilities and personnel in the light of accepted standards; sometimes to the adequacy of the volume of "output" in a given community in relation to needs; and so on. Our focus here will be on the first of these usages; the second is considered as primarily a form of administrative study of "service input" rather than "outcome"; and the third as a type of social survey.

By *evaluative research,* then, we shall here mean the study of the extent to which a social service program is contributing to defined goals of client* change (i.e., "outcome"). Some writers object to the linking of the concepts of "evaluation" and "research" on the grounds that research cannot deal directly with

---

* The term *client* is used here in the generic sense of recipient of social services, (or *client system*) whether it refers to an individual, a group, or a community.

"values" and that the process of "valuing" is apart from the scientific method. Thus Isaac Hoffman criticized the phrase "evaluative research" as a "semantic monstrosity" and a "logical contradiction."[17] While a strong case can be made for this view, and some other phrase (such as "measuring the effect of social intervention"[18]) might be more defensible, usage and simplicity seem to have sanctioned this terminology, and it now appears likely to stick.

The conceptual and technical problems confronting evaluative research in this field are many and highly ramified; perhaps no other type of social work research is so difficult and slippery to grasp and keep a fix on.* Because of its many subtleties and complications, an attempt will be made here to provide a heuristic framework for the analysis and understanding of the studies to be discussed in the following pages.[19]

## 1. IDENTIFICATION OF SERVICE OBJECTIVES

The logical starting point in evaluative research is the articulation of the program objectives for client change (or outcome) in as specific and operational terms as possible. This requirement was recognized as early as 1931 by Dr. Cabot[20] and has since been regularly urged in the research literature. In effect, the explication of program objectives becomes the basis for the "hypothesis" to be tested by the typical evaluative study; that is, the program intervention does (or does not—in the "null" version of the hypothesis) make the desired difference in client outcome. Thus the study hypothesis is "given," once the program objectives are properly delineated.

However, despite the repeated emphasis on its importance, the definition of service goals and objectives has not always been adequately spelled out for the purposes of evaluative research in social work. Such goals are necessarily implicit in any piece of evaluative research, indeed in any piece of practice, for without such direction one would have no basis for decision or action. The task of making these objectives explicit, however, is no mean one. For if they are to be useful for research, they must be in sufficiently operational form to permit accurate application to concrete situations. Broad, democratic, humanitarian principles

---

* In 1960 Martin Wolins noted that this type of study, "perhaps the most difficult to accomplish, seems also to have been in greatest demand." Martin Wolins, "Measuring the Effects of Social Work Intervention," in Norman A. Polansky, ed., *Social Work Research* (Chicago: University of Chicago Press, 1960), p. 247.

do not readily lend themselves to use as scientific yardsticks, however valid or significant they may be as professional ideals. While goals and objectives are ultimately based on such general values or ideals, it is necessary to translate the ends of service into observable terms for research purposes.*

It is also important here to distinguish between the end goals of a program and the range of "subgoals" that may be identified en route to them. Edward Suchman discusses the concept of a "hierarchy" of goals, which is helpful in clarifying such inter-relationships.[21] Thus the goal of a marital counseling service may be the increase of positive communication and affection between man and wife; subgoals may include their acceptance for joint counseling by the agency, their continuation in treatment for a series of counseling sessions, and so on. Subgoals of this type may be interpreted for our purposes as "service output" rather than "service outcome."[22]

Finally, it may be briefly noted that there is a relatively new strategy of evaluative research that places less emphasis on the identification of service goals as a basis for program assessment in relation to those goals. This is the "systems model" approach, which sharply differentiates itself from the more traditional "goal attainment model" we are stressing in this chapter.[23] The emphasis in this alternative design is on description and analysis of the program operation as a whole, including its objectives and outcomes as one of many facets of institutional maintenance and survival. This type of evaluation also places less weight on experimental manipulation and more on observation, participation, and continuing feedback into the system. However, it appears to the author that conceptual and methodological limitations at this stage in the development of the systems approach make it a less objective and hence less verifiable process than might be desirable for extensive research use. Further experience with this promising scientific strategy is urgently needed.

## 2. STANDARDIZATION OF SERVICE CONTENT

In any attempt to relate a given activity to its consequences, a clear and uniform definition of the activity and its constituent elements is essential. Unless there is such a standardization of content, which is adhered to throughout the study, any relationship may be found to exist between service and outcome is a

---

* In this connection Wolins proposed a distinction between the "effects" of services (changes regardless of direction) and their "effectiveness" (changes in the desired or "valued" direction). See Wolins, pp. 247–248.

relationship with an "unknown" variable and cannot be used for specific causal interpretation purposes. Betram Black made this point very explicitly before the 1950 National Conference:

> I have one reservation about research in measuring the effectiveness of a casework, social group work, or treatment service: there needs to be much more objectivism and standardization in the process itself than there is at present before any research techniques are likely to yield valid or reliable results in measuring effectiveness.[24]

Social work practice has yet to reach the point at which it is possible to state with sufficient certainty precisely *what* it is that a client has received in a given treatment situation. This identification may be possible, say, in medicine, where a given amount of a tested drug may be administered in a specific manner, or in certain types of social work, where the service is a tangible one, such as financial assistance. As soon as the element of *relationship* enters in, however, one is confronted with a subjective and interactional process that depends on the personality, background, and intentions of the worker, those of the client, and the unique melding between these kaleidoscopic forces. How, then, shall one describe the *unit* of service received? It may be possible to state that a treatment relationship has been established, but the concepts and techniques to assess its quality and intensity with scientific accuracy remain nebulous. In a very real sense, therefore, the social worker does not "intervene" unilaterally but, rather, offers the client or client system an *opportunity* to respond, relate, react in a constructive way. Social work is thus a bilateral or multilateral process, and the client (or client system) may be said to "intervene" voluntarily with himself (or itself) as much as the practitioner does. This crucial mutuality of interaction obviously introduces great complexity into the study and practice of a helping profession and makes the problem of evaluation extremely difficult. The great advantage of the physical and medical sciences, in which an experimental "treatment" can be administered unilaterally in uniform, interchangeable units, does not readily obtain in the social sphere, and therein lies a deep dilemma and challenge for social research.

Only relatively recently has some progress been made in conceptualizing types and levels of treatment in social casework.[25] This type of clarification needs to be carried much further so that content of practice may be adequately controlled and identified for research purposes.

Implied in the foregoing discussion of standardization in social service delivery* is the notion of *stability* of program content. Assuming that a program is sufficiently described and measured for evaluation research purposes, it is obviously also necessary that this service description and measurement hold good for a sufficient length of time to be expected to show results. If the program is rapidly evolving and changing, then one is in effect "shooting at a moving target" in attempting to evaluate it. Ideally speaking, a program should "stand still"—that is, operate in a stable fashion—for a period of months or (better yet) years in order to provide a suitable plateau for assessing its outcome.

In many cases, however, this ideal does not apply, and there are "levels" of program appraisal that can be used but fall substantially short of the full evaluation contemplated in this chapter. This situation frequently arises, for example, in demonstration programs that may be mounted for a year or two, and in other new or reorganized service approaches. The type of appraisal that is feasible in such cases is on the order of investigations of program inputs (resources, facilities, personnel) or program outputs (number of clients reached, interviews, group sessions, etc.) rather than "outcomes" in terms of client change.[26]

## 3. DESCRIPTION OF SERVICE RECIPIENTS AND TARGET CONDITIONS

The preceding two planks in our evaluative framework dealt primarily with *service* characteristics; this and the following ones pertain to the other side of the coin, that is, the *recipient* of service, and the resulting changes that may take place within the client system or its problem conditions. Many of the points made earlier in relation to the need for uniform decription of the service input apply with equal force to the service target. For if the service is standardized and stable but the clientele is not, then there will be similar difficulties in interpreting and generalizing from the findings. It is therefore equally important that the service recipients and problems be specified and stabilized before undertaking formal evaluation of the type addressed in these pages. Otherwise a less advanced level of appraisal would probably be more appropriate.

---

* The currently popular term *delivery* in reference to social services is perhaps as inappropriate as the widely used "intervention," and for the reason noted earlier, namely, the imputation of unilateral action rather than mutuality.

## 4. MEASUREMENT OF CHANGE

There are a number of important points to be considered here. If the goals are adequately defined, the service standardized, and the clientele delineated, we may turn next to the elements of change.

First, then, what are the sources of data—the nature of the evidence—regarding change in the client system? In many types of social work evaluation the essential information is obtained from agency records or by interview. In either case there is usually only a single observer available to provide a firsthand account of the object of study. Moreover, these observations are usually screened onto a case record or schedule by the primary observer, and in some instances are further selected in the form of a case summary. Obviously there are possibilities of distortion and omission at each stage of this distillation process. Each link in the data chain requires reliability and validity if the end product is to stand up as verifiable scientific evidence. One increasingly popular means of shortcutting this process is to arrange for multiple observation of the original events through panel interviews, one-way screens, tape recordings, filming, televising, and so on. Any of these devices permits repeated access to the primary observations, and some of them—notably tape recordings and video taping—have been successfully applied to the study of therapy and are being increasingly utilized. In the "macro" area, the primary observer is the major channel of research data, by means of interview, participant observation, agency records, or the like. Another important data source is official statistics regarding population change and social conditions (e.g., vital statistics, juvenile delinquency, etc.), with various potential limitations and biases.

Whatever the "facts" thus obtained, they must be interpreted if they are to have meaning. And here the values, frame of reference, and conceptual equipment of the interpreter of social data are crucially important. The way in which a client is observed and described, the significance of his behavior, the terms and values with which his status before and after treatment are assessed—these all depend largely on the orientation of the interpreter. To say that a person is "hostile," "anxious," "ambivalent," "insecure," "moody," "depressed," and so on is to go beyond the observation of isolated facts to a Gestalt judgment as to their pattern and interrelationship. Moreover, if clients are "diagnosed" as showing "rigidity" or "repressed hostility," then the particular school of psychological theory inevitably enters into the interpretation. Similarly, in group work or community work evaluation the theoretical perspective of the observer will dispose him to "see" certain components of a situation and not others. Such individual leanings should be recognized and accounted for to the extent feasible.

Finally, how are these data and interpretations to be organized into units of change, in terms of both direction and extent? What measuring rod shall be applied? Where the materials are already in quantitative form, it may be possible to adapt such scores to a measurement of change. In much evaluative research in social work, as we shall see, the yardstick is that of human judgment, applied to the information obtained. The human mind, of course, is a remarkably sensitive—yet frail and fallible—instrument.[27]

The relationship between the amount of change (if any) and the *direction* of change is of fundamental importance. For it is here, as Martin Wolins has pointed out, that the key dimension of social values enters the evaluative picture. Suppose, for example, that it is found that marital counseling increases the incidence of divorce in a study sample. Is this good or bad? If the agency is formally committed to the reduction of divorce, then the valuation obviously is negative. If, however, the agency's objectives are to strengthen constructive family relationships, then in some cases the dissolution of destructive bonds may be positive. Similarly in community work, if the goal is the increase of resident participation in planning and decision making, a positive outcome might be registered even though a particular community project fails. On the other hand, if the success of community effort is the criterion (e.g., the construction of a neighborhood housing project), then resident involvement might not be enough, and so on.

Thus the measurement of change in evaluative research is inextricably bound up with the social values of the program sponsors, the program staff and administration, the program recipients, and the research evaluators themselves. Unless there is reasonable clarity and agreement from the outset on all sides regarding the service goals, and the values on which they are based, it is unlikely that the findings will be acceptable to the major parties concerned.

## 5. THE DURABILITY OF CHANGE

It is not always enough that client change in the right direction be demonstrated in an evaluative study. A critical issue pertaining to the benefits observed is the question of their duration. In social treatment, client functioning may fluctuate from time to time, and a higher level at the close of treatment may be accidental or—if statistically significant—may not last appreciably beyond the termination of service. A parallel question in community work would be whether the mobilization of neighborhood residents stimulated by a community organizer outlived his presence in the area. In considering the cost benefits of social service, therefore, the degree of permanence of change is a key consideration. As we shall see later, the "follow-up study" technique was one device developed in social work research to throw light on this problem.

A related question that has arisen recently in connection with behavioral therapy is that of "symptom substitution." While it has been repeatedly established that specific maladaptive habit patterns (e.g., tantrums in children) can be "extinguished" through behavioral modification techniques, concern has been expressed by psychodynamically oriented observers that the elimination of such "symptoms" would tend to be followed by the emergence of others so long as the "underlying cause" was not treated. This claim has been challenged by behavioral therapists and supported by a number of follow-up studies in which the extinction of a given pathological trait was *not* replaced by other "symptoms."[28] In any case, this controversy may be viewed as another version of the central issue of the "durability" of social service results.

## 6. THE CAUSAL CONNECTION

Perhaps the most difficult of all elements in the evaluative process is the establishment of a cause-effect linkage between the program inputs and the client system outcomes. Volumes have been written on the conceptual and methodological ramifications of this problem in the social sciences. Some of the philosophic riddles surrounding causation were briefly noted in Chapter 3 (see pp. 47–49). Such issues apply in full force to the evaluation of effectiveness, since of course the concepts of cause and effect are interdependent, and if the one is in trouble then the other is equally in doubt.

In social research, the method of choice for demonstrating causal connections (and eliminating other "rival" explanations) is experimental manipulation. While useful light can be thrown on causal relationships by descriptive studies, particularly when the data can be analyzed statistically, it is generally accepted that convincing scientific evidence of social causation rests on some application of the experimental method.[29] Interestingly, this ideal does not apply universally in the physical sciences, where, for example, astronomy has reached substantial maturity with little recourse to experimental manipulation. One explanation probably lies in the greater measurability and objectivity of physical factors than of social factors.

For these and other reasons much greater difficulty attaches to social experiments than to physical ones and, consequently, to the testing of cause and effect. One experimental design the social (and medical) sciences have resorted to as a result is the familiar "control group" comparison, in which the device of matching or randomizing parallel groups is utilized in lieu of precision laboratory control. A compromise approach is the quasi-experiment, most highly developed and refined in the influential work of social psychologist Donald T. Campbell and his associates at Northwestern University.[30]

A special adaptation of the quasi-experiment has been employed effectively in psychology, namely, the single-organism (or "time series") design.[31] This technique has been widely applied in behavioral therapy, to which it lends itself readily as an integral component of treatment. This approach has been used in related schools of therapy in social work and is being actively promoted as a promising alternative to the more cumbersome traditional experimental designs.[32] Moreover, it is potentially applicable to the evaluation of "macro-level" programs as well as to "micro-level" services.[33]

Single-organism design may avoid the previously noted pitfall of the classic "control group" experiment in evaluative research, namely, the intrinsic mutuality of the helping process, whereby people tend to "select themselves" for participation (and non-participation) in a social service as much as they are selected or assigned.* For by using the same individual (or group or community) as both "treatment" and "control," the variable of self-selection vs. self-elimination is potentially held constant. Many other disadvantages of the traditional experiment are also potentially sidestepped, for example, the need for large numbers of subjects; the ethics of offering and withholding service; problems of time, cost, administration; the ubiquitous "Hawthorne" or "placebo" effect;[34] and so on. At the same time, of course, there are serious limitations of generalizability, applicability, replicability, and the like in the single-organism approach.[35] In any case, whether or not one accepts the theory or philosophy of behavioral modification, it is important to recognize the powerful research tools that they have effectively sharpened and demonstrated in their evaluative work.

* The emphasis here is on *psychological* participation rather than mere physical "presence."

The causal connection, then, is often the most problematic link in the evaluation chain we have been sketching. While the experimental and quasi-experimental designs are the most promising for attacking this obstacle, difficulties of implementation frequently require researchers to make do with descriptive approaches, sometimes including highly sophisticated statistical techniques as "surrogate" experiments, such as analysis of variance, multiple regression, path analysis, factor analysis, and the like.[36] We also noted the recent school of thought that plays down the "goal attainment model" of evaluation, with its heavy reliance on the logic of the experiment, and stresses instead the more descriptive "systems model."[37]

Against this rather idealistic backdrop of key elements in the evaluative process we may now turn to a review—partly chronological and partly thematic—of the development of this vitally important type of research in social welfare. An obvious weighting toward casework evaluation in what follows tends to reflect the published research in the field during this period.

### Early Evaluative Efforts

Aside from optimistic hopes and exhortations in the literature and conference papers, little was actually attempted in the way of specific evaluative studies in social work before the mid-1920s. However, some early efforts contained the seeds of later developments. One of the first reported studies, for example, described by Lillian Brandt in 1906, seems to embody certain aspects of the later work of J. McVicker Hunt and others. In this project workers were asked to judge the kind of progress made in a number of areas of family adjustment. These were as follows:

    I. Character
        1. Savings
        2. Industry
        3. Judgment
        4. Temperance
    II. Health of
        1. Father
        2. Mother
        3. Children
    III. Environment
    IV. Any other form of improvement

These categories of adjustment were to be checked when there were "positive gains . . . traceable in part to the action or influence of the C.O.S."[38] The workers or district agents would thus make judgments regarding change in specified areas of client adjustment on the basis of their knowledge of the case during treatment. While the categories of change were quite different in the later studies, and many refinements have been added, the basic approach—utilization of workers' judgments—persists as a major tool in present-day evaluative research.[39]

Over the next couple of decades little else was published along these lines. A Boston study was reported at the 1915 National Conference that was essentially global and unstructured, leaving it up to each individual worker to decide the way to go about answering the question of whether the work he or she was doing was worthwhile. The only systematic aspect of the project was the fact that the workers of the Boston Associated Charities were asked to undertake this evaluation at one time for every case that had been assigned to them over the preceding six months. While the findings were not reported, note was made of the "spur to greater achievement which is aroused."[40]

In 1923 a "Sub-committee on Evaluation" of the newly organized American Association of Social Workers looked into the literature on this subject and found what was referred to as a "startling scarcity" of such material. It was reported that there "had been almost no attempt, either by organizations or individual workers, to evaluate the results of social casework."[41]

## Evaluative Research, 1920–1950

As noted earlier in this chapter (p. 234), fresh impetus was given to evaluative research in social work during the 1920s by the rise of federated financing of private social agencies and the resulting demand for accountability at that level. One of the first classics in the field appeared during this period, as recounted in the following pages.

### A FAMOUS FOLLOW-UP STUDY*

While not explicitly an evaluative study, Sophie van Senden Theis' 1924 report on *How Foster Children Turn Out* embodied many of the characteristics and problems of such research and is

---

* A much earlier follow-up "classic" was Charles Loring Brace's appraisal of the outcome of his program of "farming out" tens of thousands of New York City "street children" to western farm families in the mid-1800s. This project is not further pursued here in view of its informal, prescientific na-project is not further pursued here in view of its informal, "prescientific" nature. See Charles Loring Brace, *The Dangerous Classes of New York* (1872) (New York: NASW Classic Series, 1973).

therefore included here. In 1922 the State Charities Aid Association of New York undertook to determine what had happened to the many children it had placed in foster homes over the years. What kind of people had they turned out to be in later life? To what extent were they measuring up to social, economic, and behavioral standards in the communities and families in which they found themselves? These were the kinds of questions that the study sought to answer.[42]

The focus thus was primarily on the later adjustment of the children and only indirectly on the role that the agency may have played in bringing it about. In such an inquiry, however, the two aspects were closely intertwined. If the study showed that the children on the whole performed successfully in later life, the agency's services would be seen in a favorable light; if they turned out generally unhappily, this would tend to reflect unfavorably on the agency. Therefore, while the question of effectiveness was not addressed directly, it was in a sense implicit in the study.

In brief, the method may be sketched as follows:

> Out of over 3,000 children placed in foster homes during the 25 years of the agency's existence, 910 were selected on the basis of being 18 years or older at the time of the study and having been under the care of the agency for a minimum period of one year. Most of these 910 "children" were no longer under the agency's supervision, and hence a staff of 16 field workers was organized to track down and investigate this group in order to assess their current adjustment. Only 537 individuals were personally contacted by the staff, but sufficient information was otherwise obtained for 260 additional persons, thus permitting the inclusion of a total of 797 subjects out of the original 910. This was after a most intensive search and inquiry. An elaborate schedule was filled out for those studied, consisting of eight pages of items covering family background, subject's personal life history, current adjustment, personality attitudes, interests and activities, work and marital experiences, information from relatives and other collaterals, and so on. While emphasis and selection of items might be somewhat different today, a quite comprehensive case history was thus obtained. On the average, about half a week was spent by a staff member in locating and investigating a given subject.[43]

After the above data were compiled for the subjects they were classified in various ways to reveal the major characteristics and features of the study group. The most important analysis was that of current adjustment, on the basis of which the subjects were classified as "capable," "incapable," or of "unknown capability." The definitions were as follows:

> *"Capable"*—Subjects who are law-abiding, who manage their affairs with good sense, and are living in accordance with good moral standards of their communities.
>
> *"Incapable"*—Subjects who are unable or unwilling to support themselves adequately, who are shiftless or have defied the accepted standards of morality or order of their communities.[44]

There was sufficient data for 797 subjects to permit classification into one of these two groups.

Comparisons and cross-classifications were then made between sub-groupings of the total sample. Critical ratio tests of the statistical significance of differences between categories were applied routinely, and the two-sigma level (approximately $p = .05$) was generally adopted as statistically significant.[45]

The results of this intensive study approach may be briefly summarized. Of the 797 subjects studied, 77.2 percent were classified as "capable" in their present adjustment. The remaining 23 percent were judged to be "incapable," but only about half of these were considered to be in conflict with society; the rest were harmless."[46]

About 80 percent of the study group originally came from natural family backgrounds that were classified as "bad"; 12 percent came from a "mixed" background; and only 8 percent from "good" backgrounds. On the other hand, the foster homes were classified as follows: 72 percent "average"; 13 percent "below average"; 15 percent "above average." It was further revealed that the younger the child at the time of placement the more statistically likely it was that he would achieve a "capable" adjustment in later life. Such findings were interpreted as demonstrating that "there are tremendous latent powers within an individual awaiting development, and that under favorable conditions these powers may be developed and directed toward accomplishment."[47] A particularly modern note was struck in the conclusion that "the primary condition of successful development lies in the kind of relationship which grows up between the child and his foster parents."[48] This point was given as an "impression," since few supporting data were presented.

This substantial research undertaking is all the more impressive when its early date is taken into account. The contributions it made to social work research were many. This was the field's first large-scale, formal follow-up investigation and one of the earliest systematic applications in social work of a test for the statistical significance of differences (critical ratio test). The report shows every evidence of meticulous planning and rigorous contemporary research standards throughout. The problem selected for study was a highly important one to the field, and the results cast useful light on the questions posed for inquiry.

Having stated this, it remains to enumerate a number of shortcomings, many of which were recognized in the report. Perhaps the most obvious of these is the question of the "lost" group of 113 subjects out of the original 910 (12.4 percent), for whom insufficient data were available to warrant inclusion in the study. Might this group not have differed appreciably from the others in characteristics associated with their inaccessibility? Might these differences not alter significantly the proportions and relationships observed in the "found" group of 797? It is quite conceivable, for example, that those who could not be located were on the whole a more mobile, less stable group of individuals who did not stay long enough in one place to develop roots or find a niche for themselves. If so, the 77 percent who were found to be "capable" might well be too high a proportion if the total sample were to be taken into account.

Another obvious point has to do with the adequacy of the ratings and of the classifications. How reliable and valid were the distinctions between "capable" and "incapable," for example? It was stated that "the classifications and ratings were made by experienced supervisors . . . in consultation with technical experts and with statisticians."[49] Beyond this, apparently little was done to test the judgments. The definitions, as we have seen, are quite broadly stated and lean heavily on the moralistic values that permeated early social work. It would be surprising if such general terms were applied by different judges consistently. Furthermore, the split of the study group into a "capable-incapable" dichotomy might very well have forced a number of borderline cases onto one or the other side of the fence with little justification. (It seems likely that a finer breakdown—into three or five groups— might have been desirable here.)

The accuracy of the information on which the classifications were based—the raw data—may also be called into question in such a study. Only 537 out of the total study group of 797 subjects—67.5 percent—were actually seen by the investigators; information on the remaining 260 was obtained indirectly. Despite the painstaking thoroughness with which the study was conducted, it may be fairly questioned whether the data obtained in such cases were accurate and representative. Even when the individual is contacted directly there obviously remain many difficulties and uncertainties in obtaining a true picture of the nature of his adjustment. Caseworkers, for example, often find that after several interviews a client may present a quite different aspect than in the opening contacts. Collateral information is now usually looked upon as a supplement, rather than a substitute, for material from the individual himself. Serious questions may thus be raised regarding the adequacy of the information used as a basis for evaluation in an appreciable portion of the cases. However, there is a realistic dilemma here, since eliminating such cases from the study group would further have reduced the size and representativeness of the remaining sample.

Finally, there is the basic limitation noted earlier, namely, the omission of any formal attempt to determine the causal connection of the agency's services with the later adjustment of the client. Would the children have found other living arrangements, and have turned out as well, without the activities of the State Charities Aid Association? The answer to this question would have required a much more elaborate study design, probably involving some type of controlled comparison (see pp. 264–271). It is no criticism of this pioneering achievement in social work research to point to some of the ideal objectives it was understandably not able to attain and that indeed have not yet been fully attained. It was a number of years before much technical progress along this line was made.

### An Early Behavioristic Approach

In 1926, at an institute of the American Association for Organizing Family Social Work (now the Family Service Association of America), a committee was appointed on "Measurement in Family Social Work." Its chairman, Sophie Hardy, adopted "for this purpose the 'behavioristic' viewpoint that the personality of the individual is evidenced by the sum of his habits and mental attitudes."[50] In implementing this frame of reference the committee proceeded to devise a questionnaire consisting of ninety-four items framed in the form of questions regarding the individual's habits and attitudes.[51] For example, the item "Does he remain at home in the evenings as a rule" was to be checked by the worker with a plus or a minus mark, depending on whether the answer was positive or negative.[52] All of the questions were to be answered by the worker at the beginning and end of treatment, and if there were more favorable answers at the later period than at the earlier it was concluded that there had been "growth" on the part of the client.[53] While this experiment proved to be abortive insofar as usuable findings were concerned, it made a definite impact on the field and on later research of this type. Following the classical behavioristic concept of personality, it went much further than previous studies in stressing the external observables and in dividing the individual into discrete segments for separate evaluation, ultimately combining these into an aggregative total. This early, short-lived influence of behavioristic psychology on the course of social work research is an interesting phenomenon, particularly in view of its recent resurgence via behavioral therapy.

For in essence classical behaviorism was at the opposite pole from traditional casework theory and practice. In the first place, strict Watsonian behaviorism refused to recognize the existence of mental processes and conscious meanings per se,* preferring to reduce all human reactions to neurophysical terms such as reflexes and conditioned responses. Certainly nothing could be further removed from the historic casework emphasis on client attitudes, the meaning of situations, conscious and unconscious thoughts and feelings, and the like. To be sure, in 1926 the influence of Freudian theory, with its elaborate symbolic content and stress on the interplay of conscious and unconscious ideas, was still relatively new to casework, but still there was much in the practice of the day that ran counter to the psychic reductionism of early behaviorist doctrine. Moreover, through its interpretation of personality as the sum total of the specific habits and response patterns of an individual, Watsonion behaviorism deemphasized the fuller, deeper understanding of the individual as an interrelated whole, an objective that has characterized casework from its early beginnings. Modern behaviorism—Skinnerian and otherwise—is of course a much broader and more diversified body of psychological thought, so that today its relationship to current models of casework practice is more complex and open-ended.

It is not surprising, therefore, that at the time the behaviorist approach to the study of casework effectiveness did not get very far. It did, however, arouse considerable interest and some emulation. In the following year, for example, it was applied to the evaluation of relief administration, as reported by Richard K. Conant before the 1927 National Conference.[54]

* The previously quoted statement by Hardy referring to the behaviorist viewpoint of personality as the "sum of his habits and *mental* attitudes" (emphasis added) appears to be an extension of the original school of thought. As pointed out earlier, orthodox behaviorism did not deal with mental states as such. See John B. Watson, *Behaviorism* (New York: People's Institute, 1924–1925).

It was discussed favorably in several articles in *The Family*.[55] Furthermore, its imprint may be seen in a number of subsequent evaluative research efforts, which attempted to break down the characteristics of the client and his situation into separate elements, rate these independently, and then combine them according to some formula in order to arrive at an overall score or aggregate.

## A PROBLEM-CENTERED APPROACH

After the first experiments with segmental analysis and synthesis in evaluative research, a major assault on the subject from a somewhat different standpoint was made by Ellery F. Reed in a study completed in 1931. The project was sponsored by the Helen S. Trounstine Foundation in Cincinnati and involved an ingenious procedure of rating and scoring "problems" identified in family agency case summaries in such a way as to yield a variety of evaluative measures.

The case being rated was first put into summary form. This case summary was then utilized as the basis of an elaborate tabular analysis of its content. To systematize the procedure a large tabular work sheet was set up consisting of thirteen columns calling for the rating of different factors seen in the case summary. Toward the left-hand side of the sheet was a column captioned "Problems" in which the rater was to list all problems of "deviation," "treatment," and "status" appearing in the summary.[56] The other twelve columns called for the assignment of various scores and weights to each of the problems thus listed. Five of these were for computational purposes only. The remaining seven columns were captioned and interpreted as follows:

> 1. Accomplishment—extent to which the objectives of treatment were achieved (on a scale from —100 to +100).
> 2. Weight—importance of the problem in the given case (on a scale from 1–10).
> 3. Duration—length of time during which problem was present.
> 4. Adjustment—the positive or negative change that occurred in the problem from opening to closing (on a scale from —100 to +100).
> 5. Credit—extent to which worker was responsible for change in problem (on a scale from —100 to +100).
> 6. Merit—degree of skill evinced by worker (on a scale from —100 to +100).
> 7. Tempo—the promptness and efficiency of the worker in treatment (on a scale from 0 to +100).[57]

With these basic ratings Reed was able to set up formulas with the objective of measuring various aspects of the treatment process and its effectiveness. In this way he arrived at measures for each case summary such as the following:

Accomplishment score—weighted* average of all accomplishment ratings
Adjustment score—weighted average of all adjustment scores
Merit score—weighted average of all merit scores
Tempo score—weighted average of all tempo scores
Investigation score—mean of merit and tempo scores
Diagnosis score—the investigation score computed for the diagnostic or exploratory phase of treatment[58]

One cannot help but be impressed by the ambitious and innovative nature of this attempt to quantify many of the significant dimensions of the casework process. Here, perhaps for the first time in social work evaluative research, a clear distinction was drawn among such closely related concepts as *adjustment* (used here in the sense of "change" or "movement"), *credit* (in the sense of casework responsibility or contribution), *accomplishment* (degree to which objectives were attained), *merit* (skill of worker), and so on. Even today, several decades later, social workers are not always successful in attaining this degree of conceptual clarity in their evaluative efforts. For the first time, too, this study attempts in a formal way to establish the reliability of the evaluations arrived at. A rough gauge of the reliability of the scores was obtained through the construction of scatter diagrams showing the extent of agreement between different judges in their scoring of a set of cases. While the corresponding coefficients of correlation were not presented, the scatter diagrams indicated a fair degree of agreement, sufficient in any case to give some confidence in the consistency of the data.[59]

This method was applied to over 100 case summaries in an attempt to demonstrate its potentialities. However, despite a flurry of interest and discussion in the contemporary literature, it failed to gain general acceptance by the field and soon died a natural death. Undoubtedly the inherent complications and limitations of the approach contributed to its downfall. Thus Antoinette Cannon, writing in the 1933 *Social Work Year Book,* pointed out that "the soundness of such a scheme [Reeds'] rests

---

* The weighting in each case was determined by the importance of the corresponding problem as indicated in item 2 of the preceding list.

upon the validity of the judgments which are the units to be counted. . . ."[60] Such validity was never demonstrated for the Reed scoring method, and the problem of establishing the validity of evaluative research methods has proved to be a continuing dilemma for other approaches as well.

Another problem-centered approach to evaluation was seen in a study begun in 1936 and carried on over a period of several years under the direction of A. A. Heckman of the Family Service Agency of St. Paul, Minnesota. In pursuing this approach Heckman started with the classification of problems evolved earlier by the Family Service Association of America for use by its member agencies. This consisted of a checklist of a wide range of family problems grouped under several major headings such as Employment, Family Relationships, Physical Health, and Mental Health. Each of these broad categories was subdivided into more specific types, so that the total list contained more than ninety different problems and services.

Heckman applied the foregoing framework to the answering of the following questions: "What problems are they [family casework agencies] endeavoring to treat? What success are they having in meeting these problems?"[61] Over 1000 cases were subjected to a problem analysis during the course of the study. Each case was checked semiannually by the worker handling it according to which problems were present, and for each problem noted a further rating was given as follows: (1) no improvement; (2) partial improvement; (3) definite improvement; (4) no treatment attempted. A similar rating was given to each of the major problem groupings. The decision as to the degree of improvement was acknowledged to be a subjective process, supported by the observation that "it seems . . . reasonable to assume that professional caseworkers can exercise responsible judgment."[62] Heckman reported that he had conducted several tests that tended to bear out this confidence in the use of worker judgment. For example, he had one sample of 100 cases rated by workers other than the one responsible for treatment, with the result that "This test showed no significant deviations in judgment from those made by caseworkers who had treated the cases. If anything, the workers who had not treated the cases tended to record a slightly greater degree of improvement."[63] However, the details of the test were not given.

Some of the findings obtained through the application of this procedure to approximately 1000 cases are of interest. The workers had listed a median number of over three "problems" per case, with the number of problems present ranging from one in (17.6

percent of the cases) to a maximum of seventeen. The percentage of problems in which some improvement was seen was computed for the major problem groupings, revealing that the highest portion of improvement—82.3 percent—occurred with legal problems, and the lowest—55.5 percent—with mental health problems. Family relationship problems showed improvement in 73.5 percent of the cases in which they appeared. When all problems were considered together improvement was thought to have occurred in 71.3 percent.

It may be noted that this method does not go beyond the rating of progress with specific problems to the broader question of whether or not the case has improved "as a whole." Because of the great range in type and intensity of problems, no overall calculation of the number or proportion of problems showing improvement was proposed as a means of arriving at a summary evaluation. The dissection of the case material into problems was left in segmented form with no attempt to put the pieces back together again for a total rating.

The basic notion underlying both these studies was that a case situation may be broken down into discrete "problems," that these problems can be rated in terms of their alleviation or aggravation in the given case, and finally, that such ratings together will yield an overall picture of the progress achieved.

This approach has a number of obvious advantages. The notion of a "problem" in its general sense of "difficulty" or "dysfunction" is readily grasped by professionals and laymen alike. The analogy with medical practice and its treatment of distinct pathological conditions is evident. The idea of identifying specific problems in a case and then tracing their course of progress has a strong logical appeal. Administrators and public relations personnel are likely to seize upon so tangible and clear-cut a device for analyzing and describing the work of an agency. If some types of problems are found to be more amenable to constructive modification than others (as reported earlier), then perhaps certain inferences may be drawn regarding agency policies and practice, and so on.

Despite its attractions, however, the classification and evaluation of problems did not make much headway at the time. Nor did practitioners fully accept it. As early as 1928, R. Clyde White had concluded that

> It is probably safe to say that statistics of problems and services are utterly useless as measures of the results of social casework. In mass the data are so heterogeneous that no uniformity of any sort is indicated, and in the individual case the problem units

and service units are so largely incommensurable that we can conclude nothing as to what has actually been accomplished.[64]

Moreover, the analysis of case situations into problems seemed to conflict with the dynamic concepts of behavior and personality on which the dominant theory of social work was then based. Even in Mary Richmond's day casework stressed the interactive nature of personality and environment, the understanding of the "whole" man, the "web" of interpersonal relations, the importance of individual differences, and so on. With the incorporation of Freudian and neo-Freudian theory into social work practice, additional weight was placed on an understanding of the total personality as a dynamic equilibrium of internal and external forces. To the extent that this type of approach was consistently applied in social work practice, the concept of a "problem" as a meaningful, diagnostic unit became dubious.

For in the view of classical psychodynamic theory a "problem" of the type dealt with in social work was interpretable only in the total context of the client's personality structure and his environmental situation. It was widely assumed that social workers tended to deal not so much with "employment problems" or "marital problems" as distinct objects of study and treatment as with these problems *in their relationship* to the personality of the particular client and his situation. In other words, the typical casework practitioner preferred to work with the *interactions* between individuals and their problems rather than with "problems" in isolation. Thus the significance of a problem was not clear until the client and its meaning to him were understood; problems were often seen as surface symptoms of deeper psychological processes; problems in a given case tended to overlap and interpenetrate; a given problem might have quite different etiologies and import in two different cases; and so on.

Considerations like these limited the acceptance of this type of problem-centered approach to the evaluation of social casework at that time. There has been an interesting resurgence of such interest in recent years, influenced in part by the example of behavioral modification research as, for instance in the "task-centered" casework and research model.[65]

## THE DISCOMFORT-RELIEF QUOTIENT

Another major evaluative effort was illustrated in the so-called discomfort-relief quotient (DRQ), developed between 1944 and 1947 by sociologist John Dollard and psychologist O. Hobart

Mowrer for the Institute of Welfare Research of the Community Service Society of New York.[66] This time an attempt was made, through content analysis of case records, to measure changes in overall adjustment. As a measure or index of adjustment, use was made of the concept of "tension level" couched in terms of a "discomfort-relief" dichotomy.

The approach was formulated within the framework of one form of neobehavioristic learning theory in psychology.* This school of thought utilized the principle that learning may take place under the inducement of "reward," which is considered to be the reduction of "drive" or "tension" within the individual. By viewing the client-worker relationship as a "student-teacher" relationship, with the client learning new ways of thinking, feeling, and acting from the treatment experience, the client's level of tension was seen as a likely clue to the extent of learning taking place. Since learning is supposed to be associated with reduction in tension, a measure of tension might provide an index of case "progress" in this sense. Thus if a client at intake was assessed as having a high tension level, and this level was observed to drop significantly during the course of treatment, then it might be inferred that effective learning had taken place, that is, that the case was a "successful" one from this standpoint.†

On the basis of this kind of theoretical reasoning, a concerted effort was made to devise a means of measuring the tension level at different stages of case process. The case record was utilized as the source of data, and a technique of content analysis was adapted to this type of material. In brief, the procedure consisted of counting the number of words, sentences, or clauses appearing in a case record that reflected "discomfort" on the part of the client, and the number of such units that reflected "relief." (In a given analysis only one type of unit—word, sentence, or clause—would be used throughout.) Then the DRQ as a measure of tension level was computed separately for *each page* of the total case record, according to the following general formula:

$$\frac{\text{``Discomfort'' units}}{\text{``Discomfort'' plus ``relief'' units}} = \text{DRQ}[67]$$

---

* Dollard and Mowrer acknowledged their indebtedness to Clark L. Hull, leader of this school of learning theory. John Dollard and O. Hobart Mowrer, "A Method of Measuring Tension in Written Documents," *The Journal of Abnormal and Social Psychology*, XLII, January, 1947, pp. 3–4.

† "It seemed that the report of the successful case ought to begin with 'gripes' and end with 'smiles,' that is, move from high to low tension levels." Ibid., p. 7.

The determination as to whether a given unit reflected discomfort, relief, or neither was left to the "common sense of intelligent people." Reliability was tested by having independent judges analyze the same case records and then comparing the resulting DRQs for all of the pages of the record. In one test the average intercorrelations of ten scorers in their DRQ ratings were .80, .81, and .88 for the word, sentence, and clause methods, respectively. Thus the reliability of the procedure was found to be satisfactory, with adequate agreement between results obtained by different scorers.[68]

A DRQ curve was plotted for each case, tracing graphically the course of "tension" as measured by the index from the beginning to the close of the case record. The DRQ, in values from .00 to 1.00, was plotted on the vertical axis while the abscissa was laid out in terms of pages, from the first to the last page of the case record. (Apparently the page was selected as the computational unit primarily on the ground of convenience.) Portrayed in this way, most cases tended to show a downward trend in DRQ level from the beginning to the end of the record, albeit with very wide fluctuations en route. This pattern bore out the original expectation that tension level would tend to decrease as treatment progressed.

Unquestionably, this was a highly intriguing and provocative approach to the evaluative problem in social casework research. It was rooted in psychological theory and lent itself to fairly precise quantification. The numerical scores obtained were sufficiently reliable for many practical purposes. Having pointed out these merits, the many shortcomings of the experiment are perhaps so obvious as to warrant little discussion. In the first place, the highly variable and frequently fortuitous content and verbiage in the typical social case record would appear to make so elaborate and detailed an analysis of record material rather gratuitous from the very outset. There is little basis for the implied assumption that the record contains a representative sample of emotional events in the life of a client. Moreover, as the authors themselves point out, no distinction was made as to *whose* discomfort is being measured, *when* it occurred, what the *type* or *source* of the discomfort may be, and so on. In their own words, "it is a record of all the tensions that creep into the case record."[68] It seems that any interpretation of so haphazard and diffuse a selection of material would be most difficult.

Finally, the basic concept of "tension reduction" as a necessary correlate of casework progress is subject to serious question. May not the goal of treatment be to *raise* the level of tension in some cases, for example, those in which an individual is apathetic and shows little affect, enthusiasm, or interest? Is not a reduction of tension sometimes a mark of retrogression, as in a break from neurotic conflict into a solution via psychosis, or from struggle into submission, or from painful growth into stagnation? (And in the last analysis isn't death the lowest of all tension states?) Certainly the assumption that learning and growth must be accompanied by a lowering of inner drive is a controversial one, one that is perhaps not entirely compatible with social work values and objectives which increasingly stress the highest self-expression and realization, the maximum use of capacities and potentialities, and increased zest and enthusiasm for creative living.*

After the reliability of the DRQ was adequately established, it then remained to ascertain its validity, that is, the extent to which it reflected actual progress in the case situation. In the present instance, the method of validation resorted to was that of comparing the *differences* between DRQ scores in the *first* and *last tenths* of a series of thirty-nine case records with judgments by caseworkers as to the amount of improvement occurring in these cases. The resulting correlation between DRQ score differences and the judgments of caseworkers as to the amount of improvement was .20![70] This virtually negligible correlation was not due to low reliability in the judgments of the workers, for a check of this possibility revealed a surprisingly high agreement. Apparently either the DRQ was invalid, or the workers' judgments, or both. In view of the prima facie questions that were being raised about the appropriateness of the DRQ approach, the decision was made in favor of the use of workers' judgments. From this point on, the work on evaluation of social casework at the Institute of Welfare Research was taken over by J. McVicker Hunt, a well-known research psychologist. In his work, as we shall see, Dr. Hunt emphasized the use of workers' judgments as the basis for measuring "movement" in case records.

Some time later, Philip Klein summed up the DRQ experience quite aptly in the following words: "Dollard's invention for measuring casework progress is, I think, another honorable error in our experimentation methods.[71]

---

* In considering this issue Dollard and Mowrer attribute to caseworkers the objective of "the *lowest tension levels* over the *longest periods of time*." Ibid., p. 6. For the reasons alluded to earlier, the author questions this interpretation of social work philosophy. At a later point Dollard and Mowrer acknowledge that the DRQ cannot differentiate between "adjustive" or "maladjustive" learning—a most damaging admission for what was intended to be a tool for use in evaluative research. Ibid., p. 21.

THE HUNT MOVEMENT SCALE

The highly influential and widely utilized Hunt Movement Scale* emerged, phoenix-like, from the ashes of the DRQ. In 1947, when it was discovered that unstandardized workers' judgments correlated fairly well with each other but only negligibly with the DRQ scores, the focus of the project was shifted to concentrate on this apparently more promising approach. The mean intercorrelation between the raw judgments of 10 randomly selected workers rating 38 cases was .70.[72] This degree of agreement, without standardized training or definitions, encouraged the hope that with additional refinement the judgments of workers could be made sufficiently reliable for practical research purposes. Accordingly, efforts were now bent toward the improvement and codification of the judgment process.

Through an intensive analysis of the reasons given by the judges for their ratings, a set of four general categories of evidence was eventually agreed upon as significant in judging "movement" as seen in a case record. These four categories were changes in adaptive efficiency, changes in disabling habits and conditions, changes in attitude or understanding as evidenced by the client's verbalizations, and changes in the environmental situation. The types of evidence were defined and illustrated in considerable detail. Then a seven-step rating scale was set up, ranging from −2 through 0 to +4, on the basis of which workers were to judge the degree of positive or negative "movement" seen in a given case record. By the term *movement* was meant "the change that appears in an individual client and/or his environment between the opening and closing of his case." Specific instructions for the different levels of ratings were provided, together with "anchoring" case illustrations for every other step of the scale. Finally, a special training procedure was developed for the purpose of indoctrinating workers in the proper use of the scale, involving the rating of a trial set of cases under supervision.

It should be emphasized that though four different categories of evidence were utilized in the rating process and instructions, these categories were not to be scored separately. Rather, they were guideposts to be kept in mind in assaying the case material, and while changes were to be looked for in each of these areas

* Also know as the CSS Movement Scale after the Community Service Society of New York City, where it was developed. We prefer to identify this research instrument by the name of its major author. Hunt's close collaborator in the development of the scale was a fellow psychologist, Leonard S. Kogan, so that the instrument is sometimes referred to as the Hunt-Kogan Movement Scale.

separately, the evidence had to be brought back together again to an integrated Gestalt fashion before a single, overall rating of movement could be assigned.* For this reason the Hunt study may be grouped with other studies utilizing overall case judgments as the primary evaluative tool.

This abbreviated summary of the development of the so-called Hunt Movement Scale can convey only a faint impression of the great investment of rigorous effort and elaborate care that went into the refinement of this research tool over a period of several years. With the application of this standardized procedure the level of agreement, as measured by the mean intercorrelation between workers, was raised from an average of .70 to .80.[73] The point had now been reached at which it was believed that the instrument was ready for wider application in the field. Furthermore, the variation between workers' mean judgments was found to have been reduced through the standardization process. Accordingly, a detailed manual of instructions for training judges in the use of the scale was published in 1950.

After this point further refinements were undertaken, for example, the development of an expanded scale of 70 steps for use in place of the 7-step scale, though the demonstration that this provided greater reliability in ratings was not particularly convincing.[74] In 1953 a major follow-up study aimed at validating the instrument was completed, with generally encouraging findings[75] (see excerpts, pp. 308–317). Additional studies have indicated that workers can judge their own cases as reliably as independent judges rating summaries of these cases, that worker in other agencies can be trained to judge cases as reliably as workers at the Community Service Society in New York, where the scale was developed, and that graduate students in social casework or psychology can be trained to use the scale with the same degree of reliability as experienced caseworkers.[76]

In the years following its introduction and standardization, the Hunt Movement Scale gained broad acceptance in social work research and was applied in scores of evaluative studies.[77] While its use peaked in the 1950s, it was still being employed occasionally through the 1960s as well.[78] For well over a decade it

---

* For example, the definition of the movement rating +2 is given as follows: "The client's status should improve distinctly in several areas. The amount of change between opening and closing status should appear about half that shown in the anchor for +4, as illustrated in example for +2. Improvement need not show in every type of evidence, but should show in AE (adaptive efficiency) or DH&C (disabling habits or conditions)."

dominated the measurement of change in social casework research.

In this case the many shortcomings are quite evident, at least in retrospect. First, the Hunt Movement Scale in itself was not a measure of the effectiveness of social casework or of its results; it represented only a beginning step in this direction. The scale was only intended to provide a measure of the degree of change occurring in an individual client or his situation during casework treatment, without regard to what part the treatment process may have played in bringing about the amount of movement seen. The question of effectiveness was thus bypassed pending the design of additional research such as the use of control groups, which might be able to provide an answer. Hence, any application or interpretation of the scale that implied evaluation of the *results* of social casework was premature and unfounded.*

Furthermore, while considerable evidence was accumulated in support of the reliability of the scale, its validity as a measure of movement was not fully demonstrated. The 1953 follow-up study was an attempt to test certain aspects of validity, with encouraging results.[79] It should also be pointed out that the scale did not deal with the problem of identifying in operational terms the objectives of social casework so as to provide *external* criteria of success or failure, nor did it deal with the underlying theory of psychosocial functioning on which the casework treatment was based. These fundamental matters were avoided, leaving it to the individual judges to apply their own standards and concepts. It was on such grounds that Klein took the Hunt Movement Scale to task, stating: "I do not see how a study of this type can serve the ultimate purposes of social work unless it sets up, by clear definition, the specific social value . . . which it is to serve."[80] Moreover, the author of the scale himself later acknowledged the inadequate data base on which the scale judgments rested, that is, the case record summary. In 1959 he stated at a social work research institute that "it is impossible to test the reliability of clinical judgment by having various clinicians judge a set of written documents such as we used in testing the reliability of the Movement Scale."[81]

It should be further noted that the Hunt Movement Scale applied only to individuals and did not provide any direct means

---

* Dr. Hunt and his colleagues were very explicit in their writings in emphasizing this fact. It is unfortunate, however, that they chose titles for some of their publications, such as *Measuring Results in Social Casework: A Manual on Judging Movement,* that could be misleading.

for assessing change within an overall family configuration. Finally, it presented a relativistic yardstick of change only, rather than an absolute measure of functioning at either the beginning or the end of treatment. These last two limitations, as well as others, helped spur the development of an alternative scale—the Geismar Scale of Family Functioning, first published in 1960 and subsequently revised.[82] This approach has now superseded the Hunt Movement Scale as the most frequently used gauge of change in social casework research (see next chapter).

To enumerate these shortcomings is not to detract from the great contribution that the Hunt Movement Scale made to the developemnt of evaluative research in social work.* The clarification of the crucial concept of "movement," the demonstration of substantial agreement in the subjective judgments of workers, the fruitful application of correlation methods and other statistical techniques to the analysis of such ratings, the careful and thorough systematization and standardization of the judgment process— these were significant strides toward research sophistication in this field.† It was with good reason, therefore, that Mary E. Macdonald hailed the development of the Movement Scale as a "landmark in methodology in social work research."[83]

## The Experimental Mode in Social Work Evaluation

Social work has made impressive strides with the field experiment as an approach to evaluative research, as we shall see in the following pages, but pursuit of this research strategy has been less than intense or consistent over the years. Nevertheless a considerable body of experience in this promising area has now accumulated, and an initial core of findings has begun to build up, as we shall see in the following pages.

---

* Indeed it is gratifying to note that the researchers involved in the development of the Hunt Movement Scale were their own best critics—not always the case in social work research. In addition to the above-mentioned article by J. McVicker Hunt, see Leonard S. Kogan and Ann W. Shyne, "The C.S.S. Movement Scale: A Methodological Review," in Catherine S. Chilman, ed., *Approaches to the Measurement of Family Change* (Washington, D.C.: U.S. Department of Health, Education and Welfare, June 1966).

† It may be commented in passing that at about the same time, a similar approach to the measurement of change in social group work was developed by Saul Bernstein. This parallel effort proved largely abortive, however, insofar as any extensive adoption or application in the group work field was concerned. See Saul Bernstein, *Chartering Group Progress* (New York: Association Press, 1949).

## The Cambridge-Somerville Youth Study

Though not finally published until 1951, the Cambridge-Somerville Youth Study was started in 1939 and has been widely recognized as a pioneer field experiment utilizing a control group in social sciences.[84] It has been frequently cited in the literature of psychology, psychiatry, sociology, and other allied disciplines.[85] It was conceived and implemented by a physician, Richard C. Cabot, whom we have already encountered in other connections in this field. In fact in undertaking this ground-breaking experiment Dr. Cabot was taking up his own challenge—which, as we have seen, he had laid before the 1931 National Conference of Social Work in his Presidential Address—to "measure, evaluate, estimate your results. . . ."[86] Perhaps he felt impelled to provide a demonstration of what he had in mind in the face of relative inaction in the field up to that point. In any case, we do know that Cabot was a highly dedicated and versatile cardiac specialist who lent brilliant leadership to social work in a number of areas, including the early stimulation of medical social work and, later, the mounting of this major social experiment. Cabot also had a wealthy wife whose charitable foundation supported this very significant (and expensive) study. Unfortunately Cabot died in 1939, at the outset of the project, but the work was continued by his brother and was completed in 1951 by Edwin Powers and Helen Witmer.[87]

The Cambridge-Somerville Youth Study was, as the report title indicates, "an experiment in the prevention of delinquency." It aimed at testing the efficacy of a "big-brother" type of counseling program in reducing antisocial behavior in teenage predelinquent male youths.* The sample consisted of a carefully matched "treatment" and "control" group of 325 boys each, selected on the basis of a variety of specific criteria. The 650 boys were taken from a much larger group of almost 2000 who had been reported to the study group by schools, social agencies, and the like. This initial referral group consisted of both "difficult" and "average" children, and the final group also contained both types, with about two-thirds being judged to be "predelinquents." A point of interest here is the method of separation of this final study group into "treatment" and "control" halves. An attempt was made to pair the boys (782 at the start) on the basis of 142 variables grouped into the following six categories: physical health,

---

* The following summary is highly abbreviated, since a more complete account by Edwin Powers and Helen Witmer is given in later excerpts (see pp. 278–308).

intelligence and education, personality, delinquency prognoses, factors relating to home, and factors relating to neighborhood.[88] The 142 factors were ultimately reduced to 29, based on various patterns and interrelationships as judged by two staff psychologists. Then, as referrals were made to the study group and diagnostic material was obtained, individual boys and small groups were paired on the basis of similarity in profile of ratings on these various criteria. Finally, each pair of "matched" individuals or subgroups was assigned to either the "treatment" or "control" group at the arbitrary flip of a coin. In this way the balancing effect of randomization was added to the pairing process.[89] If the precision matching was inadequate, the errors would thus tend to cancel each other out on a chance basis. The end result was the selection of two groups of 325 boys as closely matched as the techniques and knowledge of the day could provide.

Each of the boys selected for the treatment group was offered the services of a "counselor" who was employed for the purpose of developing a constructive relationship with the youngster and his family over a period of several years, taking the role of an understanding and helpful "big brother." However, only a minority of the counselors were professionally trained social workers. The service program was fully launched by 1939, ending in 1945. Less than one-fourth of the children remained in the program from start to finish.[90]

At the close of the study period an attempt was made to compare the record of behavior and adjustment of the two matched groups. The major criteria of change were (1) the official delinquency record of the children and (2) the social adjustment of the individual children at the end of the study.

On the first of these two yardsticks little difference of statistical significance was found between the two groups. Similarly, on the second criterion little overall difference in adjustment was found by Dr. Witmer in her careful review and classification of the case material. Thus the study results appeared to be negative, showing no significant differences between treatment and control groups in terms of either delinquency records or social adjustment at the end of study period. A further analysis by Witmer raised some provocative questions, however. In addition to rating the cases in terms of social adjustment, she also judged them in terms of the extent to which they appeared to have "benefited" from the counselor's services. In doing this she assessed the causal relationships subjectively, on a case-by-case basis. According to this analysis, the service was "definitely beneficial" to 19 percent of the treatment group, and of "possible," "little," or "no" help to the rest. She further found that the definitely "benefited" children differed noticeably in a number of characteristics from the rest. These results suggested that there were differential effects of the counselor's services with different types of children.[91]

Witmer's reanalysis of the Cambridge-Somerville findings provides an interesting example of the distinctive contribution of social work research to social science. Her nine chapters of text reflect the special sensitivity to the dynamics and process of individualization shown by the clinician as well as by the careful research scholar. The methodology, though essentially subjective, was sophisticated and imaginative. In some ways, perhaps, this section of the work was the most fruitful, certainly in terms of its helpful suggestions for future practice. Moreover, Witmer's critique of the experimental design was penetrating, and her steps to mitigate these shortcomings in the analysis were thoughtful and creative. This qualitative analysis may be read rewardingly today as an important supplement to the familiar quantitive presentation (see excerpt, pp. 292–308). For example, one aspect of her reconstruction of the project data identified cases in which the services offered were refused, resisted, or not needed. While only 8 percent of the clients rejected the initial offer of service, another 6 percent resisted it more or less openly during the course of the project, and a further 16 percent did not appear to be in need of the services provided.[92] Thus 30 percent or more of the study sample may, in some sense, have been inappropriate for service and the  relative outcomes affected correspondingly.

Despite its discouraging conclusions, the project had a substantial impact on the field and on related disciplines. It was one of the first to apply the experimental model to questions about the effectiveness of social services, and it thus contributed to salutary introspection and self-examination within the profession—an essential process that is still continuing and, if anything, accelerating. Equally important was the project's demonstration at a comparatively early date that a rigorous field-experiment with treatment control group comparisons can be successfully mounted in social work. As such it provided a standard and an incentive for similar ventures elsewhere and gave vital encouragement to the use of experimental designs in field settings. It should also be said on the other side, however, that the lack of positive findings, and the great cost and time involved in the experiment, may very well have served to deter some additional enterprise along this line. But these are among the risks of the research business. On balance, the weight of this monumental effort was strongly positive and constructive.[93]

THE JEWISH BOARD OF GUARDIANS STUDY

This study, which was conducted sometime after the Cambridge-Somerville Youth Project, followed a much less rigorous type of experimental model. It is reported here because its shortcomings are common ones and should be avoided if better alternatives are feasible or, if not, clearly recognized and taken into account.

Published by the Jewish Board of Guardians of New York City in 1949, the project involved a comparison of children who were receiving child guidance treatment with children who were not. The "treatment group" consisted of 196 children who had received treatment in the agency prior to March 31, 1942, and the comparison group consisted of 110 children who "had been observed and found to be within function but had not continued treatment either in an agency clinic [that is, JBG] or received any other treatment up to the time of follow-up."[94] The "nontreatment" children were in most cases withdrawn from service by their parents shortly after intake. Both of these groups of children were evaluated by a team consisting of staff members and others, which then arrived at a consensual rating regarding the degree of adjustment of the child at the close of the case and at the time of a follow-up investigation one year later. A schedule for collecting information on the children had been prepared for each of these points in time, and the panel of judges was not told which cases were "treatment" or "nontreatment" in order to avoid the possibility biasing effect of such knowledge. Two independent sets of criteria were applied to the case material—one "sociological," referring to such factors as delinquency, mental pathology, and truancy, and the other "clinical," referring to his adjustment, relationships, and symptomatology.[95] However, when it was found that the two sets of criteria "were not appreciably different," only the ratings according to "clinical" criteria were used in the study.[96]

The resulting classification of adjustment for the two groups of children at the time of follow-up is summarized in the following tabulation showing the percentage of each group falling within specified levels of adjustment:

|  | Treatment | "Nontreatment" |
| --- | --- | --- |
| Success | 50.5 | 31.8 |
| Partial success | 23.5 | 38.2 |
| Failure | 26.0 | 30.0 |
| Total | 100.0 | 100.0 |

The significance of these differences was tested by means of chi-square, with the finding of statistical significance at the .01

level. From these data the writer drew the following sweeping conclusion:

> The probability that this favorable result of treatment was due to chance was *effectively ruled out* by means of the chi square test for statistical significance. On the basis of this test, the *positive effect* of the treatment which the 196 children had received was *established beyond a doubt.*[97] (Emphasis added)

In evaluating this statement, consider the logic of this type of quasi-experimental design.* When two *matched* groups of individuals are subjected to different experiences, then it may be concluded that subsequent statistically significant differences between them are related to the difference in experience, provided that all other possible influences are "held constant." But were the groups essentially similar at the outset? Were the outside factors—other than treatment—impinging on them comparable? The data do indicate that the two groups were roughly comparable in a number of respects, and that where differences were found they were in the direction of biasing the findings in favor of the nontreatment group, thus making the differences noted all the more impressive, according to one of the authors.[98] It is, however, evident that the two groups were *not* matched in terms of all the possibly relevant variables. In particular, the basis for the selection of the nontreatment group, namely, their early withdrawal from treatment, may obviously be related to highly significant contrasts between the groups that were not taken into account at all. Thus the fact that many of the parents in the control cases refused to continue with treatment may reflect less motivation on their part, or greater rigidity, or stronger psychological defenses, and so on. If "nontreatment" parents differed in these subtle yet crucial ways from the others, then the variation found in outcome may be due to such disparities rather than to the treatment received, and the entire comparison vitiated.

The problem of establishing sufficient equivalencies between two or more groups of individuals to permit the drawing of causal inferences is difficult at best, but this particular method of "equating" groups is especially dubious. In any case, a more modest conclusion would clearly have been in order here.

Parenthetically, it should be of interest in this connection to

---

* Donald T. Campbell refers to this type of quasi-experimental model, aptly enough, as the "nonequivalent control group" design. For his critique see Donald T. Campbell and Julian C. Stanley, *Experimental and Quasi-experimental Designs for Research* (Chicago: Rand McNally, 1963), pp. 47–50.

jump ahead and take a look at a much later study (1973) that also attempted—in a more sophisticated fashion—to construct such an artificial "control" group on an ex post facto basis. Here we are referring to the recent important study conducted by Dorothy F. Beck for the Family Service Association of America, titled *Progress on Family Problems.*[99]

This was a large-scale descriptive "census" of all intake cases of FSAA member agencies for a period of one week in the spring of 1970. Eighty-one percent of the agencies participated, reporting a total sample of 3596 cases from 266 agencies in the United States. These cases were then reported on at closing, or for a period up to two years. Reports were obtained for 94 percent of the sample. In addition, a follow-up contact after closing was attempted by interview or mail questionnaire and was completed for 53 percent of the total.[100]

While a wealth of valuable analysis and findings was presented in this impressive report, we will limit our comments here to the portion of the study dealing with the evaluation of service outcome.[101] A variety of measures of client change were utilized, including worker and client global ratings, specific problem change ratings, and the like. Overall, approximately seven-tenths of the cases showed improvement, a figure similar to those found in numerous other studies of social treatment and psychotherapy.[102] The question of course has to do not so much with the level of this gross overall "improvement" rate as with whether or not it is any better than would have been achieved without any treatment. Since in this survey there was no feasible way of making a controlled comparison with an equivalent nontreatment group, a special technique was developed to derive a baseline. The method was to use the known characteristics of the families to calculate a "predicted" change score, that is, the average level of change observed in the total sample by cases with a given combination of characteristics.[103] The comparisons were made between "extensive service" cases and "minimum service" cases, the latter including six categories (such as cases receiving only one interview, cases in which only one family member was seen, etc.).[104] It was found that the "extensive service" cases significantly outdid their "predicted scores" in terms of average change, whereas the "minimum service" change scores fell short of projection. Moreover, the greater the service input as measured by number of interviews, the greater the tendency of the change scores to outperform predicted improvement. From this it was concluded that "the only logical explanation for the consistent variation in the change scores in relation to the level of service investment by the agency is that, in the main, the improvement reflected the results of agency service."[105]

But it may be seen that what we have here is a refined version of the nonequivalent "control group" design employed in the Jewish Board of Guardians Study a quarter of a century earlier. The "minimum service" cases did not go on to become "extensive service" cases for various reasons—either their own or the agency's or both. While an impressive effort was made by the researcher to equate these groups statistically, the matching was obviously limited to those "tangible" factors that were recorded on the study schedules, and this admittedly did *not* include such key dimensions as client motivation, attitude, and the like. Since these omitted variables are apt to be related to both continuance and progress in treatment,[106] the cause-effect interpretation may well be spurious. Useful and ingenious as this study may be, then, we are led once again to seek more powerful means of experimental control in order scientifically to establish the causal connection between treatment and results.

We shall now temporarily drop the trail of experimental evaluative designs in social treatment evaluation, to pick it up again in the following chapter. The path in any case broadens and proliferates so rapidly as we enter the 1960s that it is necessary to be ruthlessly (and arbitrarily) selective.* The present chapter concludes with the following section, which briefly sketches the rise of experimental evaluation in social welfare administration.

## The Administrative Experiment in Social Work

Concurrently with the emergence of experimental evaluation in social treatment, a significant series of field experiments† in social work administration were conducted that warrant some attention

---

* We omit, for example, a leading recent example of a field experiment in social work: the study by William F. Reid and Ann W. Shyne, *Brief and Extended Casework* (New York: Columbia University Press, 1969). It is not covered here because the publication is readily available and accessible. The work is strongly commended to the reader as a highly influential, technically competent, and unusually literate study report.

† Some of the following examples have been referred to in the literature as "demonstrations" rather than "experiments" on the basis of their less rigorous research emphasis and control. We have preferred to use the terms *experiment* or *quasi-experiment* to apply to any study in which there is an attempt to manipulate one or more variables systematically. See Donald T. Campbell and Julian C. Stanley, op. cit.; also, Edwin J. Thomas, "Field Experiments and Demonstrations," in Norman Polansky, ed., *Social Work Research* (Chicago: University of Chicago Press, 1960).

here. These first arose in the late 1930s in the field of public assistance, in response to the concern with heavy case loads in public welfare agencies and the mounting relief rolls and expenditures following the passage of the Social Security Act. The focus was on testing the effects of modified administrative patterns—primarily reduced caseloads—on services to recipients and their subsequent relief status.

While not the first of such efforts,[107] perhaps the best known early study of this sort was *Adequate Staff Brings Economy* (1939).[108] The project was conducted in a district office of the Chicago Relief Administration. Its purpose was to demonstrate the results of reduced caseloads and other administrative improvements in terms of "more thorough investigations, reduced relief costs, and better services to relief recipients."[109] Underlying this purpose was the desire to lift the restriction imposed by Illinois statute on administrative costs in public assistance (including all staff costs), namely, its limitation to 8 percent of total agency expenditures.

The reduction of caseloads was accomplished by more than doubling the field work staff, thus lowering average loads in the "demonstration" office from 169 to 80. Other improvements in clerical support, supervisory resources, and physical working conditions were introduced during the study period.

In order to provide a "control group" for comparison purposes a 10 percent random sample of recipient cases was selected from the other eleven district offices within the city. While this design could not provide an "equivalent" group to the demonstration district caseload, it did permit some comparative analysis within the limitations of this form of quasi-experiment.[110]

The study was conducted for three months, during which period caseload costs and turnover were monitored, services to recipients were recorded and classified, and investigation procedures were documented. A special schedule was completed on each case in the demonstration office and in the 10 percent "control" sample from other offices.

This study, like other experiments of this type conducted over the years, resulted in the finding that "adequate staff brings economy"; that is, the investment in additional field personnel yielded a net saving to the agency in terms of reduced relief expenditures. There were fewer openings, lower average grants, and more closings in the demonstration office than in the outside "control" group. This was apparently accomplished through the more efficient weeding out of ineligibles and the pruning of overpayments. There was also an increase in "rehabilitative" services and referrals of clients, though there was no direct measure of change in the social functioning of recipient families. The central goal of the demonstration was accomplished when the Illinois General Assembly raised the statutory limit on relief administration from 8 percent to 10 percent shortly after the study findings were released.[111]

There are, however, important pitfalls in such an undertaking from a technical standpoint that should be recognized. For example, in this type of demonstration there is the hazard of a strong "Hawthorne effect," in which the specially motivated demonstration workers might well be functioning at an atypically high level—even taking their reduced workloads into account—that could not be maintained over time. The brief three months' duration of the experimental conditions lent itself to such a "temporary" impact. Indeed the positive findings of most such administrative experiments might be atributed to this factor. It is not likely that such an influence would have been operating to the same extent in the "control" sample, since only a small percentage of a regular worker's caseload was included, and of course their working conditions were not altered. Moreover, it is not possible in this kind of design to isolate *which* of the experimental working conditions were most responsible for the improved output, since several changes—in addition to reduced work loads—were introduced concurrently into the demonstration office.

A much more elaborate experimental design was followed in a similar study in 1941 conducted by the California State Relief Administration[112] Picking up from the favorable conclusions of previous projects of this type, it attempted to pinpoint the optimal size of workload in relation to such results—in effect, an early type of cost-benefit analysis. To determine this relationship, three different categories of workers were given caseloads of varying size, ranging in different groups from 50 up to 200. Furthermore, there were *two* parallel "demonstration" offices in which the experiment was conducted, thus helping to eliminate idiosyncratic factors that may have affected a single location. Careful (and complicated) procedures were worked out to ensure unbiased randomization in the assignment of cases and workers, and to standardize the work pace at the several levels of operation during the three-month experimental period. The findings documented the relationship that the lower the caseloads, the greater the net savings.

A quantum leap forward in this line of investigation was taken in the highly creative experiments devised in Michigan by Edwin J. Thomas and his associates in the late 1950s.[113] Here the focus was not economy per se but, rather, on the relationship between modified administrative patterns and worker performance and family change. The project was stimulated by the 1956 amendments to the Social Security Act, which for the first time broadened the program objectives to include the strengthening of family life and self-sufficiency of recipients. The project purpose was to test the efficacy of in-service training of public welfare workers and of reduced caseloads in bringing about such improvement in family functioning and self-dependence.

The first experiment described in this report involved four groups of workers, two of which were given in-service training and two of which were not; in addition, two of these four groups were provided reduced workloads and two were not. The experimental design is schematized in the following chart, taken from the report.[113]

DESIGN OF THE FIRST EXPERIMENT

| | Status of Training | |
| --- | --- | --- |
| Workloads | Direct, specialized training of workers | No specialized training of workers |
| Reduced workloads | I. Training and reduced workloads (8 workers) | II. Reduced workloads only (7 workers) |
| Non-reduced workloads | IV. Training only[a] (6 workers) | III. No-change group (5 workers) |

[a] This *training only* group was not included in the first study, but was added to the design of the second. Logically, it belongs to the design for the first study.

This double-dichotomy design permitted not only the differentiation of training and reduced workload in terms of their effects, but also the impact of the combination of these factors.* The training consisted of direct sessions with a training supervisor for 4 hours per week over a period of 15 weeks. The reduced caseloads consisted of 50 Aid to Dependent Children cases compared to the regular average of approximately 100. The goal of caseload reduction was reflected in the level of casework activity subsequently recorded—1.82 contacts per case with the reduced caseloads, as contrasted with 0.67 contacts per case for the no-change group.[115]

In order to measure change in worker performance, several innovative and imaginative techniques were developed. Foremost

* It should be noted, however, that the groups were "nonequivalent," since they were selected from different counties. Some adjustments for such differences were attempted in the statistical analysis.

among these was the "experimental interview," in which a well-briefed and rehearsed actress played the role of a recipient in a number of standardized "episodes" while being interviewed by the worker.[116] This was the first time this flexible and promising training and research tool had been applied in social work. The worker's performance was then rated according to criteria applicable to several dimensions of casework skill. In addition, special tests of knowledge, analytical skill, motivation, and ethical attitudes were developed and used here.[117] In the area of family functioning, changes were classified according to "rehabilitative" or "nonrehabilitative" closings, family problems affected, and self-support.

The findings indicated that reduced workloads were significantly associated with positive changes for families in the three preceding areas. However, in-service training did not add significantly to such improvements in family living when combined with reduced caseloads, nor did it contribute measurably when given alone. These conclusions were interpreted as meaning that workers already knew how to do a "better job" than they were able to do with their regular workloads. Reductions enabled them to do this better job, with or without formal in-service training. The training may have been too brief, and its value was in any case masked by the overriding impact of more time and contacts per case, which the lower caseloads permitted.

The foregoing experiment was followed by a second one in which the training was done indirectly—through the training of supervisors rather than front-line workers—and in which the workload "reduction" was approached through time-saving procedures rather than through actual lowering of the number of cases. Neither of these devices worked out successfully in their implementation.

This project obviously represents a great advance over preceding ones in this line of research. The rigor and technical sophistication of experimental design were far ahead of the early studies. The measurement technology—particularly the experimental interview—was frequently original and broke new ground for the field. The period of one year for each of the two experiments was more adequate than the usual period of several months. On the negative side, the sample of workers in each group was small, making differences between groups more difficult to discern. And the pervasive "Hawthorne effect" may have been operating to some extent in the experimental groups, though it is interesting to note that the training-only group showed no significant difference in output. Any special "incentive" by virtue of being singled out for this part of the demonstration apparently was not instrumental in their productivity.

To bring this account of the administrative experiment somewhat up to date, reference should be made to the most extensive and ambitious of this series—Edward E. Schwartz's "Midway Office."[118] In view of the recency and general availability of this important work, only a brief highlighting will be attempted here. In the early 1960s the professional experienced an extremely tight labor market in the face of expanding social programs; more particularly, the optimal role of the trained social worker in public assistance was at issue within this context. The major question had to do with the comparison of the operation of a "conventionally organized public assistance staff"[119] (i.e., a supervisor overseeing several untrained caseworkers) with a newly devised team structure consisting of a professionally trained supervisor and several untrained staff who functioned on a task assignment basis rather than on the customary case assignment basis.[120] In the full design of the experiment, a secondary comparison was also set up between the foregoing two patterns in a "high-caseload situation" and a "low-caseload situation" (i.e., 90 cases per worker vs. 45 cases per worker).[121]

In essence, this complex plan called for the organization of a special experimental office of the Cook County Department of Public Aid in the vicinity of the Midway Plaisance (mall) adjacent to the University of Chicago. This experimental "Midway Office" recruited a staff of workers and supervisors, largely made up of volunteers for transfer out of other districts. The personnel were organized into four work groups, which functioned with the usual "high" caseloads, and six work groups with "low" caseloads (as defined previously). Each work group consisted of a supervisor and five untrained workers. Half of the work groups functioned "conventionally" (on a case assignment basis), while the other half functioned as "experimental teams" (on a task assignment basis). Thus the double-dichotomy design involved a total of 10 groups, 10 supervisors, and 50 workers, structured as follows:

| Caseload Size | Conventional Pattern (Case Assignments) | Experimental Teams (Task Assignments) |
|---|---|---|
| High caseload (90 cases per worker) | 2 work groups | 2 work groups |
| Low caseload (45 cases per worker) | 3 work groups | 3 work groups |

Within this format 3150 cases in the Midway district were randomly assigned to the 10 work groups. The experiment was implemented over a two-year period, from February 1963 through March, 1965. The overall study hypothesis was "the following admittedly over-simplified and rather static umbrella proposition";

1. The experimental team form of organization will provide a work situation that will engender higher morale in its members than the conventional work group will.
2. Therefore, the experimental teams will produce more work.
3. Therefore, the clients served by experimental teams will show more positive change.[122]

To abbreviate the rich and variegated findings, the first two parts of the preceding hypothesis were not statistically sustained by the evidence, while the third part was generally supported. Reduced caseloads were more effective than team patterning in increasing work performance; they were also a contributing factor in the greater progress of "team" clients over "conventional" clients. The changes in families and individuals were not measured by any of the standard scales but, rather, by a special scoring system applied to various areas of family functioning.

Attention was given to the potential operation of the "Hawthorne effect," and it was concluded that it probably did not affect the comparisons appreciably in this project. In fact the possibility of a "negative Hawthorne effect" was noted, since all of the work groups were in the experimental Midway Office and the "conventional" workers appeared to be challenged to outdo their rival "experimenters."[123]

As is often the case in applied social research, the findings of this impressive study were outpaced by changing times and conditions. Some ten years elapsed from its planning till its final publication in 1972, and by then the political climate and professional context had altered considerably. In the public assistance field, steps had been taken toward the separation of financial grant determination and social services, and the trend had shifted even further away from the employment of professionally trained social workers for such services. In social work generally, the manpower "crisis" of the 1960s was replaced by the manpower "surplus" of the early 1970s, occasioned by the early demise of the Great Society programs and the retrenchment of social priorities by the Nixon administration. Hence, the external pressure for more efficient deployment of professional personnel eased somewhat, while the desirability of the public welfare agency as a setting for such deployment diminished. Nevertheless the implications of these experimental findings to the effect that task-oriented, professional-paraprofessional teams of social workers may be more successful in bringing about client progress than more traditional patterns of service delivery stand as promising guideposts to further research and administrative practice in social welfare.

# An Experiment in Prevention of Delinquency
## EDWIN POWERS

More public and private funds are pouring into crime prevention programs every year, and yet it is currently reported that youthful criminals are increasing in numbers and in the seriousness of their offenses. To account for this perverse condition one has a choice of a wide variety of explanations, depending upon whether one's frame of reference is psychiatric, sociological, or religious. Can delinquency be prevented? Has research an answer?

Numerous statistical studies have demonstrated the close association of overt delinquent behavior with specific personal and environmental factors. Relatively few reports, however, have highlighted the effectiveness or ineffectiveness of methods of prevention. Such reports as have been written are generally based on nothing more than faith or bold assertion, buttressed by illustrative cases.

### THE CAMBRIDGE-SOMERVILLE YOUTH STUDY

Dr. Richard C. Cabot relatively early in life won a reputation in medical research as the "greatest contributor to cardiology in our generation."[1] In his later years he was equally well known and respected in the fields of social service and social ethics. He was keenly aware of the discrepancy in method between the laboratory technician and the social scientist who seldom had available adequate measures of evaluation by which to check his practice. In his presidential address to the National Conference of Social Work in 1931 he asserted:

> Many of us are now forced to base our opinions on the value of any given piece of social work largely on the character, experience, and expertness of those in charge of it. But even persons of the highest value may be doing work of far less value than they and others think, unless it can be shown to measure up reasonably to the standards which it sets for itself. [He looked forward to] the much-to-be-desired epoch when we shall control our results by comparison with a parallel series of cases in which we did nothing.[2]

From Edwin Powers, "An Experiment in Prevention of Delinquency," *Annals of The American Academy of Political and Social Science*, 261 (1949): 77–88. Reprinted with permission of publisher.

[1] Dr. Paul D. White, "Richard Clarke Cabot, 1868–1939," *The New England Journal of Medicine*, Vol. 220 (1939), pp. 1049–52.

[2] National Conference of Social Work, *Proceedings*, 1931, 3–24.

A few years later Dr. Cabot established a ten-year research project in delinquency prevention utilizing, perhaps for the first time in history, a carefully constructed control group.[3] To each of six men and four women, trained in social work or allied professional fields, were assigned a number of boys, usually 30 to 35, all under the age of 12 (with an average age of 10½), in the hope that by wise and friendly counsel supplemented by social case work techniques, these young children might be encouraged to make the most of their potential assets and become useful, lawabiding citizens. About half of the group were already showing definite signs that pointed to a delinquent career.

The plan called for an evaluation by comparing 325 T boys at the end of a contemplated ten-year program with a C group[4] similar in numbers and in all other relevant respects but receiving no help or guidance from the study, the hypothesis being that if the two groups were similar at the outset, than any significant behavioral differences between them at the end of the program could reasonably be attributed to the major variable in the picture—the counselors' treatment.

## LENGTH OF PROGRAM

Work was started at the end of 1937 with five selected boys. Seventy-one additional boys were placed in the program in 1938, and work with the remainder was commenced during the first half of 1939. After two or three experimental years, 65 boys, or 20 percent of the total group, were dropped from the program because they presented no special problems and were definitely nondelinquent.

The remaining 260 boys, including both the delinquency-prone and the nondelinquent, were retained for varying periods of time. Death of a few, removal of some of the boys from the local area, the loss of staff due to the demands of World War II, and the departure of some of the older boys for war service or enlistment in the Merchant Marine made it impossible for the counselors to continue with all of the 260 boys. Close associations were maintained and case work continued

[3] This project, located in Cambridge, Massachusetts, was called the Cambridge-Somerville Youth Study, as it embraced in its operations the city of Cambridge and the adjacent city of Somerville. It was supported entirely by funds contributed by the Ella Lyman Cabot Foundation, a charity incorporated in Massachusetts in 1935. Dr. Richard C. Cabot and Dr. P. Sidney de Q. Cabot were the original codirectors of the project until the death of the former in May 1939, when Dr. P. Sidney de Q. Cabot became the sole director. On his resignation on January 1, 1941 the author became the director of the project until its termination. During the course of the treatment program a total of approximately 75 people were employed, half of them on a part-time schedule. Approximately 22,000 pages of records have been compiled relating the story of what happened in the lives of these boys over a crucial period of their existence.

[4] T and C in this article refer to the treatment and control groups.

with 113 boys for an average period of 4 years and 2 months; with 72 boys for an average of 5 years and 11 months; and with 75 boys for an average of 6 years and 9 months. For none did the treatment program, which closed on December 31, 1945, last more than 8 years and 1 month, although many of the counselors still keep in touch with the boys assigned to them.

## WHERE THEY ARE NOW

More than a decade has now elapsed since the study's first acquaintance with these boys and their families. The group's average age is now 20—the oldest 22 and 8 months. A number of these youngsters who were in the lower grades of the elementary public schools when first known to the study are now married and fathers of a second generation. Some are earning good incomes, some are unemployed, some are officers or enlisted men in the Army or the Navy, a few are still in school, while others are in reformatories or prisons.

The study, over the years, has seen boys become delinquent in spite of its best preventive efforts, and it has likewise seen others, who seemed less promising at the outset, achieve considerable success. Take the case of Dick, for example. A counselor became Dick's friend and visited him at frequent intervals but utterly failed to prevent him from expressing his assaultive tendencies, which led him in his later adolescent years into robbery and eventually into State Prison. Assisting in the treatment plan were a psychiatrist, numerous school teachers, and two social workers from another agency called into the picture by the study. Three foster homes, though temporarily apparently successful, had no real deterrent effect on the boy.

Or there is the case of Tony, a persistent truant. The social workers, cooperating with the schools and the attendance officers, using all techniques available to them, supplemented by psychiatric advice and the counsel of a clinical psychologist, watched helplessly as this boy developed into a sly thief and was committed to a county training school for truancy and subsequently to three different correctional institutions before he reached his nineteenth birthday.

On the other hand, we see John, well on his way toward a delinquent career when first known to his counselor, now a law-abiding citizen with a good job. If his counselor had not shown a friendly interest in him, he tells us, he would today be confined in a prison or reformatory.

The fathers of these boys, too, were often appreciative of the work done for the child or for the entire family. At the end of the treatment program Joe's father wrote the counselor a letter of warm appreciation for keeping the family together and giving him the courage and confidence to carry on in spite of most adverse circumstances.

The picture of what happened in treatment—how many boys became delinquent and how many did not—will be more meaningful if the research structure is first briefly described.

## THE EXPERIMENTAL DESIGN

As the project was essentially a study in the prevention of boy delinquency, it called for the selection of boys under 12 who had not yet become delinquent but who might some day constitute part of the prison population. Who were these hypothetical youngsters, and where did they live? That was the first problem. Secondly, it was necessary to balance this group of predelinquents with boys who showed no such signs of early delinquency, for one aspect of the project was to study a wide variety of boys and to note later what kind became delinquent and what kind did not. Furthermore, for practical reasons it was necessary to include a group of presumed nondelinquents, for to deal solely with boys who would be labeled "predelinquent" would be unfair to the boys and impractical of accomplishment.

Teachers in the Cambridge and Somerville public schools and the Cambridge parochial schools submitted on request the names of many boys whom they regarded as "difficult" (in the study's scheme this meant "probably predelinquent") and many others whom they considered normal or "average" boys. All referrals were subsequently classified in accordance with the delinquency prognostic scale as described below. Approximately 1,500 names of boys under 12 were submitted by the schools.[5] At this point neither the boy nor his family knew that his name had been submitted.

Social agencies in the locality were also requested to submit names of "difficult" boys known to them. Court records were examined and police and probation officers were interviewed in order to include all boys in both cities who at an early age were considered troublesome or likely to become delinquent. From these supplementary sources 450 names (with some duplications) were received.

Thus, at the end of a two-year search, there were on file at the study the names of all boys in both cities (with the exception of boys attending the private schools or the Somerville parochial schools) who were believed destined to become delinquent, plus an equal number who were thought to be non-predelinquent.

## HOW EACH BOY WAS STUDIED

A comprehensive picture of the boy, his family, and his social environment was obtained from a variety of sources. Social workers were sent to the homes for interviews with one or both of the boy's parents. Information concerning the boy's developmental history, his habits, his recreation, his attitudes toward school, his religion, and his personality

[5] The original plan called for boys between *the ages of 6 and 7.* It was soon learned that boys in this age group were not well known by the schools, and because of their tender years were referred far less frequently than the older boys. It was necessary, therefore, in order to get the desired number of boys of predelinquent tendencies, to shift the upper age limit to 11 and later to 12 when delalys in starting the program were encountered. [Emphasis added].

was obtained and recorded. Basic information relating to the parents' education, employment history, social activities, and so on was also sought. The boy's potentialities as well as the total impact of forces upon him were described by the social workers with their own interpretations and numerous rating scales. Although they went to the boys' homes unannounced and without previous notification to the parents, they were, in most cases, cordially received. They reported that in three-quarters of the homes they were received in a very friendly spirit, while in only eight cases out of 839 homes visited did the parents definitely refuse to be interviewed in the first instance.

Extensive information was then obtained from each boy's teacher through long personal interviews conducted by a member of the staff, supplemented by the checking by the teacher of rating scales and cards listing personality traits. The teacher was also asked to give a brief personality description of the boy.

Staff psychologists gave each boy tests to measure his mental ability and school achievement, and the boy's grade placement was recorded. Dr. Richard C. Cabot himself gave the physical examinations, noting at the same time the general impressions made upon him by the child. He was assisted by a staff nurse who independently recorded her own impressions and interviews with the boys. Official reports about delinquency or criminality of boys or parents were obtained from the State Board of Probation, from the local courts, and from the police and probation officers of the two cities, all of whom were very cooperative. Information was also obtained from those agencies listed in a central Social Service Index as acquainted with the families. The neighborhoods in which the boys lived were studied and rated in terms of the probable good or bad influences on a boy living in each locality. Delinquency "spot maps" constructed on the basis of a survey of all official court records for the two cities over a four year period assisted in establishing the neighborhood ratings. A small school photograph of each boy was also available.

## SEPARATING GOOD FROM BAD PROGNOSES

The plan called for 650 boys to be divided equally into an experimental and a control group. Almost three times that number had been referred. A selection and screening process was necessary to assure the study a group of boys about equally balanced between the predelinquent and the non-predelinquent. The policy was adopted of not eliminating any boy who showed obvious predelinquent traits, provided he met the other necessary requirements of age, residence, and school attendance.

To determine which boys might reasonably be labeled predelinquent and which non-predelinquent was the next problem. Reliance could not be placed on the teachers' referral alone, for the teachers were not acquainted with the great variety of facts pertaining to the boy and his family that were available to the study. A committee of three individuals experienced in dealing with both youthful and adult delinquents made a thorough study of the comprehensive data assembled in each case, although they had no opportunity for personal interviews with the boys.

This committee consisted of one psychiatrist and two prison case workers. With a prognostic scale that ranged from plus five, indicating the greatest probability that the boy would *not* develop a delinquent career, through zero, the mid point, to minus five, indicating the greatest probability that the boy *would* develop a delinquent career, they were able to classify the 782 boys who had survived the preliminary screening process. Judgments of committee members were independently arrived at, group judgments being invoked in cases of initial disagreement. Thus, all 782 boys were finally scored on an eleven-point scale for probable delinquency.[6]

## CREATION OF TWO MATCHED GROUPS

Out of the 782 cases available, two staff psychologists created two matched groups consisting of 325 boys each. A method of matching boy with boy, combining a statistical study of more than 100 relevant variables with a clinical interpretation of the personality as a whole, divided the 650 boys into two similar groups. Two boys were considered a well-matching pair if the configurational pattern of the most important variables showed them to be psychologically similar. A coin was tossed to determine which boy of a given pair was to be placed in the treatment group and which in the control group, thus eliminating any possible "constant error" after a pairing had been made.

The most important variables, in addition to age and prediction rating (which within each pair showed little, if any, variation), were health, intelligence and educational achievement, personality, family factors, and environment. Emphasis was placed on the relationship of the variables, on the profile or "contour" of the personality, rather than on the presence or absence of a large number of independent factors. It was subsequently found that the T–C group differences in the arithmetic means of 20 selected variables were extremely small—so small as to be almost negligible. Thus, the study was provided with controls that adequately served the purpose of comparing quantitative data later ascertained for each group.

## THE TREATMENT PROGRAM

The 325 T boys were then assigned to ten counselors. The younger boys, as a rule, were assigned to the four women counselors. During the

---

[6] An analysis of the variables noted and a description of the method of prediction has been published in an article by Donald W. Taylor, "An Analysis of Predictions of Delinquency Based on Case Studies," *Journal of Abnormal and Social Psychology*, Vol. 42 (1947), pp. 45–56.

course of the program nine additional counselors were engaged to meet the unanticipated turnover of personnel due to the war demands.[7]

Treatment consisted of the application of whatever skills each counselor was capable of applying. The essence of the relationship between the boy and his counselor was personal intimacy and friendship. "What is it that keeps any of us straight unless it is the contagion of the highest personalities whom we have known?" asked Dr. Cabot in an earlier talk.[8]

Each counselor was left largely to his own resources. The agency policies, instead of being predetermined, as in most other social work agencies, were gradually evolved during the course of treatment. To social workers the "friendship" emphasis may have seemed old-fashioned and paternalistic; in practice, counselors were permitted and encouraged to utilize any of the modern techniques of social work with which they were familiar.

Although some counselors considered the job to be that of an orthodox social case worker, others did not. One counselor, for example, believed that genuine, personal friendship was of greater value to a boy than all the technical skills that a more objective social worker could bring to the case. Inspiration, practical help, and persuasion were more commonly used by this counselor than was the traditional method of searching for the basic causes of the maladjustment. Others believed that the skill of the psychiatric social worker was indispensable in treating delinquency as a symptom of the boy's maladjustment. Certainly no one point of view prevailed, either as to therapy or as to the interpretation of the concepts used.[9]

[7] Only two of the original ten served during the entire treatment period, from 1937 to 1945. It was necessary, therefore, to assign approximately one-third of the 75 boys who were carried through the entire program to four or five different counselors; another third to three; while the remaining third were not reassigned more than once. Of the nineteen counselors, eight were professional social workers, six had completed part of the academic requirements for a degree in social work, two were experienced boys workers, one was a trained nurse, and two were psychologists. The counselors represented a wide distribution of ages, with an average of approximately 31 years. Three of them were about the same age as the boys' parents; nine were under 30.

[8] In an address called "The Consecration of the Affections," given before the American Social Hygiene Association, February 3, 1911.

[9] It became increasingly evident that the concept "delinquent boy" was misleading. A single act (minor or serious) might make a boy delinquent in the legal sense, but one could not draw valid generalizations about a group of boys who were similar in respect to a legal judgment but who differed among themselves in almost every conceivable way, each responding to a different combination of forces. The medical analogy that a delinquent boy is a "sick" boy leads one further astray. The evidence seems to show that delinquent behavior, as a rule, is more likely to be related to a normal, impulsive response to a particular culture or specifically to the restrictions of that culture, or the yielding to the adolescent's urge for exciting adventure rather than to any serious emotional conflict or abnormality. Most delinquents be-

Attention was given to each boy individually. Many visits were made to his home and to his school. Group work was seldom used. Sometimes the boy was taken on trips or to the counselor's home, or (particularly in the later years of the study) to the office of the study for scheduled interviews with the counselor. Some boys were seen two or three times a week for long periods of time; most of them at less frequent intervals. An important feature of the program was its coordination with available resources and agencies in the community.[10]

## Areas of Emphasis

Treatment comprised a wide variety of activities. An analysis of the records at the end of the program showed that major emphasis had been placed on the boy's adjustment to school. The co-operation of the school officials was good throughout the history of the study. Counselors continually visited each school to seek information or to enlist the co-operative efforts of the teachers in treatment planning. Frequently it was important to interpret to the teachers the boy's difficulties and to acquaint them with the conditions in the boy's home which so frequently were unknown to them.

So many of the boys in trouble were retarded in school that the staff employed special tutors, who had had public school teaching experience, to give individual attention to 93 of the boys during or after school. Special attention was given to reading difficulties commonly found among retarded children.

Another area of treatment constantly receiving the attention of the counselors was the boy's health. The counselors arranged for more thoroughgoing physical examinations for the boys, and many of them were taken to clinics or hospitals or were treated by the staff pediatricians. For eight summers camping was made available through local camping associations or other youth organizations. Two hundred and four boys were sent to camps for two-week periods or longer. Counselors, too, frequently took the boys on overnight or week-end camping trips. They guided them to recreational opportunities and in some cases obtained for them scholarships or memberships in various organized youth groups. Boys were encouraged to develop their own religious ties.

The study initiated the placement of twenty-four boys in foster homes; sent ten to private schools, the expenses being underwritten by the study if the families could not meet all the costs. Much family case work was called for to gain the co-operation and understanding of the

---

come relatively law-abiding after the age of 18. Those who persist in their antisocial behavior constitute a highly selected group. Generalizations might be made with greater validity about the persistent delinquent who, on the whole, seems to be neurotic and unhappy.

[10] For a brief case study demonstrating the co-ordination of the services of the school and other local agencies, see Margaret G. Reilly, R.N., and Robert A. Young, Ed.D., "Agency-Initiated Treatment of a Potentially Delinquent Boy," *The American Journal of Orthopsychiatry*, Vol. XVI, No. 4, Oct. 1946.

parents and to assist them in dealing with their own or their children's problems. In fact, the counselors realized that winning and retaining the friendship and confidence of the parents was essential.

### Professional Services

During the last three or four years of the program there were available for consultation a pediatrician, a psychiatrist, and a clinical psychologist. During the early days of the study the counselors were not supervised by a trained social worker, although for a period of a little over a year an experienced social worker and director of a local children's agency was available once a week for consultation on especially difficult problems. During the last four years of the study the Director placed the entire treatment program under the supervision of a clinical psychologist who had had long experience in dealing with boys' problems. A counselor with special skills in dealing with family problems supervised that aspect of the work for a period of four years.

In brief, it can be said that the treatment program, utilizing some of the best professional advice obtainable, comprised an unusually wide diversity of special services to boys and their families, from removing nits from boys' heads (and their siblings' heads, too!) to preparing them for higher education.

### DISTINGUISHING FEATURES OF THE STUDY

It is so unusual for one to carry on research with boys with whom one is at the same time attempting treatment that the project was faced with a number of unprecedented situations. As there has not been, to the writer's knowledge, any other research project comparable to the study, some of its unique aspects may be pointed out.

*Aid unsought*—Boys receiving guidance from the study had not asked for it. The counselor's first visit to the boy and his family occasioned surprise in some cases, while in others it was taken as a matter of course, the assumption being that the counselor came from the school. Would a boy or his family profit by help if they were not motivated to seek it in the first place? The answer was "yes" and "no." Experience showed that in a few cases the offer of help was received with polite tolerance. In these instances case work was not possible. In a great majority of cases, however, a friendly relationship was very easily and early established. The personality of the worker seemed to be the determining factor.

If rapport were achieved, then the boy usually expressed his most obvious needs. If there were no need, expressed or even implied, over a long period of time, the case was usually dropped. It is evident that boys of eight to eleven in need of help do not ordinarily turn to a social agency. Their names do not come to the attention of social workers, as a rule, until something of an emergency nature has happened. There is some advantage, therefore, in becoming acquainted with the boy before a problem arises. It cannot be denied, however, that the plan of offering unsolicited help was financially extravagant.

*Not linked to special need*—The closing of a case did not follow upon the solution of a specific problem, as is usually true in social agencies. Most boys, in fact, had not been referred because of the existence of an acute problem. The case work relationship was, then, generally maintained beyond or in disregard of any special need, and in this respect was more akin to friendship than to conventional social work. The counselor stood by the boy "for better or for worse."

*Before the act*—Most studies of delinquents are made only after a boy has been in court or committed to an institution. The study was in the unusual position of observing the development of delinquent behavior in boys who, when first known, were not overt delinquents and in some cases not even considered predelinquents.

*Nonproblem boys*—The facilities of the study were not limited to those who were in need, but included a wide variety of boys, both "good" and "bad." The inclusion within the T group of boys whose problems were the normal problems of an average boy (or whose parents were adequate to meet any problem that arose) occasionally left the counselors in a state of confusion. It was frequently stated in case conferences that "the boys without problems are our greatest problems." Although there were obvious research advantages in including within the T group, for observation at least, all kinds of boys, the trained social workers were not eager to develop a relationship that seemed, from a professional point of view, to have no point. Nevertheless the project probably would not have been able to develop good public relations if it had not included "all kinds of boys." However, 18.7 percent of the "nonproblem" boys were carried through the entire treatment period.

*Objectivity*—Ordinarily, the very existence of an agency depends upon convincing a board of directors that its money has been well spent. Under such circumstances one is sometimes blinded to failure and is thus denied the benefit of searching self-criticism. The study, on the other hand, had ten years to go—and no longer—regardless of its effectiveness in preventing delinquency. It was trying to test, not to prove, the hypothesis that delinquency might be prevented by an indong what was best for the boy, on the keeping of accurate records, and on a fair evaluation. It is now in a position to give its first report on its successes and failures.

## DID THE C.S.Y.S. PREVENT DELINQUENCY?

Looking at the record at the end of the treatment program, *without reference to the C group,* the counselors could point to several very satisfying reports:

### The Treatment Group

1. There are 70 T boys who are now well past the age of 17 whose careers have been closely followed and who, as boys under 12, appeared to the predictors to be more likely than not to develop delinquent careers. That is, they had been rated on the "minus" side of the prediction scale. After these boys had been through the treatment program,

not more than one-third (23 boys) committed serious or repeated delinquent acts, while 31 of them proved not to be delinquent at all.

2. There are 163 T boys who, when under 12, were rated on the "minus" side of the prediction scale as "probable" predelinquents. How many of these boys in the ensuing years committed delinquent acts that led to their commitment to a correctional institution?[11] Inspection of the registers of the two Massachusetts correctional institutions for juveniles, the reformatory for older offenders and the House of Correction for the county in which Cambridge is located, shows that only 23 had been committed as of March 1, 1948. This rate, of 14.1 percent, seems a surprisingly low figure in view of the fact that the study, it was believed, included practically all boys in the two cities, with a combined populuation of 213,000, who showed early signs of future delinquency.

3. Counselors' opinions were sought—an unusual research procedure, and yet who would be in a better position to know the effect of their own treatment on their own boys? Each counselor, during the middle period of the program, was asked on three or four different occasions to list all T boys who he or she thought had been "substantially benefited by their contact with the study." Of the 255 boys then in the program, 166, or about two-thirds, were so listed. About half of the 166 were recorded by the counselors as having been "outstanding" in respect to benefit received.

4. Let us turn to the T boys themselves. They are much older now. They are in a position to look back upon their years of association with the study and to evaluate the experience with some insight. One hundred and twenty-five boys who in 1946 and 1947 were still in the Cambridge-Somerville area and who were available for a personal interview were questioned by special (nonstaff) investigators who had had no prior information about the study. The boys were asked direct questions concerning the part the study may have played in their lives. More than half (62 percent) of this large, unselected sample stated that the study had been of value to them. Jim's declaration that "they helped me keep out of trouble" was typical of many of the replies. Henry summed up the impact of the study upon his life by saying, "I used to be backward but they snapped me out of it and got me interested in so many different things and finally I got to college."

By such evidence alone, one might reasonably conclude that the study had been successful in preventing delinquency. Many illustrative cases could be given to "prove" the point in the traditional manner. Such evaluation, though of the customary type, is inconclusive.

### The Control Group

At the core of the plan was the *control group.* What had happened to boys who had received *no* help at all from the study during the years

---

[11] About nine out of every ten of these boys are now over 17; a few over 21. Most of the remaining are 16, the youngest 15 years and 5 months.

in question? Had they become delinquent with greater or less frequency and seriousness than the T boys? We now look at the record.

1. The records of the Crime Prevention Bureau, established in 1938 by the police department in the city of Cambridge, reveal some interesting facts relating to the T and C boys who lived in Cambridge. Practically all boys who are reported by citizens or officials for minor offenses come to the attention of this bureau. Some recorded offenses were relatively trival, such as "upsetting bags of ashes" or "taking rope from a flagpole"; others were serious enough to be referred to the local court for disposition.[12] Without differentiating degrees of seriousness, a tabulation of offenses from 1938 to 1945 (while treatment was in progress) lists the names of 267 T boys but only 246 C boys. It appears, at first sight, that treatment was ineffectual.

2. Two evaluations were made, also while treatment was in progress, by comparing samples of T boys with their paired controls. Comparisons of scores on a wide variety of tests, questionnaires, and rating scales pertaining to character, personality, social behavior, and achievements showed that while, as a general rule, the T boys excelled the C boys, the group differences were uniformly so small that they could be attributed to chance.

3. Studying the records of the 68 C boys who have passed the age of 17 and who were characterized as predelinquents in their early years (that is, they had been rated "minus" on the prediction scale in the same manner as the 70 T boys above referred to) but who were not subjected to the study program, we find that an almost equal proporation had refrained from serious delinquency. The record shows that 27, or 39.7 percent, of the older C boys had become more or less serious delinquents, compared to 23, or 32.9 percent, of the comparable group of T boys. The difference of 6.8 percent in favor of the T boys is obviously not great.

4. Taking the 165 C boys who had been predicted on the "minus" side (in the same manner as the 163 T boys above referred to), we find on an inspection of the registers of the same correctional institutions where we sought the names of our T boys, that 22, or 13.3 percent, of the C boys had been committed for delinquent behavior—about 1 percent *less* than the percentage of committed T boys.

5. A comparison can also be made of the frequency of delinquent offenses that brought the T or the C boy to the attention of the court (although court appearance may not have led to an institutional commitment). The State Board of Probation that compiles data recording the

[12] Many boys, of course, who committed delinquent acts were not known to the police. An estimate was made from the records of the study of the number of unlawful acts committed by boys that did not result in an official complaint, for one reason or another. A study based on the records of 114 boys showed that there were approximately 4,400 minor offenses. Less than 1 per cent of these were prosecuted. See Fred J. Murphy, Mary M. Shirley, and Helen L. Witmer, "The Incidence of Hidden Delinquency," *American Journal of Orthopsychiatry*, Vol. XVI, No. 4, Oct. 1946.

appearance of boys in any court of the state discloses the following facts:

Of the 325 T boys, 76 are listed as having a court appearance for a relatively serious offense, compared to 67 of the 325 C boys.

If we include minor offenses along with the serious, the score stands: 90 T boys, 85 C boys.[13]

## FIRST CONCLUSION

A T–C comparison of official records made within a few years after the termination of the treatment program shows that the special work of the counselors was no more effective than the usual forces in the community in preventing boys from committing delinquent acts.

The utilization of a control group thus casts a sharply revealing beam of light on the record. The effectiveness of the professional staff in preventing delinquency was clearly below anticipations, although it must be conceded that the difficulties of carrying out a well-planned and consistent program were considerable, in view of the impact of the war and the resulting turnover of personnel.[14]

Before we conclude that the treatment program was completely ineffectual, let us look deeper. There is evidence to suggest that, given a further lapse of time, greater differences between T and C groups in the seriousness of official offenses may appear in favor of the T boys. It begins to look as though the C boys are the more serious and the more persistent offenders. We find, for example:

1. The Crime Prevention Bureau statistics show that the C boys are more frequently brought in for repeated violations.

2. The records of correctional institutions show that more C boys (8 in number) have been sent to more than one institution than T boys (4 in number).

[13] By "minor offense" is meant: traffic violations, breaking glass, using profane language, hopping a ride on a streetcar, or the like. The Board of Probation records were cleared as of July 1, 1947.

[14] Although relatively meager records were kept relating to the behavior of the C boys, it might be deduced from the T-C comparison that what was happening to the predelinquents in the T group was happening to the predelinquents in the C group. If counselors were successful in preventing some boys from becoming delinquent, then it would be reasonable to infer from our statistics that certain deterrent forces in the community were operating with equal effectiveness on the C group during the same period of time. One is prone to overlook the strengthening influences of the home, the church, the school, and the public and private agencies in combating the forces of evil. It is reasonable to assume that without such influences the entire group of 165 predelinquent C boys might have developed into serious, offenders. Seldom do we hear the question—"Why is there not more delinquency?" Seldom does one know or appreciate the extent of preventive work constantly going on. Indeed, there is less need for concern over the fact that there is so much delinquency than there is reason for optimism over the fact that there is so little, in the face of so many adverse circumstances.

3. Eight of the more serious offenders were committed to the Massachusetts Reformatory, an institution for older male criminals between the ages of 17 and 30. Seven of these were C boys.

4. Again, in comparing the number of boys who had committed more than four serious offenses (known to the authorities), we find the names of five T boys and nine C boys.

5. In a list of the 108 relatively serious offenses (arson, sex offenses, burglary, assault with a dangerous weapon, robbery, and manslaughter), 46 were committed by T boys, 62 by C boys.

## SECOND CONCLUSION

Though the counselors were unable to stop the rapid advance of young boys into delinquency with any greater success than the usual deterrent forces in the community, some of the boys were evidently deflected from delinquent careers which, without the counselors' help, might have resulted in continued or more serious violations. Thus, the evidence seems to point to the fact that though the first stages of delinquency are not wholly averted when starting treatment at the 8-to-11-year level, the later and more serious stages are to some degree curtailed.

This conclusion must, of course, be subject to a further check at a later time.

These facts, based on group statistics, do not necessarily imply that the counselors were not helpful in individual cases. Furthermore, delinquency was not the whole story. The making of good citizens—"social adjustment" in the language of the social worker—was the broader objective on which the study was based. An examination of the records and interviews with the boys themselves offer evidence that in many cases, even in the lives of many of the delinquent boys, emotional conflicts were alleviated, practical problems were dealt with successfully and boys were given greater confidence to face life's problems.

An analysis of the less tangible effects of treatment is now being made. The Ella Lyman Cabot Foundation is planning a series of publications to include a complete account of the treatment program and a more extensive evaluation of it. Answers will be attempted to such questions as—"What types of treatment were most effective?" "What kinds of boys were responsive—what kinds unresponsive to the counselors' services in general and to specific types of treatment measures?" "Can delinquency be predicted?" "Do delinquent boys come from 'delinquent areas'?" "From this experiment, what implications for social work can be drawn?" Case studies will describe how some boys became delinquent in spite of treatment and how other boys were helped to build constructive lives, emphasis being put on factors in the boys' lives and in treatment measures that differentiated these two types.

As indicated at the close of Edwin Power's article, a further analysis of the "less tangible" effects of the treatment program was undertaken. The researcher who carried this out was Helen Witmer (later research director of the U.S. Children's Bureau). Her intensive "case study" emphasis exemplifies the frequent contrast between a *social work* research approach and a *social science* research approach. In the following excerpt the actual individual case summaries have been omitted.

# Value of the Study to Individual Boys

## HELEN WITMER

To determine which boys were helped by the study services requires the making of difficult decisions. "Helped" to what? "Value" for what? Those are the basic questions. Reference to the narrow objectives of the Study suggests that the answer should be "helped to avoid delinquency"; reference to the broad objective suggests "value for character development." The impossibility of determining in any particular case so negative a factor as help in avoiding something led to the control-group plan, for surely one can seldom say that such-and-such a boy would have been delinquent if the Study worker had not been on the scene. As to value for character development, neither the control-group nor one of individual analysis would seem of much use, for strength and depth of character cannot be measured, in spite of the implication of the terms, nor is it possible to demonstrate that any particular event or series of events contributed to the development of a boy's character.

The value or the help that is in question when judgments about the usefulness of a social agency's services are being made can, however, be defined by reference to the function of social work. This can be seen when the "value for character development" argument is pursued a bit further. Stated most generally, the function of social work is to help individuals deal with the difficulties that stand in the way of their playing their required part in organized social groups or in making use of those groups' services. Youth has a culturally prescribed role to play in relation to family, school, job, neighborhood, government, and informal associations of friends, but not all individuals are able to play their part adequately or to take advantage of the opportunities afforded by the various social institutions, such as schools and recreational associations. The value of a social agency's services to a particular individual should be judged, then, by whether it helped him play his socially assigned role better—whether, for instance, in consequence of the agency's services he could function better in school, be more law-abiding, relate himself better to his companions, and so on.

From Helen Witmer, "Value of the Study to Individual Boys," in Edwin Powers and Helen Witmer, *An Experiment in the Prevention of Delinquency: The Cambridge-Somerville Youth Study* (New York: Columbia University Press, 1951), chap. XXV, 421–455. (Reprinted with permission of publisher and Dr. Witmer.)

Obviously, services can be of value without having such consequences. For example, a boy may go to camp, take art lessons, acquire a good friend without any noticeable change in his general behavior or in his relations with people; the value may lie in his enjoyment of the activities and in the broadening and enrichment of his life. Educational and recreational institutions operate on this basis: their services are given, not to help the individual deal with difficulties that stand in the way of the socialization process, but to further that process by direct methods, and the value of their services is to be judged thereby. The Study, however, was not such an institution, although it used some of those institutions' methods. For example, the Study provided tutoring if boys needed it. Its aim in doing so, however, was not only the direct one of improving the boy's ability to read or understand arithmetical processes, as would be a school's aim. The Study provided this service if the counselor thought that lack of ability to read was handicapping the boy in his social adjustment; the service, therefore, would be judged of value not on the basis of the boy's improvement in reading but by reference to his behavior in school and elsewhere.

The value of the Study services had to be judged, then, not by whether the boys enjoyed the opportunities afforded or by whether their range of interests was broadened or by whether they became closely attached to the counselors, but by whether, through the services, the difficulties that stood in the way of their socialization were lessened and they operated better in family, school, job, and so on. In a sense, then, the value of the Study in individual cases was judged by improvement in what is commonly called "social adjustment." A boy, however, was rated as helped only if it could be shown that obstacles to his social adjustment, either in the boy himself or in his environment circumstances, were dealt with by the counselors, and the boy, apparently in consequence, functioned better in social relations. Moreover, in the classification system described below, we took into account how sure we were that it was the Study services that had produced the change, a distinction being made between cases in which we were sure that counselors had been helpful and those in which the value of their services seemed dubious.

It will be noted that we are not proposing that a given boy be regarded as helped merely because his adjustment became better, which is the test used in many psychiatric follow-up investigations. We are saying that it is expected that a boy handicapped in a certain way will improve if that handicap is removed. If, therefore, the provision of Study services did remove the handicap and the boy's adjustment did improve, we say that the improvement was due (in part, at least) to those services. In other words, our judgments refer not only to the boy's behavior but to the conditions believed to influence that behavior. These judgments are validated, to some extent, if it can be shown that the boys who were rated as benefited differed from those who were not benefited, both in the nature of their handicaps and in the measures that were used to aid them.

In this evaluation, emphasis was placed on how sure we were that the boy had been helped, not on how good his adjustment became. A boy who was originally very much maladjusted might have received much help and still not be functioning as adequately as another boy who apparently was helped only slightly or perhaps not at all by the counselors' efforts. The extent of relation between amount of help received and terminal social adjustment will be shown later through comparison of the two series of ratings.

A classification of "value of service" requires that each category be sufficiently defined and its limits set sufficiently clearly that competent judges can agree fairly well in the rating of cases. In this study, however, the judgments were made only by the writer; they were not tested by formal submission to other judges, although there was a certain amount of informal checking by reason of the fact that case records were abstracted and rated by several readers (of whom the writer was one) before final judgment was passed. Such a procedure was followed because it was thought that adequate judgments could not be made unless all the records were studied and compared with as much care as was given by the writer to the task; for a larger number of judges that would be too time-consuming a job.

In the following descriptions of categories the considerations that led to the placing of cases in particular groups will be stated, and the cases themselves will later be described and compared. The reader will have at hand, therefore, some of the facts on which the writer's judgments were based and can check the ratings for himself.

## VALUE-OF-SERVICE CATEGORIES

In order to compare the boys in these various ways it was necessary, of course, to divide them into groups on the basis of the extent to which they appeared to be benefited by the Study services. We accordingly set up the following descriptive categories, which were arrived at through careful comparison of the individual case records.

    A. Boy clearly aided by the services.
    B. Services possibly of some assistance but not much change in behavior effected.
    C. Little accomplished in spite of friendly relations.
    D. Services ineffectual:
       1. Boy or parents refused help.
       2. Work of counselors slight or of poor quality.
       3. Other reasons.
    E. Boy did not need help.

Definitions and examples of each of these types will be given below, while in later chapters analyses of all the cases within each category will be made.

It is to be emphasized that it is not the type of service but the changes effected by it that are under consideration here; if we mention type of service, it is only to elaborate upon the nature of its effect. Similarly, we are not primarily classifying the boys' adjustment, although that necessarily entered into the evaluation of how influential the work was. The work might be influential, however, even though a boy did not become well adjusted; conversely, a boy might become well adjusted for reasons other than the receiving of the service. With these reservations, then, the following are the value-of-service categories.

*A. Boy Clearly Aided by the Services.* In these cases the connection between the boy's improvement in social adjustment and the help given him by the counselors seemed indisputable. This is not to say that the Study was the only beneficial factor in the situation or that the boy became thoroughly well adjusted; in some cases, in fact, the boy had many favorable factors in his environmental situation and never was very maladjusted, while in others he was severely handicapped and made only moderate gains. What we mean, then, by an A rating is that the services appeared to be genuinely helpful and that without them it seems unlikely that the boy would have done as well as he did.

The basis on which such judgments were made varied considerably from case to case. In some the improvement in adjustment followed rapidly when, through the counselor's efforts, certain specific handicaps were removed; in others the good results seemed attributable largely to the work of social or psychiatric agencies whose services the counselor secured for the boy. . . .

*B. Services Possibly of Some Assistance But Not Much Change in Behavior Effected.* Three types of cases were grouped together in this category—the first two listed in subsequent tables as B1, the other as B2. In B1 were put the cases in which (a) a relatively well-adjusted boy appeared to derive some slight benefit from the concrete services the counselors were able to afford him, and (b) a more maladjusted boy was probably helped but the total effect seemed rather slight. . . .

*C. Little Accomplished in Spite of Friendly Relations.* The cases in this category were rather misleading in that the parents or the boys regarded the counselors as good and helpful friends, sought their services frequently, and expressed much gratitude for what was done for them. There was little indication, however, that the boys' behavior or personality problems, which were never very severe, improved much or that the boys in any demonstrable way were greatly aided by the counselors' efforts, though the work could not be judged wholly ineffectual. . . .

*D. Study Ineffectual for One or Another Reason.* In setting up the sub-categories under this heading we did not attempt to take into account all the kinds of reasons for the lack of effectiveness of the Study's work. In fact the more important of them, from the viewpoint of this evaluation, can be ascertained only by inter-group comparisons. For instance, one cannot say, on the basis of a series of unsuccessful cases alone, that it was the severity of the boys' emotional maladjustment that was the barrier to effective work. Such a conclusion can logically be reached only if comparisons with a series of successful cases show many fewer such boys among the ones who were benefited. . . .

*E. No Need for the Study's Help.* Finally there was a considerable number of cases in which there was little or no need for the services of the Study; hence it was impossible to judge the value of the services that were given. For the most part the boys in this category had been referred to the organization to meet its request for "average" or well-adjusted youngsters. To many of the boys in this category only slight service was given but some were seen at fairly frequent intervals over a considerable period of time. More than half of these cases were dropped when war conditions forced the organization to retrench. . . .

The distribution of boys according to these categories of value of service, sub-divided to indicate whether the case was dropped or was carried through to completion (that is, to the end of the Study or to the boy's 17th birthday), is set forth in Table 1. Before considering the significance of these figures, however, we want to show the extent of correspondence between these ratings and two other types of data by which the accomplishments of social agencies are frequently judged.

## CORRESPONDENCE WITH OTHER TESTS OF ACCOMPLISHMENT

Social agencies frequently test the effectiveness of their services by describing either how well adjusted their clients became by the time work with them ended or how much they improved during the period of contact. Figures with respect to these two points have been presented in the preceding chapter, where it was shown that about a third of the boys were very well adjusted and another third fairly well adjusted when last known, and that this represented improvement over the original situation in about 40 percent of the cases. Since much the same situation was found in the control group, however, it was not at all certain that this fairly good showing could be attributed to the counselor's efforts.

Table 1 **Distribution of Boys by Value and Duration of Study Service**

|  | Duration of Service | | | |
|  | Dropped | Completed | Total | |
| Value of Service | | | *Number* | *Percent* |
|---|---|---|---|---|
| A. Definitely beneficial | 16 | 33 | 49 | 19 |
| B. Possibly beneficial | | | | |
|    1. Slight benefit | 2 | 22 | 24 | 10 |
|    2. Temporary benefit | 3 | 10 | 13 | 5 |
| C. Little accomplished in spite | | | | |
|    of friendly relations | 5 | 15 | 20 | 8 |
| D. Clearly ineffectual | | | | |
|    1. Offer of service refused | 18 | 2 | 20 | 8 |
|    2. Work insufficient or poor | 27 | 17 | 44 | 17 |
|    3. Other reasons | 10 | 34 | 44 | 17 |
| E. No need for help | 24 | 16 | 40 | 16 |
|      Total | 105 | 149 | 254 | 100 |

In Table 2 the extent of correspondence between the terminal adjustment ratings and those referring to value of service is indicated. It will be noted that only a third of the well-adjusted boys and less than a fourth of those rated fairly good in adjustment were boys whom the Study clearly appeared to have benefited. At the same time, a fifth of the boys whose terminal adjustment was rated poor seemed possibly to have been helped somewhat by the counselors. The table thus shows that the value-of-service judgments were not based on terminal adjustment alone. It also suggests that, in spite of the control findings, the good showing of some boys may have been attributable, in part at least, to the counselors' services.

In Table 3 this possibility is further explored by comparison of the value-of-service ratings of the boys who improved greatly during the period of Study contact with those who made little improvement or became less well adjusted. We have earlier pointed out the impossibility of making accurate judgments about improvement in social adjustment or character, since most children have their ups and downs and since standards vary from one age to another. Nevertheless, an attempt at judgment on this point was made by noting the extent of difference between initial and terminal adjustment ratings,[1] the following scale being used:

I. *Boy became better adjusted*
   a. Initial rating 5; terminal rating 1, 2, or 3
   b. Initial rating 3 or 4; terminal rating 1 or 2
   c. Initial rating 2; terminal rating 1

Table 2 **Relation Between Value of Service and Terminal Adjustment**

| Terminal Adjustment | Value of Service | | | | | | | |
|---|---|---|---|---|---|---|---|---|
| | A | B | C | D3 | D1 | D2 | E | Total |
| 1. Good | 26 | 2 | 2 | — | 5 | 11 | 30 | 76 |
| 2a. Fairly good | 13 | 12 | 6 | 5 | 7 | 16 | 6 | 65 |
| 2b. Fairly good; neurotic | 9 | 9 | 5 | 2 | 1 | 5 | — | 31 |
| 3a. Rather poor | — | 3 | 4 | 1 | 1 | 4 | 1 | 14 |
| 3b. Rather poor; neurotic | — | 5 | 2 | 9 | 2 | 4 | — | 22 |
| 4a. Poor | — | — | 1 | 3 | — | — | — | 4 |
| 4b. Poor, neurotic or psychotic | — | 6 | — | 8 | — | 1 | — | 15 |
| 4c. Chronic delinquent | — | — | — | 14 | — | 1 | — | 15 |
| Not known | 1 | — | — | 2 | 4 | 2 | 3 | 12 |
| Total | 49 | 37 | 20 | 44 | 20 | 44 | 40 | 254 |

[1] It will be recalled that the initial ratings were made on a five-point scale, in which values 3 and 4 differed in quality but perhaps not in degree of maladjustment, while the terminal adjustment ratings were made on a four-point scale.

   II. *Boy became less well adjusted*
     a. Initial rating 1; terminal rating 3 or 4
     b. Initial rating 2; terminal rating 3 or 4
     c. Initial rating 3 or 4; terminal rating 4
   III. *Boy remained the same*
   IV. *Terminal adjustment not known*

Table 3 again demonstrates that the value-of-service ratings were not based primarily upon adjustment or change in adjustment, for of the 101 who became better adjusted only 35 were rated as clearly benefited by the organization's services, while four of the 24 who became worse seemed possibly to have been helped somewhat. Among those who became better adjusted, those whom the counselors appeared to have aided were more likely to be boys who made a slight change (and that form a fairly good to a good adjustment) than the boys who changed greatly. This rather important finding is in line with data to be presented later. If correct, it would help to explain the lack of difference between the Study and control series, for such slight improvement might well have taken place in the absence of the counselors' help.

A third test of results sometimes employed by social agencies is that secured by asking the clients, sometime after service is ended, whether they had benefited. Material on this point for the present study was provided by an independent investigation conducted by graduate students, this study being made one to two years after the Study period of service had ended.

For this follow-up investigation boys were selected by the Study executive on the basis of availability. One hundred and eighteen boys were interviewed. Tabulation of their distribution among the value-of-service categories indicated that, while they did not constitute a proportional sample of all the categories (very few, for example, of those

Table 3 **Relation Between Value of Service and Degree of Change in Adjustment**

| Change in Adjustment | Value of Service | | | | | | | | | |
|---|---|---|---|---|---|---|---|---|---|---|
| | A | B | C | D3 | Total | D1 | D2 | E | Total | Total |
| I. Became better | | | | | | | | | | |
| a | 3 | 4 | 1 | 7 | 15 | 1 | 1 | — | 2 | 17 |
| b | 17 | 14 | 7 | 5 | 43 | 2 | 7 | — | 9 | 52 |
| c | 15 | 1 | 1 | — | 17 | 3 | 10 | 2 | 15 | 32 |
| Total | 35 | 19 | 9 | 12 | 75 | 6 | 18 | 2 | 26 | 101 |
| II. Became worse | | | | | | | | | | |
| a | — | — | 1 | — | 1 | — | — | 1 | — | 2 |
| b | — | 3 | 2 | 5 | 10 | 1 | 4 | — | 5 | 15 |
| c | — | 1 | 1 | 4 | 6 | — | 1 | — | 1 | 7 |
| Total | — | 4 | 4 | 9 | 17 | 1 | 5 | 1 | 6 | 24 |
| III. Remained same | 13 | 14 | 7 | 21 | 55 | 9 | 19 | 34 | 62 | 117 |
| IV. Not known | 1 | — | — | 2 | 3 | 4 | 2 | 3 | 9 | 12 |
| Total | 49 | 37 | 20 | 44 | 150 | 20 | 44 | 40 | 103 | 254 |

who refused to participate being included), marked "successes" and marked "failures" were equally represented among them.[2]

The investigators presented themselves to the boys as persons who were unconnected with and largely ignorant of the Study program. In soliciting opinions of it they said either that somebody was considering setting up such a program in another city or that the people who had provided the money for the Study's activities wanted to find out what the boys thought of the program. They asked the boys, among other questions, what the organization's purpose was, how they happened to be invited to join in its activities, who their counselors were, how they liked the program, what they thought its value to themselves and others had been.

All but one or two of the 118 boys selected for interviewing were willing to talk to the investigators. The great majority appeared to express their opinions very frankly, though there was, of course, much variation in their articulateness. Widely different opinions about the value of the Study were expressed. Categorized, they were as follows:

1a. Some boys were highly enthusiastic about the program, thought the services had been of great benefit to them, and stressed especially the value of their personal relationships with the counselors and the intangible benefits secured.

> *Lester.* When asked whether he thought this program was some-thing that could keep a fellow straight, Lester replied, "Yes, it's hard not to, when you know they'll ask you why and how—ask you for the story. You're in good with them, so you just don't do things. You know them so well you tell them the inner things— they get them out of you. Yah, they make you feel at ease; they're easy to talk to. And sometimes when you're trying to say some-thing, they help you say it."

1b. Others talked chiefly in terms of the "concrete" assistance. These boys stressed such services as tutoring, medical care, recreation, aid when in difficulty with the police, and said that they had been definitely helped thereby.

> *Spike.* "I have nothing but good to say for the Study." He went on to describe the program largely in terms of recreation, the good

| [2] Value of Service | In Sample | Total | Percent in Sample |
|---|---|---|---|
| A | 27 | 51 | 53 |
| B | 23 | 35 | 66 |
| C | 13 | 20 | 65 |
| $D_1$ | 2 | 20 | 10 |
| $D_2$ | 13 | 44 | 30 |
| $D_3$ | 24 | 44 | 55 |
| E | 16 | 40 | 40 |
| Total | 118 | 254 | 46 |

times he had with the counselors and the boys he met at the Study. He also mentioned the help given him in finding jobs.

*Eliot.* This boy stressed recreation, help with schoolwork, help when he was in court. "The aim of the Study was to make a regular guy out of you." It was chiefly useful, he said, for "kids that haven't got much—money, intelligence, things other kids have, such as bikes. It keeps them busy and off the streets."

1c. Still others were not quite so explicit about being helped. They said they appreciated greatly the counselor's friendship but did not say specifically that they had followed the advice they received.

*Julius.* "N was one of the best friends I ever had. If I ever needed him, I could always rely on him. A lot of times I went to him with problems and asked him what to do. When I quit school, my brother got mad, so I asked N and he told me the best thing was to go back. But I quit because my mother needed the money. . . . A lot of times I could get along better with N than with my brothers and sisters. They'd tell him to tell me what to do and I'd do it faster than for them."

2. Other boys were somewhat less enthusiastic. Some of them spoke in affectionate terms of their counselors but were a bit uncertain as to whether they had been helped. Others were rather vague about the value of the program as a whole but mentioned some services that had been helpful.

*Pasquale.* "The aim of the Study was to make good citizens, to develop talents." It was of use to him because of the tutoring provided and because "they had my ears fixed, so people don't laugh at me so much anymore." "The program can lead a guy but the rest is up to him." He apparently was not sure that he had been helped greatly.

*Cornelius.* His counselor was very nice, this boy said, and helped him with schoolwork and by securing medical care and sending him to camp. The Study "helped some kids to get self-confidence"; for himself he "didn't have much to do with it."

3. Some boys were more dubious about Study benefits. "It was okay," some of them said, unenthusiastically. "It was a good thing, I suppose, but I didn't go there much," said others. "It was all right for kids who were in trouble but I didn't need it." Such remarks, as well as the rather frequent comment that they remembered little about the organization, were characteristic of these boys.

4. Finally, some boys (4a) were either very ambivalent about the organization or (4b) said its services were of little value to them, though in some single aspects its work may have been useful, or (4c) were certain that the whole program was valueless.

*Buddy.* "They kept me out of trouble—they thought!" The boy went on to tell about various escapades then and now, making it clear that he paid little attention to what the counselors or his parents thought. "Most of the fellows went along for the ride. That's what

I did. We used to go different places. It gave you something to do. I'd make things in the woodworking shop. I liked to do those things. I miss them now."

Nearly half of the 118 boys interviewed expressed opinions of the first type, nearly a third made replies of the second or third type, while about a fourth were clearly skeptical of the organization's value. These proportions cannot be immediately generalized to refer to the total group of boys served by the Study, since the sample of boys interviewed contained somewhat disproportionate shares of the various value-of-service groups described above. If attention is confined, however, to the 87 boys in the most significant groups (A, B, C and D3), and the boys who either did not need, did not want, or were not adequately given service are omitted, this discrepancy between the sample and the total population almost disappears. We find, then, in this representative sample of boys who needed and more or less accepted help and were given service in line with the organization's intentions that about a half thought the service of value, a third were more or less dubious, and about a fourth said they had received little, if any, benefit from it (see Table 4).

Just what were the characteristics of the boys who expressed these various types of opinions is a question of interest, but our desire here is to show to what extent the boys' opinions coincided with the judgments arrived at by the writer on the basis of the case record material. The relationship is shown in Table 4.

Apparently almost all the boys whom the writer rated as having been definitely benefited by the organization's services would have agreed with that judgment. Twenty-three others also described the Study as very worth while, but most of them did not make it so clear that they thought their conduct had been influenced by the counselors' efforts. Apparently a boy might have the highest regard for his counselor and appreciation of what he had done for him and yet not credit the counselor with having changed his behavior greatly. This was the sort of

**Table 4 Boys' Opinions and Writer's Judgments of Value of Study Service**

| Boys' Opinions | Writer's Judgments of Value of Service | | | | | | | |
|---|---|---|---|---|---|---|---|---|
| | A | B | C | D1 | D2 | D3 | E | Total |
| 1. Study very worth while | | | | | | | | |
| a. Conduct influenced by relationship with counselor | 14 | 1 | 1 | — | — | 1 | 1 | 18 |
| b. Benefited by material services | 10 | 2 | 1 | — | 3 | 3 | 5 | 24 |
| c. Services appreciated; effect on conduct not mentioned | — | 3 | 3 | — | — | — | — | 6 |
| 2 Somewhat worth while | 3 | 8 | 4 | — | — | 4 | 1 | 20 |
| 3. Dubious value | — | 3 | 2 | — | 2 | 4 | 6 | 17 |
| 4. Little or no value | — | 6 | 2 | 2 | 8 | 12 | 3 | 33 |
| Total | 27 | 23 | 13 | 2 | 13 | 24 | 16 | 118 |

appreciation of the Study expressed by most of the boys not rated as being clearly benefited.

Two-thirds of the boys who had not benefited (D3) were dubious about the value of the Study or said that it had been of little or no use to them. The boys who refused the offer of service and those with whom little or poor work was done (D1, D2) were also largely in agreement with the writer that the organization had not helped them. Characteristically, most of the boys in Category C, those who had had very friendly relations with their counselors but did not appear to have benefited significantly, reported that they liked the Study very much, as did about a fourth of those in Categories B1 and B2, whose case records seemed to indicate that what benefit they had received had been slight or only temporary.

A review of the most striking exceptions to the agreement between the boys and the writer (the four cases in Category D3 in which the boys said they greatly appreciated what their counselors had done for them) provides some clues as to reasons for the divergence in opinion.

Two of these four boys described the value of the Study in terms of their personal relations with the counselors. One said briefly, "They were like your own folks." The other, a very verbose individual, said, "I wouldn't be where I am today if it weren't for Mr. B. He taught me to understand loyalty and trust and respect. He was like a father—no, like an official. He didn't tell me I had to do anything—just gave me advice and suggested. . . ." The case records showed both of these boys to be very unstable emotionally, perhaps of psychopathic personality, as judged by their "smooth" ways, their constant promises to do better, their ability to use people for their own interests. The one boy had a long record of delinquency and was in the state reformatory at the time of the follow-up interview. The other had joined the Merchant Marine and was passionately devoted to the seamen's union; shortly thereafter he quit the service and stayed around home, as irresponsible and immature as always.

The two other boys stated explicitly that they considered the Study chiefly worth while because it helped them to stay out of delinquency by keeping them busy. The testimony of one of them seemed rather unreliable, for he was somewhat drunk at the time of the interview; taken at its face value, the benefit he derived was that of "encouragement" when "in trouble" (meaning when delinquent) in return for which he was willing to tell the counselor "anything he wanted to know." The other, a boy with a long history of emotional maladjustment and inability to relate well to people, said that the Study was important to him for its help when he was in difficulty with the police and for providing a place where he could play. "There's nothing to do around these streets," he said. "The nearest playground is a mile and a half off in the 'nigger' section and they beat you up if you go there."

From this it seems clear that the boys' opinions of the value of the Study cannot be accepted at face value but must be judged in relation to the whole story of the organization's contact with them and their personality make-up. An enthusiastic endorsement of the organization may mean only that the speaker is one who is accustomed to telling adults what he thinks they want to hear, or it may indicate a dependent individual's liking for being kept in line or out of difficulty, or it may mean that the client greatly enjoyed certain of the organization's activities or appreciated the counselors' friendship without necessarily being greatly influenced thereby. Or there may be other explanations that the cases so far examined do not reveal. The point of importance is that testimony as to an organization's value to an individual must itself be evaluated—which leaves the research worker in the awkward position of maintaining that his own judgments are more valid than those of the persons who received the organization's services.

In spite of this rather disappointing conclusion, Table 4 is of value in confirming to a considerable extent the judgments arrived at in the previous section of this chapter. One of our objectives in that analysis, it will be recalled, was to find the boys who were clearly benefited by Study services so that we might compare their terminal adjustment with that of their control twins. It was reassuring, therefore, to discover that all but three of the boys in the sample who had been classified as clearly benefited stated that the Study had helped them very much, and that those three (boys with whom the Study had worked briefly) said that they had been aided by some particular service. At the other end of the scale, two-thirds of the boys classified as not having benefited (D2 and D3) stated frankly that they were dubious about the value of the services or that the services had been more or less useless; most of the others were the maladjusted boys described above. The opinions of most of those in the other categories (those who claimed more value from the organization than the writer thought justified by the case records) could be accounted for by facts much like those described in the divergent cases above. It is with considerable confidence, therefore, that we proceed with the further analysis of the findings with respect to these values-of-service groups.

## IMPLICATIONS OF THE FINDINGS

Returning now to an analysis of the figures in Table 1 (the distribution of boys according to these categories of value-of-service, sub-divided to show whether the case was "dropped" or completed), we note that the data can be considered from two angles: (1) that of the group as a whole, which would indicate what the Study accomplished with the total series of boys under consideration here,[3] and (2) that of the boys who needed and accepted the organization's help and were given service of the type the organization deemed adequate.

Viewed from the first angle, about a fifth of the boys appeared to have been definitely aided by the Study and another tenth got some

[3] Here, as elsewhere in this second part of the volume, "total" refers to the 254 boys, not to the 325 on the Study's original list.

slight benefit from its services. The rest, for one reason or another, did not appear to have been appreciably helped by the organization's work. This latter fact—that two-thirds or more of the boys were not significantly affected by the help given—would seem to go far toward explaining why the later social adjustment of the T-boys did not differ from that of the controls.

The second angle from which the figures may be considered is of chief importance to those who are interested in the social work implications of the data. Such persons want to know (1) what proportion of boys responded to this offer of service, which was so contrary to present-day social work practice (that is, soliciting the interest of the boys and their parents rather than waiting for them to seek the organization's help); (2) what was accomplished with those who especially needed the organization's help; (3) were better results obtained with those the Study worked with to the end than with those who were "dropped?"

> 1. The figures indicate that only 20 boys of the 254 (8 percent) who were approached by Study counselors either refused to have anything to do with the organization or soon lost interest. In some cases this was their own decision; in others, that of their parents. These were, of course, not all the boys who were "resistive"; they were, however, the only ones who were so resistive that the counselors did not have an opportunity to demonstrate what their services might consist of. It would seem, therefore, that "difficult" boys and their parents are not likely to object to being approached by a social worker who offers help.
>
> In drawing this conclusion, one must consider, however, the kind of help the Study offered, as described in Part I. Briefly, it was an offer to provide some recreational opportunities, help with school work, access to health services, and the like. Parents and boys, in the main, accepted such offers with pleasure. This response was in marked contrast to one reported by a skilled social case worker.[4] This case worker visited parents of delinquents and offered them help with their troubles. She did not secure nearly so favorable a response as did the Study counselors. Apparently, then, it was the specificity of the Study's offer, as well as the nature of it, that secured the favorable response.
>
> 2. In determining what proportions of boys were significantly aided by the Study, the 20 boys who refused the offer of service should be omitted from the total. So, too, should the 40 who were found to be so well adjusted that what the organization could do for them could be of little or no benefit from the viewpoint of social-work objectives. Then, if we are interested in learning what could have been accomplished rather than what was accomplished

[4] Bertha Capen Reynolds, "Between Client and Community," *Smith College Studies in Social Work*, V (1934), 43–97.

by work of this kind, the 44 boys with whom the work was below the agency's standards should also be dropped from consideration. Such omissions constitute 41 percent of the total series of cases and leave us with 150 boys who needed and accepted Study service and were given assistance of the type that seemed to be in keeping with what the organization aimed to provide. One-third of these boys (see Table 1) were clearly benefited by the help they received, about a fourth got slight or temporary benefit, and the rest (42 percent) got little or no help, as far as the writer could see. Whether this is a good or poor showing is difficult to determine, for comparable figures from other types of social agencies are lacking, though it is known that child guidance clinics usually fail to help about a fourth of their patients.[5]

3. There were some differences in accomplishments with the boys were were dropped[6] and those with whom work was carried on until completion, as defined in the plan of the Study. There were, of course, among the dropped cases more boys who refused the offer of service and more who had little or no need for it. These constituted 40 percent of the dropped boys and only 12 percent of the others. With such cases omitted, as well as those with whom inadequate work was done, the proportion of boys who benefited definitely or slightly was 41 percent in the dropped series and 29 percent in the series in which service was carried on until the planned-for termination. The proportion of cases in which the Study clearly failed, even though the work was carried on in accordance with the agency's standards, was higher in the latter group than in the former. Stated another way, a third of the boys whom the Study clearly helped were boys who were dropped rather early in the course of service.

These findings suggest that the long-time contact the Study planned on is not always necessary, that some boys can be aided in a relatively short time. To this may be added the fact (revealed through the analysis of cases) that to many boys the really effective service was given, and improvement in their social adjustment was secured, long before contact with them ended. With some exceptions, then, the lengthy period of contact called for by the Study plan did not appear to be needed by all the boys.

All in all, these findings suggest that if the intake of the Study had been limited in accordance with usual social-agency practice (to those who need and want the service) and if all the work had been up to the

[5] Helen L. Witmer, "A Comparison of Treatment Results in Various Types of Child Guidance Clinics," *American Journal of Orthopsychiatry,* V (1939), 351–361.

[6] Our figures for "dropped" boys, as stated earlier, omit the six who died or moved away soon after work with them started. Evaluation of results with these boys was clearly impossible.

Study's standards, the boys who clearly benefited would have been fairly numerous. Their proportion in the total might have been even higher than the one-third noted above, for "wanting help" would probably have been defined in such a way that some of the boys with whom the Study failed would not have been accepted as clients. Such a limiting of intake, however, was contrary to one of the basic principles of the Study; in fact, it was this practice of most social agencies that was one of the points at issue when the organization was set up. From that point of view, then, one of the chief findings is that only 8 percent of the 254 boys and their families definitely refused or lacked interest in the Study's offer of help. This would imply that the Study's plan of going out to the families of boys who are thought to be in need of help is usually successful in arousing interest. Such an offer results, however, in only about a third of the boys being helped to improve in social functioning. We are left, then, with the conclusion that the Study's plan cannot be universally recommended; and we want to know, more than ever, who were the boys whom it did help.

## COMPARISON WITH THE CONTROL GROUP

As will be recalled, in determining the value of the Study service to individual boys, we had two objectives aside from that of judging the program's effectiveness. The one objective was to provide a basis for discovering the distinguishing characteristics of the circumstances under which the Study's type of program can be helpful to difficult boys. This question will be answered in the subsequent chapters. The other objective was to provide data for analyzing further why the T-boys were apparently doing no better than their C-twins at the time their social adjustment was rated. At the end of the preceding chapter it was pointed out that this statement was true only when the two series of boys were considered as wholes, that there were pairs of cases in which the T-boy was functioning better than his twin. The question was raised whether these were the boys who had benefited significantly from the organization's work. The classification according to value of service makes it possible to answer that question.

Unfortunately for definite findings, the number of boys available for comparison is small. Of the 51 boys rated A (definitely benefited by the Study) there were only 15 whose C-twins' social adjustment was ascertained at the same age. (In 15 other cases the C-twin was located but there was a difference of more than a year in the ages of the pair when social adjustment was rated.) These 15 form about the same proportion of the total sample of 91, however, as the 51 do of total population, so they are probably representative of the whole.

When these 15 pairs of boys were compared with respect to terminal adjustment, it was found that in 11 pairs the T-boy had a better rating than his control, in only one pair did he have a poorer rating, and there were three pairs in which the rating was similar. These 11 boys accounted for more than a third of the cases in the total series in which the T-boy was doing better than the control. (See Table 5.) Much the same was true when the comparison was made without respect to age. There were then 30 boys to be compared. In that case, 16 of the T-boys had a higher rating and four a lower rating than their C-twins. These 16 again constituted a third of the pairs of that type. In spite of the small number of cases involved, these differences were found to be statistically significant.

At the other end of the scale the opposite condition obtained. Among the 19 pairs of boys of the same age in which the T-boys were not benefited by the Study (rating D3) the C-boys made the better adjustment in 10 cases and the T-boy in three; in six pairs the ratings were similar. When the comparison was made irrespective of age, the C-boy was found to be doing better in 16 out of 27 pairs, the T-boy in four, while similar ratings appeared in seven pairs.

In Table 5 comparable figures are presented for all the value-of-service categories, these being grouped in descending likelihood of the T-boys' adjustment being favorably influenced by the Study. It will be seen that in the first two categories (that in which the boys did not seem to need the organization's services and that in which they clearly benefited) the number of pairs in which the T-boy excelled in adjustment far outnumbered those in which the C-boy excelled. In the second group of categories (that in which the boys either benefited only slightly or refused the offer of service) there was the distribution of ratings that was to be expected by chance. In the third group, in which little if anything was accomplished with the boys, the C-boys made a much better showing than did the T-boys.

In spite of the rather small number of cases the consistency of these findings lends weight to the conclusion that when the Study services were effectual most of the boys did function better socially than their C-twins. This conclusion can be accepted, however, only if its opposite is also accepted: that some of the boys who were not benefited may

Table 5 **Distribution of Relative Adjustment Ratings of T- and C-Boys by Value-of-Service Categories**

| | Terminal Adjustment | | | | | | |
|---|---|---|---|---|---|---|---|
| | T and C of Similar Age | | | | Irrespective of Age | | |
| | T | C | | | T | C | |
| Value of Service | Same | Better | Better | Total | Same | Better | Better | Total |
|---|---|---|---|---|---|---|---|---|
| A. Clearly benefited | 3 | 11 | 1 | 15 | 10 | 16 | 4 | 30 |
| E. Help not needed | 6 | 6 | 1 | 13 | 9 | 10 | 3 | 22 |
| B1. Slight benefit | 4 | 3 | 6 | 13 | 6 | 5 | 6 | 17 |
| B2. Temporary benefit | 1 | — | 3 | 4 | 1 | 1 | 4 | 6 |
| C. Benefit dubious | 4 | 2 | 3 | 9 | 4 | 2 | 5 | 11 |
| D1. Refused help | 1 | 1 | 2 | 4 | 2 | 3 | 5 | 10 |
| D2. No benefit: poor work | 4 | 3 | 7 | 14 | 6 | 7 | 12 | 25 |
| D3. No benefit | 6 | 3 | 10 | 19 | 7 | 4 | 16 | 27 |
| Total | 29 | 29 | 33 | 91 | 45 | 48 | 55 | 148 |

have been handicapped in social adjustment by the organization's efforts. If this is true, we can conclude that the apparent chance distribution of terminal adjustment ratings noted in the preceding chapter was due to the fact that the good effects of the Study were counterbalanced by the poor. . . .

# A Follow-up Study of the Results of Social Casework

LEONARD S. KOGAN, J.McV. HUNT, and PHYLLIS F. BARTELME

## SUMMARY AND CONCLUSIONS

The follow-up method is generally considered to occupy a preeminent position among evaluative techniques designed to assess the effectiveness of such helping services as social casework and psychotherapy. Although other methods, for example, pre-tests and post-tests applied opening and closing of cases, analysis of interview protocols or case records, counselor opinions, and so on, may play an important role in providing evidence about changes in clients and their circumstances occurring during the course of a counseling process, only the follow-up method goes beyond the circumscribed period of contact and attacks directly the critical question: Do any apparent effects of the helping service continue to show in the life of the client after his case is closed? The follow-up method alone can provide ultimate criterion data against which to validate measures of results obtained during the period when service is rendered, unless the problem-begging position is taken that the goals of helping service are limited in temporal scope to what happens to the client between the time his case is opened and the time it is closed.

Historically, we were first led to the follow-up method as a logically necessary basis for assessing the validity of measures of change in clients and their circumstances which occurs in association with casework help. Two procedures for measuring such change had been developed at the Institute of Welfare Research of the Community Service Society of New York as the result of a collaborative effort between research workers and casework practitioners: the Distress-Relief Quotient and standardized judgments of movement in clients. We were interested in determining what value ex-clients would place upon the service they had received and whether or not apparent changes in adjustive and adaptive status observed to occur during contact persisted for some time after the cases were closed. From the standpoint of the validity of our measures of change, we wished to see how closely these measures are related to ex-clients' valuations of service and the persistence of change.

As the committee of caseworkers and researchers discussed the plan for a follow-up study, however, other purposes were added. We became interested in the following list of topical questions which in turn served as the basis for fairly intensive follow-up interviews that took place some five years after the cases were closed: (1) How well are the individuals in each family getting along at the time of follow-up? (2) What has happened in their lives since their cases were closed? (3) How well do the individuals who participated recall their casework experience? What aspects of it do they emphasize or de-emphasize? (4) What evaluative attitudes do the ex-clients exhibit toward the help they had received, toward their caseworkers, and toward the agency as a name or symbol? (5) Why do the families feel that their contact with the caseworkers did or did not help?

## METHOD

In its general outline the method of this follow-up study is uncomplicated. It consisted of having a highly experienced clinical psychologist find and interview, some five to six years after their cases were closed, accessible members of a sample of 38 families, who had received casework service from the agency. The follow-up interviewer was kept in ignorance about what had happened during the period of casework contact, except for information considered necessary to protect the welfare of both the ex-clients and the interviewer. This sample of 38 cases had been originally selected to represent three degrees of movement for the *case as a whole:* very little change, moderate change, and significant change. The 38 families were comprised of 139 individuals, 90 of whom the caseworkers attempted to help. Of these 90 individuals, 80 were actually interviewed during the casework contact. Nearly half the families were judged to be of the lower-middle class according to adaptation of the Warner system of classification, but they ranged from the upper-middle class (two families) to lower-lower class (three families). They mentioned all kinds of problems and probably more problems than was typical of families coming for family service. The number of different problems with which the caseworkers attempted to help them ranged from one to 15 with a median of nine. The families were also highly selected from the standpoint of the amount of service received. They derived from the minority of family service cases who received seven or more interviews. They were also provided with more financial assistance on the average than would probably be typical of a sample of cases from family service today. In terms of movement, some 75 percent of the clients judged showed positive improvement during the period of casework contact.

Because Americans are highly mobile people in the geographic sense, locating many of these 38 families was an exceedingly challenging task. It took the follow-up interviewer to the Midwest, the Far West, the

Southwest, and the South, as well as to most of the boroughs of New York City. In view of the fact that the sample of cases was fairly small, a strenuous effort was made to locate *at least one client* from each family. In this the follow-up interviewer succeeded. Of the 80 individuals whom the caseworkers had interviewed and attempted to help, the follow-up interviewer succeeded in directly interviewing 73 and had a telephone conversation with one more.

We attempted several innovations of follow-up method in this study. The follow-up interviewer located the family and appeared unannounced whenever possible, although at all times taking great precautions to protect the feelings and confidence of each ex-client. The initial follow-up contact, whenever possible, consisted of approaching the ex-client in a direct, face-to-face manner without previous communication by letter or otherwise. A standard opening question, when feasible, was asked of each client: "I'm from the Community Service Society. Do you remember us?" This approach was chosen, first, to permit a better chance of interviewing at least one member of every family in the sample, and second, to permit the follow-up interviewer to get the unprepared emotional reactions of as many clients as possible as these were registered by words and gesture. The follow-up interviewer succeeded in seeing 61 ex-clients in such an unannounced fashion. This method raised qualms on the part of some of the committee members and agency staff, but our experience indicates that in most cases the ex-clients were not distressed by such an approach. The follow-up interviewer met with co-operation from the great majority of the interviewees and what resistance occurred usually showed only in the form of hesitant response to the inquiry. The reaction of the ex-clients to the method of direct approach and the follow-up process is indicated by the fact that the idea of the study, when it was explained, was accepted by all but six of the 69 ex-clients for whom such a judgment could be made. Of these six, four were noticeably ambivalent while only two failed to co-operate beyond the initial meeting.

A second innovation was the condition that the follow-up interviewer should work without knowledge of the casework process or of the status of the clients at closing. She did not know who had apparently improved and who had not. Her information consisted of, in general, the nature of the problem at intake, a minimal description of the composition of the family, and the last known address. In some cases, however, the follow-up interviewer was provided with limited additional information felt to be necessary to protect both herself and the welfare of the client. This precaution of keeping the interviewer by and large without specific information about what had happened during the casework contact was taken to avoid the possible contamination of her inquiry and any judgments she would have to make by knowledge of which clients had shown improvement and which had not.

Typically, then, the follow-up interviewer located the client and presented herself with the statement, "I'm from the Community Service Society. Do you remember us?" She talked about the purposes of the study and made an appointment for a follow-up interview at the client's convenience. These follow-up interviews, which took from two to as long as six hours in two or more sessions, usually covered the following areas: (1) a description of how the various members of the family were getting along at the time of the interview, (2) what had happened in their lives since the time their cases had been closed, (3) what they recalled of their casework experience, and (4) answers to questions concerning whether the casework had helped, why it had or had not helped, and so on.

## RESULTS

### How Did the Ex-Clients Value Their Casework Experience?

The value attitudes of the ex-clients toward their casework experience were obtained in two ways. One method was to secure an immediate quantification of their opinions during the actual course of the interviews. This was a third innovation in the follow-up plan. The follow-up interviewer stimulated the ex-client to talk freely about whether or not the casework had helped him, what he thought of the caseworker(s) wo had served him, and how he felt about the agency. On the basis of the ex-client's free responses, the follow-up interviewer reflected several previously scaled statements approximating the attiude that the interviewee had exhibited in the free discussion. The ex-client then chose a particular scaled statement epitomizing his valuation.

Because a very high proportion of the ex-clients selected from the reflected statements the two statements representing the greatest degree of approval, it was decided to test the validity of the reflecting-back procedure against the content of the free discussion. The detailed, frequently verbatim, follow-up records contained many freely offered valuative statements. These were copied on separate slips of paper, sorted on a scale by five independent judges, and then the scaled values for the individual statements were reassembled to yield value attitude scores for each individual ex-client. The correlation between the valuations as obtained by the reflecting back of scaled statements during the interview and by means of the analysis of free statements was .82 for valuation of help, .68 for valuation of the caseworker(s), and .40 for valuation of the agency. The short-cut method of quantifying ex-client attitudes by immediate reflecting back of scaled statements during the interview appears to be satisfactorily valid, especially in the case of valuation of help by the ex-client. In any case both approaches to the quantification of client valuations clearly indicated that the majority of the ex-clients placed a high value upon their casework experience. Over four out of every five interviewees tended to select scaled statements that expressed highly positive valuations while three out of every five interviewees gave free valuation that fell at the ap-proving end of the valuative continuum. Only four out of 66 ex-clients expressed valuations indicating that they felt the casework help had been on the harmful side.

### The Predictive Validity of Movement and D.R.Q. Judgments

No significant relationships were found between the ex-clients' valuations of their casework experience with respect to help, caseworker(s), or agency and the movement judgments depicting the direction and amount of change that had occurred in the client and/or his circumstances during the period of casework contact. A similar lack of significant relationship was found to exist between the amount of distress relieved as measured by the D.R.Q. method and composite family valuations at follow-up. This is to say that clients who were judged to show no improvement are just as likely to place a high valuation on the help they received, their caseworker(s), and the agency as are clients who were judged to show great improvement. Neither is the degree to which the help is valued correlated with the amount of financial relief given or with the length of time the case was open.

To the extent, then, that client valuations secured at follow-up are considered to be significant criteria for determining the validity of movement and D.R.Q. judgments, the latter measures must logically be regarded as exhibiting insignificant validity. On the other hand, many considerations argue against the arbitrary designation of client valuations as satisfactory criterion data for validating measures of client change associated with the period of the casework contact. Client valuations may tend to reflect the manner in which help is given or attempted rather than the actual effectiveness of the help. Having someone listen sympathetically when a person is in distress may be a helpful experience in itself. The attitude of the ex-client may reflect to some degree a feeling of obligation on his part for the attempt that was made to help him. The expressed opinion of the ex-client may even reflect deep-seated personality characteristics or the degree to which he is charmed by the follow-up interviewer. Unfortunately, without further refinements, the follow-up method employed does not permit choice among these and other explanations for the failures of the measures of change to be significantly predictive of ex-client valuations.

### Can Follow-up Valuations Be Predicted?

Despite the finding that movement and D.R.Q. judgments do not show significant correlations with the client valuations of their casework experience, certain evidence indicates that it may be possible to make significant predictions of such valuations by means of other direct judgments made on the basis of case record material. Although the reliability of their judgments has not been established, two experienced caseworkers read the case records of the 38 cases and made predictions about how they thought each client would value the service he had been given if he were interviewed five years after the closing of his case. These predictions showed statistically significant correlations of .52 with the averaged valuative ratings for each ex-client based on his free statements and .36 with his averaged scaled statements. Moreover, ratings of the over-all level of adjustment of each client at opening and at closing also showed statistically significant correlations with the clients' free valuations at follow-up. These relationships have positive implications both about the accuracy of case records and about the ability of the experienced worker to make valid judgments about the client's attitude toward the service he has received. It seems clear that the client's valuations of his casework experience are not capricious even though they may not be related to the judged change that occurred in him and/or his situation during the time of contact with the agency.

## Was Improvement Sustained?

In many ways this question is the central issue of the present follow-up study. If one makes the assumption that the movement judgment reflects to a significant degree the actual change that occurred in the client and/or his circumstances during the period of casework contact, it still remains to be seen what happened after his case was closed. Without some variation of follow-up method, it is impossible to know, for example, that a client who showed apparent improvement during the course of contact did not backslide after his case was closed and revert to his former status.

To answer this question we employed the Movement Scale. Two judges trained in its application judged the movement shown by each client during the period between the closing of the case and the follow-up contact some five or six years later. These judgments were based upon specially prepared descriptions of the families at the time the cases were closed (from the case records) and independent descriptions of the families at the time they were seen by the follow-up interviewer (from the follow-up records).

The answer, on the whole, is that the gains associated with the period of casework were apparently sustained during the period from the closing of the cases to the time of follow-up. As would be expected, however, if casework has a beneficial influence, more of the ex-clients showed some deterioration between closing and follow-up than during the period of casework contact. Thus, whereas only six of the clients were judged to exhibit negative movement during the time of contact with the agency, some 26 of them showed negative movement subsequent to the closings. On the other hand, only three individuals actually deteriorated by more than one step-interval on the Movement Scale between closing and follow-up. This in turn was balanced by the fact that 13 individuals were judged to have improved by one or more scale-intervals from closing to follow-up. The general picture for the 76 individuals on whom relevant data were obtained was an average improvement of two-tenths of a step on the scale during the time from closing to follow-up. Even this $+.2$ of a step-interval is statistically different from zero, however, and there is evidence to conclude that on the whole the group showed a slight improvement after closing. The adjustive and adaptive status that the sample as a whole had attained by the time their cases were closed was evidently sustained in the subsequent five-year period before the follow-up interviews.

### Is Movement Subsequent to Closing Related to Movement During the Time the Case Was Open?

The amount of variation in movement scores in the period from closing to follow-up is almost as great as that which occurred during the case-work contact. This fact indicates that the picture is not the simple one of each individual tending to sustain or slightly improve his adjustive status between closing and follow-up. If this had been so, the majority of clients would have shown relatively little movement between closing and follow-up. Actually, only 39 of the 76 movement ratings for this period fell within the range from −.5 to +.4 step-intervals of movement. The remainder showed greater change.

The question thus arises as to whether there is a relationship between the direction and amount of movement shown by a client during the casework contact and the direction and amount of movement that occurs subsequent to closing. The distribution of movement scores judged to occur during the period from closing to follow-up does not reflect whether or not there is any dependence between movement subsequent to closing and movement prior to closing. If, for example, individuals who improved during the casework contact continued to improve, individuals who did not change during the contact continued to remain static, and individuals who deteriorated during the contact continued to deteriorate, the over-all distribution of movement scores for the period from closing to follow-up could have given the picture that was found. On the other hand, if in the period from closing to follow-up some of the individuals showed appreciable amounts of positive or negative movement, but such changes were unrelated to direction and amount of movement during the course of casework contact, the distribution of movement scores could also have given the same over-all picture.

On theoretical grounds it might be argued that new adaptive skills and understanding acquired during the period of casework contact should continue to bear fruit in a client's life and that he should continue to grow, that is, show further positive movement in the period from closing to follow-up. Similarly, one might expect that clients who showed deterioration during the casework contact would tend to show even further deterioration. This hypothesis would imply high positive correlation between movement from opening to closing and movement from closing to follow-up. According to a second hypothesis it might be expected that those clients showing the greater amounts of positive or negative movement during contact would not continue to maintain such a pace, with the greater amounts of movement in the follow-up period tending to be characteristic of individuals who showed moderate change during contact. In this event the correlation between the two sets of movement scores (opening to closing and closing to follow-up) might still be positive but of considerably lower magnitude. As a third possibility, if the effects of casework were largely limited to the period of contact, those improving during contact tending to lose their gains and those failing to improve tending to solve their problems, the correlation between the two sets of movement scores should tend to be negative.

None of these hypotheses, however, is adequately supported by the findings. The correlation between movement during contact and movement between closing and follow-up was found to be .18 for 76 individuals. This correlation is positive but it falls short of statistical significance. The safest inference to draw within the framework of the available evidence is that gains associated with casework are generally sustained, but that the direction and amount of change that occurs during casework has relatively little to do with the direction and amount of change that occurs after the case is closed.

## Is the Improvement During Casework a Result of Casework?

Throughout our publications on the Movement Scale, we have pointed out that it is a way to answer only the first evaluative question: Is there an appropriate change in the helped person associated with his having received service? Negative inference is much stronger than positive inference in drawing further conclusions from apparent gains associated with service. If desired change fails to be associated with the helping service, the service fails to that extent. On the other hand, if desired change is associated with the helping service, the evidence is necessary but not sufficient for concluding that the change is a result of the helping service. The problem of obtaining logically incontrovertible evidence that any apparent improvement associated with psychotherapy or casework is the result of such helping services is exceedingly difficult.

The most definitive approach to demonstrating that a given service is the main determinant of a given outcome is via the so-called *control group design,* where one group of clients is provided with the service while a second, comparable group does not receive the service. Our follow-up approach to the problem of exploring possible causal relationships between the provision of casework help and results in terms of movement shown by clients is admittedly less convincing than would be the application of a control group design. *It consists in having the 76 available individuals within the follow-up sample serve as their own controls.* The average amount of movement shown by these individuals during the period of casework contact is compared with the average amount of movement shown by these same individuals in the period from closing to follow-up. The logic of this comparison is based upon the assumption that improvement and deterioration in the adaptive and adjustive status of the individuals in a given group of families can be expected to be distributed uniformly over the temporal course of their lives unless some fairly strong beneficent or deleterious influence is brought to bear upon them. We have used the direction and amount of change that occurs in ex-clients during the five years subsequent to the closing of their cases as a kind of control in establishing a base line for evaluating the direction and amount of change that occurred during the casework contact. [Emphasis added.]

If the casework were not a definitely beneficent influence, we reasoned that the average amount of movement in our sample during the period of contact should be approximately the same as that which occurred between closing and follow-up. Obviously, any positive effects of social casework persisting beyond termination of cases tend to minimize this contrast. The mean amount of movement during the period of casework contact was +.9 of a step-interval, whereas the mean amount of movement for the same 76 individuals in the period from closing to follow-up was only +.2 of a step-interval. The difference between these mean amounts of movement in favor of the movement occurring during contact is statistically significant beyond the 1 percent level of confidence.

Furthermore, a comparison of the two distributions of movement scores indicates that the larger amounts of improvement in terms of positive movement occurred during the period of casework help. Thus, if it is assumed that the period from closing to follow-up can be used as a kind of control for evaluating what happened during the period of casework contact, the evidence argues that the apparent general improvement noted during casework was at least partially attributable to the help received.

Certain considerations, however, tend to diminish the strength of this conclusion. In the first place, movement judgments of the kind described are probably biased by certain limitations in the usual nature of case recording. Movement judgments derive in general from a comparison of two pictures of how an individual is getting along, that is, at opening and at closing. Although social caseworkers are trained to check the facts reported by clients, it is still true that the picture of an individual which appears in the case record or follow-up record is to a considerable degree dependent upon what the individual reports. It may be assumed that people usually come for casework help when they are in crisis situations. When an individual is distressed to the extent of seeking help, he may be inclined by virtue of the motivating power of his anxieties to impress his need and his family's need upon the caseworker by reporting his situation in an unfavorable light. Thus, the opening picture of the individuals in a case study is generally derived from data obtained at a time of felt crisis. This opening picture is then compared with the picture at closing (by means of the movement judgment) when, presumably, the client is no longer as strongly motivated to impress his need for further help. Similarly, the picture at follow-up derives from reports obtained when the client is most likely not particularly distressed or at least is not in most cases actively seeking help. From this standpoint, the greater amount of improvement judged to occur between opening and closing than that which occurred between closing and follow-up might be regarded as depending to an unknown degree upon the emotional state of the client at the time the opening report was secured.

A second factor weakening the inference that the general improvement found resulted from casework is the fact that the sample of cases studied was not obtained by random sampling from the population of longer-term cases carried by the agency. It was rather picked so that approximately two-thirds of the cases had shown apparent improvement during the course of contact. When a sample is so picked, it is hardly to be expected that the group will show an equivalent amount of improvement during an immediately subsequent period of their lives.

Thus, while our adaptation of the follow-up method yields a fairly strong implication that at least some of the gains were casually related to casework, the logic of inference is not unequivocal and we must return to the proposition that the follow-up method as used is not a substitute for control group design. In the last analysis it seems clear that an adequate evaluative study must involve both some form of control group design (Are the results attributable to the service rendered?) and provision for follow-up (Do the results persist beyond the period of contact?).

## CONCLUSIONS

1. Families and individuals who came for help to a family service agency could generally be located five years after their cases were closed, but the operation was expensive and time consuming, especially because a reasonably complete follow-up of the designated sample was stipulated.

2. The ex-clients seldom seemed to resent being approached directly by the follow-up interviewer without prior preparation and in general they readily accepted participation in the study.

3. A predominant majority of the ex-clients appeared to place a high positive value on the help they had received, the caseworkers who were known to them, and the agency.

4. Judgments of change in the form of movement that occurred during the course of contact with the service or D.R.Q.-differences did not correlate significantly with the evaluative attitudes of the ex-clients. There was evidence, however, that such evaluative attitudes can be predicted to a significant degree by an experienced social caseworker on the basis of case record material assembled during the course of service.

5. Movement judgments for the period from the opening to the closing of cases did not correlate significantly with movement judgments for the period from closing to follow-up. There was evidence, however, that an experienced social caseworker can predict subsequent movement to a significant degree on the basis of case record materials.

6. The gains in terms of a general positive movement judged to occur during the time casework was offered tended, on the whole, to be sustained during the period subsequent to closing of cases.

7. The evidence from the follow-up study yields a strong implication of a causal relationship between the general gains shown by the clients and the rendering of casework services, but the evidence is not incontrovertible.

8. To yield definitive evaluative evidence, the follow-up method should be combined with some form of control group design.

## Chapter Summary

This chapter was intended to give historical perspective to the critical problems of evaluation in social work, and to the research strategies that have been utilized in grappling with it. The profession did not move eagerly or without misgivings into the task of evaluation. Some of its foremost leaders questioned the appropriateness and feasibility of applying evaluative yardsticks to its human subject matter. Slowly but surely, however, the pressure of the scientific climate of the time, the questions raised by centralized financing, and the growing scientific interest within the profession itself led to the belated emergence of a growing body of research effort in social work directed toward this problem.

Before 1920, despite considerable interest expressed in the literature, only a few limited gestures in the direction of evaluation had actually been made. For the most part these involved informal judgments of change by the worker on the case and were used mainly for agency staff information and staff development. By the end of the 1920s, however, considerable activity had evidenced itself and some progress had been made in evaluative research; since that time this type of study had occupied an increasingly prominent position in social work research.

An early classic in social work research with evaluative overtones was Sophie Van Senden Theis' *How Foster Children Turn Out*, which for decades stood as the outstanding example of follow-up study in this field. Some three-quarters of the children placed by the New York State Charities Aid Society were found at the time of follow-up to be exhibiting a "capable" adjustment, a figure that was taken as reflecting favorably on the program.

Measurement of client change during social work treatment was approached variously over the years. An early attempt was made under the auspices of the Family Service Association of America in 1926, in which a "behavioral" definition of personality was translated into a checklist of "yes" or "no" questions for the worker to fill in. Other approaches included Reed's case-scoring system, in which the segment selected for separate rating was the "problem"; the Heckman-Stone checklist, also based in part on the "problem" unit; and the Discomfort-Relief Quotient of Professor John Dollard, in which case records were subjected to content analysis and scored. The major emphasis in this type of evaluative research in social work has been on the use of the overall case judgment of raters (usually practitioners themselves) regarding the change observed in a given case. In the latter category was the well-known Hunt Movement Scale (1950), which surpassed its predecessors by virtue of the rigor and technical sophistication with which it was developed by psychologist J. Mc-Vicker Hunt and his associates. Dr. Hunt picked up from the Discomfort-Relief Quotient when its results conflicted with worker judgments, and succeeded in fashioning these subjective judgments into a reliable and practical yardstick of client change. Its validity was tested with promising results in a later follow-up of cases rated by this method. However, serious shortcomings in this instrument—its reliance on case records, its bypassing of service goals and values, its focus on the individual rather than the family unit, its relativistic nature, and so on—led to its gradual decline in favor and its replacement by other measures, such as the Geismar Scale of Family Functioning (1960).

Thus far in this recapitulation, evaluative efforts were limited to descriptive ratings of client adjustment without experimental manipulation or "control group" comparisons. In the 1949 Jewish Board of Guardians study a quasi-experimental design was used, involving a "nonequivalent" control group approach in which children continuing with treatment were matched with a similar group who had withdrawn from treatment. Though the results allegedly reflected favorably on the efficacy of the child guidance services, the study design was vulnerable on the grounds of potential bias in this method of obtaining a "control." A recent (1973) FSAA study has attempted to refine such comparisons, with controversial conclusions.

In the justly famous Cambridge-Somerville Youth Study a more rigorous method of "matching" groups was followed, involving the pairing of individuals on the basis of a large variety of objective measures and then randomizing assignments. The results of this comparison were equivocal in terms of both delinquency statistics and judgments of social adjustment. However, a supplementary intensive case-by-case analysis of the study group by Helen Witmer yielded some promising clues regarding the causal role of the "counseling" services provided particular children and the conditions under which these services may be beneficial.

A related cycle of experimental evaluation in social work is the administrative experiment, in which a series of studies stemming from the late 1930s sought to test the results of varying models of service delivery. The major dimension of manipulation was that of reducing worker caseloads in public assistance with the intent of demonstrating that—as one early American Public Welfare Association study title put it—"Adequate Staff Brings Economy" (1939). Several such experiments (actually quasi-experimental in design) over a period of years provided evidence that reducing public welfare caseloads yielded net gains in relief costs and client progress. A significant step forward in this line of research was seen in Edwin Thomas' *In-Service Training and Reduced Workloads* (1960), in which the focus in results was not on "economy" but, rather, on worker and family performance. In addition to the effects of reduced workloads, the experimental design also provided for the impact of in-service training programs for workers. An important innovation in this project was the introduction of the experimental interview as a promising device for the measurement of worker performance. The most recent, and perhaps most ambitious, undertaking of this type was Edward E. Schwartz's *The Midway Office: An Experiment in the Organization of Work Groups,* in which the primary variable was the pattern of staff deployment in public assistance—conventional case assignments vs. experimental task assignment teams. In addition, the results of reduced workloads were also tested.

During the course of this chapter a structure was presented and elaborated upon for the purpose of conceptualizing the evaluative task in social work. The outline developed was as follows: (1) identification of service objectives; (2) standardization of service content; (3) description of service recipients and target conditions; (4) measurement of change; (5) the durability of change; and (6) the causal connection. These points are believed to represent key components of full evalaution and, it is hoped, provide a useful framework for the interpretation of the strengths and shortcomings of specific evaluative approaches. The "single-organism" evaluative design, adapted from behavioral modification research, was noted as particularly promising.

In the 1960s evaluative research in social work proliferated in diverse directions, as indeed did social work itself. The large-scale entry—with its demands for accountability—of the federal government onto the social service scene greatly accelerated the pace and progress of research in this field. Aside from the related research to be taken up in the following chapter, no attempt will be made to do justice to this fast-shifting picture.

Excerpts from the *Cambridge-Somerville Youth Study,* by Edwin Powers and Helen Witmer, and from *The Follow-up Study of The Results of Social Casework,* by Leonard Kogan and J. McVicker Hunt, concluded the chapter.

## NOTES

[1] See, for example, Richard B. Stuart, "Research in Social Work: Social Casework and Social Group Work," *Encyclopedia of Social Work,* II, 1106–

1122. This article is devoted almost entirely to a consideration of evaluative research.

² E.g., David G. French, *An Approach to Measuring Results in Social Work* (New York: Columbia University Press, 1952); Henry J. Meyer et al., *Girls at Vocational High* (New York: Russell Sage Foundation, 1965); Richard B. Stuart, *Trick or Treatment* (Champaign, Ill.: Research Press, 1970); Gordon E. Brown, ed., *The Multi-Problem Dilemma* (Metuchen, N.J.: Scarecrow Press, 1968); Edward J. Mullen, James R. Dumpson, et al., *Evaluation of Social Intervention* (San Francisco: Jossey-Bass, 1972); Tony Tripodi et al., *Social Program Evaluation* (Itasca, Ill.: F. E. Peacock, 1971); Joel Fischer, *The Effectiveness of Social Casework*. (Springfield, Ill.: Charles C. Thomas, 1976).

³ Margaret Blenkner, "Obstacles to Evaluative Research in Casework: Parts I and II," *Social Casework,* 31, nos. 1–2 (January-February 1950), 18 pp.

⁴ June Purcell-Guild, "But What Good Came of It at Last?" *The Survey,* January 1928, p. 515.

⁵ See Blenkner, op. cit.

⁶ C. C. Carstens, "The Statistical Test in Children's Work," *Proceedings of the National Conference of Charities and Corrections,* 1908, p. 253.

⁷ Margaret E. Rich, "Editorial," *The Family,* 7 (December, 1926): 247.

⁸ Ibid.

⁹ Frank J. Bruno, "Objective Tests in Casework," *Proceedings of the National Conference of Social Work,* 1926, p. 303.

¹⁰ Ibid., p. 304.

¹¹ David H. Holbrook, "The Relativity of Casework Measurement: Discussion," *Proceedings of the National Conference of Charities and Corrections,* 1915, p. 523.

¹² Blenkner, op. cit.

¹³ Carstens, p. 253.

¹⁴ Walter W. Whitson, "What Measures Do We Have for Growth in Personality?" *The Family,* 7 (July 1926): 142.

¹⁵ Ellen F. Wilcox, "The Measurement of Achievement in Family Case Work," *The Family,* 8 (April 1927): 46.

¹⁶ Richard C. Cabot, "Presidential Address," *Proceedings of the National Conference of Social Work,* 1931, p. 21.

¹⁷ Isaac L. Hoffman, *Toward a Logic for Social Work Research* (St. Paul: Amherst Wilder Foundation, 1952), p. 31.

¹⁸ See Martin Wolins, "Measuring the Effect of Social Work Intervention," in Norman Polansky, ed., *Social Work Research* (Chicago: University of Chicago Press, 1960), pp. 247–272.

¹⁹ In developing this listing the writer drew in part on Edward A. Suchman, *Evaluative Research* (New York: Russell Sage Foundation, 1967).

²⁰ Cabot, p. 18.

²¹ Suchman, p. 55.

²² For a useful differentiation of the concepts of service "input," "throughput," "output," and "outcome" see Claire M. Anderson, Edward E. Schwartz, and N. Viswanathan, "Approaches to the Analysis of Social Service Systems," in Edward E. Schwartz, ed., *Planning, Programming, Budgeting Systems and Social Welfare* (Chicago: University of Chicago, School of Social Service Administration, 1970).

²³ For a discussion of the systems model approach to evaluation see Herbert C. Schulberg and Frank Baker, "Program Evaluation Models and the Implementation of Research Findings," in Francis G. Caro, ed., *Readings in*

*Evaluative Research* (New York: Russell Sage Foundation, 1971). Also see Herman Stein et al., "Assessing Social Agency Effectiveness: A Goal Model," *Welfare in Review,* 6, no. 2 (March–April 1968): 13–17, and Perry Levinson, "The Evaluation of Social Welfare Programs," *Welfare in Review,* 4, no. 10 (December, 1966): 1–11.

[24] Bertram Black, "The Function of Research in Social Administration" *Proceedings of the National Conference of Social Work, 1950,* New York: Columbia University Press, 1950, p. 197.

[25] See, for example, William J. Reid and Ann W. Shyne, *Brief and Extensive Casework* (New York: Columbia University Press, 1969), pp. 70–72. Interestingly, in this study the widely accepted classification of social casework methods in terms of "modifying" (insight-oriented) and "supportive" techniques proved not to be reliable—i.e., judges were not able to agree closely with workers as to which type of casework was being applied in particular interview passages. Ibid., pp. 89–90. Also see Florence Hollis, *Women in Marital Conflict* (New York: Family Service Association of America, 1949), and *A Typology of Casework Treatment* (New York: Family Service Association of America, 1968).

[26] For a useful outline within which various "levels" of program evaluation may be considered, depending on the stage of service development and operation, see Tripodi et al., pp. 3–60.

[27] For a still valuable series of papers on the place of judgment in social work research, see Ann W. Shyne, ed., *Use of Judgments as Data in Social Work Research* (New York: National Association of Social Workers, 1959).

[28] See for example, Arnold A. Lazarus and Gerald C. Davidson, "Clinical Innovation in Research and Practice," in Allan E. Bergin and Sol L. Garfield, ed., *Handbook of Psychotherapy and Behavior Change: An Empirical Analysis* (New York: Wiley, 1971), pp. 200–201; also, Julian Meltzoff and Melvin Kornreich, *Research in Psychotherapy* (New York: Atherton Press, 1970), p. 197; and T. Allyon, "Intensive Treatment of Psychotic Behavior by Stimulus Satiation and Food Reinforcement," in Phillip Fellin, Tony Tripodi, and Henry J. Meyer, *Exemplars of Social Research* (Itasco, Ill.: F. E. Peacock, 1969), p. 269.

[29] See, for example, Hubert M. Blalock, Jr., *Causal Inferences in Non-Experimental Research* (Chapel Hill: University of North Carolina Press, 1964); Morris Rosenberg, *The Logic of Survey Analysis* (New York: Basic Books, 1968); and Donald T. Campbell, *Experimental and Quasi-Experimental Designs for Research* (Chicago: Rand McNally, 1963).

[30] Campbell and Stanley, pp. 34–63.

[31] Ibid., pp. 37–42.

[32] For example, Stuart, op. cit.; Michael Howe, "Casework Self-Evaluation: A Single Subject Approach," *Social Service Review,* 48, no. 1 (March 1974): 1–23.

[33] See Donald T. Campbell, "Reforms as Experiments," *American Psychologist,* 24, no. 4 (April 1969): 409–429.

[34] See Margaret Blenkner, "Control Groups and the 'Placebo' Effect in Evaluative Research," *Social Work,* January 1962; also, Jerome Frank, *Persuasion and Healing,* rev. ed. (Baltimore: Johns Hopkins Press, 1973), pp. 136–164.

[35] For a detailing of such limitations, see Campbell and Stanley, pp. 34–43 (esp. chart, p. 40).

[36] E.g., Blalock, op. cit.; also Fred Kerlinger, *Foundations of Behavioral*

*Research,* 2d ed. (New York: Holt, Rinehart and Winston, 1973); and Hubert M. Blalock and Ann B. Blalock, *Methodology in Social Research* (New York: McGraw-Hill, 1968).

[37] For an example of the systems approach to program evaluation, see Howard Polsky and Daniel Caster, *The Dynamics of Residential Treatment* (Chapel Hill: University of North Carolina Press, 1968).

[38] Lilian Brandt, "Statistics of Dependent Families," *Proceedings of the National Conference of Charities and Corrections,* 1906, p. 440.

[39] See Shyne, op. cit.

[40] Elizabeth L. Holbrook, "A Survey of a Month's Work Made Six Months Afterwards," *Proceedings of the National Conference of Charities and Corrections,* 1915, p. 81.

[41] Elinor Blackman, "Some Tests for the Evaluation of Case Work Methods," *The Family,* 6 (July 1925): 132.

[42] Sophie van Senden Theis, *How Foster Children Turn Out* (New York: State Charities Aid Society, 1924).

[43] Ibid., pp. 165–183.

[44] Ibid., p. 23.

[45] Ibid., p. 210.

[46] Ibid., p. 161.

[47] Ibid., pp. 163–164.

[48] Ibid., p. 164.

[49] Ibid., p. 182.

[50] "Editorial," *The Family,* 7 (January 1927): 278.

[51] Richard K. Conant, "How Shall We Measure the Results of Our Poor Law Administration," *Proceedings of the National Conference of Social Work,* 1927, p. 485.

[52] Sophie Hardy, "What Measures Have We for Growth in Personality?" *The Family,* 7 (December 1926): 257.

[53] Walter W. Whitson, "What Measures Do We Have for Growth in Personality?" *The Family,* 7 (July 1926): 139.

[54] Conant, op. cit.

[55] See Whitson, op. cit.; also, Hardy, op. cit.; and "Editorial," *The Family,* op. cit.

[56] Ellery F. Reed, "A Scoring System for the Evaluation of Social Case Work," *Social Service Review,* 5 (June 1931): 216.

[57] Ibid., p. 216.

[58] Ibid., pp. 225, 236.

[59] Ibid., 214.

[60] M. Antoinette Cannon, "Social Case Work," *Social Work Year Book,* 1933, p. 469.

[61] A. A. Heckman and Allan Stone, "Forging New Tools," *Survey Midmonthly,* October 1947, p. 267.

[62] A. A. Heckman, "Measuring the Effectiveness of Agency Services," *Journal of Social Casework,* December 1948, p. 396.

[63] Ibid., p. 397.

[64] R. Clyde White, "Integrity in Social Work Publicity: A Platform of Facts and a Platform of Ethics," *Proceedings of the National Conference of Social Work,* 1928, p. 603.

[65] William J. Reid and Laura Epstein, *Task-Centered Casework* (New York: Columbia University Press, 1972).

[66] John Dollard and O. Hobart Mowrer, "A Method of Measuring Tension

in Written Documents," *The Journal of Abnormal and Social Psychology,* January 1947, pp. 3–32.

[67] Ibid., p. 7.

[68] Ibid., p. 12.

[69] Ibid., p. 21.

[70] J. McVicker Hunt and Leonard S. Kogan, *Measuring Results in Social Casework: A Manual on Judging Movement* (New York: Family Service Association of America, 1950, p. 11.

[71] Philip Klein, "The Contribution of Research to the Progress of Social Work," in Philip Klein and Ida C. Merriam, *The Contribution of Research to Social Work* (New York: American Association of Social Workers, 1948), p. 20.

[72] Hunt and Kogan, p. 10.

[73] Ibid., p. 23.

[74] Nathan S. Kogan, Leonard S. Kogan, and J. McVicker Hunt, "Expansion and Extension of Use of the Movement Scale," *Social Casework,* 33 (January 1952): 10–12.

[75] Leonard S. Kogan, J. McVicker Hunt, and Phillis F. Bartelme, *A Follow-up Study of the Results of Social Casework* (New York: Family Service Association of America, 1953).

[76] Leonard S. Kogan, "Evaluative Techniques in Social Casework," *Social Service Review,* 26 (September 1952), p. 308.

[77] Edna Wasser, "Classified Bibliography: CSS Movement Scale" (New York: Community Service Society of New York, 1960), mimeographed.

[78] See, for example, Meyer et al., op. cit., and Brown, op. cit.

[79] Kogan, Hunt, and Bartelme, op. cit.

[80] Philip Klein, "Past and Future in Social Welfare Research," *Proceedings of the National Conference of Social Work, 1951* (New York: Columbia University Press, 1951), pp. 130–147.

[81] J. McVicker Hunt, "On the Judgment of Social Workers as a Source of Information in Social Work Research," in Shyne, op. cit.

[82] Ludwig L. Geismar, *Family and Community Functioning: A Manual of Measurement for Social Work Practice and Policy* (Metuchen, N.J.: Scarecrow Press, 1971).

[83] Mary E. MacDonald, "Social Work Research: A Perspective" in Norman A. Polansky ed., *Social Work Research* (Chicago: University of Chicago Press, 1960), p. 14.

[84] Meltzhoff and Kornreich, p. 146.

[85] See, for example, Matilda White Riley, *Sociological Research: A Case Approach* (New York: Harcourt Brace Jovanovich, 1963), pp. 572–580; also, Hans J. Eysenck, *The Effects of Psychotherapy* (New York: International Science Press, 1966); and Meltzhoff and Kornreich, p. 210.

[86] Cabot, p. 21.

[87] Edwin Powers and Helen Witmer, *An Experiment in the Prevention of Delinquency: The Cambridge-Somerville Youth Study* (New York: Columbia University Press, 1951).

[88] Ibid., pp. 61–64.

[89] Ibid., pp. 72–78.

[90] Ibid., p. 153.

[91] Ibid., p. 454.

[92] Ibid., pp. 450–453, 502.

[93] For a revealing follow-up (with further "negative" findings) of the Cambridge-Somerville sample ten years later, see Wm. McCord and Joan

McCord, *Origins of Crime: A New Evaluation of the Cambridge-Somerville Youth Study* (New York: Columbia University Press, 1959).

[94] Louis J. Lehrman et al., *Success and Failure of Treatment of Children of the Jewish Board of Guardians, New York City* (New York: Jewish Board of Guardians, 1949), p. 25.

[95] Ibid., pp. 29–30.

[96] Ibid., p. 32.

[97] Ibid., p. 80.

[98] Ibid., p. 86.

[99] Dorothy Fahs Beck, *Progress on Family Problems* (New York: Family Service Association of America, 1973).

[100] Ibid., p. 2.

[101] For a related critique see John R. Schuerman, "Do Family Services Help? An Essay Review" *Social Service Review,* 49, no. 3 (September 1975): 363–375.

[102] Cited in ibid., p. 12.

[103] Ibid., sec. 9.

[104] Ibid., p. 8.

[105] Ibid.

[106] See, for example, Lilian Ripple, Ernesteina Alexander, and Bernice Polemis, *Motivation, Capacity, and Opportunity: Studies in Casework Theory and Practice* (Chicago: University of Chicago, School of Social Service Administration, 1964).

[107] See, for example, Ellery F. Reed, *An Experiment in Reducing the Cost of Relief* (Chicago: American Public Welfare Association, 1937); and Rebecca Staman, "What is the Most Economical Case Load in Public Relief Administration?" *Social Work Technique,* 4 (1938): 117–121.

[108] *Adequate Staff Brings Economy* (Chicago: American Public Welfare Association, 1939).

[109] Ibid., p. 1.

[110] Campbell and Stanley, pp. 47–50.

[111] Ibid., p. 4.

[112] Herbert A. Simon et al., *Determining Work Loads for Professional Staff in a Public Welfare Agency* (Berkeley: University of California, Bureau of Public Administration, 1941).

[113] Edwin J. Thomas et al., *In-Service Training and Reduced Workloads: Experiments in a State Department of Welfare* (New York: Russell Sage Foundation, 1960).

[114] Ibid., p. 22.

[115] Ibid., p. 25.

[116] Ibid., pp. 36–42; see also Edwin J. Thomas, "The Experimental Interview," *Social Work,* 5, no. 3 (July 1960): 52–58.

[117] Thomas et al., pp. 33–36; see also Edwin J. Thomas, "Role Conceptions and Organizational Size," *American Sociological Review,* 24 (February 1959): 30–37.

[118] Edward E. Schwartz and William C. Sample, *The Midway Office: An Experiment in the Organization of Work Groups* (New York: National Association of Social Workers, 1972).

[119] Ibid., p. 10.

[120] Ibid., pp. 11–14.

[121] Ibid., p. 11.

[122] Ibid., pp. 25–26.

[123] Ibid., p. 155.

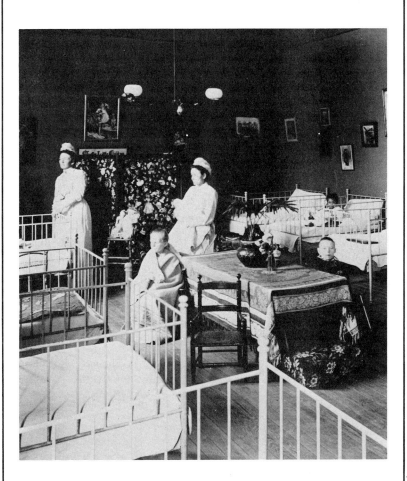

# Chapter 8
# From Multiproblem Family to Multideficit Society: A Research Odyssey

---•---

## Introduction: The Setting

Perhaps the last large round of research continuity in social work that can be discerned from the present vantage point is the series of studies of the "multiproblem family" that emerged in the late 1940s and early 1950s and held sway in the field for over a decade. Just as it could be said of the earlier social survey movement that it was identified with a particular city ("What a famous town Pittsburgh was in those days!"[1]), so might it be said of multiproblem family study that it was a later research gospel according to St. Paul, Minnesota. From this source the concept and its analysis spread rapidly across the country, and indeed into other countries as well.

The Truman-Eisenhower era was an increasingly prosperous and complacent time for the nation and a time of growing professionalization and refinement of technique for social work. The persistence and expansion of public assistance caseloads into the post-World War II period was a matter of recurring public concern, as was the rise of juvenile delinquency and youth gang activity in the major cities. In this atmosphere, a social welfare leader we have had occasion to discuss before—Bradley

Buell, director of the private community planning and survey firm known as Community Research Association—sought and found a city receptive to a "new" approach to the social problems of the day. Some years earlier, as we saw in Chapter VI, he had developed and popularized for a time the controversial barometer of community pathology known as the "social breakdown index."[2] Now, in 1947, Buell was invited by a group of civic leaders and agency representatives to visit St. Paul, Minnesota, for consultation on the city's growing complex of community problems and programs.[3]

His recommendation seemed straightforward and logical enough, namely, to conduct a study of the cases known to the large number of 108 public and voluntary social agencies making up the health and welfare network of this typical metropolitan area.[4] However, this was not a typical caseload inventory that Buell proposed; he was after a very special sort of quarry, nothing less, in fact, than the source and wellspring of the dependency and delinquency that was disturbing the social fabric of the postwar period.

He proposed a study that was to take stock of all the families served by these agencies during a given month (November 1948). He urged that a systematic, concurrent analysis of the agency loads of an entire community—a task that had never been carried out in a major urban area—should throw new light on the extent and nature of its social problems and point toward potential solutions through more effective concentration of its health and welfare resources. Key cooperation and support were provided by the Greater St. Paul Community Chest and Council, the Planning and Research Council, and the Grant Foundation. Buell's Community Research Associates was to provide overall direction and technical assistance.[5]

The subsequent implementation of the study involved the completion of some 58,000 case schedules by the several scores of agencies, reflecting (owing to overlapping caseloads) some 43,000 separate families. A crucial aspect of the research plan was the focus on the *family as the unit of study*, rather than on the individual client or patient—hence the title "Family Unit Report Study" (FURS). Its proposed design and rationale were spelled out in an article by Buell, entitled "Know What the What Is," that appeared in 1948 in the popular welfare journal of the time, the *Survey Mid-Monthly*.[6] According to Leonard Rutman (who has recently reviewed this project as evidence of the incompatibility of "demonstration" vs. "research") this early publicizing of the proposed plan was part of a deliberate effort to promote and disseminate the approach, despite the fact that it was yet to be tested.[7] We have had occasion to note such tendencies in the field before.

## The Original St. Paul Study Report

The findings of this first community caseload analysis were published in 1952 by Columbia University Press in a 464-page volume written by Buell and his associates.[8] The title—*Community Planning for Human Services*—indicated that its scope was much broader than a study report per se, and in fact the research methods and data were touched upon lightly, as a sort of backdrop to a comprehensive diagnosis and prescription for the social ills of American cities.

By way of anticipation of the breadth of the conclusions, Buell explained in the Preface that "of great value was the fact that our corps of project consultants had behind them prior association in local community studies and surveys—which for the most part extended over a decade and a half—with a strong thread of continuity and thought."[9] He went on to state (somewhat immodestly perhaps):

> The research project upon which this volume is based was designed to produce a definitive treatise on the major issues underlying community organization efforts in four interrelated areas of community service: dependency, ill-health, maladjustment. and recreation need.[10]

It should be underscored here and throughout this discussion that the perspective within which this project and its sequels were conducted was that of the *local community*—the modern urban area. This angle of vision gave direction to the problems identified and the solutions proposed. Buell and the Community Research Associates were nationally known consultants to communities in their health and welfare planning activities, and this perception of the locus and arena of effort both infused and limited their work, as we shall see. Thus we find the following viewpoint expressed:

> Planning and organizing the community's services for an attack upon the major problems of dependency, ill-health, maladjustment and recreation need is essentially a matter of logistics. In terms of what is known about the characteristics of these enemies, their methods of community infiltration, and the nature and

disposition of their forces, the right service in sufficient amount must be brought to bear at the right places at the right time with a maximum of efficiency and economy. The fruits of victory are the preservation and enhancement of individual and family capacity for social self-maintenance and self-sufficiency. . . .

The community is in truth the battle area. . . .[11]

With this premise, the boundaries of both diagnosis and treatment of human problems were clearly predetermined and circumscribed. The contrast between this local service-centered approach to social needs and the societal reconstruction emphasis of certain aspects of the later War on Poverty may be readily noted. (Interestingly, however, the military metaphor was used by both.)

METHODOLOGY

The study procedure was described briefly as follows (no technical appendixes, copies of schedules, or statistical reference tables were provided):

A unique feature of the reporting process was that each of the 108 agencies filled out a schedule on every case known to it, giving identifying information about the whole family, even though the agency might be serving only one family member. Thus it was possible to consolidate data (utilizing IBM equipment) from different agencies into a composite picture of the problems presented and the constellation of services being rendered to the family.[12]

Questions of reliability or validity of the data thus obtained were not raised. The case records of the agencies—plus the memories of the workers—were the primary sources of the information registered on the study schedules. The criteria of maladjustment, ill health, and dependency were quite broad; for example, in the case of maladjustment two main types of evidence were accepted: (1) antisocial behavior "as reflected by the formal judgments of society, that is, records of crime, delinquency, child neglect and other types of behavior in respect to which society takes official action" (note the echo here of the Social Breakdown Index), and (2) "diagnostic evidence"—primarily of a judgmental nature—from case records and the like.[13]

In effect, the study design was very summarily disposed of; the stress was clearly on demonstration and interpretation, rather than on research, in this exposition. As we shall have occasion to note, this slighting of method was severely criticized in the subsequent literature.

FINDINGS

The specific results of the Family Unit Report Study were also briefly presented by Buell. For example:

> The St. Paul Study showed that in a single month [November 1948] 41,000 families, 40 percent of the families in the community were being served by the city's 108 public and private agencies.[14]

Buell went on to present the provocative crux of the data analysis:

> The most dramatic evidence of vicious circling in St. Paul's families came with the discovery that a group of 6,600 families, about 6 percent of the city's families, were suffering from such a compounding of serious problems that they were absorbing well over half of the combined services of the community's dependency, health and adjustment services.[15]

Here we encounter the nub of the study results, and the springboard for a major current of research and demonstration in social work over the following decade and more. The community's welfare problems were thus tracked down to a seeming "handful" of problem-ridden families. Hence the prescription—rehabilitate this "hard core" of 6 percent of families who account for the bulk of the burden on the community's health and welfare facilities, and much of the source of social problems will be cut off. How simple—and how deceptive—this solution turned out to be! Buell continued as follows:

> More than three-quarters of the families dependent [on public assistance] in that month were part of a group of 6,466 families (6 percent of all families in the community) whose life was complicated by constellations of the major problems of ill-health, maladjustment, and dependency. . . .
>
> In other words here was what we might call a group of "pathological families," each with its own constellation of serious problems and disabilities. Not all were dependent on the community for assistance during that particular month but nearly 80 percent were, *and it seems reasonable to predict that most of the others will be in similar need as time goes on. . . . These facts, we believe, help to explain the reasons for the residual load of relief recipients in a time of high employment.* They help to explain why disabilities in one large group of families *may produce a substantial proportion of the dependency load.* Equally important, they illustrate certain characteristics significant to a community-wide program for the prevention of dependency. . . .

A community-wide program for the *prevention and control of a residual load* of this kind calls for three types of procedure: (1) prevention of particular disabilities; (2) systematic concentration on the most disorganized families; and (3) systematic use of the [social] insurance services.[16] (Emphasis added)

## THE "HARD CORE"

Thus the quarry had been tracked to its lair. At the end of the search for the source of the community's social pathology was spotlighted "a hard-core of seriously disorganized families," comprising a relatively small fraction of the total population, who were the object of the bulk of the social agency effort in the urban area. The heart of the problem was the so-called "multiproblem family"—a term that Ludwig Geismar ascribed to Isaac Hoffman, research director of the Wilder Foundation of St. Paul.[17] As interpreted by Buell, these chronic, multiply beset families were considered to be those in which "there was some combination of two or more of the three problems, dependency, maladjustment, and ill-health."[18]

He then went on to spell out what he had in mind by "prevention and control"[19] of such pathology. Apparently, Buell's earlier foray into social breakdown measurement had convinced him that these problems were handed down from generation to generation, and that in order to break this vicious cycle and relieve the consequent burden on the community it was necessary to zero in on the offending families with concentrated, coordinated health and welfare services. Referring to his earlier studies, he stated:

> Facts from certain cities that have kept the social breakdown index for a number of years indicate that from 40 percent to 50 percent of those who each year given official evidence of behavior disorders come from families with a previous record. This suggests that possibility of developing procedures for identifying families *whose background indicates a predisposition toward disordered behavior, and for maintaining an alertness toward the successive recurrence of new symptoms.*[20] (Emphasis added)

As a specific example he cited the case of Stanford, Connecticut, where social breakdown had been analyzed first in 1937 and then followed up in 1946. "In the span of less than a generation," he concluded, "constellations of these different symptoms appeared in the same families with extraordinary frequency and variety."[21]

On the basis of such data and inferences Buell underscored the centrality of the chronic, hard-core, multiproblem family in the social pathology of the American city, and urged the targeting of community resources on their rehabilitation in order to prevent the spread and transmittal of the condition. Better integration of fragmented, episodic agency services to these families was vital, since "at least two and often many more agencies were working currently with practically every family in this [6 percent] group."[22] Thus *multiproblem* families were also seen as *multiagency* families in most instances.*

To recapitulate briefly, then, the wave of multiproblem family research arose within the context of local community concern over persistent dependency and delinquency trends after World War II. The leader of the project at its inception was Bradley Buell (and his Community Research Associates), who persuaded prominent citizens and agency representatives in St. Paul, Minnesota, to undertake a community-wide inventory of caseloads with a focus on the family unit as the basis of study. The analysis revealed that around 6 percent of the city's families were absorbing over half the health and welfare services of the community's public and voluntary agencies. These "multiproblem" families were thus identified as the source of the bulk of social pathology in the area, and the focal point for a concerted effort through coordinated social services to reduce their incidence and prevent their recurrence.

With the momentum of this study and the impact of its publication in 1952, an initial grant of $90,000 was made by the Hill Foundation to the Greater St. Paul Community Chest and Council to mount a demonstration aimed at improving the conditions highlighted.[23] More specifically, the grant was "made for the purpose of developing a community plan for the prevention of maladjustment among multiproblem families."[24] The multiproblem family movement was now formally on its way and launched on its meteoric rise across the field and nation through the 1950s and early 1960s.

## Refinement of the Multiproblem Family Concept

Up to this point the notion of the multiproblem family had evolved rather pragmatically. For a more conceptual delineation and definition we may look to the researcher who came on the scene soon thereafter and gave technical direction to the sub-

---

* It should be noted that the methodology utilized, namely, the identification of multiproblem families through agency sources, might well have predetermined such an association.

stantial research investment that followed. He is Ludwig L. Geismar, whom we encountered in Chapter VII as the author of the Scale of Family Functioning[25] and whose prolific writings and competent research productivity dominated this subject for over a decade.

As we have seen, Buell referred in his 1952 report to multiproblem families as those with some combination of two or more of the three major problem groupings—dependency, maladjustment, and ill health.[26] To these criteria Geismar added a further requirement, namely, the presence of one or more children under 18 years of age.[27]

In an effort to translate this revised operational definition into a more theoretical framework for greater generality, Geismar later (1964) reformulated the definition conceptually as

> A family with disorganized social functioning of an order that adversely affects the following sets of behavior: (1) relationships inside the family; (2) relationships outside the family group, particularly neighborhood and community relationships; and (3) the performance of tasks such as those concerned with health, and with economic and household practices that are designed to maintain the family as a physical unit.[28]

The foregoing operational and conceptual versions of the term are not readily convertible into one another. The former was obviously more amenable to statistical surveys on a community-wide basis and was so utilized; the latter, according to Geismar, was found to be more useful for hypothesis formulation, and for case measurement and the assessment of social functioning.[29]

### The Statistics of Multiproblem Families: Their Prevalence

Definitions obviously affect the count of a given phenomenon, and since statistics were widely quoted in the promotion of the multiproblem family movement it will be well to scrutinize the figures that were frequently cited. The most popular, of course, was the famous "6 percent" given currency by Bradley Buell's 1952 book on the St. Paul project findings. This was based on the original definition referred to earlier, a more inclusive one than the later modification by Ludwig Geismar. As we have seen, the "6 percent" represented the portion of families in St. Paul in November 1948 conforming to the criteria of two or more agency-reported problems out of the three categories: dependency, ill health, or maladjustment. With the addition of the Geismar qualification that these families must also contain one or more children under 18 years of age, a smaller percentage was of course obtained. A later rerun of the 1948 St. Paul data by Isaac Hoffman of the Wilder Foundation yielded a figure of 2 percent of all the city's families in the multiproblem group.[30] Subsequent surveys in 1957 in St. Paul and Vancouver, British Columbia, utilizing a simplified checklist approach by local agencies resulted in estimates of 2.2 percent and 2.3 percent, respectively.[31] The 1957 "epidemiological" surveys were tested for reliability, and percentages of agreement on problem categories between agencies with the same cases ranged from 60 percent to 93 percent.[32] External validity was tested in several ways, including comparisons with other groups such as Aid to Dependent Children families, generally with statistically significant results.[33]

The smaller percentage of multiproblem families derived from Geismar's revised definition would be expected to have the effect of lending greater saliency to the "hard-core," since it was now more concentrated—and presumably more manageable thereby—than if it were larger. A somewhat different focus in a New York City study at about the same time, limited to "delinquency-producing" families, came up with a figure of 1 percent, and a later delinquency survey in Indianapolis pinpointed "less than 1 percent" of families as the source of delinquent youths.[34] Any such figures have to be taken in perspective, however. Since only 2 or 3 percent of youth may be "officially" delinquent in a given community in a given year, it may not be particularly sensational to learn that they come from 1 percent (or less) of the total families in the area. Statistics of this type often have more public relations value than scientific import.

A related comment on the St. Paul "6 percent" was made by the executive secretary of the Wilder Foundation as follows:

> The [1948 St. Paul] project reveals that out of a total of 20,264 problem families and non-problem families [known to agencies], 6,466 or 32 percent* absorbed up to 50 percent of the volume of service in the study month—admittedly a less dramatic statement.[35]

## The Treatment and Study of the Multiproblem Family

The next stage in the St. Paul multiproblem family program, after the receipt of the Hill Foundation grant in 1952, was the implementation of the "Family-Centered Project." However, rather than focusing on the development of a *community plan* for the prevention of family disorganization—as originally in-

---

* Of the families *known to agencies,* as contrasted with the *total* number of families *in the community.*

tended—the emphasis was soon shifted to the rehabilitative *treatment* of multiproblem families and the research evaluation of such treatment.

An explanation as to how this happened was given by Charles Birt, then director of the Greater St. Paul Community Chest and Council, in his account of the experience. In the attempt to design approaches to prevention, an "experimental detection center" was set up as a sort of early-warning system for identifying potential multiproblem families. However, such efforts "demonstrated the futility of discovering families needing help *unless treatment could be provided them, and emphasized . . . the need for working agreements with agencies for providing this treatment*" (emphasis added).[36] Apparently the helping impulse of the welfare professional and lay leadership overrode other priorities, and it thus came about that the thrust of the Family-Centered Project turned to family treatment and its measurement rather than "planning and prevention."

The challenge of rehabilitation of the multiproblem family to the social worker of the 1950s should, however, not be underestimated. Social work treatment up to that time was centered almost exclusively on the individual client, with much emphasis on the motivated client who takes initiative in seeking and coming to the agency for service. Now a veritable revolution in technique was called for: a focus on *family* diagnosis and treatment; aggressive, *reaching-out* services to resistant, often hostile clients; the close *collaboration* of many autonomous health and welfare agencies at the policy level and in jointly serving individual families; the incorporation of demanding and sometimes burdensome *research reporting requirements;* and so on. A new body of concepts, skills, and attitudes on the part of workers was patently and urgently needed. Agencies had to be convinced that the proverbial untreatable, chronic, problem-ridden family was worth the salvage effort; workers had to be won over from their frequent stance of suspicion and avoidance of these high-risk, high-frustration cases. The task facing the fledgling Family-Centered Project was not an easy one from any standpoint. In choosing this unmapped road the St. Paul project leaders were by no means taking the path of least resistance, and their courage and persistence should be recognized.

To direct the Family-Centered Project, Alice Overton was brought in from the New York City Youth Board, where she had been coordinator of a similar experimental program.[37] The two original research associates were Malcolm Stinson (succeeded in 1954 by Ludwig Geismar) and Beverly Ayres. Overton tackled the task with enthusiasm and sensitivity to its complex operational, conceptual, and research requirements. Her later text based on this experience, published with the unassuming title *Casework Notebook,* was widely utilized across the country, explicating as it did the "new" social casework—family centered, reaching out, coordinative, and persevering in the face of long odds and discouragement.[38] Her role was indeed a highly creative one, employing of necessity untested theory and methods.

At the same time, as expressed in retrospect by Geismar, "in this area, as in most applied professions, social action has a tendency to outrun precise knowledge and research."[39] It fell, of course, to the hands of the research staff—primarily Geismar, with the able collaboration of Ayres—to attempt to close this gap between practice and knowledge. The study of the "epidemiology" of the multiproblem family, the first area of investigation, has already been discussed. Now, in the course of the Family-Centered Project's demonstration of rehabilitative treatment, the research was aimed at *evaluation* of the effectiveness of the treatment program.

One impressive result of this effort has been referred to in the preceding chapter, namely, the Geismar Scale of Family Functioning,[40] probably still the most widely accepted and utilized measuring instrument of its kind in the field. The first version of this scale was published in full in 1960.[41] A slight revision for use with more "normal" families was developed in conjunction with a related project in New Haven several years later.[42] Finally, the refined and definitive edition of the scale was published in book form in 1971 (with the addition of a new "Scale of Community Functioning").[43]

This considerable contribution by Geismar to measurement in social work, and his several significant applications of the Scale of Family Functioning to the evaluation of the St. Paul Family-Centered Project and related demonstrations elsewhere, will not be described in detail here. They are competent, careful, sophisticated technical achievements that are relatively recent and readily accessible works for the interested reader. (An exception will be made in the case of the question "Was it effective?"—a research theme that harks back to the unresolved issue of the last chapter and that will be picked up again at the close of this one.)

## The Explosive Spread of the Multiproblem Approach

From these limited experimental beginnings in St. Paul, the mid-1950s and early 1960s witnessed the rapid spillover of the multiproblem idea to scores of cities in the United States and beyond. This contagion caught fire while the demonstration was in early process, and well before any of the conclusions or test results were in.

In the 10 years between 1952 and 1962, over one-half of the 260 cities with populations over 100,000 in the United States and Canada reported "some phase of programing" for multiproblem families! This was the amazing result of a survey completed in 1962 by Joseph C. Lagey and Beverly Ayres.[44] They found that 143 cities were seriously interested in this subject, which included 117 in "advanced planning, in operation, or recently concluded."[45] (The other 26 were in earlier phases of planning and exploration.) Sixteen of these 117 communities were pursuing *community development* as an alternative to the social *treatment* approach to the multiproblem family.[46] In New York State alone, 10 different programs for multiproblem families were counted in 1960.[47]

Benjamin Schlesinger of Toronto University completed a comprehensive annotated bibliography on the subject in 1962, and published a revised second edition in 1965.[48] In the latter report a total of 321 articles, books, or monographs were cited, of which only 196 were from the United States. England and Canada were next in frequency of publication on the subject, with 51 and 44 items, respectively. Holland, France, Australia, and other countries were represented.

Apparently, then, the field potentially had another "movement" on its hands by the late 1950s and early 1960s. However, from the research standpoint there was much to be desired in this surge of enthusiasm. According to Lagey and Ayres, writing in 1962, "few projects are employing standardized 'objective' measurement scales. Fewer still are employing control groups and rare are the projects which use before-after design with a control group."[49]

What accounted for this explosive growth of a new program idea? Certainly not the evidence of its effectiveness, nor the tested validity of its methods or theory, since, as Leonard Rutman has emphasized, the most rapid dissemination of the approach took place well *before* any definitive findings were in hand.[50] To be sure, as we have observed, the soil of the profession was ready for such a seed during its consolidation phase after World War II; moreover, the social and political climate of the Truman-Eisenhower years may have favored such a "retail" case-by-case approach to the reduction and prevention of the residual dependency and delinquency in our advancing economy.

But beyond this there was a concerted and effective attempt to promote and publicize the St. Paul effort as widely as possible. In addition to the previously cited 1948 article by Buell in the

*Survey Mid-Monthly* and his 1952 book, there were numerous speeches, national conference papers, meetings, and workshops around the country to spread the word. In 1949 the first findings of the project were presented at a National Conference on Appraising Family Needs held in St. Paul in 1949.[51] It is no surprise to read that, according to Schlesinger, "in the United States [the] outstanding leadership has come from the Community Research Associates" in the subsequent dissemination of the approach.[52] Shortly after the St. Paul Project was launched, related demonstrations were organized under the direction of Community Research Associates in Winona, Minnesota (dealing with economic dependency); in Washington County, Maryland (dealing with physical disability); and in San Mateo, California (dealing with behavioral disorders). These developments were avidly picked up in the literature.[53] This evangelical zeal, together with the readiness of the field and lay leadership for a fresh assault on perennial social problems, apparently resulted in the rapid growth just described. The fact that a similar approach had been evolving independently during this period within the New York City Youth Board also helped give national visibility to the idea and impetus to its spread.[54]

But then, almost as abruptly as the concept caught on, after its enthusiastic adoption in scores of cities across the country during the 1950s, it quickly dropped off in the early 1960s. For example, up to 1962 Schlesinger was able to locate 306 bibliographical references to the multiproblem family subject. However, in the 3 years from 1962 to 1965 only 15 new items appeared. "This would seem to indicate that interest in the multiproblem family has subsided . . . ," he observed.[55] The Family-Centered Project itself, after a cutback in foundation support and scope of operation in 1959, finally terminated in 1967.[56] What were the factors that led to this sharp decline, so that by the early 1960s another major wave of social work research had crested and by the mid-1960s the movement had largely spent itself? In the following section we will take a look at some of the counterforces that ultimately undermined and put a halt to the trend as a distinct entity.

### Reaction and Reappraisal

Is It "New?"

In the first place, it was soon noted that the multiproblem family— while a new term—was actually an old and venerable challenge to social work and social work research. In fact Schlesinger pointed out that "there can be little doubt that the multiproblem family wãs to be found among Charles Booth's 'submerged tenth' at the turn of the century."[57]

The New York State Charities Aid Society issued a 1960 report on the subject prepared by its Research Consultant, Roland Warren, entitled *Multi-Problem Families: A New Name or a New Problem?* After comparing the notion of the multiproblem family with the early genetic theories of familial defects in the famous studies by Dugdale of the Jukes, Kallikaks, and other chronically dependent and handicapped lineages, he concluded that "today's Jukes are called multiproblem families" and that "there is little new about the multiproblem families as such. . . ." He went on, however, to recognize that "there is a great deal that is new and significant in increased awareness of the nature of the problem and in increased concern that something be done about it."[58]

In this sense the focus on the multiproblem family may be seen as similar to the later War on Poverty in that a persisting social dilemma was lifted for a time to the forefront of public attention and priority for attempted solution. The fact that a new phrase had been devised, and the challenge was viewed in a new context, did not alter the realization that an age-old problem—exacerbated by modern industrialized society and an increasingly fragmented welfare system—was being tackled once again. This perception need not in itself have lessened the commitment and enthusiasm behind the movement, but it probably added a degree of caution and sobriety in recognition of the historic and deep-rooted nature of the realities being faced.

## ARE ITS PREMISES SOUND?

More fundamental questions were raised by Irving Lukoff and Samuel Mencher in a 1962 article in *Social Service Review*.[59] After analyzing some of the assumptions of the "conceptual foundation" of the work of Buell and the Community Research Associates, they concluded that

> The methods and philosophy of [Community Research Associates], when closely examined, present nothing new and much that has been discarded in the development of the social work profession. . . . Relative to the issues examined, the focus of [Community Research Associates] provides too narrow an orientation for constructive social welfare effort. The result can only be a parochial view of the social work role and an abdication of professional responsibility for the functions and direction of welfare policy.[60]

The grounds for this broad repudiation of the organization behind the multiproblem family approach were several, but first and foremost was the critique of the restrictive concentration on the multiproblem family as the key to the prevention and control of the pathology. The critics rejected this strategy as excessively conservative, simplistic, and based on a false medical analogy. In essence, they pointed out that the focus on the multiproblem family unjustifiably assumed that the "causes" of the pathological condition lay in its victims and diverted attention from the broader societal and institutional inadequacies that may have created the pathology in the first place. As they put it, for example,

> The genes for "problem families" lie not in the immediately identifiable group but in the vast complex of social, psychological, biological, and economic factors which may result in individual, family, and community maladjustment.[61]

And further:

> The improved coordination [between health and welfare agencies] in a community [that Community Research Associates] institutes may well be worthwhile, but the real problems in the community may escape the net if all the fishing is done in agency files.[62]

Conceptually, their quarrel here was partly with Buell's notion of "prevention." In public health terms, they noted, the approach he proposed was not one of primary prevention. That is to say, the limitation to the identification and treatment of multiproblem families does little to "prevent" their breakdown in the first place, unless one accepts the theory that the condition is somehow transmitted from one generation to the next. Buell was essentially narrowing his scope to one of reducing recidivism, they maintained, rather than preventing the problem in the primary sense. In their words,

> In social work, [Community Research Associates] contends, prevention takes place after the onset of symptoms and is limited to the prevention of further breakdown—which corresponds to the secondary and tertiary levels of prevention in public health. Some sense of the meaning of the word prevention is retained . . . although this comes close to the usual discussions on recidivism rates and their control.[63]

The critics' case against Buell and the multiproblem family approach, therefore, was that it shifted the locus of public concern from broader social inequities and deficits to the consequences of these conditions. "The emphasis on the family may have as one consequence," they maintained, "the obliteration from social work consciousness of the rich diversity of groups and institutions that need to be considered in dealing with social problems."[64]

It should be pointed on the other side that the difference here is perhaps more one of degree than one of kind. For example, in his 1952 book on the St. Paul Project Buell went at considerable length into the need for improved national systems of income maintenance through expanded social insurance programs and the like.[65] At the same time, Lukoff and Mencher would no doubt have supported the attempt to help multiproblem families on a case basis, along with broader improvement of societal conditions.

Lukoff and Mencher also go into a number of other short-comings of the work of the Community Research Associates, including the confounding of community *services* with family *problems,* since it "may well be that families that use community services are making a much more adequate adjustment to the difficulties of living than those who do not";[66] the hazards of "stigmatizing" families so identified and thus providing a ready scapegoat on which to project public responsibility; the limitations of the local community frame of reference; the untested theories of diagnosis and treatment employed; and finally, the fact that the research methods and findings of the Community Research Associates project were seldom reported with sufficient detail to permit independent judgments to be made of their conclusions, as noted earlier.[67] (An important contrast in multiproblem family research, as we have seen, may be found in the well-documented studies by Geismar after he arrived on the St. Paul scene. Technically speaking, however, he was not actually working with Community Research Associates but, rather, with the local St. Paul Family-Centered Project, so the Lukoff-Mencher criticism of that organization is not affected thereby.)

A couple of years earlier Roland Warren, director of social research of the New York Charities Aid Association, had expressed a related caution about the narrow scope of the multiproblem family focus, stating that "social agencies cannot 'do it all.' Housing, employment opportunities, schools, churches—all have an important part to play in creating an environment conducive to healthy living."[68] More explicitly, he emphasized that

> There seems to be a growing realization that multiproblem families are a product of the total community, and that it is unrealistic to expect social agencies alone to remedy conditions

whose roots are deeply imbedded in basic community inadequacies. According to this point of view, what should be expected from social agencies is that they make known the community lacks and needs they encounter, and that they join with other agencies and community groups in joint planning for community development and for the provision of such services and facilities as are needed.

It is only as this takes place that specific agency efforts in direct service to multiproblem families can be expected to succeed in the long run.[69]

While this 1960 statement anticipated the Lukoff-Mencher critique of the microlevel concentration of the multiproblem approach, its author, Warren, took the issue one major step further. He went beyond general criticism per se and undertook a large research experiment to test the effectiveness of the social work treatment of multiproblem families.[70] We shall review and excerpt this significant study shortly (see pp. 345–348 and 373–398).

Is It Effective?

As noted earlier, the research priority in the St. Paul Family-Centered Project—when the program turned to the treatment of multiproblem families after 1952—became the measurement of family functioning and its effectiveness. Leonard Rutman points out, logically enough from a basic social science point of view, that this research emphasis was premature inasmuch as the *components* and *process* of the treatment program had not yet been analyzed or conceptualized. Therefore the evaluative effort was in a sense attempting to study a "black box" of unknown content.[71]

However, the applied emphasis inevitably influenced the accompanying research focus, and the urgent concern of the project's staff and leadership was to demonstrate and test the *treatability* of the multiproblem family. Hence, after the preliminary studies of the "epidemiology" and some analysis of the characteristics of multiproblem families,[72] the primary research energies were devoted to the development of the Geismar Scale of Family Functioning and its utilization in assessing case movement and the efficacy of the treatment services.

It was recognized that the ideal evaluative research plan would involve some type of experimental design, including the use of control groups to isolate the impact of the treatment program. However, this approach was not implemented in the St. Paul Project for a variety of pragmatic reasons, including the higher priority necessarily given to the original development and refinement of the Scale of Family Functioning. Moreover, according to Leonard Rutman, it was realized that the aggressive dissemination of the Project's concepts and methods in the St. Paul area and beyond meant that it would be difficult to find an "uncontaminated" comparison group of cases treated by more conventional methods:

> In other words, if a control group had been established and if the results showed that their outcomes did not differ greatly from the families in the experimental [family-centered treatment] group, this would not necessarily imply that family-centered treatment was ineffective. Such results could also suggest that families in both groups received similar treatment because the techniques of family-centered treatment were widely transmitted.[73]

For such reasons as these, the use of control groups was bypassed, and attention was concentrated on the measurement of the social functioning of the treatment group of multiproblem families, and on changes in its level during the period of service. A type of compromise was suggested by Geismar wherein it was argued that the treatment group itself might be considered its "own control" to the extent that these cases exhibited an extended history (or "baseline") of dependency and maladjustment prior to treatment, and then often improved noticeably during treatment. (This approach may of course be recognized as an approximation to the "single-case" quasi-experimental model discussed in the preceding chapter.)[74] In Geismar's own words,

> The three aforementioned factors—prolonged problematic functioning of the families prior to intake, significant changes during treatment coincidental with movement in areas of greatest inadequacy, and the maintenance of treatment gains during follow-up—do provide converging evidence for the utility of services given.[75]

Conservatively, he went on to add that these data "do not make an airtight case."[76] His findings showed that 65 percent of a sample of multiproblem families treated showed positive movement, 19 percent showed no change, and 16 percent showed negative change.[77] Once again, then, we encounter the familiar "two-thirds" of clients in "therapy" showing improvement, but perhaps with particular interest here inasmuch as we are dealing with long-term malfunctioning families. However, the attempt at "quasi" control over a baseline period was retrospective only, and the circumstances lent themselves to the operation of a substantial Hawthorne effect in view of the special enthusiasm and motivation of the Family-Centered Project workers in the five participating agencies. In essence, therefore, the results may be said to have been encouraging but far from conclusive in testing the project's impact on these families.

It remained for a more definitive test of the multiproblem family treatment approach to be conducted elsewhere. This was the outstanding Chemung County (Elmira, New York) demonstration-research project instigated by Roland Warren of the State Charities Aid Association. Here an advanced experimental design was carried through in rigorous fashion from 1961 through 1964:

> The objective of this study was to assess the effects of intensive social casework on a group of 50 multiproblem families, in contrast with the effects of normal public assistance services given a control group of 50 similar families. The intensive service was given by caseworkers who had earned the Master of Social Work degree, and who had previous field experience. Caseloads in the demonstration group were limited to less than half the usual number carried by public assistance workers, and greater emphasis was put on using other available community services. The treatment phase was planned for 36 months and ultimately ran 31 months.[78]

While not a "crucial experimental test" of the effectiveness of multiproblem family treatment, for reasons to be noted, this study probably represented an outstanding state-of-the-art field experiment within the resources available to it. Thorough precautions were taken to preserve the integrity of the design (including a second, "hidden" control group)* and of the resulting findings.[79] It employed the two foremost measures of change in adjustment— the Geismar Scale of Family Functioning and the Hunt Movement Scale, which were used as cross-checks on each other. A comparison of the rating by the two instruments showed an "astonishing" degree of symmetry and consistency with each

---

* This extension of the traditional experimental control group design involved the drawing of a third random sample of 50 multiproblem families in addition to the regular experimental and "known" control group. The reason for this refinement is that the regular control group was necessarily known to the public assistance workers, and they therefore may have—knowingly or not—modified their role with them. The "hidden" group was not known to them, since they were not interviewed at the start of the project but only at its close. Thus any "Hawthorne effect" was thought to be minimized (see excerpt, pp. 392–395).

other.[80] In a sense this may also be seen as a test of the "external" validity of the two scales.[81]

The conclusion drawn from the analysis of demonstration and control group changes was quite sobering—and by now familiar:

> The essential finding was that while the demonstration group attained a slightly better degree of family functioning, its margin of progress over the control group was not significant in the statistical sense. That is, the demonstration group's greater advance could be attributed to chance alone.[82]

The book in which the Chemung County project was reported consisted of chapters written by various authorities in the field as well as by the project staff and leadership. The different presentations reflected a many-dimensional analysis and interpretation of the study and its results. Needless to say, there was a wide diversity of viewpoints and reactions.

The main spokesman of those critical of the study was Helen Harris Perlman of the University of Chicago's School of Social Service Administration. She questioned the suitability of the multiproblem idea in the first place, the adequacy of the research approach, and the far-from-ideal circumstances under which the project was carried out from the standpoint of desirable casework treatment conditions.[83] But her heaviest challenge was directed toward the unrealistic expectation that casework alone should be looked to for significant rehabilitation of such chronically deprived families: "Let us not assess the efficacy of casework in helping people to lift themselves by their bootstraps when they have no boots," she remonstrated.[84] More specifically, she inveighed against

> the use of casework in public assistance agencies when such agencies are themselves hampered by conditions of inadequate funds and lack of social resources. Under such circumstances, can casework work? . . . are these psychological and social conditions that make a casework all but futile? The Chemung County findings . . . force one honestly to look at these questions.[85]

She concluded that, "in short, the *multiproblem family* is usually a *multi-deficit family*"[86] (emphasis added), by which she meant one multiply bereft of the societal opportunities, advantages, and resources necessary for participation in the American mainstream.

Interestingly enough, by the time of this 1966 colloquy Geismar had also entered the lists against such evaluation on similar grounds:

> It is my opinion that the overall research action plan was deficient in not developing the best input variables at the time

services were being rendered. Best in this context is not to be understood as [intervention by professionally trained experienced caseworkers].[87]

What he had in mind as an alternative was the following: "Evaluation research in social welfare stands much to gain by expanding the theoretical horizons to include forces both within the individual and *in the larger socio-economic environment*,"[88] that is to say, going beyond social treatment to the modification of resources in the broader society (emphasis added).

However, as Wayne Vasey pointed out in his commentary on the Chemung County study, the claims and actions of social work in past years had at least implicitly assumed that casework treatment could make a difference "in helping such families toward the attainment of a more adequate level of functioning."[89] He noted that

> This is the pattern of thinking that led to the enactment of the service provisions in the 1962 Amendments to the Social Security Act dealing with public assistance. Under these amendments, states have been encouraged to step up professional services, reduce caseloads, and to provide specific evidence of services rendered. . . . Successful amendments have fostered this emphasis.
>
> There has persisted the thought that one primary hopeful step would be that of bringing to bear a concentration of more skilled professional work on the problems of people in such circumstances. *It would not be accurate to say that such services have been suggested as a substitute for bread, but they certainly have been prominently featured in [social work] proposals for improvement of the public welfare system.* One cannot, as a matter of public policy, advocate measures without including in such advocacy some hope of a productive outcome.[90] [Emphasis added.]

It will be recalled that Warren himself had raised such questions in 1960, prior to the Chemung County Project.[91] However, he was enough of a social researcher to want to test the issue empirically; he therefore gave leadership to the subsequent experiment. He responded to the Perlman critique in the following terms:

> Like all rhetorical questions [they] answer themselves. Today, that is! They did not answer themselves seven years ago. As a matter of fact they were not being asked seven years ago with any such explicitness as they are raised here. I do believe a lot of learning has taken place in this respect in the last few years, and that studies such as this provide a desirable stimulus for such questions.

I would go so far as to say that such thinking was not only prevalent at the time of the 1962 amendments, but remains prevalent today, even though the explicit anwser to Helen Perlman's questions would take the expected form.[92]

And so, once more, social work appeared in the space of less than two decades to have come around close to 180 degrees, from an enthusiastic embrace of the multiproblem family as the special target of social rehabilitation to a prior focus of concern. Attention was being shifted (as during the 1930s) to the unmet community and national needs for social reconstruction and economic provision. In this circling, the reaction to and critical reappraisal of the multiproblem approach had made major contributions—the recognition of its persistent, familiar nature; the challenging of its limited scope and case-centered premises; and the research questioning of its effectiveness.* Underlying these factors, perhaps, was the natural "rhythm" that we have come to expect in research priorities in this applied field—the internal dialectic that appears to affect the ebb and flow of professional interest over the years. But in addition there was another factor that might well have overshadowed the multiproblem family movement in any event.

### The "Final Blow"—The Social Activism of the 1960s

In the early 1960s, when the multiproblem family projects had already passed their peak, a quite different approach on social problems was crystallizing at the national level in some of the major foundations and in the federal government. This new perspective was first seen in the "gray areas," projects, the urban neighborhood programs of the Ford Foundation in the 1950s, and in the later juvenile delinquency prevention projects of the Ford Foundation and then of the Federal government in the early 1960s.[93]

---

* The controversial article by Joel Fischer ("Is Casework Effective? A Review," *Social Work*, 18, no. 1 (January 1973): 5–21) drew strongly negative conclusions regarding casework efficacy in general, based on Fischer's analysis of eleven available "experiments" in the literature. The Chemung County study was one of these. Another was a multiproblem family research project directed by Ludwig Geismar in New Haven, Connecticut, in the late 1950s and early 1960s—the Neighborhood Improvement Project. (Ludwig L. Geismar and Jane Krisberg, *The Forgotten Neighborhood: Site of an Early Skirmish in the War on Poverty*, Metuchen, N.J.: Scarecrow Press, 1967). This time Geismar used a nonequivalent control group experimental design. As an interesting postscript, Geismar subsequently challenged such negative conclusions regarding casework effectiveness. See Ludwig Geismar, "Correspondence," *Social Service Review*, 47, no. 1 (March 1973): 105–107.

Perhaps the most influential of these projects, at least insofar as its impact on social work is concerned, was the Mobilization for Youth project on the lower east side of Manhattan. If one were to attempt to characterize the "activist" social work of the 1960s, the following features would probably be included: aggressive social advocacy on behalf of the disadvantaged; "new careers" in helping roles for indigenous workers; organized confrontation of the "establishment" by staff-supported slum resident and welfare-recipient groups; support of neighborhood control of social institutions; emphasis on more equitable distribution of social opportunity and resources, including welfare reform and new transfer payment programs (i.e., a stress on an "income" strategy vs. a "service" strategy); and so on.[94] A further feature would also be assertive, intensive, reaching-out casework and referral services to chronically dependent, malfunctioning multiproblem families.

Practically all of the foregoing components—with the exception of the last, developed of course by the St. Paul Family-Centered Project, were initiated by the Mobilization for Youth program. This highly creative project, which was initiated with federal and foundation financing in 1962, had a marked impact on the subsequent social experimentation of the Great Society programs generally and the War on Poverty in particular. Suffice it to say here that the Mobilization for Youth and its later counterparts around the country proceeded from a set of premises and frame of reference diametrically opposed to those of the St. Paul program. The conceptual base was the "opportunity structure" theory of sociologist Robert Merton, as elaborated by Richard Cloward and Lloyd Ohlin,[95] which pointed to inequities of the external social system and its rewards and constraints as the source of antisocial behavior. The major thrust, therefore, was toward social action and reform of social institutions—the opposite pole, basically, from that of the multiproblem family approach. The multiproblem family emphasis was thus replaced by the drive to document and correct the multiple deficits of society. This new activism in social welfare quickly swept the field in the 1960s, fueled by heavy injections of federal largesse; it delivered the final *coup de grace*— if one was still needed—to the St. Paul gospel.

## A Stock Taking

It is, in a way, too easy today, hardly more than a decade later, to perceive the many flaws and gaps in the multiproblem family movement. Indeed its research leadership was largely cognizant of its main shortcomings from the outset, and quite explicit about them in later writings. For example, in 1960 Geismar stated that "in planning studies which rely chiefly upon symptomatology we should be aware of their limitations with regard to the possible goal of research aimed at prevention and *early* treatment of multi-problem family functioning."[96] Somewhat later he wrote, somewhat ambivalently perhaps:

> The ideal objective . . . —the substantial modification of the environment of the deprived population—is an exceedingly big order. Such modification is more typically the product of social revolutions . . . [than of "community development" projects of the type then reported in the Lagey-Ayres survey]. The emphasis [in these] tends to be on youth and centers around education, employment, and recreation. . . .[97]

At that time, in 1964, he was posing the conceptual issue as "multiproblem *families* or multiproblem *welfare system*" (emphasis added).[98] His emphasis at that point was on the view that "problematic family functioning and inadequate agency functioning may be viewed as two sides of a coin."[99] He recognized expressly, however, that "such [agency] efforts are circumscribed by the opportunities provided by the community"[100] and went on to maintain that

> Social welfare in this country operates in fact with a very limited mandate: to help the socially handicapped. It is not charged with removing the conditions which gave rise to social handicaps.[101]

This restrictive interpretation of social welfare's mission would no doubt be challenged by most professionals.

Finally, in 1972, in referring to particular multiproblem family projects, Geismar wrote:

> Under the very best of circumstances professional intervention was able to bring to bear on the client only a limited number of influences that would be needed if his overall social functioning were to be substantially altered. And so the pessimism expressed in the report on their findings is often the result of failure to countenance the lack of realism in the hypotheses.[102]

He further stated that

> No profession and certainly not social work can be blamed for expressing itself optimistically regarding the power of its professional methods. It seems, however, that much of the infectious

optimism of practitioners has been carried over to a large proportion of researchers, *the present ones included,* leading them
to postulate hypotheses holding exaggreated views of social work
capabilities. Significant improvements in total social functioning
and the prevention of economic dependency not only strain the
imagination of man but also make demands on many systems.[103]
(Emphasis added)

Perhaps this is as much of a *mea culpa* as should be looked for
from any researcher! Interestingly enough, a similar "confession"
was expressed by Warren in 1974, as follows:

> Do we really take seriously what has been learned in the social
> sciences about multiple causation? What it indicates is that in
> most problem situations there is no single element which either
> causes the problem condition or can be used to correct or measur-
> ably ameliorate the problem condition. In many problem areas,
> informed, rational analysis is sufficient to cast grave doubt on
> single-intervention techniques designed to make significant im-
> pacts on admittedly complex situations.
>
> Let me present *an outstanding example of what I consider to
> be the essential naiveté and myopia* which I have described. A
> number of years ago a rather extensive demonstration project
> was developed, directed at so-called multiproblem families. The
> intervention technique was that of intensive casework with con-
> siderable inter-agency cooperation and many of the other
> desiderata which at the time were considered to be at the cutting
> edge of new developments in family casework. A careful evalua-
> tion research design was developed, which contained not only a
> utilization of the classical controlled field experimental model
> but many of the other appurtenances of sophisticated field re-
> search methodology. It was, in its design, "one for the books,"
> and has frequently been cited in the evaluation research litera-
> ture. The principal investigator in the research later wrote that
> both researchers and caseworkers were well aware that no effec-
> tiveness might be shown by the demonstration program. I quote:
>
> > "We even joked about it in a sort of macabre fashion, but
> > I don't think any of us really anticipated such an outcome.
> > Nevertheless we all had our own little ways of hedging.
> > Mine was to say, 'If the demonstration proves effective, we
> > will have to rewrite all the books.' To my way of thinking,
> > intensive casework services could offer, even under the best
> > circumstances, such a small part of the total configuration
> > of attitudes, behavior patterns, and institutional configura-

tions surrounding these troubled families that it would seem miraculous if casework could have a sufficient effect to be registered on the admittedly crude instruments we planned to use. The instruments were the best available."

But this notion that "if the demonstration proves effective we will have to rewrite all the books" did not deter the evaluation researcher from proceeding. The project and the evaluation research were carried through as planned. No significant differences on the outcome measures were found between the experimental group of target families and the control group.

If it appears that I am pointing a self-righteous, holier-than-thou finger at this researcher, let me be the first to assert what many of you already know: that *I was the evaluation researcher.* And so quite obviously, to the extent that my remarks are critical they certainly apply to me.[104] (Emphasis added)

The foregoing extended quotations in this "stock-taking" section of the chapter may serve to illustrate that the key researchers in the study of the multiproblem family were in a very real sense their own best critics, and therefore the limitations of their research efforts can often best be summarized in their own words.*

However, there were positives as well as negatives in the multiproblem family effort in social work. In the late 1940s and early 1950s the field lacked momentum; it was marking time in a traditional mode of worker-client treatment relationship. It centered largely on the motivated client, who applied for service within the scope and criteria of agency program priorities and was generally ready, willing, and able to come in for periodic interviews during regular hours for service by a single more or less specialized agency.

The multiproblem family approach changed that rather passive posture drastically. Assertive, collaborative, reaching-out casework services, in the client's home, at odd hours of the day or night became the "new frontier" of the profession. The previously "hopeless," half-forgotten, many-troubled, chronically dependent family moved to center stage from the shadowed fringes. And this focus persisted through the 1950s, the activist 1960s, and now into the 1970s for special categories of need, such as the abused child, the neglected aged, the discharged mental patient, and ex-

---

* To conclude this string of confessionals, the author should acknowledge that he too was an ardent supporter of and participant in the multiproblem family movement over a number of years. See Sidney E. Zimbalist and Walter W. Pippert, "The New Level of Integration in Community Welfare Service," *Social Work,* 5, no. 2 (April 1960): 29–34.

prisoners. Previously fragmented, single-agency services were brought together into more coordinated networks. Thus a vital ferment was introduced (or reintroduced) into social work over two decades ago that has served to galvanize and strengthen practice and programming since then. A sharper and broader sense of social work function emerged.

The research contributions of the movement were also many and significant. The Geismar Scale of Family Functioning itself represented a substantial advance beyond the Hunt Movement Scale as a measure of change in adjustment, and remains today—despite its limitations—the best available instrument of its kind in the field. The large number of community studies and agency case inventories it spawned added to knowledge, experience, and methodology in analyzing multifaceted, intractable cases. And the Chemung County study by Warren remains a model of field experimental design in social work. Moreover, its negative findings regarding the impact on multiproblem families of intervention by trained social workers—together with similar conclusions from other such experiments—helped raise fundamental issues regarding both the effectiveness of social work and the adequacy of existing research methodology that reverberate and remain essentially unresolved today. Current trends and strategies in social work continue to reflect such challenges and their far-reaching ramifications.

Thus even in its failures the multiproblem family approach had valuable consequences. As it ran its course and revealed its own limitations, these in turn pointed toward more promising directions for the profession and the nation. In a certain sense, then, the movement—with all its pros and cons—helped usher in the next great wave of public and social welfare concern, the "activist" social work and social reform programs of the 1960s.

# Delineating the Problem
## LUDWIG L. GEISMAR and MICHAEL LA SORTE

In this book Geismar and La Sorte undertook to synthesize and conceptualize what had been learned about the multiproblem family over some fifteen years of research and demonstration. The selections here are from Chapters 1 and 3, pp. 15–21, and 52–93.

From Ludwig L. Geismar and Michael La Sorte, *Understanding the Multiproblem Family: A Conceptional Analysis and Exploration in Early Identification* (New York: Association Press, 1964). Reprinted with permission of publisher.

It is no accident that research and social action focused on the disorganized or multi-problem family for the first time during the 1950s. Though earlier decades of the twentieth century witnessed the rapid growth of the social sciences and the development of social work into a full-fledged profession, certain major events during this period overshadowed the crisis situations which occurred in the lives of a small segment of the population. The economic depression of the 1930s and the global war of the forties left little room for society to concern itself with those of its members whose problems, however severe and persistent, were neither felt nor shared by the community at large.

In the postwar period, however, general economic prosperity, broken only by relatively brief recessions, and a rise in the standard of living brought into sharp relief the fate of one portion of our population which did not benefit from the blessings of a booming economy or from the provisions of an improved system of social security. Moreover, the growth process of the social work profession itself, as we shall show, has been a determinant in the shift of focus to, and then away from, problems such as those presented by the multiproblem family.

The supposition held by health and welfare agencies that a small number of families in a given community were beset by a multiplicity of serious problems was supported by several surveys which are cited in subsequent pages. However, what magnified the problem in the eyes of the large community was the finding from a St. Paul, Minnesota, study done in 1948 that over half of the combined services and budget allotments of the major health and welfare agencies of the city were being absorbed by a small proportion of families which were being served simultaneously by several community welfare resources.[1] Subsequent surveys in St. Paul and a number of other urban communities produced supporting evidence that between two and three percent of the families in the community are seriously disorganized, take up the bulk of social services, and also account for a disproportionate share of deviant behavior, such as abuse and neglect of children, juvenile delinquency, adult crime, and adult alcoholism.

An analysis of the use of social services made by these families reveals that their relationships with agencies have been poor, ranging from indifferent to hostile. Most of these families are known by their pattern of going from agency to agency, in search of one which will meet their immediate need. Agencies note that the families make repeated application for service but fail to follow through with the plans offered to help them. The relationships of the multiproblem families to the community can best be described as "anomic," that is, as having a lack of identification with and integration into the community, and a nonadherence to community values. The relationships which they do have lack the strength and stability necessary for nealthy identification. Contacts with the neighborhood are tenuous. There is little participation in church, school, and recreational activities. A mutual alienation appears to be characteristic of the relationship between the community agencies or institutions and these families.

Public welfare agencies and those providing correctional and protective services have been most aware of the existence of the multiproblem family. Although rarely analyzed in conceptual terms, such a family is characterized by recidivism, deviant behavior, frequency of crisis situations, and chronicity of assistance and services. The last named has taken strikingly tangible form in voluminous case records going back frequently over several generations.

The ever-growing concern of the American social work community with the multiproblem family has led the authors of this volume to attempt a systematic analysis of its functioning and an exploration of ways in which social welfare might move toward prevention of the problems the family presents to the community and to itself. An effort has been made to present the disorganized family within a framework of classifications which is consistent with leading concepts on the nature of the American family system, drawn from both social science and social work. The particular conceptual approach used here was selected for its pertinence to treatment planning at various levels of community organization.

The contents in this book are drawn from a number of studies, particularly the research done in the Neighborhood Improvement Project of New Haven, Connecticut, and the Family Centered Project of St. Paul, Minn. Chapters 4 and 5 comprise a detailed report on a New Haven study comparing a group of disorganized families in a public housing project with a group of stable families in the same project. Comparisons encompass contrasts in present patterns of social functioning and in modes of behavior early in the family life cycle. The main theme of this study is the development of knowledge which may lead to an early identification of the multiproblem family.

The authors' general purpose is to give the reader a conceptual clarification of the multiproblem family and an acquaintance with data on the subject that have been uncovered by research, and thus enable him to gain a better understanding of a problem whose urgency has come to be acknowledged by the social work profession and many communities throughout the country.

## A QUESTION OF TERMINOLOGY

The term "multiproblem family" appears to the authors to be the most appropriate term by which to designate the phenomenon discussed in this volume. In view of the fact that many papers and articles on the subject of problem families dispose of the question of terminology as being of minor importance (after all, what's in a name?) we deemed it necessary to discuss the concept in its larger perspective, that is, to consider the term "multiproblem family" from the viewpoint of its conceptual adequacy.

A heightened awareness of, and concern with, the problems of the seriously disorganized family have led public and private welfare agencies all over the nation to establish projects and services on behalf of these families. A survey by the State Charities Aid Association listed ten different programs in the state of New York alone.[2] No complete roster of such undertakings for the entire country seems to be available at this writing (1962), but a survey by the Communty Chest and Councils of the Greater Vancouver (B.C.) area revealed that as of 1962, at least 143 communities out of 260 surveyed in the United States and Canada are engaged in some kind of activity designed to cope with the problem of the multiproblem family.[3] There is practically no communication among these undertakings, and most of them appear to be struggling on their own without the benefit of knowledge and findings from other communities. The growing concern with the problems of such families is also expressed by the increasing number of sessions devoted to the subject at national and regional welfare conferences.

It would appear from all these activities that this area of concern is in the process of becoming a major field of practice in social welfare. In the face of this situation, the question arises whether the lack of adequate terminology and definitions does not represent a major obstacle to the development of such a field of social work practice.

A number of descriptive terms have been used in the literature to designate the seriously disorganized family. They include hard-core, socially delinquent, deprived, distrustful, hard-to-reach, and others. Each in its way singles out for description a given characteristic of these families. The term "multiproblem family" has perhaps been used more widely than the other designations. Yet, referring as it does to problems rather than to specific family traits, the term poses some problems of its own with regard to definition.

Without disclaiming the possibility of independent invention, the authors recall that the expression "multiproblem family" was first proposed as a descriptive term for seriously disorganized families by Isaac Hoffman, Research Director of the Wilder Foundation in St. Paul, Minnesota, in connection with the 1948 St. Paul study, noted above. The term was adopted by the survey team for this study, entitled the *Family Unit Report Study,* carried out under the auspices of Community Research Associates, Inc., of New York. In this survey the term was used to designate families with serious problems in more than one of the following areas: social adjustment, health, economic behavior, and recreational need.[4]

The obvious difficulty with this definition is its vagueness. As seen in the *Family Unit Report Study* a problem was a pathological condition which needed treatment. The borderline between pathology and normal behavior is difficult to delineate. Furthermore, the four areas designated are so broad that a breakdown in only one of the areas might result in a serious impairment of the family's capacity to function as a unit. Yet in the view of many practitioners, the term "multiproblem" seems suggestive enough of certain characteristics and behavior patterns found in family disorganization to merit continued use when defined more sharply.

The Family Centered Project of St. Paul, which was one of the intended outgrowths of the *Family Unit Report Study,* concentrated much of its research work upon an effort to develop a conceptual foundation for studying the nature of, and the giving of service to, the multiproblem family. This effort was perceived as a precondition for any attemt to evaluate the work with multiproblem families. The definition of multiproblem family, developed in the Family Centered Project and refined in the New Haven Neighborhood Improvement Project, and the general conceptual framework in which the definition is cast serve as a base for the present discussion of the work with, and findings about, multiproblem families.

The term "multiproblem family," as used in this book, denotes a family with disorganized social functioning of an order that adversely affects the following sets of behavior: (1) relationships inside the family; (2) relationships outside the family group, particularly neighborhood and community relationships; and (3) the performance of tasks such as those concerned with health, and with economic and household practices that are designed to maintain the family as a physical unit. To our mind, the value of defining the multiproblem family in this way lies in the relatedness of the definition to social practice and its potential for measurement.

The adequacy of a concept can be judged only in relation to its uses. In this instance we needed to ask ourselves what are the specific purposes which might be served by the concept and definition selected. The purposes may be summarized under the following headings: (1) understanding of family functioning, (2) identification, (3) diagnosis, (4) treatment, and (5) evaluation of change. The present volume is chiefly concerned with the first two purposes and with the search for a method leading to early detection of multiproblem behavior.

## NOTES

[1] Bradley Buell and Associates, *Community Planning for Human Services* (New York: Columbia University Press, 1952), pp. 9 ff.

[2] State Charities Aid Association, *"Multi-Problem Families," a New Name or a New Problem?* (New York: State Charities Aid Association, May, 1960).

[3] Joseph C. Lagey and Beverly Ayres, *Community Treatment Programs for Multi-Problem Families* (Vancouver Community Chest and Councils of the Greater Vancouver Area, Dec. 1962), pp. 1–6.

See also Joseph C. Lagey and Beverly Ayres, "Community Treatment Programs for Multi-Problem Families," in Benjamin Schlesinger, *The Multi-Problem Family, A Review and Annotated Bibliography* (Toronto: University of Toronto Press, 1963), pp. 55–71.

[4] Bradley Buell and Associates, op. cit., pp. 9–11.

# Problems of Identification and Measurement

## THE PREVALENCE OF FAMILY DISORGANIZATION

If family disorganization or multiproblem functioning is viewed by the community or by society as social pathology the question of its prevalence must be raised. This needs to be done for two reasons:

· The scope of any process or even harmful to the welfare of man and society should be known in order that it can be dealt with by any method known to and accepted by society. Whether such action takes the form of direct treatment, legislation, or quarantine is not important in this context. What matters is that the relationship between the scope of the problem and the magnitude of the action should be known in order to permit realistic planning.

· An assessment of the effectiveness of any action also presupposes knowledge of the scope of a problem. In the long run effectiveness can be measured by whether or not the action undertaken serves to decrease, increase, or contain the phenomenon under consideration.

The availability of precise data about the prevalence of pathology is taken for granted in medicine and public health. Adequate data about social pathology are scarce because the field of social work has not developed the same expectations relative to such information. Instead, it has been reasonably satisfied with dealing with the most urgent problems and/or giving services where resources were available.

This situation has not been conducive to the growth of epidemiology, that is, the study of pathology in relation to population characteristics and processes, in the area of social problems. Existing efforts at procuring epidemiological knowledge have been handicapped by loose terminology of given phenomena. For example, some advocates of community-wide reporting in social work have dealt with the term "economic dependency" as if it were a serious disorder that needs to be eradicated. To cite another example, the term "social maladjustment" has been treated like a clearly identifiable disease such as diabetes or polio. Social work as a whole, however, has shown relatively little interest in systematic and reliable stock taking of existing welfare problems.

It is not far-fetched to suppose that the problems inherent in defining social pathology have been a hinderance to the development of social epidemiology to the same extent that the absence of an orientation aimed at pinpointing welfare problems has retarded efforts at conceptualizing community-wide pathology. In other words, one might postulate here a reciprocal relationship between orientation and knowledge rather than a one-way influence.

The pursuit of epidemiology requires, in addition to adequate conceptualization, some provision for collecting data on a community-wide basis. The two requirements unfortunately do not often go hand in hand. The most comprehensive kind of reporting usually relies on data that are readily available. Yet, the process of defining social pathology and operationalizing data collection must, of necessity, work independently of whatever information may be at hand through administrative channels. Administrative data gathering is generally very specific in terms of the requirements arising out of the operation of a given program. The process of conceptualization, by contrast, is theory related and demands data collection in keeping with the theoretical frame of reference.

The investigator who wishes to study the prevalence of a community-wide problem is faced with a dilemma: to refrain from data collection until means can be found to procure thoroughly meaningful information, or to collect data which raise questions as to their significance but are available on a community-wide basis. The decision as often as not is one of compromise between these two extremes.

The family functioning approach may, as we hope to show later, suggest a way of studying family disorganization in a meaningful manner. It is equally clear that the data required for such an analysis can be obtained only with some effort in training social workers and/or skilled interviewers in procuring and writing up such information. Short of this or an equally promising approach for gauging the scope of a community problem, certain compromise techniques may be used. An example of these techniques are two checklist studies carried out in St. Paul, Minnesota,[1] and Vancouver, British Columbia,[2] in recent years. Mention of the latter has been made in the previous chapters.

Both surveys were designed to establish the approximate number of multiproblem families in the respective communities as a basis from which to gauge the need for reaching-out services. In both studies it was agreed, for reasons of practicability, to confine the surveying to institutional channels, that is, to utilize the agencies and organizations most likely to be in contact with disorganized families. It was assumed that this approach would yield data about the bulk of multiproblem families who are in some ways dependent upon the community. In both cities the major public and private welfare agencies were canvassed. There were, however, differences in the scope of health, educational, recreational, and correctional agencies surveyed. The Vancouver canvass was broader (8,017 cases as against 4,980 in St. Paul) but did not yield a higher proportion of multiproblem cases, perhaps because the disorganized families, many of whom had multiple agency contacts, were picked up even in the St. Paul survey through at least one of the agencies serving them.

The survey technique used in both places differed only in some minor respects and was essentially as follows: All social workers giving service to families in the agencies participating in the study received instructions in completing a schedule or checklist on every one of their client families with at least one parent and one or more children under 18 in the home. The checklist, which was accompanied by instructions containing definition of terms, required the review of each case and the checking of categories appropriate to the objectives of the survey.

For purposes of both surveys, and with recognition of the limitations in the data-gathering process, a crude but operational definition of multiproblem family was decided upon. This definition was a modification of that used by Community Research Associates, Inc., in their 1948 St. Paul Family Unit Report Study.[3] A multiproblem family was defined in both the St. Paul and Vancouver surveys as one with one or more children under 18 which is characterized by (1) serious behavior disorders as evidenced by verified neglect, delinquency, mental disorders, emotional disturbances, severe conflicts in interpersonal relations, and the like; and (2) problems in one or both of the following areas: economic functioning, which included continuous or intermittent relief or public assistance, excessive debts, problems around money management, and health functioning, particularly a serious health condition in adults and children.

Both studies concerned themselves with the question of reliability of reporting by comparing differences in categories checked on all cases with multiple agency contacts. Percentages of disagreement ran from 7 to 40, depending on whether information required was objective, such as family status, or whether it was more judgmental, such as behavior problems in the family. The fundamental weakness in both surveys lay in the fact that agency recording is for the most part not family centered but focuses on programs or specific problems dealt with.

Thus, a probation officer carrying a case load of 120 may not know much about the family of orientation of one of his charges placed in an institution. Or a public assistance worker may have only the vaguest notion about the nature of the marital relationship in a family under his care.

These defects in reliability of data seriously limit their validity. As an index of family disorganization in the community, two assumptions might be made in interpreting and utilizing any survey results:

· Even if our average error in reliability runs as high as 33 percent, our estimate about total incidence of multiproblem families in the community brings us within a sufficiently close range of the actual figure to evolve a strategy for coping with the problem.

· The chances are that the most disorganized families were reported in the survey because these families have a tendency to become known to the social worker. The remedy for such hazardous postulating lies obviously in equipping social agencies with the tools for collecting meaningful and reliable data.

Having accepted the limitations inherent in the survey method of the St. Paul and Vancouver studies, what do they tell us about the prevalence of family disorganization?

When the total population of the two cities was used as a base, the estimated proportion of persons identified by the above-mentioned method as belonging to disorganized families was 4.5 percent for St. Paul and 4.6 percent for Vancouver. The figures were arrived at by counting the average multiproblem family as a six-person group, an estimate supported by preliminary studies in both communities. The estimate for multiproblem families as percentages of all families in the two communities was found to be 2.2 and 2.3, respectively.

These survey findings are not too different from those established in the 1948 Family Unit Report Study done by Community Research Associates,[4] which had covered 37,369 families as a result of wider agency participation. The 1948 study, in contrast to the two later surveys, included a considerable number of recreation and group work agencies.[5] A total of 6,466 families, roughly 6 percent of the families in St. Paul, were identified as multiproblem in the 1948 study.[6] The definition used was more inclusive than that used in the 1957 checklist survey and comprised some families who had no adjustment problems. Moreover, the term "family" was used in a less restricted manner than in the two other later studies.[7]

Unfortunately the 1948 survey provided no information on the reliability of data. A subsequent analysis of the data by the Research Department of the Amherst Wilder Foundation of St. Paul in terms similar to those of the later checklist studies yielded an estimate of roughly 2 percent of families identified as disorganized in St. Paul in 1948.

In a progress report on human welfare in New York City, a study committee reported that "at most 5 percent of the city's families with children under 18 can be regarded as multiproblem units."[8] This ratio would be smaller if all the families in the community were used as a base for computation.

In 1960 the Neighborhood Improvement Project of New Haven, Connecticut, conducted an intensive survey of all the households, numbering 300, in a low-income public housing project, in an effort to locate every seriously disorganized family with children under 18 in the project. The survey preceded the establishment of a treatment program for these multiproblem families. Using the criteria employed in the 1948 St. Paul study, 25 families were found to be clearly multiproblem. This number is about 8 percent of the families in this particular neighborhood, which is known for its high rates of economic dependency and delinquent behavior. Though it is not known how representative this housing project is of other deteriorated areas, it can safely be said that deprived neighborhoods contain the bulk of multiproblem families in a community.[9] This conclusion is borne out by the Vancouver survey, in which eight census tracts out of a total of forty-nine were reported to have multiproblem families constituting between 3 and 6.2 percent of all families in the area, whereas twenty other tracts had rates below 1 percent.[10]

What do these various findings add up to? Allowing for a considerable margin of error due to low or unknown reliability in reporting, we do get converging evidence that the proportion of the most disorganized families in the urban community who are *known* to the community is relatively small, ranging perhaps between 2 and 3 percent of all the families in the community. However, this small group receives a great many services, as was shown in a study of one hundred St. Paul families by Geismar and Ayres[11] and in the findings of Bradley Buell and Associates which state that these families "were absorbing well over half of the combined services of the community's dependency, health, and adjustment agencies."[12]

We do not know whether St. Paul and Vancouver are representative with regard to the prevalence of known community disorganization. It is possible that economic and social factors accounting for demographic patterns different from those in these two cities exist elsewhere and are associated with different ratios of disorganization. This question could be answered by checklist-type surveys in a cross section of communities repeated at given time intervals, designed to study differences resulting from variations in socio-economic forces. Basic to any such effort—and this appears to be the most important lesson emanating from the checklist studies—are provisions to assure adequate reliability of reporting data. Any community which is interested in determining the prevalence of multiproblem functioning as reflected in multi-agency contacts can take certain steps to improve the reliability of reporting data.

These steps include the acceptance, by agencies participating in the survey, of a family centered focus in serving clients, the provision for continuous data collection on family functioning, and some in-service training of social workers in the method of data gathering. An ongoing reporting operation built into agency practice is likely to yield more reliable data because it permits the establishment of a consistent focus and the development of reporting skills. Such a focus geared to a ready perception of breakdown in the psychosocial functioning of a family would hardly appear to be at odds with the basic goals of social work endorsed by most agencies.

The checklist type of survey technique for identifying multiproblem families is based upon the assumption that the great bulk of them can be located by a review of agency case loads. Multiproblem families are thought to be "known" to the community because their disordered behavior brings them to the attention of agencies and authorities concerned with economic, health, adjustment, and correctional functions.

The study by Geismar and Ayres of one hundred St. Paul families diagnosed as seriously disorganized revealed, indeed, that these families were known not to one but to many agencies in the community. The medium number of registrations during the family life cycle was thirteen, and the families had received services from nine *different* agencies, on the average. The mean number of years during which the families were known to the agencies was fifteen.[13]

This pattern of multiple registration was not surprising because it had served as the means by which identification and selection for treatment was carried out. Therefore it would be accurate to state that families known to many agencies tend to be multiproblem in functioning. The converse may be true, but we are not aware of any comprehensive studies which have investigated this relationship. To do so it would be necessary to study the social functioning of a cross section of a given population and relate malfunctioning to the agency registration pattern.

Little is known regarding the prevalence of family disorganization in middle-class families, although the records of any therapist or mental health clinic will show that multiproblem behavior in the middle and upper strata of society is not isolated phenomenon. Families in the higher socioeconomic groups differ significantly from those in the lower ones by their ability to shield problem behavior from the community at large by the purchase of services which are private and confidential in nature.

We omit here some three pages that summarized studies of Social Service Exchange registration patterns of multiproblem families. The excerpts continue with an overview of Geismar's approach to the measurement of "family functioning."

## A PERSPECTIVE FOR ASSESSING FAMILY FUNCTIONING

Effective assessment of family or social functioning must rest upon clear definitions of the kind of behavior that is to be assessed. As suggested earlier, this may be done by viewing the family not merely as an aggregate of individuals but also as an interacting group of persons playing mutually complementary roles and carrying out certain basis tasks or functions which are necessary for the welfare of the family and are in keeping with the expectations of society. Earlier, family functioning was presented in a broad theoretical frame of reference. Our purpose here is to consider family functioning in terms that are useful in assessing it.

This approach suggests that we examine the roles which each person is playing and ask whether they contribute to his own and is family's well-being, whether they are in line with his potential for social functioning, and whether they are in keeping with societal expectations. Moreover, we must consider to what extent those tasks which can be identified as family functions are being performed in a manner which is conducive to the welfare of the family as well as the community.

The Family Centered Project of St. Paul developed a model for assessing family functioning of disorganized families.[14] This model was named the Profile of Family Functioning. The Profile is a chart of a family's social functioning in nine categories or areas and 26 subcategories on a seven-point continuum ranging from adequate to inadequate behavior. Data for the chart are collected by means of open-ended interviews with family members and reading of agency records pertaining to the family's functioning. The narrative information, after being entered in the Profile schedule under the appropriate categories and subcategories, is rated by two or more judges on the seven-point continuum mentioned above.

The Profile of Family Functioning was tested for reliability and applied in the study of 150 St. Paul families who had received family centered treatment.[15] The Profile has also been used in the Neighborhood Improvement Project of New Haven, Connecticut, the Research Demonstration Project with Dependent Multiproblem Families of Elmira, New York, and several other research action programs. Since the details of this particular method of analyzing the functioning of problem families were presented in several publications, we shall review here only its conceptual underpinnings and sketch its basic outline.

## Individual Behavior and Adjustment

In presenting the two aspects of family functioning, we inquired first into the nature of each individual's functioning. We term this category of observations "Individual Behavior and Adjustment." It comprises each family member's personality structure, which includes his physical appearance, attitudes, and behavior, and also pathological characteristics of a physiological, psychological, and social nature. Examples of the latter are physical and mental handicaps, anxieties, pathogenic conflicts, and character disorders.

The second aspect of the category "Individual Behavior and Adjustment" covers sets of roles which family members play in daily life. Typical roles include those of husband, wife, parent, homemaker, breadwinner, child, sibling, student, member of peer group, member of an organization. Since every member of a family plays a great number of roles both inside and outside the family, assessment takes into account how well these roles are being performed and integrated within the personality structure of each family member. Integration refers to the compatibility and complementarity of roles which either may permit the individual to function in keeping with the expectations of the group and enjoy good mental health, or may make him experience conflict between roles or between roles and expectations and may affect his personality adversely.

## Areas of Social Functioning Involving Role
## Performance in the Family Group

As stated earlier, an area of social functioning represents a concept that groups together all those sets of activities or roles performed by family members with the aim of getting a certain job done. The primary concern in appraising the convergence of roles by areas is how well the tasks are performed rather than who performs them. One group of areas involves role playing within the primary social system called family. This means that contacts, whether of an expressive or of an instrumental nature, are with members of the family only.

Three areas represent functiong in such intrafamilial roles. The first is termed *Family Relationships and Unity*.[16] It comprises the subareas of "marital relationship," "relationships between parents and children," "relationships among children," and "family solidarity" or family cohesiveness, as indicated by likeness or difference in values, beliefs, and goals among family members. The second area of intrafamilial functioning is termed *Care and Training of Children,* which includes physical care and training methods. The latter includes data covering such questions as these: how do parents think children should behave, how and by whom is approval shown, how are limits set and enforced, are parents consistent in training and discipline and do they work together. The third area covers *Home Conditions and Household Practices.* Information is sought regarding the neighborhood, physical facilities, including the condition of the home; household equipment; accommodations for sleeping, bathing, cooking; housekeeping standards, which refers to the way the household is managed; the nature of the diet enjoyed by the family; and related subjects.

## Areas of Social Functioning Involving Roles Both Within and Outside the Family Group

One area in this group is *Social Activities,* comprising role playing by family members both within and outside the family system. The subcategory "information associations" refers to social and recreational activities with members of the immediate or extended family, social contacts with friends and neighbors. It calls for information on the question, "What does the family do together, or what do its members do separately during their leisure time; what do they do to have fun?" The subcategory "formal associations" inquires into the participation of family members in more structured activities such as church, clubs, neighborhood centers, unions, PTA's. It has been our observation that the area of Social Activities is neglected in the records of caseworkers. A possible reason for this might be found in the fact that social work, because of its problem orientation, has shown concern mainly for the negatives or weaknesses in psychological and social behavior and has underemphasized the positives or strengths in social functioning.

The area of *Economic Practices* likewise calls for role performance both within and outside the family. The latter is represented by the subarea "source and amount of family income" which covers such questions as these: where is the money coming from, is it adequate for the needs of the family, what is the job situation of the main income provider. The subarea "job situation" calls for information on the nature of work, job satisfaction, irritants and frustrations at work. Functioning within the family is represented by the third subarea entitled "use of money," which calls for answers on how well money is managed, who controls the purse, priorities in spending money, amount of debts, and the like.

Another "mixed" area with regard to roles played in and outside the family is *Health Conditions and Practices.* The subarea "health problems" covers information on the health of the family members, whereas the subarea "health practices" seeks information as to how health problems are being met and how the family protects the health of the family members. This covers functioning within the family, such as activities to improve the health of sick members in the home or to assure good health and prevent illness of those who are well. "Health practices" also pertains to the use of resources in the community for for both curative purposes and the prevention of illness.

## Areas of Social Functioning Involving Role Performance Outside the Family

Social functioning involving role performance largely beyond the family group covers the area *Use of Community Resources,* which deals with the way the family sees and uses the school, the church, health resources, social agencies, and recreational agencies. It also covers the area *Relationship to the Social Worker*, of special relevance to the multiproblem family in treatment, since the relationship to the worker and the family's use of the worker may be seen to reflect in some measure the ways its members relate to the community and are able to use help in resolving their problems.

### Areas of Family Functioning Involving Social Relationships or Instrumental Goals

A further distinction can be made between family functioning characterized by social relationships and functioning in which such relationships are subordinated to the attainment of instrumental goals. The expressive-instrumental dichotomy discussed earlier does not clearly differentiate among the areas of family functioning.

All functioning involving social relationships has expressive components, but relationship areas such as *Care and Training of Children* and *Use of Community Resources* are to a large extent also instrumentally oriented. A two-way categorization stressing the predominance of social relationships or their subordination to instrumental goals is therefore more appropriate for handling the data with which we are concerned. By placing this categorization against the intrafamilial-extrafamilial categorization described above we obtain the schemata given below. The eight areas of family functioning in the schemata plus the category *Individual Behavior and Adjustment* are the basic working tools in the studies reported here. It should be noted that the category *Individual Behavior and Adjustment* must of necessity be viewed separately from the fourfold conceptualization shown in the schemata since the functioning of an individual in a family generally combines more than one type and often all four types of functioning in the roles he plays.

### SCHEMATA OF FAMILY FUNCTIONING

|  | Functioning That Is Largely Intra-familial | Functioning That Is Largely Extra-familial or Mixed |
|---|---|---|
| Functioning Character-ized by Social Relationships | Family Relation-ships and Unity | Social Activities |
|  | Care and Training of Children | Use of Community Resources |
|  |  | Relationship to Social Worker |
| Functioning in Which Social Relationships are Subordinated to the Attainment of Instrumental Goals | Home Conditions and Household Practices | Economic Practices Health Conditions and Practices |

It should be remembered that the organization of areas for the Profile of Family Functioning has been specially geared to the multiproblem family which is generally in the lower socio-economic stratum of society. This is to say that in describing conceptually the functioning of any other type of family in our society, the organization of the Profile might have to be changed in relation to the degree of prominence of certain types of functiong in the total behavior pattern of family members. For instance, in describing middle-class family functioning, political and religious functioning might be covered under main rather than subcategories, and relationship to the social worker might not merit the important focus assigned to it in our scheme.

Following our effort to outline areas of social functioning, we are now faced with the task of evaluating given patterns of behavior which have been sketched in terms of the profile scheme suggested here. Evaluation requires standards with which to compare the functioning of the families studied. Earlier we discussed the need for evaluation in social work and pointed up some obstacles in the way of having the principle of evaluation accepted by the profession. The view has been expressed that the growing interest in research has given impetus to efforts at evaluation of client functioning. Indeed, special interest on the part of practitioners has been aroused to the extent that evaluative methods have come to show some relevance to treatment.

The Family Centered Project of St. Paul devoted a major part of its research effort to developing a scheme of levels of functioning which could serve as a model against which to compare the functioning of multiproblem families. This scheme had been tested in a reliability study[17] and was used for assessing family functioning in St. Paul and the Neighborhood Improvement Project of New Haven, Connecticut.

Without going into the details of the evaluation method, it is pertinent to recapitulate briefly the rationale for the levels of functioning approach. In view of the fact that social welfare in general and social work in particular are constantly impelled, for purposes of treatment, to evaluate clients and client families on the basis of what the profession views as acceptable behavior, an evaluation of groups of families can hardly be considered a departure from professional practice. Nevertheless, we need to be mindful of the risk inherent in applying standards which reflect norms of behavior of a status group higher than the one to which the family whose functioning we are evaluating belongs.

To avoid doing this, the standards or levels of functioning selected must not be so narrowly circumscribed as to constitute prescriptions for class behavior. A model for evaluation should, in fact, set up base lines against which behavior can be judged to be seriously at odds with the law and inimical to the welfare of the family and commnity, or in line with broad expectations of the status group and conducive to the welfare of the family and community. The intent is obviously to define levels which are broad enough to meet the latter specifications.

A definition of minimum levels of social functioning is actually implicit in all social work with seriously disorganized families. The granting of public assistance, the filing of neglect petitions, the placement of children, and the other decisions carried out by the social worker, all require a judgment as to whether or not functioning in one or more areas is at a level at which intervention by the community is in order. Protective services are rendered whenever an assessment of the family situation suggests that the family is unable without professional help to provide the minimum standards of child care for their offspring.

The concept chosen here for defining levels of functioning is one suggested by the discussion above. It may be most appropriately termed community concern. It pertains to the success or failure of the family group to function in such a way as to ensure the welfare of its own members or those of the community around it. Community concern may be aroused by the impairment of, or threat to, the well-being of family members, especially the children. This might take the form of socially and psychologically deviant behavior on the part of parents and/or children. Community concern may also result because of serious problems in physical and mental health, economic performance, family relationships, and other areas of family functioning.

A second facet of community concern is behavior which adversely affects the welfare of the community. In its most extreme form this means the violation of laws designed to protect the community. Less easily definable but of some importance as a factor of community concern is the extent to which the family has been violating mores which are part of the basic value system, for example, not toilet training children until after the usual ages, or failing to permit them to join peer groups.

A joint effort by researchers and caseworkers in the St. Paul Family Centered Project resulted in the Levels of Social Functioning scheme. The general criteria for evaluation of family functioning upon three levels—inadequate, marginal, and adequate functioning—which were used as anchor points of a seven-point scale in the evaluation studies, are as follows:[18]

> *Inadequate Functioning* (Community has a right to intervene.) Laws and/or mores clearly violated. Behavior of family members a threat to the community. Family life characterized by extreme conflict, neglect, severe deprivation or very poor relationships resulting in physical and/or emotional suffering of family members; disruption of family life imminent, children in clear and present danger because of conditions above or other behavior inimical to their welfare.
> *Marginal Functioning* (Behavior not sufficiently harmful to justify intervention.) No violation of major laws although behavior of family members is contrary to what is acceptable for status group. Family life marked by conflict, apathy, or unstable relationships which are a potential threat to welfare of family members and community; each crisis poses the danger of family's disruption, but children are not in imminent danger.
> *Adequate Functioning* (Behavior in line with community expectations.) Laws and mores are observed; behavior is acceptable to status group. Family life is stable, members have a sense of be-

longing, family is able to handle problems without facing disruption, children are being raised in an atmosphere conducive to healthy physical and emotional development. Socialization process carried out affirmatively; adequate training in social skills.

These criteria, when they are broken down into their components corresponding to the profile areas of family functioning, provide a guide line for evaluating the functioning of disorganized families. Although the Levels of Functioning scheme provides a structure for facilitating classification and subsequent measurement, it does rely upon the judgment of those charged with processing the data. Within this structure, as has been shown in the St. Paul Manual,[19] fairly reliable judgments may be obtained. At the same time, the flexible character of the scheme and the need to have it adapted to different settings and population groups must be strongly emphasized.

Most of the remainder of this chapter, dealing wtih specific applications of the Geismar Scale of Family Functioning to sample populations, is here omitted. More recent detail on the use of the Scale, and later revisions therein, is available in Ludwig L. Geismar, *Family and Community Functioning: A Manual of Measurement for Social Work Practice and Policy* (Metuchen, N.J.: Scarecrow Press, 1971). We close these excerpts with the final section of the chapter, involving tests of the Scale's validity.

The previous prediction about differences in functioning based on knowledge of types of client families is borne out by the differences found in mean scores of family functioning and in the Profiles placed on the social functioning grid. Differences between ADC and St. Paul multiproblem families were statistically significant.[20]

Further evidence of external validity of the scale is provided in a study done at the University of Minnesota's School of Social Work.[21] Scores on the scale of family functioning were found to differentiate clearly between a sample of multiproblem families for whom a neglect petition and been filed and a random sample of such cases not charged with the neglect of children. Low scoring on the scale was found to be directly related to a situation where action had been taken by the community to bring neglect charges against the family.[22] Finally, a comparison of Profiles based on the independent interviews of husbands and wives in ten New Jersey families showed that the marriage partners described family functioning in similar terms. Main category scores were identical on 58.8 percent and one scale step apart on 33.7 percent of the ratings. The scores differed by more than one scale step in only 7.5 percent of the responses.[23]

We have presented here some evidence that the Profile of Family Functioning is an instrument which is able to measure properties of behavior that are used diagnostically in scoal work. Furthermore, it differentiates among client groups which on an a priori basis are seen to differ from one another. With this evidence on the validity of the scale let us now apply it to an analysis of the functioning of a group of seriously disorganized families and compare their functioning pattern with that of families showing greater stability and adequacy in role relationships.* The demonstration of differences in present family functioning, which will be statistically documented, is not seen as an end in itself but as a means of launching research into factors in the early life cycle of families associated with later family stability or disorganization. This effort at early identification of multiproblem families is seen as a beginning attempt to develop tools with which social work may examine its performance in the area of prevention.

* The study referred to in the last paragraph is presented in the next chapter of the Geismar-La Sorte book (Chapter 4), which is not given here.

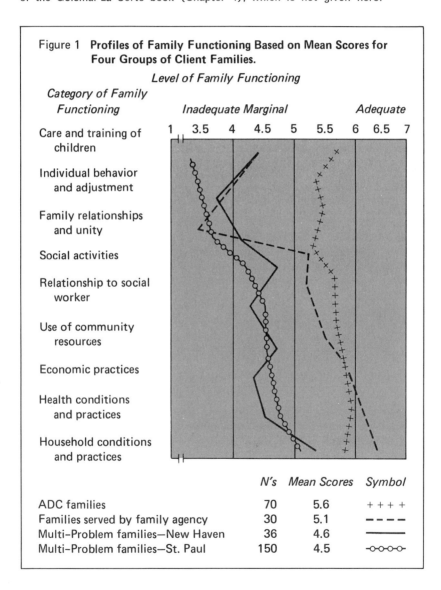

Figure 1  **Profiles of Family Functioning Based on Mean Scores for Four Groups of Client Families.**

*Level of Family Functioning*

|  | N's | Mean Scores | Symbol |
|---|---|---|---|
| ADC families | 70 | 5.6 | + + + + |
| Families served by family agency | 30 | 5.1 | - - - - |
| Multi–Problem families—New Haven | 36 | 4.6 | ———— |
| Multi–Problem families—St. Paul | 150 | 4.5 | -o-o-o-o- |

Table 1 **Mean Scores of Social Functioning and Standard Deviations for Four Client Populations**

| Category of Family Functioning | ADC Service (N=70) | | Family Service (N=30) | | Service to M-P Families New Haven (N=36) | | Service to M-P Families St. Paul (N=150) | |
|---|---|---|---|---|---|---|---|---|
| | Means | S.D.'s | Means | S.D.'s | Means | S.D.'s | Means | S.D.'s |
| Care and Training of Children | 5.7 | .95 | 4.4 | .83 | 4.4 | .96 | 3.7 | 1.04 |
| Individual Behavior and Adjustment | 5.3 | 1.04 | 3.9 | .71 | 3.9 | .94 | 3.8 | .81 |
| Family Relationships and Unity | 5.4 | 1.02 | 3.6 | 1.02 | 4.2 | 1.02 | 3.9 | .93 |
| Social Activities | 5.3 | .99 | 5.3 | .97 | 4.9 | .77 | 4.6 | .79 |
| Relationship to Social Worker | 5.7 | 1.08 | 5.3 | 1.05 | 4.6 | .81 | 4.7 | .84 |
| Use of Community Resources | 5.7 | .95 | 5.5 | .80 | 4.9 | .81 | 4.7 | .86 |
| Economic Practices | 5.8 | .77 | 5.8 | .80 | 4.5 | .89 | 4.8 | .88 |
| Health Conditions and Practices | 5.9 | .99 | 6.1 | .83 | 4.6 | 1.01 | 4.9 | 1.06 |
| Household Conditions and Practices | 5.8 | 1.23 | 6.4 | .87 | 5.3 | 1.45 | 5.1 | 1.42 |
| Mean of Column Means | 5.6 | 1.00 | 5.1 | .88 | 4.6 | .96 | 4.5 | .96 |
| S.D.'s of Mean of Means | .22 | .12 | .90 | .11 | .39 | .19 | .48 | .19 |

## NOTES

[1] L. L. Geismar, *Report on Checklist Survey* (St. Paul, Minn.: Family Centered Project, 1957, mimeographed).

[2] Beverly Ayres and Joseph Lagey, *A Checklist Survey of Multiproblem Families in Vancouver City* (Vancouver, B.C.: Community Chest and Councils of the Greater Vancouver Area, 1961, mimeographed).

[3] Bradley Buell and Associates, *Community Planning for Human Service* (New York: Columbia University Press, 1952), pp. 11–17.

[4] See Community Research Associates, *Matters of Fact for the National Conference on Appraising Family Needs* (New York: Community Research Associates, 1949).

[5] The St. Paul 1948 survey included 16 recreation and group work agencies; the Vancouver checklist survey covered 4; and the St. Paul 1957 checklist survey, none.

[6] Community Research Associates, op. cit., pp. 50–53.

[7] For details, see Ibid., Geismar, op. cit., and Ayres and Lagley, op. cit.

[8] Community Service Society, *Searchlight on New York: A Progress Report on Human Welfare in New York City* (New York: Community Service Society, 1960), p. 37.

[9] Interestingly enough, another survey of a low-income housing project in Syracuse, New York, showed that approximately 8 per cent (54 out of 678) of the families were identified as problem families. See Charles V. Willie, Morton O. Wagefeld, and Lee J. Cart, *The Effect of Social Service upon Rental Paying Patterns in Low Income Problem Families* (Syracuse, N.Y.: Youth Development Center, Syracuse University, 1962, mimeographed), p. 1.

[10] Ayres and Lagey, op. cit., p. 34–40.

[11] L. L. Geismar and Beverly Ayres, *Families in Trouble* (St. Paul, Minn.: Family Centered Project of St. Paul, 1958), p. 48 ff.

[12] Bradley Buell and Associates, op. cit., p. 9.

[13] Geismar and Ayres, *Families in Trouble,* op. cit., p. 48 ff.

[14] L. L. Geismar and Beverly Ayres, *Measuring Family Functioning. A Manual on a Method for Evaluating the Social Functioning of Disorganized Families* (St. Paul, Minn.: Family Centered Project, 1960).

[15] L. L. Geismar and Beverly Ayres, in association with K. Tinker, *Patterns of Change in Problem Families* (St. Paul, Minn.: Family Centered Project, 1959).

L. L. Geismar and Beverly Ayres, "A Method for Evaluating the Social Functioning of Families Under Treatment," *Social Work,* Vol. 4, No. 1, Jan., 1959, pp. 102–108.

L. L. Geismar "The Multiproblem Family: Significance of Research Findings," *The Social Welfare Forum,* 1960 (New York: Columbia University Press, 1960), pp. 166–179.

Ludwig L. Geismar, "The Social Functioning of the ADC Family," *The Welfare Reporter,* Vol. XIV, Number 3, July, 1963, pp. 43–54.

[16] For details see Geismar and Ayres *Measuring Family Functioning,* op.cit.

[17] Ibid., pp. 7–20.

[18] The three levels spelled out here are: the midpoint—marginal functioning; the left anchor point—inadequate; the right anchor point—adequate functioning. Additional scale points not defined in the Levels of Social Functioning scheme but designed to provide for finer gradations of judgment between the anchor points were called: near inadequate; below marginal; above marginal; near adequate functioning. The method of evaluation was thus based

upon a seven-point continuum which was applied to nine areas and 26 subareas of family functioning.

[19] Geismar and Ayres, *Measuring Family Functioning,* op. cit.

[20] With reference to the statistical significance of findings the question can be asked whether the differences among the means scores of family functioning are greater than might be expected by chance. An answer is possible if we accept the assumption, at least partially defensible, that the client groups selected in this study are representative of larger universes of client families served in the respective agencies. The median test of the significance of difference yields a chi square value of 65.70 (1 d.f. p $<$.001), which permits a rejection of the hypothesis that differences in functioning are due to chance.

[21] E. Garinzi, N. Larson, L. Miller, P. Rekstad, N. H. Ian, *A Study of Multiproblem Families from the St. Paul Family Centered Project: Factors Distinguishing Multiproblem Families for Whom a Court Petition of Neglect Was Filed from Those for Whom It Was Not Filed* (Minneapolis, Minn.: School of Social Work, University of Minnesota, June, 1961, M.S.W. thesis, unpublished).

[22] Chi squares for a $2 \times 2$ table were 6.38 (p. $<$ .01) at the beginning of treatment and 34.81 (p $<$ .001) at the time of closing.

[23] Walda Ciafone, Florence M. Bernstein, et al., *Relationship of Family Functioning to Anomie, Social Class, and Other Related Factors* (New Brunswick, N.J., Graduate School of Social Work, Rutgers: The State University, June, 1963, unpublished M.S.W. thesis), p. 20.

# A Multi-Problem Confrontation

## ROLAND L. WARREN

This book is a report on a "Seminar" meeting held on the results of the Chemung County (Elmira, New York) Project, and consists of papers by program participants presented as individual chapters. The following selections are drawn from the chapter by the original project director, Roland L. Warren, and from the chapter by his successors, David Wallace and Jesse Smith. This study is an outstanding example of modern experimental design in evaluative research in social work, and might as such have been excerpted in the preceding chapter (Chapter VII) on this topic; it is, however, included here because of its close connection with the multiproblem family "movement."

Perhaps this is an appropriate place to review briefly the purpose and rationale of the project and to supplement the project report, particularly regarding decisions made in the planning and developing of the project before David Wallace came on the scene. Insofar as possible

From Roland L. Warren, "A Multi-Problem Confrontation," and David Wallace and Jesse Smith, "The Study: Methodology and Findings," in Gordon E. Brown, ed., *The Multi-Problem Dilemma: A Social Research Demonstration with Multi-problem Families* (Metuchen, N.J.: Scarecrow Press, 1968), pp. 91–95, 107–151. Reprinted with permission of editor and publisher. Copyright © 1968 by State Communities Aid Association.

I will confine myself to quoting directly from the original project proposal, letting the passages speak for themselves, without the benefit of hindsight.

> The aims of the project are to attempt to secure improvement in the adequacy of family functioning among families who come within the project's operational criteria; to measure the changes made, using pre-defined measures to be described later in this prospectus; to compare statistically the changes made with those made by a control group of families selected from the same population but to whom the special service will not be offered; and to analyze, within the demonstration group, factors which appear to be associated with a substantial degree of improvement as measured by the project criteria. . . .
>
> The demonstration program herein described incorporates aspects whose advisability is indicated by the many programs for multiproblem families which have been reported from various parts of the country. There is good reason to hypothesize that such a program may be effective. However, there is little knowledge based on adequate research projects to verify this. . . .
>
> In the casework process, the whole family—as defined—will be considered the client, rather than a single individual. Its total living configuration will be of concern, thus including factors not customarily considered in the usual administration of the public assistance programs. Thus, the demonstration program will include the four constituents previously mentioned: interagency collaboration as indicated; "reaching out"; the whole-family approach, and intensive casework with sustained contact.
>
> The two demonstration workers will both be professionally trained, experienced caseworkers. A unit of this type designed to give special services to multiproblem families is perfectly feasible for local welfare departments in many parts of the country. It represents not a "dream" program or super-agency far beyond the realistic possibilities of most communities, but a perfectly plausible arrangement.
>
> But how effective can such a set-up be? We simply do not know, for similar programs have not been adequately researched. . . .
>
> Since social welfare agencies are coming more and more to accept intensive casework and interagency collaboration as the basic, if not the exclusive, aspect of their approach to multiproblem families, it is important to know the extent to which such a program is actually effective in achieving its stated objectives. . . .
>
> In addition to evaluating the aggregate effectiveness of the program through the control group design described above, the research design provides for internal analyses of the demonstration group itself.

With the exception of the internal analysis of the demonstration group, these aims were achieved. It can be seen from the above that the objective was neither to place casework on trial (in the sense of asking whether it is desirable, or necessary, or in any or all cases effective), but rather to examine rigorously whether casework in a situation as described above would have measurable results in terms of the criteria employed.

While no one would claim that the criteria were perfect, I believed, and still believe, that the items in the CSS Movement Scale and in the Geismar Family Functioning Scale are in the main relevant and reasonable criteria. If change is not registered along such dimensions as these, I am at a loss to see what other types of possible change would be considered relevant.

Of course, it was theoretically possible to develop a set of criteria designed specifically for this particular project, based on a specific set of strategies within the broad criteria of reaching out, considering the whole family rather than just Johnny's delinquent behavior, coordinating the efforts of various agencies dealing with the family, and so on. But casework was not at the time developed to the point where more specific intervention strategies for such families were being talked about and put into operation.

We were not concerned with hypothesizing as to what particular strategy might under ideal circumstances be expected to have a measurable impact on some carefully delineated group within the multiproblem family category (although this might be a perfectly desirable objective). Rather, we were concerned with testing a type of organization of agency services which was coming to be considered broadly relevant for dealing with multiproblem families.

And to repeat, we were not interested in testing the "ideal" situation. We wished to steer between the Scylla (which many professional people pointed out) that any so-called "demonstration" could not afford to offer inordinately high salaries to attract the "best" caseworkers, and could not afford to be in a community which was rich in available services as most communities are not, and to have such a small caseload as to be utterly unrealistic in terms of future applicability to practice; and the Charybdis of mounting an effort which would be so palpably minimal that it would be rediculous to expect it to make any difference.

We think we did steer between these extremes, although others may feel that we either set our sights too high or too low, or in some other way scored far from the mark.

All three of the caseworkers on the project (the second was replaced by the third) were professionally trained workers with a number of years' experience. We definitely had in mind that one worker, with greater experience, would handle a smaller caseload than the other and act as supervisor, and of course that she must have the qualifications of experience and training suitable for this responsibility. For this reason, the first worker recruited, who was younger and had had fewer years' experience, was not made supervisor, and had to function without supervision while the supervisor was being recruited.

But of course it did not occur to us that we should avail ourselves of expert consultation in order especially to train these workers for their difficult caseloads. No one expected miracles—only that the casework would be of help, and that this help would be evident. Again, it might well have been possible to "beef up" the input variable by recruiting the most experienced caseworkers, by putting special funds at their disposal, by reducing their caseloads even farther, and by making available to them a battery of high-powered consultants. But our objective was to assess not such a situation, but one much more relevant to the realities of present day agency resources and practice— at all time, and even now.

To say what we did wish to test is, of course, to say also what we did *not* purport to test: the most highly-skilled casework under optimum conceivable circumstances with exceptionally great resources. Such casework may or may not be effective. We did not set out to study this, we did not study it, and we did not claim (and do not claim) that under such circumstances, or under the circumstances that Helen Perlman* outlines, it would be ineffective. I for one would not even hazard a guess. What we are prepared to say is what we have said, that caseworkers, under the circumstances of this demonstration, did not prove effective in terms of the measures we used.

* In another chapter of Brown, op. cit., which is not given here.

# The Study: Methodology and Findings

## DAVID WALLACE and JESSE SMITH

In 1948 an exhaustive study of the St. Paul, Minnesota, public assistance rolls produced a statistic which gave focus to a condition that long had been suspected by welfare officials. It was that six percent of the families on public assistance were accounting for nearly fifty percent of all welfare expenditures.

Most of these families were found to be receiving assistance from more than one agency, in some cases four or five agencies. Their problems extended through a range of areas: schools, courts, housing, health, and so on. Many had been recipients from multiple sources for as long as three generations. Thus the term "multiproblem" family was born, a euphemism synonymous with the "hard-core" family which had been used by less delicately-minded officials.

In Chemung County, New York, the Commissioner of welfare and the Exectuive Director of the Chemung County Council of Community Services had since 1956 been concerned with multiproblem families there. They had organized a special Difficult Case Committee of the community's forty-odd assistance agencies to help study and resolve the problem. By 1959 plans were made to organize a special unit within the Council as a demonstration project. The unit was approved by the New York State Department of Social Welfare (now the State Department of Social Services) as well as by the County Board of Supervisors. In this effort the community was assisted by the Deputy Director of the State Communities Aid Association, Mr. Lowell Iberg, whose chief interest is in welfare activities, and who served also as the executive secretary of the New York State Association of Councils and Chests. Dr. Roland L. Warren, Director of Social Research of the State Communities Aid Association, also had met with the Chemung Committee on several occasions to formulate possible research plans.

At this point in history—it was in early 1961—the Social Security Administration of the U.S. Department of Health, Education and Welfare announced a new program of supporting research-demonstration projects in social and family behavior. Because the Chemung group was advanced in its thinking about just such an effort it was one of the very first applicants for support under the new research-demonstration program. In June, 1961, the application was formally accepted. The award was made to the Chemung Council of Community Services. Dr. Warren was designated as the Project Director, in view of his key role in the project's design and submission for support.

It is worth noting that the endeavor comprised federal, state and local agencies, public as well as private, working together in a concerted effort. From the very start the Chemung County Multiproblem Family Project was regorously conceived from a research standpoint. Under the guidance of Dr. Warren, the plans called for a series of specifications seldom found in this kind of effort, where all too often fuzzy good intentions override the colder requirements of objective research. In brief, the chief research specifications included:

1. The group under study must be a defined population; it must be described. There must be specific criteria by which some families are included in the group while others are not.

2. There must be a control group drawn from the same population of families as the demonstration group. The former must be the same in all pertinent respects as the latter, so that the effect of what is done in the demonstration group can be measured over time against the control group.

3. The research and treatment operations of the project must be carried out independently of each other—as it turned out by entirely different staffs—so that the evaluation is free of any subjective involvement of those who administer the treatment.

There were the over-all research specifications of the project, designed to avoid the conflict of interest between service and research that had plagued so many efforts to assess social behavior. Within each area, of course, there were many sub-specifications which came to be worked out.

Treatment variables were principally three in number. They were: a) trained caseworkers defined as having a Master's degree and previous field experience in social work would give the demonstration group intensive casework service; b) caseloads in the demonstration group would be limited to a maximum of 20 cases for the supervisor and 30 cases for the junior worker; and c) the demonstration caseworkers would have greater than normal cooperation from the range of the community's resources. In addition to these major variables there were several technical specifications to be followed in the demonstration group. These were: d) the entire family rather than any single individual would be considered as the client, e) case closing would be in relation to the satisfactory total functioning of the family rather than to the resolution of economic dependency, f) treatment goals would be planned, articulated, and systematically conducted.

These variables stood in sharp contrast to generally prevailing conditions in public assistance agencies, where workers perform largely dispensing functions and are principally concerned with satisfying legal requirements of eligibility; where caseloads average from 80 to 100 or more clients per worker; and where only minimum claims are made on other commuity agencies, often because these consider that providing financial maintenance is the sole proper realm of public welfare departments.

The demonstration, then, was to assess the effects of intensive professional casework under optimal conditions of having adequate time to spend with each case, and with the maximum cooperation of the community. The caseworkers were to operate within existing agency policies and community resources, but otherwise were given full professional freedom as to the use of their skills. The control group of similar families, meanwhile, would receive only the regular public assistance service.

## THE SAMPLE AND STUDY DESIGN

Description of the project population was the first requirement. After much discussion with the Difficult Case Committe, the local Commissioner, officials of New York State Department of Social Welfare and of its area office, agreement was reached on the following criteria for inclusion in the project: 1) The family must be receiving either Aid to Dependent Children or Temporary Aid to Dependent Children or Home Relief (a residual general assistance category in New York State). 2) There must be a mother figure in the family and at least one child. 3) The family must have received services at some time in the present or past from at least two additional agencies on specified list. 4) The family must have received services from at least one of these agencies three years or more before the date of screening. From the approximately 1200 ADC, TADC, and Home Relief cases active with the Chemung County Department of Welfare in the summer of 1961, 195 met these specifications. They were placed in a pool from which the demonstration and control groups were drawn.

By a table of random numbers equal quantities of cases were drawn from the pool for the demonstration group and the control group. Ultimately there would be 50 cases in each, but they were assigned in "takes" because time was required in which to prepare the opening summaries for the research evaluation (see below). But now arose a technical problem in this classical protest-posttest design for a laboratory experiment. An assessment of each case was to be made independently by the research staff at two points in time: before casework started and again at the conclusion of casework. The intervening period was envisioned as approximately three years. But it was impossible to prepare an opening summary for the control cases, requiring a research interview with the family and the gathering of materials from the public files, without revealing the identity of the control cases to the regular assistance workers. Being known, there was the possible danger that the control cases would receive something other than normal routine treatment from the public assistance workers. The danger was minimal in caseloads averaging 90 to 100 cases per worker, but should some sort of "Hawthorne effect"—or change produced by no more than awareness of participating in a special program—take place in these cases their value as controls would be lost. Consequently, it was decided to draw a second group of 50 cases from the pool to serve as a "hidden control" group. The latter would be known only to the research staff. They would not be interviewed for an opening protocol; only for a closing protocol when the project was completed. The closing protocols for the two control groups could then be compared for indications of possible contamination of the known control group. In diagram, then, the project groups looked like this:

|  | Demonstration | Control$^1$ | Control$^2$ |
|---|---|---|---|
| Opening Summary | D-op | C$^1$-op | — |
| Closing Summary | D-cl | C$^1$-cl | C$^2$-cl |

Ideally, at the close of the project C$^1$-Cl would equal C$^2$cl. If so, there would be assurance that no measurable contamination had occurred in the known control group through knowledge of its identity. Then the difference between C$^1$-cl and C$^1$-op becomes a valid baseline against which the difference between D-cl and D-op can be measured.

## THE RESEARCH INSTRUMENTS

The principal instrument to be used in recording the condition of the demonstration and control cases was the research summary. This was typically an eight to twelve-page description of the family's functioning on nine major and twenty-five minor dimensions developed by Dr. Ludwig Geismar in the earlier St. Paul study. Materials for the summaries would come primarily from an interview with each family by the research staff, but other information was drawn from the records of outside agencies, such as schools, courts, the probation office, etc., from the case records of the welfare department, as well as from interviews with public assistance workers who were familiar with the families. There would be two summaries from each case, one prepared at the opening of the project, the other at closing. The nine major Geismar dimensions are:

Family Relationships and Family Unity
Individual Behavior and Adjustment
Care and Training of Children

Social Activities

Economic Practices
Household Practices
Health Conditions and
   Practices
Relationship to Project
   Worker
Use of Community
   Resources

The before-and-after profiles would later be given to independent teams of trained judges who would rate each dimension of family functioning. There thus would be a score at opening, and another at closing, with the difference between the scores being degrees of "movement." The research staff would then analyze the rating scores.

It should be mentioned here that at no time did the caseworkers see, or have knowledge of, the contents of the summaries. They were research documents exclusively.

There was need, however, for some record of what went on during the course of the project: how many contacts were made per week; who initiated them; what was discussed, etc. For this purpose "treatment logs" were kept by the workers, week by week for each case. The logs of the demonstration workers were more detailed than those of assistance workers for two reasons: first, the demonstration workers were to prepare a definite plan of approach to each case, but secondly because of their greater sophistication on the kinds of treatment they were offering. The two logs are not directly comparable but they are parallel in their content.

A first task of the research group was to measure the differences between the cases who by our definitions were "qualified" to enter the project as multiproblem families, and those who met the family structure criterion but because they were not serviced by the specified number of agencies or were not long-term cases, were "not qualified." Briefly, the "qualified" as compared with the "unqualified" families were slightly more urban, more likely to be in the ADC category, more often deserted or separated in marriage, and had received service from more agencies for a longer period of time (the latter two characteristics by definition). There were no significant differences in age of family head or number of children under 18 years of age in the home.

Meantime, a recruitment drive was opened to obtain the necessary two trained caseworkers for the demonstration. This proved to be more difficult than expected. Several months were consumed in interviewing. Finally, the first caseworker was hired to begin work on November 1, 1961. At this point 75 cases from the pool of 195 "qualified" cases were randomly assigned to the three study groups: demonstration, control 1, and control 2; 25 cases to each. A second supervising caseworker was retained to begin work on February 1, 1962, when additional cases would be assigned. Caseworker difficulties were not over yet, however, Unfortunately, it soon became apparent that the supervisor's concept of the project, and of her role and function in it, were not compatible with the project's aims. For one thing, her insistence on interjecting a highly psychiatrically-oriented personal philosophy into the treatment process reached such an extreme that it jeopardized other community relations. After a hearing in May 1962 this worker's resignation was tendered and accepted. At approximately the same time Dr. Warren accepted a new post and submitted his resignation to State Communities Aid Association as of May 31, 1962. He was succeeded by Dr. David Wallace, whose initiation to the project began with the above hearing.

The search now resumed for a replacement of the caseworker supervisor, a task not completed until September, 1962. Meantime, however, the original pool of "qualified" cases had been depleted through assignments and closings. The remaining original number was augmented with a second screening of "qualified" cases which, when compared with the contemporary "unqualified" groups, showed the same basic differences between groups.

With casework underway, the research staff then made a comparison of the characteristics of the families which had been randomly assigned to the demonstration, control 1, and control 2 groups. Characteristics were as of the time of original sampling. There were no significant differences among the groups in urban residence, assistance categories, marital status, number of children in the home under 18 years of age, number of agencies from which services were received, time of earliest agency service, or time on public assistance rolls. In two comparisons of age of family head (Dem. vs. $C^2$, and $C^1$ vs. $C^2$) there were no significant differences, but in one (Dem. vs. $C^1$) the family head was older.

The treatment aspects of the project had started for a few cases shortly after the hiring of a first caseworker in November 1961, and they terminated for all cases with the closing of the project on May 31, 1964. Thus the entire time span of caseworker service was a little over two and one-half years. However, due to different dates of caseworker hiring, changes in personnel, and time required to prepare opening summaries prior to case assignment, few cases were under continuous service that long. The full quotas of 50 cases in each group were not completed until August 1962. The two workers who ultimately completed the project had terms of service of 31 months and 20 months, respectively. As for the cases themselves, their time in the project is shown by an extract from the treatment logs:

Weeks in the Project

|  | Demonstration | Control |
|---|---|---|
| 125 weeks and more | 16% | 18% |
| 100–124 | 30 | 26 |
| 75–99 | 48 | 40 |
| 50–74 | 6 | 16 |
| Median Weeks | 98 | 96 |

It would be pleasant to report that the term of the project was uneventful, that service proceeded on regular schedule with all personnel performing at peak efficiency, that no issues or problems arose that were not immediately resolved, and that everything worked smoothly, as sometimes is gathered from casework texts. This was not the case. There were lumps and bumps aplenty as the weeks passed.

A bothersome matter was personnel turn-over. Aside from the senior caseworker and Project Director already mentioned, there were three directors of the Council of Community Services and two chairmen of the Difficult Case Committee during the project's course. A Director of Social Services entered the welfare department in mid-term. Of the key administrative figures at the project's start, only the Commissioner of Welfare and the Deputy Director of the State Communities Aid Association were present at its conclusion. These repeated changes were not conducive to the best administration, which, being shared was nebulous at best.

Within the shared administration, a division of labor gradually developed. The Council of Community Services, as grantee, assumed principal responsibility for the disbursement and accountability of grant funds. The Welfare Commissioner concentrated on the legality of daily operations. The Difficult Case Committee assumed over-all policy making for other than day-to-day matters. The State Communities Aid Association, through its Social Research Service, focused on the conduct and analysis of the research.

Several problems arose from this fractionization. Chiefly they affected the caseworkers in their relationships and accountability to the administrative groups. Being professionally trained workers, they were allowed freedom to apply their social casework techniques without undue restriction by the welfare department. Yet their caseloads were the responsibility of the department and the workers were required to be accountable to the Commissioner in respect to state and local regulations. Frustration sometimes developed as to whom they should turn for the resolution of special problems—the Commissioner, Project Director, Executive Director of the Council, or the Difficult Case Committee?

A continuing problem area was the workers' day-to-day relationship with "management" (the Commissioner and Director of Social Services of the welfare department). From the workers' viewpoint, the denial of special services not available to other cases was often looked upon as unreasonable; they had been given a special job to do, why should they be shackled by universal policies? From "management's" viewpoint, these requests took on the character of special pleading which had to be weighed against agency policy and the Commissioner's responsibility to approve aid, as well as to see that the requests were kept within the project design. On occasion, requests not falling within agency policy had to be denied. Many of the workers' frustrations were due to their inability to accept limitations inherent in a public welfare program.

Another point might be mentioned. During the project's term several changes were made in the operations of the welfare department. A new Commissioner had come in just before the project opened. In the early days he was reorganizing the agency and evaluating policies and procedures. The new professionally-trained Director of Social Services was brought in. Caseloads were reassigned from an integrated to an adult and family caseload basis. Geographical assignments were abolished, budgeting practices revised, and a limited in-service training program instituted. During the project period the Federal Defined Services Program also came into being. Few three-year periods in any agency are completely static, but these and other events put the control cases in a somewhat different environment at the project's end than at its opening.

Midway in the project, the Commissioner called upon a special consultant from Albany to review the caseworkers' records in terms of eligibility and legal requirements. The consultant found what she termed "deficiencies" in the currency of dictation, determination and recording of eligibility data, and the interpretation of case conditions. The shortcomings were discussed with the workers.

As a result of this social "audit" the Commissioner, in concert with others in the project, sought the assistance of the State Department of Social Welfare in obtaining a consultant to supervise the workers' record-keeping on a sustained basis. Because, however, of staffing shortages and other pressure occasioned by the Special Federal Review of all ADC cases of that time the request could not be met. Nor was a qualified person available outside of state sources.

At this point the Director of Social Services of the Chemung Department of Welfare, who previously had refrained from direct involvement in the project, agreed to take over weekly after-hours consultation sessions with the workers. This arrangement continued to the termination of the project.

Differences in treatment philosophies occurred principally during this period of consultation with the Director of Social Services. Briefly, he advocated an effort to "reach out" more aggressively to the project cases. The workers, on the other hand, generally favored a policy of developing initiative in the cases themselves to seek help. They felt that greatest support effectiveness could come only when the ground was prepared to receive it.

The active "treatment" phase of the project, then, averaged just under two years for most cases. What now about its outcome?

At the conclusion of casework service on May 31, 1964, the research staff revisited all demonstration and control cases prior to preparing the closing summaries. At this time, too, the Control[2], or "hidden control" cases were interviewed for the first time, and a closing summary was prepared for them. To recapitulate, we now had an opening and a closing summary for each of the 50 demonstration cases, and the same two protocols for each of the original 50 Control[1] cases. In addition, there were 50 closing-only summaries for the Control[2] cases. In total, these came to 250 separate documents averaging about ten pages of description in length.

The protocols were then delivered to Dr. Ludwig Geismar for assignment to independent trained judges. Dr. Geismar's procedures call for movement judges to work in pairs. Each reads and rates a protocol individually, then confers with the other over any difference, and the pair comes to a consensus. Hence there are three ratings on each dimension in each protocol, two by the judges working individually, plus the consensus by the judge pair. Dr. Geismar distributed the work for this project among three judge pairs. With 250 opening or closing protocols, each containing 9 major dimensions of family functioning, there thus are 250 × 3 × 9, or 6,750 single-position, and 7,500 movement ratings on the 25 sub-dimensions. In all, a total of 35,700 ratings are available for analysis.

But that is not all. The investment of the time and effort to obtain the before-and-after protocols had been enormous. As completion time neared an idea only loosely considered earlier was reexamined: why not have a second crew of judges make an addition evaluation of the same materials? The Community Service Society of New York City has a research unit which had developed the Hunt-Kogan method of measuring social change. True, the Geismar and Hunt-Kogan methods are somewhat different inasmuch as Geismar uses the family system as his basic unit, while Hunt-Kogan focuses on individual persons in the family. But both are concerned with social change over time.

Accordingly, a small additional sum was requested from and granted by the U.S. Welfare Administration to have four CSS judges make a second independent evaluation of the protocols. The CSS judges, under the direction of Dr. Siroon Shahinian, were asked to make two kinds of judgments. First, they were to follow the regular Hunt-Kogan procedures and make an over-all movement rating of change among *individuals* in the family. Then they were to reread the proctocols and re-rate them following the Geismar *family* procedures. The CSS judges also replicated the "after only" rating of the three groups (Demonstration, Control 1, and Control 2) using the Geismar procedures. A minor point of difference between the procedures for the judge crews was that it was impractical to have the CSS judges work in pairs. Therefore the CSS judgments are by a single rater working alone, while the Geismar measures include those of two judges working independently, plus their resolution of any differences. In summary, the rating scheme was as follows:

Geismar Procedures

| | | |
|---|---|---|
| Opening | Judge A    Judge B | Net Movement |
| | Consensus | Family Functioning |
| Closing | Judge A    Judge B | |
| | Consensus | |
| Closing Alone | Judge A    Judge B | Closing Score |
| | Consensus | |

CSS Procedures

| Opening | | CSS Movement of In- |
| --- | --- | --- |
| | Judgc A | dividual Family |
| Closing | | Members |

(CSS Rating, Geismar Dimensions)

| Opening | Judge A ⎫ | |
| --- | --- | --- |
| | | Net Movement of |
| Closing | Judge A ⎬ | Family Functioning |
| Closing Alone | Judge A | Closing Score |

Another further technical difference between the Geismar and CSS procedures is that Geismar judges normally rate opening and closing summaries for a given case separately, recording a score for each point in time. The degree of movement is the arithmetical difference between the two scores. The CSS measure of movement, on the other hand, is obtained by reading the opening and closing protocols together to obtain an estimate of the difference according to certain criteria. When the CSS judges followed the Geismar procedures they rated the protocols separately.

## THE RESULTS BY RATING OF GEISMAR JUDGES

Well, what happened? Did the demonstration cases, which for almost two years were under the care of trained caseworkers, with reduced caseloads, and given access to more than the usual range of community services—did these demonstration cases show a greater degree of movement toward better family functioning than the control cases, which received only regular public assistance services?

To answer this question we will want to look first at the condition of the two groups at the opening of the project on the particular measures we will use for the ultimate comparison. The two groups were drawn at random from the same population of multiproblem families, and we already have seen that they were essentially the same in demographic and other respects for which information was available in the opening case records. But non-differences in characteristics not directly related to the central topic of investigation—in this case levels of family functioning—are merely suggestive of randomness in the central area of family functioning; they do not prove it. It has often happened that two groups have been similar in demographic and other attribute respects but have been quite different internally. We will want to look directly at the two groups on the specific dimensions of family functioning. The opening levels of functioning as rated by the consensus of Geismar judge pairs on the nine principal Geismar dimensions are shown in Table 1.

The range here is a seven-point scale reaching from totally inadequate, at the lowest extreme, to adequate, at the upper extreme. "DK, DNA" signifies "don't know" or "does not apply." From inspection, it

Table 1 **Level of Family Functioning at Opening of Project, Geismar Dimensions—by Consensus of Paired Judges**

| Weights | Inadeq. (1) | Near Inadeq. (2) | Below Marg. (3) | Marginal (4) | Above Marg. (5) | Near Adeq. (6) | Adequate (7) | DK/DNA (4) | New Weight Score |
|---|---|---|---|---|---|---|---|---|---|
| *Demonstration* N = 50 | | | | | | | | | |
| Family Relationships | 2 | 1 | 4 | 9 | 12 | 18 | 3 | 1 | 4.9 |
| Individual Behavior | 1 | 4 | 6 | 12 | 18 | 8 | 1 | — | 4.4 |
| Care, Training of Children | 1 | 1 | 4 | 8 | 17 | 18 | — | 1 | 4.9 |
| Social Activities | — | — | — | 6 | 13 | 17 | 14 | — | 5.8 |
| Economic Practices | — | 5 | 10 | 9 | 20 | 5 | — | 1 | 4.2 |
| Household Practices | — | 2 | 6 | 2 | 11 | 16 | 13 | — | 5.4 |
| Health Conditions | — | — | 5 | 15 | 14 | 10 | 6 | — | 4.9 |
| Relation to Worker | — | — | 3 | 13 | 16 | 10 | 7 | 1 | 5.1 |
| Community Resources | — | — | 1 | 5 | 16 | 19 | 9 | — | 5.6 |
| (450) | 4 | 13 | 39 | 79 | 137 | 121 | 53 | 4 | 45.2 |
| *Control* N = 50 | | | | | | | | | |
| Family Relationships | — | 1 | 2 | 7 | 15 | 19 | 4 | 2 | 5.2 |
| Individual Behavior | — | 2 | 6 | 14 | 19 | 8 | 1 | — | 4.6 |
| Care, Training of Children | — | 2 | 2 | 6 | 20 | 10 | 6 | 4 | 5.0 |
| Social Activities | — | — | — | 3 | 18 | 17 | 11 | 1 | 5.7 |
| Economic Practices | — | 4 | 6 | 11 | 21 | 6 | — | 2 | 4.4 |
| Household Practices | — | — | 1 | 8 | 15 | 17 | 8 | 1 | 5.4 |
| Health Conditions | — | 1 | 2 | 8 | 17 | 15 | 7 | — | 5.3 |
| Relation to Worker | — | — | 3 | 11 | 14 | 12 | 8 | 2 | 5.2 |
| Community Resources | — | — | 1 | 3 | 16 | 22 | 8 | — | 5.7 |
| (450) | — | 10 | 23 | 71 | 155 | 126 | 53 | 12 | 46.5 |

can be gathered that the demonstration cases were slightly lower than control cases on most dimensions at the opening of the project. When we weight these scores by a seven-point range from 1 for "inadequate" through 7 for "adequate" (counting "don't knows" and "does not apply" at the mid-range of 4), we get a group score of 45.2 for the demonstration group, and a score of 46.5 for the control group, a difference of 1.3 in favor of the control group. In so doing, we have, of course, given all dimensions equal weight in the group average, which may or may not be warranted. But for the moment the mean of all dimensions considered equally gives us a single convenient term. The demonstration and control groups thus started at comparable levels of family functioning at the start of the project.

We might now glimpse something of what went on during the two years of the treatment phase of the project. Earlier we spoke of the "treatment logs" kept in some detail by the two demonstration caseworkers, and in lesser detail by the regular assistance workers for the control cases. These were week-by-week records of the number of contacts with each case, where the contact took place, with whom, and a brief notation of what took place on each occasion. The logs also contain descriptive information about each case, some of which was obtained from the case records at the start of the project, but other which was recorded during the project. Excerpts from the treatment logs are shown in Table 2.

Several comments are in order for Table 2. The first is that differences between the demonstration and control groups in "number of workers on case" and "terminal status of case" are due to the nature of the demonstration. In the demonstration group the caseworkers stayed with their cases throughout the duration of the project, the only exceptions being the reassignment of a few cases after the departure of the original casework supervisor. The control group, on the other hand, operated under more normal conditions of worker turnover. These had a median of just under two workers per case throughout

## Table 2 Selected Items from Summary of Treatment Logs, Demonstration and Control Groups (Percents)

| | Dem. | Cont. | | Dem. | Cont. |
|---|---|---|---|---|---|
| N = | (50) | (50) | N = | (50) | (50) |
| Number of workers on Case | | | Activity History | | |
| | | | Open throughout | 96% | 52% |
| 1 | 92% | 32% | Open throughout | 96% | 52% |
| 2 | 6 | 26 | Closed once, p. at end | 0 | 12 |
| 3 | 2 | 14 | Closed once, cl. at end | 4 | 24 |
| 4 | 0 | 12 | Closed twice, op. at end | 0 | 6 |
| 5 & more | 0 | 16 | Closed twice, cl. at end | 0 | 4 |
| Terminal Status of Case | | | Other | 0 | 2 |
| Open | 96% | 70% | Average Total Contacts | | |
| Closed | 4 | 30 | Per Week | | |
| Welfare Classification— | | | 1.5 & more | 10% | 0% |
| Start of Project | | | 1.0 –1.49 | 12 | 4 |
| ADC | 72% | 66% | .5 – .99 | 46 | 26 |
| TADC | 24 | 26 | .25– .49 | 26 | 46 |
| HR | 2 | 8 | Less than .25 | 6 | 24 |
| ADC and HR | 2 | 0 | Average Contacts/Week | | |
| Education, Head of | | | Initiated by Worker | | |
| Household | | | 1.0 & more | 12% | 0% |
| Some College | 4% | 4% | .5 – .99 | 34 | 6 |
| High School Grad. | 20 | 12 | .25– .49 | 38 | 16 |
| High School Attend. | 16 | 32 | Less than .25 | 16 | 78 |
| Grade Sch., 4 yrs. + | 38 | 18 | Total Contact Events Per | | |
| Grade, Less 4 yrs. | 2 | 0 | Week in Project | .79 | .33 |
| Don't know | 20 | 34 | —Wiht Mother | .28 | .18 |
| Years in Chemung County | | | —With Father | .06 | .03 |
| Born here | 40% | 40% | —With Children | .01 | .00 |
| 10 yrs. & more | 24 | 20 | —With Others | .17 | .04 |
| 5–9.9 yrs. | 4 | 0 | —Multiple | .26 | .09 |
| Less than 5 yrs. | 0 | 0 | —Initiated by Worker | .50 | .16 |
| Don't know | 32 | 30 | —Initiated by Client | .19 | .15 |
| Weeks in Project | | | —Initiated by Other | .06 | .02 |
| 125 & more | 16% | 18% | —In Office | .19 | .08 |
| 100–124 | 30 | 26 | —Face to Face | .29 | .11 |
| 75 – 99 | 48 | 40 | —By Telephone | .28 | .14 |
| 50 – 74 | 6 | 16 | —By Letter, Other | .03 | .01 |

the project. Also, the criteria for "closing" a case were different in the demonstration and control groups. In the demonstration group the entire family was considered the client rather than a single individual. Demonstration closings occurred only when the total family situation, rather than the resolution of economic dependency, had been satisfactorily improved, or when the family left the county. Hence many demonstration cases were carried on as "open" which would have been regarded as "closed" in the control cases.

In several items, notably education of head of household, years in Chemung County, and weeks in the project, there appear to be no differences between the demonstration and control groups. These are a reflection of the random assignment of cases to the two groups.

The first important difference between the experiences of the two groups is seen in the average number of contact events between the workers and the case. In the demonstration group the caseworkers made more than twice as many contacts with the cases as was done in the control group. Better than twenty percent of the demonstration cases were seen once a week or oftener, as contrasted with only four percent of the control cases. Further, the more frequent contacts with the demonstration group were far more often initiated by the caseworkers than by the clients. Demonstration contacts also usually involved several family members, compared with the predominantly single-person contacts with the control group. The demonstration contacts also ranged over a broader number of family problems.

This, then, is a brief measure of what was done during the course of the project. The picture of the demonstration group, in a quantitative sense at least, is one of more frequent and more comprehensive contact events initiated by the caseworkers.

We come now to the crucial matter of the condition of the two groups at the closing of the project some two years later. What happened as a result of these great efforts?

We were not surprised to see little difference in family functioning between the demonstration and control groups at the start of the project—in fact, this gave us assurance that the two were essentially similar on the pertinent dimensions with which our evaluation ultimately is concerned. But it is a clear surprise to find that the "movement" between opening and closing of the two groups is almost identical. *In short, nothing much seems to have happened in the demonstration cases that did not also happen in the controls.* The picture of "movement" of the two groups between opening and closing is shown in Table 3.

Looking at the distribution of total scores for the nine dimensions, it can be seen that the demonstration group is slightly higher than the control group in almost all degrees of positive scores, while it also has fewer of all degrees of negative scores. To reduce these distributions to a single score for direct comparison we will again weight the columns, this time by a nine-point range, from 1 for four or more steps of negative movement, through 5 for no movement, to 9 for four or

Table 3 **Movement Between Opening and Closing of Individual Cases on Geismar Dimensions—by Consensus of Paired Judges**

| | | | | | | | | | | Whole Numbers | |
|---|---|---|---|---|---|---|---|---|---|---|---|
| | Degrees | of | Movement | | | | | | | | Weighted |
| Demonstration N=50 | −4 | −3 | −2 | −1 | 0 | +1 | +2 | +3 | +4 | DNA | Move |
| Weight= | (1) | (2) | (3) | (4) | (5) | (6) | (7) | (8) | (9) | (5) | |
| Family Relationships | — | — | 2 | 12 | 20 | 12 | 1 | — | 1 | 2 | 5.0 |
| Individual Behavior | — | — | 1 | 11 | 20 | 17 | — | — | 1 | — | 5.2 |
| Care of Children | — | — | 4 | 6 | 24 | 12 | — | — | 1 | 3 | 5.0 |
| Social Activities | — | — | — | 6 | 27 | 15 | 1 | 1 | — | — | 5.3 |
| Economic Practices | — | — | 2 | 5 | 20 | 13 | 4 | 1 | 1 | 4 | 5.4 |
| Household Practices | 1 | — | — | 8 | 20 | 12 | 3 | 2 | 2 | 2 | 5.4 |
| Health Conditions | — | 1 | 5 | 7 | 22 | 10 | 4 | 1 | — | — | 5.0 |
| Relation to Worker | — | — | 2 | 6 | 15 | 14 | 10 | 2 | — | 1 | 5.6 |
| Community Resources | — | — | 1 | 8 | 25 | 12 | 3 | 1 | — | — | 5.2 |
| (450) | 1 | 1 | 17 | 69 | 193 | 117 | 26 | 8 | 6 | 12 | 47.1 |
| Control N=50 | | | | | | | | | | | |
| Family Relationships | — | — | 3 | 9 | 15 | 14 | 3 | 1 | — | 5 | 5.2 |
| Individual Behavior | — | — | — | 13 | 11 | 18 | 4 | 2 | — | 2 | 5.4 |
| Care of Children | — | — | 4 | 7 | 19 | 11 | 2 | 1 | — | 6 | 5.1 |
| Social Activities | — | — | 1 | 4 | 33 | 9 | — | — | — | 3 | 5.1 |
| Economic Practices | — | — | 1 | 6 | 19 | 14 | 3 | 3 | — | 4 | 5.4 |
| Household Practices | — | 1 | 4 | 8 | 19 | 11 | 1 | 2 | — | 4 | 5.0 |
| Health Conditons | — | 1 | 2 | 8 | 21 | 12 | 4 | — | — | 2 | 5.1 |
| Relation to Worker | — | 2 | 3 | 9 | 18 | 10 | 3 | 1 | — | 4 | 5.0 |
| Community Resources | — | — | 1 | 10 | 21 | 13 | 3 | — | — | 2 | 5.1 |
| (450) | — | 4 | 19 | 74 | 176 | 112 | 23 | 10 | — | 32 | 46.4 |

more steps of positive movement. And, as in the table at opening, "don't know" or "does not apply" scores are weighted at the mid-range, which in this table is 5. The weighted scores of movement are 47.1 for the demonstration group and 46.4 for the control group, or a difference between the groups of but .7. It is not necessary to elaborate that the difference is not statistically significant.

While we are on this table, attention should be drawn to the six scores in the demonstration group showing extreme movement between opening and closing of +4 steps or better. The reason is that these six scores account for a major part of the small difference between the groups. In detailed analyses of the data considerable attention was focused on these and other extreme scores. Some findings are too complex to be discussed here, but one can be mentioned. Of the six +4 scores shown in that column, four are for a single demonstration case. Should this one case have shown a lesser degree of movement the total difference between the demonstration and control groups could have been indiscernible instead of merely non-significant.

In summation, then, it must be concluded that very little improvement in family functioning can be demonstrated by the project. The groups were similar at opening and they were little changed at closing. In some respects, even, the control cases appear to have done better than the demonstration cases.

But now a technical matter. Up to this point we have used a weighting scheme that includes cases with zero movement as well as those in which some information is missing: the "don't knows" and "does not apply." It is possible to *accentuate* the differences between the demonstration and control groups by dropping these cases and by employing a weighting system that focuses on only positive and negative degrees of movement, the extremes of the distributions. To do this we will re-weight the "movement" table just shown by $-4$, $-3$, etc. on through $+3$ and $+4$, with "0" movement given a value of zero, or omitted. The resulting scores are the net arithmetical weighted values of positive and negative degrees of movement. They are shown in Table 4.

These accentuated scores of net positive and negative movement are 2.20 for the demonstration group and 1.16 for the control group. Even these scores of difference between the groups are not statistically significant. Also note that on the important dimensions of "family relationships," "individual behavior," and "care of children" the control cases show more positive movement than the demonstration cases. The superiority of the latter is largely on the demonstration of "social activities," "household practices," and "relations to workers."

For the record, we will note that the scores of the two groups at the closing of the project—using the same weighting system as was used at opening, in which all cases including "don't knows" were given a value between 1 and 7—was 47.5 for the demonstration group and 47.2 for the control group. True, the demonstration cases were a bit behind the controls at opening (45.2 for the demonstration group and 46.5 for the controls), while now they are slightly ahead. But the difference between opening and closing is only a gain of 2.3 for the demonstration group and .7 for the control group, which again is not statistically significant.

Because the accentuated scores—in which zero movement and "don't knows" and "does not apply" are omitted—give a magnified view of the difference between the groups, these scores will be employed for detailed analyses throughout the balance of this report.

Remember, too, that these are net scores. The weighted negative

Table 4 **Movement Between Opening and Closing of Individual Cases— by Weighted Positive and Negative Degrees of Movement Only**

| | Extremes of Net Weighted Movement | |
| --- | --- | --- |
| | Demonstration Group | Control Group |
| Family Relationships | .04 | .16 |
| Individual Behavior | .16 | .38 |
| Care of Children | .04 | .06 |
| Social Activities | .28 | .06 |
| Economic Practices | .36 | .44 |
| Household Practices | .40 | −.04 |
| Health Conditons | .10 | .08 |
| Relation to Worker | .60 | −.10 |
| Community Resources | .22 | .12 |
| Total Net Weighted Movement | 2.20 | 1.16 |

values (−1, −2, −3, −4), have been subtracted from the weighted positive values (+1, +2, +3, +4). Hence their lower magnitude than when all cases are given a positive weight.

But here we must pose interjection. Does the generally negative outcome of the project indicate that social casework should be abandoned as having no effect? We do not think so, not on this or other empirical evidence to the same end, at least. There are too many factors in human behavior, and in our present skills for measuring such a cosmos, to hold that any negative evaluation should take full precedence over services that many devoted workers feel are beneficial. If people feel that good has been done, who is to say that this feeling itself is not beneficial? In this project, for example, both the caseworkers, as well as the Director of Social Services, conscientiously felt that a great deal of good was done in some cases, whatever our attempted measures might show. All we can say is that we could not measure the benefit.

Nor do we have a satisfactory definition of what "casework" is in this and other efforts. There are many theories about the nature of effective casework, few of which agree in their basic premises. In this project alone, there were differences of opinion between the workers, and between the workers and the department. Which was right? In what respects? Under what circumstances? We cannot say. In fact, although there was elaborate specification for the design and instrument aspects of the project, there was no specification for what the caseworkers might choose to do, other than that they must work within the general framework of a department of public assistance. It was assumed from the start that a Master's degree in social work would provide whatever is known as "casework."

For all these reasons, then, perhaps the most accurate statement that can be made about the outcome of this (or other similar projects) is:

> <u>Whatever was done by these workers for these clients</u>
> <u>cannot be demonstrated to have had a beneficial effect</u>
> <u>by the particular procedures we chose to apply.</u>

It could be that the caseworkers did a great deal of good for some cases that our measures failed to reveal. Certainly the research methodology used in this project is vastly more sophisticated than that which would have been employed a generation ago. And just as certainly, the methodology that may be used in some future time will make ours look as if it came from the stone ages. All we can say now is that this earnest and rigorously-designed project failed to demonstrate any significant degree of success by what we choose to define as success in our particular culture.

The next eight pages of this chapter have been omitted; they go into more refined analysis of the data, the results of ratings by Community Service Society judges utilizing the Hunt Movement

Scale, and their comparison with the Geismar Scale results. The findings did not serve to modify the conclusion just presented. We pick up with the final pages of the chapter, in which the "hidden" control group, and the issue of the quality of the case-work, are discussed.

## CONTROL GROUP 1 VS. CONTROL GROUP 2

Built into the project design was a second, "hidden" control group of which we have but briefly spoken. This group was drawn at random from the same pool of eligible multiproblem families as were the demonstration and principal control groups. It was, however, merely designated by the research staff, no worker knew which cases were in it, and it was not interviewed until the project was closed. It was to be used as a control upon the known control group which, because the cases in this group had to be interviewed to obtain opening summaries, was at least known to the public assistance workers. It was not thought likely that the known control group would be contaminated by reveal-ing the cases within it—that is, that they might be given more than ordinary attention and thus cause a "Hawthorne effect"—but the pos-sibility was foreseen. The hidden control group would be free of any such effect because it was completely unknown. Now we are ready to compare the hidden control group with the known controls.

The method of rating for this comparison differs somewhat from that used earlier. Up to now the judges had seen both the opening and closing summaries for each case, even though, as in the Geismar pro-cedure, they had rated each summary separately. But the Control 2 cases, the hidden controls, had only one summary—at closing. To insure comparability on this point, the closing-only summaries of both the demonstration and Control 1 cases were re-rated after the regular rating was completed and turned over to the research staff. We thus have a new comparison of the closing summaries for the demonstration, Con-trol 1, and Control 2 groups independent of anything shown before. The independent re-rating was made by both the Geismar and CSS judges.

First, we will look at the total weighted scores for the three groups. These are the sum of the scores for the nine Geismar dimensions. Two scores are shown for each team of judges. Those in the first column (for the demonstration and Control 1 cases) are when the closing sum-maries were rated in company with the opening summaries; the second —and new—scores are when the same closing summaries were rated alone. These totals are shown in Table 5.

A number of things are observable here. First is that Geismar judges rated generally higher in all categories than did CSS judges. Second is that both sets of judges rated all groups higher when the closing summaries were seen alone than when the closing and opening sum-maries were seen together. A possible reason is contextual: with less information on long-standing or related problems, the judges may see

Table 5 **Comparison of Total Weighted Group Scores for Closing Summaries When Rated Jointly with Opening Summaries and When Rated Alone**

|  | Geismar Judges | | CSS Judges | |
|---|---|---|---|---|
|  | Jointly | Alone | Jointly | Alone |
| Demonstration Group | 11.46 | 12.88 | 8.80 | 9.14 |
| Control 1 Group | 11.16 | 14.51 | 8.58 | 9.24 |
| Control 2 Group | — | 13.14 | — | 7.06 |

the closing-only situation as less serious than when its duration is exposed. The difference is greater among Geismar judges but it is present as well with the CSS judges. The third point of note is that both sets of judges rated the Control 2 Group *lower* than the Control 1 Group; conspicuously so by CSS judges, but also by Geismar judges.

Now let us move to the closing ratings on individual dimensions. These are shown in Table 6. In general, the average difference between the control groups persists through most dimensions. And in the case of the Geismar ratings, the differences become large enough to be statistically significant on three rather important dimensions, although significance is not obtained on the remaining six. On all significantly different dimensions—Family Relationships, Individual Behavior, and Economic Practices—the Control 1 group is rated higher than the Control 2 group. For an analysis of subdimensions within the major dimensions (not otherwise presented in this report) it appears that "family solidarity" is the major contributor to the difference in Individual Behavior, "behavior of parents" to the difference in Individual Behavior, and "income" and "use of money" to Economic Practices.

In any event, so long as we adhere to the criterion of statistical significance it is clear that in at least some ways Control 1 group was rated higher than Control 2 group at the close of the project. Several explanations are possible:

1. The two groups might have been different from the onset of the project. Although all cases were drawn at random from the same population, and although they did not differ in case record respects, the lack of an opening summary for the Control 2 cases precludes an answer to this supposition. Maybe they were different.

2. The "Hawthorne effect" we were hoping to avoid may have occurred. Perhaps the regular assistance workers did give the known control cases more than routine attention (although it is not clear why greater attention per se should have produced improvement in these cases when it did not in the demonstration cases, especially when we also found that frequency of contact is negatively associated with movement, even in the control cases). Still, maybe it did.

3. The difference may have been produced by differing amounts of informaiton available for the closing summaries. In general,

Table 6 **Weighted Scores for Individual Geismar Dimensions in Closing Summaries When Judged Jointly with Opening Summaries and When Judged Alone—Geismar and CSS Judges**

|  | Geismar Judges | | CSS Judges | |
|---|---|---|---|---|
|  | Jointly | Alone | Jointly | Alone |
| Family Relationships |  |  |  |  |
| Demonstration | .96 | 1.10 | .70 | .88 |
| Control 1 | 1.32 | 1.72 | 1.10 | 1.06 |
| Control 2 | — | 1.20 | — | .84 |
| Individual Behavior |  |  |  |  |
| Demonstration | .56 | .70 | .56 | .68 |
| Control 1 | .88 | 1.30 | .58 | .68 |
| Control 2 | — | .62 | — | .20 |
| Care, Training of Children |  |  |  |  |
| Demonstration | .92 | 1.12 | 1.16 | 1.10 |
| Control 1 | 1.04 | 1.43 | 1.18 | 1.18 |
| Control 2 | — | 1.50 | — | 1.10 |
| Social Activities |  |  |  |  |
| Demonstration | 2.06 | 2.06 | .86 | .94 |
| Control 1 | 1.74 | 2.15 | .88 | 1.02 |
| Control 2 | — | 2.30 | — | .68 |
| Economic Practices |  |  |  |  |
| Demonstration | .54 | .66 | .44 | .40 |
| Control 1 | .76 | 1.00 | .82 | .86 |
| Control 2 | — | .34 | — | .16 |
| Household Practices |  |  |  |  |
| Demonstration | 1.82 | 1.98 | 1.38 | 1.52 |
| Control 1 | 1.34 | 1.74 | 1.06 | 1.28 |
| Control 2 | — | 1.58 | — | .96 |
| Health Conditions |  |  |  |  |
| Demonstration | 1.04 | 1.28 | 1.02 | 1.04 |
| Control 1 | 1.30 | 1.60 | .90 | .98 |
| Control 2 | — | 1.44 | — | 1.02 |
| Relation to Worker |  |  |  |  |
| Demonstration | 1.72 | 2.08 | 1.36 | 1.36 |
| Control 1 | 1.06 | 1.57 | .88 | 1.04 |
| Control 2 | — | 2.14 | — | .96 |
| Community Resources |  |  |  |  |
| Demonstration | 1.84 | 1.88 | 1.32 | 1.22 |
| Control 1 | 1.72 | 2.00 | 1.18 | 1.14 |
| Control 2 | — | 2.02 | — | 1.14 |

Control 1 cases had more information in the case records than did Control 2 cases. It is possible that assistance workers may have recorded more positive information for known control cases than for others, and it is possible that the research interviewer gained more information from cases he had interviewed three years earlier than he did from the hidden controls which he interviewed only at closing. However, we have surmised above in rating closing summaries "jointly" with opening summaries rather than "alone" that amount of information is negatively associated with high rating. Still, we do not know. Whatever the reason, our procedures compel us to accept Control 1 group as superior in over-all functioning to the "hidden" Control 2 group at the close of the project.

Yet, if we look at Control 2 group as a purer baseline against which to compare the demonstration group we get a mixed result. If we use the Geismar ratings when the closing summaries were judged alone, we find that Control 2 is now slightly higher than the demonstration group. If we make the comparison with the demonstration group when Geismar judges rated "jointly" with opening and closing summaries, the superiority of the Control 2 group widens. Only in the view of CSS judges does the substitution of Control 2 group for Control 1 improve the margin in favor of the demonstration cases. And here we might note that whereas there were statistically significant differences between Control 1 and Control 2 on three dimensions in the rating of Geismar judges, there is only one dimension—Individual Behavior—in which the difference between Controls 1 and 2 is statistically significant in the ratings of CSS judges.

In summary of this point, then, there is some evidence that the Control 1 group may be an adulterated baseline. However, the same materials offer no clear mandate for holding that the demonstration cases would show greater improvement were the Control 2 group substituted for Control 1 as a purer baseline. Hence, any alternative measure could change only in a modest degree the basic conclusion already stated: the demonstration group showed a slightly greater, but not statistically significant, margin of improvement in family functioning over the control group(s).

## QUALITY OF THE CASEWORK

As envisioned originally, the project was completed at this point. But with this essentially negative outcome an additional question was raised. It was: "How good was the casework? Perhaps the reason nothing happened was that the casework was somehow deficient."

To provide an answer to this query, a *post hoc* investigation was instituted. Two respected authorities in the field of casework teaching— Dr. Carol H. Meyer, Professor of Social Work at the Columbia University School of Social Work, and Dr. Benjamin Lyndon, Dean of the

School of Social Work at the State University of New York at Buffalo—
consented to evaluate the quality of casework as evidenced in the
official records. Note that these are different materials from the research summaries rated earlier by the Geismar and CSS judges for
"movement." The case records were used as one source for preparing
the summaries, but the main materials for the summaries were research interviews with the clients. The caseworkers never saw these
summaries, nor did the judges of "movement" have direct recourse to
the case records. The two are related but independent documents.

In keeping with the project's previous aims of objectivity, preliminary
discussions in this new phase of evaluation centered around establishing specific criteria of casework. Before a judgment of "good" or "bad"
could have meaning, it must be "good" or "bad" in respect to something. What then? The evaluators agreed that whatever else casework
might involve, seven dimensions should be reflected in the case records. These are:

> 1. Description of the situation; adequacy of recording relevant
> facts in the opening situation.
> 2. Assessment of client problems and potentials; the selection
> of those which are subject to treatment within the available re-
> sources of the client and of the community.
> 3. Relatedness of what was done by the caseworkers to the in-
> dicated needs and potentials of the client.
> 4. Evidence of "reaching out" by the worker to serve case-
> related needs.
> 5. Alertness of the worker to available community resources.
> 6. Adequacy in recording of the treatment process.
> 7. Evidences of the worker's professional objectivity in treating
> individual clients.

The above were not deemed exhaustive. Rather, they were viewed
as necessary but not sufficient conditions of good casework. To add
further objectivity, each dimension would be rated on a seven-point
scale ranging from "very poor" to a mid-point of "average" to a top
value of "very good."

Judgment of the quality of professional casework is pertinent only
to the demonstration cases since, as a chief variable under measure,
such casework was not given to the control cases. So it is only with
the fifty demonstration cases that we are now concerned. Also, all
measures previously shown have been for the aggregates of demonstration and control groups. In total, they showed but small differences. Yet
within both groups there was a considerable range of difference by
individual cases. In the demonstration group, for example, the highest
individual score of "movement" was +23, while the lowest score, indicating regression between the opening and closing of the project, was
−11.

In the present evaluation, cases were selected in "takes" to represent maximum dispersion of the movement scores. First, the fifty

demonstration cases were stratified into three groups totalling 15, 15, and a residue of the 20 remaining cases. The first group of 15 cases contained five which showed the greatest degree of positive movement, five which remained at about zero, and five which showed the greatest negative regression. The second group of 15 cases contained the next greatest dispersion, while the remaining 20 were a relatively homogeneous residue.

The "takes" were to be judged blind. That is, the casework evaluators did not know the movement scores for the individual cases. The two judges also were to rate the same cases independently from each other. As a start, the first group of highly dispersed cases was to be judged. Then, if found necessary, the second and perhaps the third group would be examined.

The conclusion was that the quality of casework evident from the case record was, at the best, "slightly above average for regular public assistance workers and slightly below average for trained case-workers," in the consensus of the two judges.

But the variation among individual cases provided the most inter-esting—and possibly significant—result. For when the blind ratings of quality of casework were keyed to the independent scores of move-ment, there was a direct association between high, medium, and low scores by both measures. In short, although the aggregate of demon-stration cases did little better than the control cases in movement, there appeared to be an association between the amount of movement in individual cases with the quality of casework evident for the same cases.

There are several ways to express the degree of association between the movement and casework scores. One is by the rank correlation coefficient. When the cases are ordered from 1 to 15 according to the amout of their positive movement and compared with the order of their casework scores through the appropriate procedures and formula, the result is a rank order coefficient of .44. This is not overly impressive, but in the calculating process it was seen that the two extreme cases (1st and 15th) are contributing the major weight to the modest correla-tion. When these are removed and the remainder ($N=13$) re-calculated, the correlation rises to .68, a quite respectable association.

Another way to see the association between the movement and case-work scores is through a succession of arithmetic means. First the scores of the two judges for each case were averaged. Then a mean score was obtained for each dimension within the high, medium, and low movement groups, plus a further mean of all dimensions within the movement groups. These are shown in Table 7.

Clearly the score for quality of casework are higher in the group of cases with greatest movement than they are in the group with zero movement, or than they are in the group with negative movement. But these, again, are the most extreme cases. The result was so en-couraging that it was decided to extend the casework evaluation to the second group of fifteen demonstration cases with the next greatest

### Table 7 Means of Quality of Casework Scores—Fifteen Cases with Greatest Dispersion of Movement

|  | Movement Groups | | | |
|  | High | Medium | Low | Total |
| --- | --- | --- | --- | --- |
| Situation | 4.6 | 4.3 | 4.1 | 4.3 |
| Assessment | 4.5 | 4.2 | 3.8 | 4.2 |
| Relatedness | 4.3 | 4.4 | 3.8 | 4.2 |
| Reaching Out | 4.8 | 5.1 | 4.6 | 4.8 |
| Community Resources | 4.8 | 5.0 | 4.9 | 4.9 |
| Recording | 4.1 | 3.6 | 3.0 | 3.6 |
| Objectivity | 4.7 | 4.3 | 3.7 | 4.2 |
| Mean of means | 4.6 | 4.4 | 4.0 | 4.3 |
| N= | (5) | (5) | (5) | (15) |

dispersion of movement. Should the association between movement and quality of casework continue to be found, it would greatly support the original association, as well as furnish an additional finding in its own right. Ideally, the second association should be present, but on a lower level from the first. Unfortunately, however, as is shown in Table 8, the association disappeared completely with the less extreme demonstration cases.

### Table 8 Means of Quality of Casework Scores—Fourteen* Cases with Second Greatest Dispersion of Movement

|  | Movement Groups | | | |
|  | High | Medium | Low | Total |
| --- | --- | --- | --- | --- |
| Situation | 4.1 | 4.3 | 4.1 | 4.2 |
| Assessment | 4.4 | 4.5 | 4.2 | 4.4 |
| Relatedness | 4.3 | 4.4 | 4.1 | 4.3 |
| Reaching Out | 4.3 | 4.1 | 4.6 | 4.3 |
| Community Resources | 4.6 | 4.5 | 4.7 | 4.6 |
| Recording | 3.5 | 3.6 | 3.7 | 3.6 |
| Objectivity | 4.1 | 4.0 | 4.2 | 4.1 |
| Mean of means | 4.2 | 4.2 | 4.2 | 4.2 |
| N= | (5) | (4) | (5) | (14) |

* The file of one case—in the "medium" group—failed to get copied for casework rating.

And that, in sum, is the end product of the project's findings. After two years of service to multiproblem families by trained caseworkers, operating with reduced caseloads and with special cooperation of the community's resources, but within the framework of public assistance policies and procedures, the demonstration group showed a small but statistically non-significant margin of improvement over the control group(s) which received only routine service from regular public assistance workers. In addition, a small but fleeting association was found among the most extreme cases in the demonstration group between the degree of movement and the indicated quality of casework.

## Chapter Summary

It is probably not amiss to refer to the relatively recent multi-problem family phenomenon in social work as a social movement (or at least a "minimovement"!). It had for a time, between around 1950 and 1965, the zeal, the contagion, the cohesion, and the faith of a "cause" in social welfare.

Beginning with Bradley Buell's St. Paul Family Unit Report Study in 1948, it soon gained momentum. In the early 1950s, the key phrases—"hard core," "multiproblem," "disorganized," "malfunctioning," "resistive," "reaching out," "aggressive service," and of course the well-known "6 percent"—had spread far and wide across the land and beyond. By 1960, over half the larger cities in the United States and Canada were in some stage of planning or implementing multiproblem family programs. However, by the mid-1960s much of the air had gone out of the balloon in the self-limiting pattern shown by other research and action cycles in social work.

Multiproblem families were first defined as families known to social agencies that were characterized by problems in two or more of three areas: economic dependency, ill-health, or maladjustment. Later the criterion that children under 18 years of age must be present in the home was added, and the concept was elaborated in terms of social functioning and role theory.

A research emphasis paralleled the planning and action demonstrations from the start, first stressing the prevalence and characteristics of multiproblem families, and later, under the leadership of Ludwig Geismar, shifting to focus on the measurement of social functioning and on changes in its level associated with "family-centered treatment" by cooperating agency workers. While such inquiries were informative and encouraging, they could not provide any semblance of an "acid test" of effectiveness in view of the absence of an adequate experimental design.

This lack was eventually made up in the early 1960s with the launching of the Chemung County Study under the guidance of Roland Warren of the State Charities Aid Association. This project utilized an advanced experimental model with control groups and the best research instruments available, including the Geismar Scale of Family Functioning and the Hunt Movement Scale. The results, though variously interpreted, failed to show significantly greater progress among multiproblem families treated by professionally trained social workers with reduced caseloads as compared with those treated by "normal" public assistance services. This setback was accompanied by questions in the literature regarding the "newness" of the multiproblem family notion, and by challenges to its underlying premises, such as concentration on the family as the potential source and cure of the pathology, rather than on the shortcomings of economic and social systems within the broader society.

But with or without such reactions to the movement, another set of priorities had been brewing within the field and the nation —namely, the social activism of the mid-1960s, as typified in the trail-blazing Mobilization for Youth in Manhattan, and in the Great Society's War on Poverty. This new swing of the pendulum toward the community and societal deficits underlying family pathology gave the final quietus to the multiproblem family approach as a distinct trend in social work, though its demise due to natural causes was probably imminent in any case. Nevertheless, the multiproblem family approach has had a continuous impact on the field in its more aggressive out-reaching, family-centered treatment techniques, as well as in its research methodology.

Selected readings from Ludwig Geismar's *Understanding the Multiproblem Family* and from Roland Warren's Cheming County study were presented.

## NOTES

[1] See Chapter 5, p. 000.

[2] See Chapter 6, pp. 000–000.

[3] Charles J. Birt, "Family-Centered Project of St. Paul," *Social Work*, 1, no. 4 (October 1956): 41.

[4] Ibid.

[5] Ibid.

[6] Bradley Buell, "Know What the What Is," *Survey Mid-Monthly*, 84 (October 1948): 299–302.

[7] Leonard Rutman, "The Demonstration Project as a Research and Change Strategy," *Journal of Sociology and Social Welfare*, 2, no. 2, suppl. (Winter 1974): 259–270.

[8] Bradley Buell et al., *Community Planning for Human Services* (New York: Columbia University Press, 1952).

[9] Ibid., p. ix.

[10] Ibid., p. 6.

[11] Ibid., pp. 6–7.

[12] Ibid., p. 16.

[13] Ibid., p. 238.

[14] Ibid., p. 7.

[15] Ibid., p. 9.

[16] Ibid., pp. 84–85.

[17] Ludwig L. Geismar and Michael A. La Sorte, *Understanding the Multiproblem Family: A Conceptual Analysis and Exploration in Early Identification* (New York: Association Press, 1964), p. 19.

[18] Buell et al., p. 336.

[19] Ibid., p. 85.

[20] Ibid., p. 260.

[21] Ibid., p. 254.

[22] Ibid., p. 87.

[23] Birt, p. 42.

[24] Rutman, p. 267.

[25] See Chapter 7, p. 000.

[26] Buell et al., p. 336.

[27] Geismar and La Sorte, p. 56.

[28] Ibid., pp. 74–75.

[29] Ibid., p. 20.

[30] Ibid., p. 57.

[31] Ibid.

[32] Ibid., p. 56.

[33] Ibid., p. 87.

[34] Sidney E. Zimbalist and Walter W. Pippert, "The New Level of Integration in Community Welfare Services," *Social Work,* vol. 5, no. 2 (April 1960): p. 31.

[35] Cited in Rutman, p. 265.

[36] Birt, p. 42.

[37] See, for example, *Reaching the Unreached Family,* Monograph no. 5 (New York: New York City Youth Board, 1952).

[38] Alice Overton, Katherine Tinker, et al., *Casework Notebook* (St. Paul: Greater St. Paul United Fund and Council, 1957).

[39] Ludwig L. Geismar, "The Multiproblem Family: Significance of Research Findings," in *Social Welfare Forum, 1960* (New York: Columbia University Press, 1960), p. 179.

[40] See excerpt in Chapter 7, p. 264.

[41] Ludwig L. Geismar, Beverly Ayres, et al., *Measuring Family Functioning: A Manual on a Method for Evaluating the Social Functioning of Disorganized Families* (St. Paul: Greater St. Paul United Fund and Council, 1960).

[42] See Ludwig L. Geismar, *Preventive Intervention in Social Work* (Metuchen, N.J.: Scarecrow Press, 1960), and Ludwig L. Geismar et al., *Early Supports for Family Life: A Social Work Experiment* (Metuchen, N.J.: Scarecrow Press, 1972).

[43] Ludwig L. Geismar, *Family and Community Functioning: A Manual of Measurement for Social Work Practice and Policy* (Metuchen, N.J.: Scarecrow Press, 1971).

[44] Joseph C. Lagey and Beverly Ayres, *Community Treatment Programs for Multiproblem Families* (Vancouver, B.C.: Community Chest and Council of the Greater Vancouver Area, 1962), pp. 55–5.

[45] Joseph C. Lagey and Beverly Ayres, "Community Treatment Programs for Multiproblem Families," in Benjamin Schlesinger, *The Multiproblem Family: A Review and Annotated Bibliography,* 2d ed. (Toronto: University of Toronto Press, 1965), p. 57.

[46] Ibid., p. 56.

[47] Cited in Geismar and La Sorte, p. 18.

[48] Schlesinger, op. cit.

[49] Lagey and Ayres, op. cit. (1962).

[50] Rutman, p. 266.

[51] Ibid., p. 265.

[52] Schlesinger, p. 6.

[53] Ibid., p. 266.

[54] E.g., *How They Were Reached,* Report no. 2 (New York: New York City Youth Board, 1954).

[55] Ibid., p. i.

[56] Rutman, p. 260.

[57] Schlesinger, p. 4.

[58] State Charities Aid Association, *Multiproblem Families: A New Name or a New Problem* (New York: State Charities Aid Association, 1960), pp. 1–2.

[59] Irving Lukoff and Samuel Mencher, "A Critique of the Conceptual Foundation of the Community Research Associates," *Social Service Review,* 36, no. 4 (December 1962): 433–444.

[60] Ibid., p. 443.

[61] Ibid., pp. 441–442.

[62] Ibid., p. 438.

[63] Ibid., p. 434.

[64] Ibid., p. 432.

[65] Buell et al., pp. 101–124.

[66] Lukoff and Mencher, p. 437.

[67] Ibid., p. 439.

[68] State Charities Aid Association, p. 9.

[69] Ibid., p. 4.

[70] Gordon E. Brown, ed., *The Multi-problem Dilemma: A Social Research Demonstration with Multi-problem Families* (Metuchen, N.J.: Scarecrow Press, 1968).

[71] Rutman, p. 262.

[72] See (in addition to the studies by Ludwig L. Geismar and associates previously cited), Ludwig L. Geismar and Beverly Ayres, *Families in Trouble* (St. Paul: Greater St. Paul Community Chest and Council, 1958).

[73] Rutman, p. 264.

[74] See Chapter 7, p. 245.

[75] Geismar, "The Multiproblem Family," p. 177.

[76] Ibid.

[77] Ibid., p. 176.

[78] Brown, p. 7.

[79] See David Wallace and Jesse Smith, "The Study: Methodology and Findings," in Brown, pp. 107–161.

[80] Ibid., p. 141.

[81] Geismar, *Family and Community Functioning,* pp. 139–140.

[82] Brown, 7–8.

[83] Helen Harris Perlman, "Casework and the Case of Chemung County," in Brown, pp. 47–71.

[84] Ibid., p. 70.

[85] Ibid., p. 61.

[86] Ibid., p. 66.

[87] Ludwig L. Geismar, "Implications for Research," in Brown, pp. 74–75.

[88] Ibid., p. 85.

[89] Wayne Vasey, "Implications for Social Work Education," in Brown, p. 33.

[90] Ibid.

[91] See p. 342.

[92] Roland L. Warren, "A Multi-Problem Confrontation," in Brown, p. 103.

[93] For a masterful account of this evolution from the 1950s into the mid-1960s, see Peter Marris and Martin Rein, *Dilemmas of Social Reform* (New York: Atherton Press, 1967).

[94] See the four-volume series on the Mobilization for Youth by Harold H. Weissman, ed., *The New Social Work* (New York: Associated Press, 1969). For an essay review of these volumes the reader is referred to Sidney E. Zimbalist, "Mobilization for Youth: The Search for a New Social Work," *Social Work*, 15, no. 1 (January 1970): 123–128.

[95] Richard A. Cloward and Lloyd E. Ohlin, *Delinquency and Opportunity: A Theory of Delinquent Gangs* (New York: Free Press, 1960).

[96] Geismar, "The Multiproblem Family," p. 168.

[97] Geismar and La Sorte, p. 198.

[98] Ibid.

[99] Ibid., p. 201.

[100] Ibid., p. 188.

[101] Ibid., p. 190.

[102] Geismar, Ayres, et al., p. 186.

[103] Ibid.

[104] Roland L. Warren, "The Social Context of Evaluation," in William C. Sze and June C. Hopps, *Evaluation and Accountability in Human Service Programs* (Cambridge, Mass.: Schenkman, 1974), pp. 20–21.

# Chapter 9
# Retrospect and Prospect

## RETROSPECT

It is hardly feasible or necessary here to summarize the detailed material and excerpts presented in the preceding chapters. The summaries provided at the end of each chapter may serve the purpose of such a review if desired. Instead, this section will consist of some personal impressions and commentary gleaned from the foregoing work. Potential areas for further investigation will also be pointed out in the process. The reader should be mindful throughout of the limitations of scope and procedure noted at the outset.*

The most obvious generalization that can be drawn from this inquiry is that social work research can indeed be organized into more or less cohesive themes or cycles in research emphasis over the decades. The six research cycles that have emerged from the present analysis are not the only ones that could have been identified; other investigators going over the same ground may very well have come

---

* For example, the restriction to social work sources in this inquiry suggests the desirability of parallel studies stressing the contribution of other social sciences—e.g., sociology, psychology, anthropology, and economics—to research in this field.

out with different results. Through several such studies by different researchers a more definitive and balanced picture may emerge. Replication through review of the development of social work research from a number of vantage points and by a number of scholars is therefore urgently needed in this as in most other areas of social work research.

The six themes identified represent a major portion of the research effort of the field, but far from the whole of it. Administrative research, historical investigation, case studies, and theoretical inquiry have been largely excluded for the reason that they appeared to this writer to lack a sufficient pattern of cohesion and continuity. Nevertheless they each warrant review and analysis in their own right as research trends of particular interest and significance.

The research topics that were chosen are not parallel in terms of categories. While in a sense they reflect research *goals,* a couple tend to be centered on methodology (i.e., quantification and index making, and evaluative research); a couple are more substantive in nature (i.e., poverty causation and multiproblem family research); and at least a couple are a combination of both (i.e., poverty measurement and the social survey). Because of the close interrelatedness of method and content in social work research, a "pure" or single-dimensional classification system did not seem applicable to what has actually evolved in the field.

A crucial question inheres in the *reasons* for these trends or cycles. Why do we find such wide swings in research emphasis over the years? In part, these fluctuations are to be expected in an applied social art, which depends in the last analysis on public opinion and its vicissitudes for support. As a consequence the field must in some degree follow where public perception leads, and this guide to social needs and problems is a notably fickle one. The more basic sciences have their fads and fashions too, but these are more likely to be influenced by theoretical developments and empirical findings than by external pressures; that is, they appear to be more "inner" and less "outer" directed, at least in terms of degree.

But given this difference between the applied and the basic, there still appears to be an excessive tendency for social work to "go overboard" with the latest wave of research—when one succeeds in catching on in this generally research-resistant profession. Perhaps the periodic overenthusiasm is fed by the relative neglect of research at other times, so that the one extreme is a reaction to the other. In any case, there has been an obvious readiness to embrace a promising research approach as a potential panacea and ready solution to highly intractable and deep-seated ills. We saw this long ago in the research on the causes of poverty, in the social survey movement, in the drive for social work measurement, and more recently in the study of the multiproblem family. Closer study of the dynamics and sources of such oscillations in research interest and activity should be rewarding. What is clearly needed is a more evenly balanced and steady commitment to research and to research criticism throughout the profession over the long haul.

One key to the fluctuation in social work concern and its related research emphasis is the well-known individual vs. societal polarity that has marked American social history and the social work field since its inception. Before 1900, "scientific" charity and the search for causes stressed the study of the family and the individual as the source of poverty and other social problems. The early 1900s ushered in an era of social reform—represented in social work in the classic social survey and the rapid spread of the settlement house movement. After World War I, "normalcy" in social work was reflected in the professionalization of social work practice and the growing influence of Freudian and psychodynamic concepts. The Great Depression of the 1930s of course forced the nation and the young profession to attend to social and economic needs external to the individual. The post-World War II period saw a resurgence of social work technique in the diagnostic-functional casework controversy, the refinement of social group work (e.g., detached street work with gangs), and the rise of the multiproblem family movement and its research component. The 1960s rediscovered poverty and other societal deficits, while the 1970s appear to have reverted to a more individualized concern, this time featuring a proliferation of casework and group interactive models. From this perspective it may be argued that the phenomenon of research themes in social work is in part attributable to the American (and professional) penchant for going to extremes in the effort to deal with changing social challenges. Perhaps there is an intrinsic Hegelian dialetic underlying these moves and countermoves in American social thought, in which social work and social work research are inextricably caught up.

In the same vein, a given wave of research would often carry within it the seeds of its own decline and the emergence of the following cycle, much in the manner of a typical social movement. Thus the quest for "causes" within the indigent themselves revealed the limitations of this approach and pointed the way to the study of external "conditions" in the social survey; similarly, research on the multiproblem family circled inward on itself and through its own fall helped usher in the societal reforms of the 1960s.

Another overall conclusion that can be adduced from what has gone before is the thorough permeation of social work research—like social work itself—with the value dimension. The criteria for the measurement of poverty, the standards for survey conclusions and recommendations, the essence of evaluative research (that "semantic monstrosity"), and so on—each variant of research analyzed was found to have a value-laden core. Moreover, the study of the causes of poverty, the measurement of social work, and the research on the multiproblem family also reflect value premises in terminology, study design, and content. Values pervade not only the interpretation of findings, the techniques for obtaining those findings, and the underlying parameters in which they couched but also—and perhaps most significantly—the very perception and choice of the research problem qua problem in the first instance. This value grounding of empirical inquiry is not unique to social work—it no doubt characterizes all of the applied social arts and the basic social sciences as well;[1] it may also underlie the physical sciences.[2] But perhaps nowhere are science and value more directly and inextricably joined than in social work, at the very nexus of constructive interaction between the individual or group and the surrounding social environment. Fuller and more explicit study of this critical relationship and its implications for social work research is clearly needed.

The recurring dilemma of the role and nature of research in an applied helping art continues to plague and divide the limited research resources of the profession.[3] Should it be primarily specific, fact finding, and operational on the one hand, or more basic, conceptual, and theoretical on the other, or some combination of the two? In actuality, the historical weight appears to be clearly on the side of the former type of research in the themes identified, and as we shall see, continuity in theoretical research in social work thus far seems to be conspicuous largely by its absence. At the "macro" level of planning, policy formulation, administration, and community action, *applied* research and fact finding seem to be more widely accepted (as in the community survey approach) than at the "micro" levels of social treatment and its evaluation, where theory and process are given greater stress—at least in aspiration. The day when this debate with its semantic pitfalls is past will be welcome indeed. (The *relative* nature of the issue is illustrated by the fact that in social work evaluative research is often viewed as more "basic," whereas in the social sciences such as sociology or psychology it tends to be seen primarily as "applied" research.) For this writer the preferred solution is the acceptance of *both* types as equally legitimate in this field.

From its very inception social work research has obviously been shaped by the structures and people involved in it. We have had occasion to note that the genesis of the National Conference on Social Welfare as a section of the American Social Science Association a century ago had its significance for research in this field, as did its break away from it several years later. Similarly, the charity organization movement, the federated fund-raising movement, the growing role of the states and later the federal government each made its impress. Specific organizations such as the Russell Sage Foundation, the U.S. Children's Bureau, the Family Service Association of America, the Child Welfare League of America, the Social Work Research Group,* the National Association of Social Workers, and the Council on Social Work Education, as well as the Charities Publications Commitee, *The Survey, Social Work*, and other professional journals left their mark and in many cases continue to exert influence today. Each of these entities warrants thorough study in terms of its bearing on social work and social work research.[4] By the same token, the major *researchers* over the course of the field's development should be reviewed in depth and their contributions analyzed in detail for the "models"—and cautions—that every discipline needs to document and recognize. Early leaders such as Frederick Wines, Amos G. Warner, John Koren, Kate Claghorn, Robert Chapin, Isaac M. Rubinow, Neva Deardorff, Paul Kellogg, Raymond Clapp, Philip Klein, Julia C. Lathrop, Richard C. Cabot, Ralph Hurlin, Grace Abbott, Edith Abbott, Helen Witmer, Wayne McMillen, and others might well be studied in this way.[5]

In this connection it should be noted that—despite the fact that the focus of this work has been on an "inside view" of the development of social work research rather than on the contributions of other social sciences—many of the leading researchers in this field have had part or all of their training outside of social work. This was of course inevitable in the early decades of social work history, since social work education did not fully crystallize until well into this century. Indeed Charles Booth was a largely

* Now incorporated within the National Association of Social Workers as its Council on Social Work Research.

"self-taught" businessman; Amos Warner was an economist; and so on. However, throughout this century as well the key people in this field have often had one or both feet in another discipline. Thus (to identify our "landmark" authors only), Paul Kellogg was a journalist; Helen Witmer has her doctorate in sociology; J. McVicker Hunt and Leonard S. Kogan are psychologists; Ludwig Geismar and Roland Warren are sociologists; and so on. Other prominent examples discussed in this volume include William E. Gordon (from biology) and Norman A. Polansky (with psychology as well as social work training). The intent of this observation is not to tally a "box score" of inside vs. outside researchers in social work but, rather, to stress the major role played in this field by people with at least part of their scientific background in other disciplines. While this pattern is undoubtedly related to the relatively recent emergence of the research specialization (and doctoral training) in social work education, there are probably implications here regarding the continuing value of an interdisciplinary "mix" in the further development of social work research.

Finally, in this brief backward glance at the road we have traveled, there are many indications that social work research is at last "coming of age," if it has not already reached that point in its evolution. Ever since its separation from generalized "social research" a scant 30–40 years ago, it has rapidly expanded in quantity and advanced in quality, though much, obviously, remains to be done. There are several bases for this judgment:

1. There is growing sophistication of research methodology in this field.[6] The increasing use of empirical studies, experimental and quasi-experimental models (including single-case design), and such statistical techniques as multivariate analysis, factor analysis, path analysis, and nonparametric statistics represents significant progress. While these approaches have usually been borrowed from other social sciences, some have been honed and sharpened in social work research, as in the use of judgments as data in research.[7] While the application of more advanced and more powerful research tools does not in itself ensure fruitful research, it at least provides greater potential for it. At the same time, it is essential that such techniques be applied appropriately, which has not always been the case in social work. A critical review of the application of these more current statistical and research procedures in this field should have considerable instructive value.

2. We have observed the growing capacity of social work to recognize and contain its own research excesses, and so to provide a more effective set of checks and balances for its sound development. Perhaps the first modern successful emergence of this crucial

capability took place in the late 1930s and 1940s in the healthy reaction to and rejection of the Social Breakdown Index and its overly ambitious pretensions. More recently, the study of the multiproblem family soon aroused a spate of controversy and correction within the field. In earlier days—as with the social survey movement—it will be recalled that the first attacks came from without, rather than from within (and belatedly at that).

3. Social work research has increasingly specialized and shifted and narrowed its focus with the passage of time—as has social work itself. Starting with the coverage of the whole of social welfare and "civic conditions," there has been a progressive delimitation of scope to the study of the social services and the professional core concerns of social work at the time. This selectivity has been accompanied by the yielding of older research topics to other specializations, such as much of poverty research to economists, infant mortality studies to biostatisticians, social surveys to sociologists, and so on. Such "losses" have permitted greater concentration on the study of the social services per se, their evaluation, their theoretical foundations, and related social policy issues and administrative questions by social work researchers, who have themselves become increasingly specialized in particular facets of the field.[8]

4. We are beginning to see the more direct impact of research on social work practice, in place of the rather distant separation that often characterized them in the past.* Thus the development of the family-centered casework approach was heavily influenced by research on the multiproblem family. Related community action efforts were also in part an outgrowth of these studies and demonstrations and their findings. More recently, the impressive field experiment of William J. Reid and Ann W. Shyne on *Brief and Extended Casework* (1969) has—together with other forces— had a marked bearing on current trends in time-limited and task-focused social treatment models.[9] Even the predominantly negative findings of most evaluative studies in social work have had salutary consequences in the self-searching and the exploration of less pretentious helping modalities that have resulted. The intensive study of this closer interweaving of research and practice in social work is a significant and promising area of inquiry.

---

* However, research was not without its impact on social work trends in the past. The early "primitive" studies of poverty causation, for example, pointed toward the key practice concept of multiple causation and toward the inadequacy of looking to the poor themselves as the source of their impoverishment. Similarly, the social survey movement helped shape the era of social reform in social work in the early 1900s.

In these several ways, it may be fairly inferred that social work research—once marginal to the mainstream of professional development—is attaining sufficient maturity and recognition to influence and illuminate its future direction.

## Prospect

Though the past is at best an imperfect and ambiguous guide to the future, the temptation is irresistible—after this extended review of the field's past research record—to hazard some speculations regarding the shape of things to come in the anticipation of a more scientific social work. What might be looked for in the way of future research trends, based on what has been seen thus far?

One tentative projection, of course, is that there will continue to be changing themes in social work research. Such cycles of scientific interest and emphasis might well be expected in the decades ahead. This projection follows not only from past patterns but also from their grounding in the applied and public nature of the social work profession. Fluctuation of public interest will probably continue to affect not only the periodic swings in programatic focus but related research concerns as well.

More recent examples of this intermeshing of public priorities and social work research may be seen in the burgeoning of poverty-related research in the mid-1960s, in the drug abuse studies and the crime and corrections research emphasis of the early 1970s, in the growth of research relating to the aged and services for them, and in the current resurgence of evaluative research efforts in the face of renewed demands for "accountability" from the sponsoring public. While the preceding examples may not meet our criteria for a new and distinct theme in social work research, they can serve to illustrate the close connection and responsiveness of research in this field to recent shifts in social concerns.

It is probably not feasible to be any more specific than this in terms of future research fashions, since these will turn upon changes in the political and social climate of the nation that it would be hazardous to try to forecast. The possibility also exists that social work in the future may be *less* subject to such wide swings of focus. Greater stability and continuity in research effort would obviously be highly desirable in terms of cumulative knowledge building. In order for such a change to materialize, however, a couple of conditions at least would need to be met: first, the increasing independence of social work as a more self-sufficient and prestigious profession, and second, the development of more effective scientific methodology and theory relevant to the helping disciplines. While it is hoped that these developments will be forthcoming over the long term, in the short run it seems likely that social work and its research arm will continue largely to follow, rather than lead, the shifts of public opinion in this area.

If this is the case, we should have our "scientific guard" up, so as not to be entirely swept away in the research enthusiasm and contagion of the moment, while still lending appropriate support to the new priority. We should be wary of scientific prophets promising nostrums, and of tackling research problems clearly beyond the existing state of the art with the expectation of early results. At the same time, we should be mindful of the fact that research, no less than practice, "learns by doing"; we therefore need to maintain active pressure on the growing edge of knowledge and methodology, and to be prepared for new ventures while avoiding premature claims or pretensions.[10] These are obvious platitudes, perhaps, but there is the weight of several generations of social work research experience behind them. In these efforts, too, we should continually be guided and informed by the experience and findings of the basic social sciences bearing upon the research issues at hand.

Finally, as we have seen, some of the most significant advances in social work research have been in its technology, usually "imported" from other fields but at times developed or deepened from within. It is, of course, impossible to predict what future breakthroughs might be made in this area, though current trends might be observed. In this connection it may be noted that a couple of "new" methodology chapters were added to the *Social Work Research* volume under Norman Polansky's editorship between the first edition in 1960 and the second in 1975: "Applications of Computer Technology," by William J. Reid—including information systems, simulation techniques, and the like—and "Uses of Research Methods in Interpersonal Practice," by Edwin J. Thomas, covering "single-case" designs and other quasi-experimental models.[11] These are obviously promising and potentially powerful tools for significant progress in our field, as they have proved to be in others, and their further application to social work inquiry is urgently needed.

Beyond such innovations, further headway in the philosophy of science as it bears upon the study of social phenomena may be the most critical challenge of all. As noted a number of times in this text, the poor match between the prevailing mechanistic scientific models and premises and the interactive, organic realities with which social work deals has placed frequent obstacles in the way of its research endeavors.

### Research on Social Work Theory—A Chapter Yet to Be Written

It has been emphasized that none of the research themes or landmarks in the body of this text deal squarely with the development and testing of social work *theory*. This objective was, to be sure, an underlying motivation of many research efforts in the field as early as the nineteenth-century foray into "causes" by Amos Warner in his attempt to build a science of "philanthropology."* But a sustained, cumulative, incremental building of concepts, constructs, and theories has been largely lacking in this field. What has been done to date along these lines is for the most part on an ad hoc and fragmented basis.[12]

In part, this lack may be explained by the fact that theory testing and development is the primary function of the more fundamental social sciences† from which social work has typically drawn—sociology, psychology, economics, anthropology, and so on—while an applied profession such as social work has other priorities for its limited research capacities. However, this traditional differentiation has become increasingly obscure and overlapping in recent times as the basic social sciences have moved into problem solving and application (e.g., clinical psychology, applied sociology, economic planning, etc.) and as social work has addressed itself more persistently to the theory testing and knowledge building needed to underpin its practice.

A couple of decades ago the theoretical emphasis in social work research was given a strong impetus in the writings of William E. Gordon, a biologist who gained experience in social work research and subsequently joined the faculty of the George Warren Brown School of Social Work at Washington University. His 1951 monograph *Toward Basic Research in Social Work*, articulately setting forth the need for and proposing a program of theory-based research, was widely cited in the field. Later he collaborated with

---

* It may perhaps be maintained that the periodic research efforts traced in Chapter 3, dealing with research based on changing notions of causation, constitutes a type of "theoretical" research stretching over many decades. However, the wide swings and frequent shifts of terms and concepts belie the continuity and coherence that is vital to the empirical development of theory.

† For a recent view and critique of the uneven and controversial "state of the art" in the major social sciences, see Rollo Handy and E. C. Harwood, *A Current Appraisal of the Behavioral Sciences,* rev. ed. (Great Barrington, Mass.: Behavioral Research Council, 1973).

Harriet Bartlett and others in the study and "working definition" of social work practice.[13] A key conceptual formulation, for example, which had been introduced earlier by Werner W. Boehm and was carried forward by these efforts, was that of "social functioning" as the focus of social work practice.[14] As we have seen, Ludwig Geismar further developed and operationalized this notion in his Scale of Family Functioning (see Chapter VIII).

Though Gordon and his associates conducted a number of empirical inquiries in line with these theoretical ideas, the weight of their impact was conceptual and philosophical, and it can hardly be claimed that a substantial, ongoing program of basic research has yet materialized from these promising beginnings. Similarly, while Geismar's instrumentation of related concepts has contributed much to research methodology in social work, his energies were largely directed to applying these measurement tools to the evaluation of family-centered treatment and the assessment of early intervention rather than more theory-centered questions.

Perhaps the major example of sustained research on social work concepts in recent times is the impressive series of "Motivation, Capacity, and Opportunity" studies by Lilian Ripple and associates at the Research Center of the School of Social Service Administration at the University of Chicago from 1953 through the mid-1960s.[15] Dr. Ripple credited Charlotte Towle with the initial formulation of this conceptual triad, and for over a decade she devoted her exceptional talents and those of her students and associates to the operationalization of these concepts and the study of their characteristics and correlates. Despite the substantial progress gained, her spadework appears not to have been picked up on extensively by others, and since her departure from the Research Center in the late 1960s little further study of these matters has been done. The present program of the Research Center, now directed by William J. Reid, has an entirely different conceptual focus, namely, the study and development of task-centered casework.[16]

And herein lies the familiar pitfall of theory-based research in social work, namely, its episodic, transient, and highly personalized character. As Norman Polansky recently expressed it,

> Sooner or later, a responsible scientist recognizes that conducting a single study, unrelated to his other work, is like tossing a rock into a pond. It is not that it makes no difference at all; it is that it makes so little difference as to be hardly worth doing. It used to be customary to end a study with some variation of, "And

thus, we see, more research is needed. . . ." In fields still as thinly staffed as social work research, *if one does not stoop to retrieve his own gauntlet, himself, no one else picks up the challenge.* So it is a sign of maturity in both the scientist and his science when problems are increasingly formulated in terms of a program, or a potential program of studies . . . interlocked in such a fashion that they lead to increasing depth and comprehensiveness in theory, and in study design.[17] (Emphasis added)

Polansky goes on to cite the leadership of Charles Gershenson, who was instrumental in the federal government in developing a pattern of funding open-ended research programs such as the highly productive series of longitudinal studies of foster care and adoption by David Fanshel and associates at the New York School of Social Work of Columbia University.[18] However, Alfred Kadushin, professor at the University of Wisconsin (Madison) School of Social Work and a leading child welfare researcher over a period of many years, reviewed this field of research as of 1971, including some of the programatic funding projects of the U.S. Children's Bureau.[19] He regretfully concluded* that

There is apparently no general theoretical system applicable to child welfare problems that holds the allegiance of any sizeable group of researchers. Having lost our innocence about psychoanalytic theory, we have nothing as systematic and comprehensive to take its place as a guide to research.

Perhaps this is to be expected. The phenomena with which different researchers are concerned are too diverse to expect that a single comprehensive theory would have explanatory power for all. . . . More often than not . . . no theoretical basis is offered for selection of the question to be researched, for the methodology . . . or for the explanation of the research results. Much of the research is thus an ad hoc enterprise rather than being related to efforts to confirm or validate some theoretical preconceptions.

The research available often speaks with a forked tongue. Often it is contradictory and non-cumulative. . . .[20]

Polansky—a social worker who also received training in psychology—is himself a prime example of a creative and prolific researcher in social work theory, with his many influential studies

---

* This negative judgment might now be modified in the light of the later productivity of Dr. Fanshel and his associates, and other recent work in this area.

of "group contagion," "verbal accessibility," and the like.[21] Yet, as has been noted, he is quick to acknowledge that such probes into social work theory are rarely if ever pursued by others and are typically limited to the enterprise of a lone research worker with perhaps a few students or associates.

As a result the author has been unable to identify a sufficiently extended and cohesive body of research to present a coherent narrative of the growth of empirically based social work theory. To be sure, there has been a great amount of fruitful and productive activity at this level—and a number of "landmarks"—but it has not reached the stage of integration or cumulation to enable this author to trace a substantial, continuous trend of the sort portrayed in previous chapters.

Therefore we must conclude with the observation that research on theory is a chapter "yet to be written" in social work. Its preparation still awaits the emergence of sufficient momentum in this area to carry beyond the work of individual researchers, and the testing of particular theories or concepts, to the construction of an empirically based framework of theories applicable to practice by collaborating researchers. It may also depend on the rise of fresh research strategies and philosophic perspectives more pertinent to the subtle, humanistic art and aspiring science that is social work.

## NOTES

[1] E.g., Gunnar Myrdal, "A Methodological Note on Facts and Valuations in Social Science," in his *An American Dilemma* (New York: McGraw-Hill, paperback edition, 1964), II, 1035–1064.

[2] See, for example, Michael Polayi, *The Tacit Dimension* (Garden City, N.Y.: Anchor Books, 1967); and J. Bronowski, *Science and Human Values* (New York: Harper Torchbook, 1959).

[3] See, for example, Norman A. Polansky, "Research in Social Work," in Robert Morris et al., eds., *Encyclopedia of Social Work: Sixteenth Issue* (New York: NASW, 1971), pp. 1098–1106; and Mary E. Macdonald, "Social Work Research: A Perspective," in Norman A. Polansky, ed., *Social Work Research* (Chicago: University of Chicago Press, 1960), pp. 1–23.

[4] Some have already been the subject of published works. See, for example, Clark A. Chambers, *Paul U. Kellogg and the Survey: Voices for Social Welfare and Social Justice* (Minneapolis: University of Minnesota Press, 1971); Charles L. Mowat, *The Charity Organization Society, 1869–1913* (London: Methuen, 1961); Dorothy Bradbury, *Five Decades of Action: A History of the Children's Bureau* (Washington, D.C.: GPO, 1962).

[5] Examples of some biographies that have been written include Jane Addams, *My Friend Julia Lathrop* (New York: Macmillan, 1915), and Chambers, op. cit.

[6] See, for example, Merlin Taber and Iris Shapiro, "Social Work and Its Knowledge Base: A Content Analysis of the Periodic Literature," *Social*

*Work,* 10, no. 4 (October 1965): 100–106; and Roslyn Weinberger and Tony Tripodi, "Trends in Types of Research Reported in Selected Social Work Journals, 1956–65," *Social Service Review,* 43 (December 1965): 439–447.

7 Ann Shyne, ed., *Use of Judgments as Data in Social Work Research* (New York: NASW, 1959).

8 See Norman A. Polansky, ed., *Social Work Research* (Chicago: University of Chicago Press, 1975), p. 14. 2d ed.

9 William J. Reid and Ann W. Shyne, *Brief and Extended Casework* (New York: Columbia University Press, 1969); and William J. Reid and Laura F. Epstein, *Task-Centered Casework* (Chicago: University of Chicago Press, 1972).

10 Donald T. Campbell, "Reforms as Experiments," in Francis G. Caro, ed., *Reading in Evaluative Research* (New York: Russell Sage Foundation, 1971), p. 258.

11 See Polansky, rev. ed., 1975, pp. 229–253, 254–283.

12 For a somewhat more sanguine though generally corroborative discussion of this topic, see Norman A. Polansky, "Theory Construction and the Scientific Method," in Norman A. Polansky, ed., *Social Work Research* (Chicago: University of Chicago Press, 1975), pp. 18–37.

13 See William E. Gordon, *Toward Basic Research in Social Work* (St. Louis: Washington University, George Warren Brown School of Social Work, 1951), "A Critique of the Working Definition," *Social Work,* 7, no. 4 (October 1962): 3–13, "Toward a Social Work Frame of Reference," *Journal of Education for Social Work,* 1, no. 2 (Fall 1965): 23, and "Knowledge and Value: Their Distinction and Relationship in Clarifying Social Work Practice," *Social Work,* 10, no. 3 (July 1965): 32–39. See also National Association of Social Workers, Commission on Social Work Practice, "Working Definition of Social Work Practice," *Social Work,* 3, no. 2 (April 1958): 5–8; and National Association of Social Workers, *Building Social Work Knowledge* (New York, 1964).

14 For a later elaboration of this important concept, see Harriet Bartlett, *The Common Base of Social Work Practice* (New York: National Association of Social Workers, 1970), pp. 84–117. For an earlier formulation, with somewhat different interpretation, see Warner W. Boehm, "The Nature of Social Work," *Social Work,* April 1958, pp. 10–19. vol. 3, no. 2.

15 See, especially, the summary monograph by Lilian Ripple, Ernestine Alexander, and Bernice Polemis, *Motivation, Capacity, and Opportunity: Studies in Case Work Theory and Practice,* Social Service Monographs, 2d ser. (Chicago: University of Chicago, School of Social Service Administration, 1964).

16 See William J. Reid and Laura F. Epstein, *Task-Centered Casework* (Chicago: University of Chicago Press, 1972).

17 Polansky, rev. ed., 1975, p. 33.

18 See, for example, David Fanshel and Eugene B. Shinn, *Children in Foster Care* (New York: Columbia University Press, in press); David Fanshel, "Parental Visiting of Children in Foster Care: Key to Discharge," *Social Service Review,* 49, no. 4 (December, 1975): 493–514; David Fanshel, "The Exit of Children from Foster Care: An Interim Report," *Child Welfare,* February 1971, pp. 61–81; David Fanshel and Eugene B. Shinn, *Dollars and Sense in Foster Care of Children: A Look at Cost Factors* (New York: Child Welfare League of America, 1972); David Fanshel, "Parental Failure and Consequences for Children: The Drug-Abusing Mother Whose Children Are

in Foster Care," *American Journal of Public Health,* June 1975, pp. 604–612; also, Shirley Jenkins and Elaine Norman, *Filial Deprivation and Foster Care* (New York: Columbia University Press, 1975), and *Beyond Placement: Mothers View Foster Care* (New York: Columbia University Press, 1975); also, Deborah Shapiro, *Agencies and Children: A Child Welfare Network's Investment in Its Clients* (New York: Columbia University Press, in press).

[19] Alfred Kadushin, "Child Welfare," in Henry Maas, ed., *Research in the Social Services: A Five-Year Review* (New York: National Association of Social Workers, 1971), pp. 13–69.

[20] Ibid., pp. 62–63.

[21] A number of Dr. Polansky's research and theoretical contributions are incorporated in his *Ego Psychology and Communication* (Chicago: Aldine-Atherton, 1971).

# Index

77 78 79 80 9 8 7 6 5 4 3 2 1